D1601662

Egypt During the Sadat Years

Egypt During the Sadat Years

Kirk J. Beattie

palgrave

First published 2000 by
PALGRAVE™
175 Fifth Avenue, New York, N.Y. 10010 and
Houndmills, Basingstoke, Hampshire, England RG21 6XS.
Companies and representatives throughout the world.

PALGRAVE™ is the new global publishing imprint of St. Martin's Press LLC Scholarly and Reference Division and Palgrave Publishers Ltd (formerly Macmillan Press Ltd).

ISBN 0-312-23246-2

Library of Congress Cataloging-in-Publication Data
Beattie, Kirk J.
    Egypt during the Sadat years / by Kirk Beattie.
        p. cm.
    Includes bibliographical references and index.
    ISBN 0-312-23246-2 (cloth)
        1. Egypt—Politics and government—1970-1981. 2. Sadat, Anwar, 1918-
I. Title.

  DT107.85 .B43 2000
  962.05'4—dc21

                                                            00-040465

A catalogue record for this book is available from the British Library.

Design by Westchester Book Composition

First edition: December, 2000
10 9 8 7 6 5 4 3 2 1

Printed in the United States of America.

For my wife, Elizabeth,
My daughters, Zoë and Taya,
And in loving memory of my mother,
Hazel Katherine Findlay Beattie

Contents

Preface

This book, an analysis of Egypt's political history from 1970-1981, is in many respects a sequel to my first book, *Egypt During the Nasser Years* (Westview Press, 1994). As with that book, I have tried to write in a style that makes the material more accessible to non-specialists. Thus, I use theory to inform the book's framework of analysis, but I have kept theorizing and the use of political science concepts to a minimum. Readers not interested in theoretical matters may wish to skip the next paragraph.

A Brief Theoretical Note

The principle concept used to direct this study is Antonio Gramsci's notion of hegemony, which Gramsci defined as a situation in which a ruling class has "succeeded in persuading the other classes of society to accept its own moral, political, and cultural values." [See James Joll, *Antonio Gramsci* (New York: Penguin Books, 1977, 129.] To achieve hegemony, a ruling group must go beyond controlling the institutions of the state; it must establish widespread acceptance of its values in such institutions of "civil society" as the educational system, major religious institutions, the press, sociocultural clubs, professional associations, and trade unions. Such an effort requires the support of a corps of intellectuals and the development of a political philosophy spelling out those values. Individuals who embrace those values must carry the struggle for hegemony into the aforementioned arenas of civil society, converting or defeating their hegemonic rivals to assure that their values are dominant. The struggle for hegemony's importance derives from two factors: (1) any political regime's long-term viability hinges on its ability to convince others of its value; (2) for any particular socioeconomic development strategy to succeed, concordant political institutions must be established. In consequence, it is essential to chart the struggle for hegemony over state and civil societal institutions, as well as scrutinize all domestic and international factors influencing that struggle, to understand the political-economy of a "developing country" like Egypt.

Additional Prefatory Remarks

The introductory chapter of this book contains several passages taken from my first book. I do present "fresh" material there, but the primary purpose of the introduction is to set the stage for detailed coverage and analysis of Sadat's presidency. In short, the heavy lifting, in so far as new research and analysis is concerned, begins in chapter two. From chapter two onward, the book follows a chronological order.

The reader will detect an imbalance in coverage of U.S.–Egyptian relations in the book; coverage is more extensive in the beginning, and lighter thereafter. To begin, the focus of the book is on Egyptian domestic politics, not foreign relations. That said, I couldn't resist sharing the information I found in recently declassified U.S. State Department and National Security Council documents. However, while most of the documents for the 1970-1973 period have been declassified, they are in general not yet available beyond that period.

I have used a very simple style of transliteration. An apostrophe has been used for both the *'ayn* and the *hamza*. Anyone who knows Arabic can readily discern which is intended by the context. My apologies are offered to those Egyptians whose names appear differently from the way they spell them in English. I have respected the wishes of those who specifically asked to have their names spelled in a familiar manner.

This book is the product of many years of field research. It draws heavily on extensive personal interviews with Egyptians, most of whom were members of the broad political-economic elite during Sadat's presidency, as well as interviews with a few well-placed Americans. Although a limit of fifty interviews was in effect during much of the research period in Egypt, well over a dozen trips to Egypt over the past twenty years have enabled me to acquire a large set of key elite interviews. Multiple interviews were held with a select group of past and present political elites, ministerial officials, bureaucrats, party cadres, religious figures, lawyers, journalists, economists, engineers, academics, businesspersons, and workers representing a broad cross-section of ideological viewpoints. This list includes interviews with representatives of the broad Islamist current, although the clandestine nature of Islamist extremists' activity and/or their imprisonment rendered that group less accessible than representatives of other currents. I can honestly say that every interviewee received me with great hospitality and respect, for which I will remain forever grateful.

This book is also the product of thousands of hours of research conducted in various libraries, newspaper and magazine "morgues," and research centers, where I pored over sundry secondary sources and memoirs in Arabic, English, and French. Particularly careful readings were made of *Rose al-Yusuf, al-Musawwar, al-Muhamat,* and *al-Da'wa.* Access to the archives of the major newspapers, especially *al-Ahram* and *al-Akhbar,* proved very useful, and I thank the staffs and management there for "opening their doors." I also spent a great amount of time working in the library at the United States Embassy in Cairo, where Nadia Rizq, Nadia al-Kilani, and their assistants were very helpful, as well as at the library of the American University of Cairo, to whose staff I am also grateful.

Funding from Simmons College, the American Research Center in Egypt, and the U.S. Office of Education made it possible to cover most of my travel to Egypt and living expenses there. Needless to say, this assistance was very beneficial, and I am greatly appreciative.

Several individuals have provided various forms of assistance with this book over the years, and to them I owe a special debt of gratitude. Special thanks go to 'Ali al-Din Hilal Dessouki, Rif'at al-Sa'id, Hermann Eilts, Salah Dessouki, Hamdi Fuad, Ricky Romano, Magda al-Sanga, Diane Singerman, "Naldo" Haddad, Clement Henry, Robert Springborg, John Waterbury, Sa'd al-Din Ibrahim, Magdi and Barbara Hatour, Muhammad al-Mismari, 'Abd al-Latif al-Boghdadi, Kemal al-Din Hussein, John Viste, Muhsin 'Abd al-Khaliq, Mrs. Jehan Sadat, Kemal Hassan 'Ali, Nayrouz Tatanaki, Shibley Telhami, Michael Sterner, and Ann Lesch.

At Simmons College, Cheryl Welch, Deborah Nutter, Zachary Abuza, Toni-Michelle Travis, Erik Jensen, and Denis McLean provided friendship, moral support, and professional advice. I received essential administrative assistance from Karen Talentino, Chet Haskell, and John Robinson, as well as help from the Simmons reference librarians. The staff at Palgrave, especially Donna Cherry, Ruth Mannes, Gabriella Pierce, Sonia Wilson, and Meredith Howard, was highly efficient and helpful. Finally, I would also like to thank my dear friends scattered about the planet for their good humor, kindness, and understanding, as well as my father and his wife, Kathleen, Richard and Joellen Bennet, and all the members of the Beattie and Hagge clans for all their love and support.

Kirk J. Beattie

1

Introduction

On September 28, 1970, following a marathon effort to put an end to fighting between Jordan's army and Palestinian guerrillas, Egypt's legendary leader, Gamal 'Abd al-Nasser, died. If funerals and funeral processions can serve as a measure of a political figure's impact on humankind, then Nasser's burial procession, with few rivals in contemporary history in terms of attendance and mass demonstrations of grief, spoke volumes. Most of those who mourned his loss did so out of abject love and admiration. Others did so because he represented a father figure, perhaps too stern and harsh in his treatment at times, but one who literally worked himself to death trying to provide the grand Egyptian family with a better future.

But to be a political animal is to incur enemies as well. Animosity and opposition go with the turf, it being impossible, as Abraham Lincoln so aptly stated, "to please all the people all the time." And so on the day of Nasser's burial, there were others both in Egypt and abroad, albeit a distinct minority in Egypt at the time, who quietly rejoiced and wondered whether the lion's passing would enable Egypt to move in new political, economic, and sociocultural directions.

In this introductory chapter, my objective is twofold. First, I hope to provide the reader with an idea of where Gamal 'Abd al-Nasser's leadership had taken Egypt, shedding light on who did or did not mourn his death and why. Second, I will present a background sketch of the origins of Muhammad Anwar al-Sadat. I will cover Sadat's early political socialization, as well as the numerous roles he played during the Nasser presidency. In so doing, I wish to set the stage for a discussion of Egypt's political history under Sadat, including his determination as Nasser's successor, his showdown with regime elites who were rivals, and his subsequent reorientation of Egypt's major domestic and foreign policies. I also hope to demonstrate how the policies of the Sadat regime affected the quest for a stable and fructuous political-economic order.

Nasser's Legacy

In the Beginning, There Was Nasser's Coup Turned "Revolution"

On the night of July 22-23, Nasser led his carefully crafted, clandestine group called the Free Officers in a successful military coup d'etat. Mostly in their early thirties, the officers held a mishmash of ideological orientations, but were united by an ardent nationalism and profound discontent with Egypt's constitutional monarchy. Their nationalistic fervor had been galvanized by the humiliating defeat by Israel in the 1948 Palestine war and their revulsion from over seventy years of British imperialism. Their domestic political concerns derived from the existing constitutional monarchy's inability to address the problems of widespread poverty, disease, and illiteracy.

To understand the political stagnation of the pre-1952 regime, one must realize that beyond several small parties supporting the monarchy, civilian political actors were divided into four disparate ideological camps. The two largest camps were: (1) the largely secular, pro-capitalist, liberal democrats; and (2) pro-capitalist Islamists, who desired full implementation of Islamic (*shari'a*) law. These camps were represented by the Wafd party and the Muslim Brotherhood (MB) organization, respectively. Wafdists enjoyed broad societal support and were most effective at mobilizing voters. The Brothers, who mostly shunned electoral competition, were popular among professionals, state bureaucrats, and entrepreneurs. By the late 1940s, they had become equally or more capable than the Wafdists of mobilizing what Egyptians call the "political street" in urban areas. Alongside these two forces stood two smaller, yet highly vocal camps of transitional authoritarians and Marxists. Among the transitional authoritarians were parties inspired by European fascist models, especially the Young Egypt party (which metamorphosed into the Egyptian Socialist party). Their members were entrepreneurs, professionals and agriculturists who rarely embraced a full fascist ideology, but did believe that only a powerful state could engineer Egypt's socioeconomic development. The Marxists, formally banned from the political playing field, were divided into a myriad of small parties and groupings that recruited most effectively among intellectuals, "Europeanized" Egyptians and some workers.

The ideological differences separating these four camps made concerted opposition to the king or fruitful cooperation all but impossible; they also enhanced the king's divide-and-conquer capabilities. These ideologically diverse political forces vied for popular support, and many competed in elections for control of parliament. The king, however, was able to dissolve parliament at will, and both Fuad, who ruled from 1923 to 1936, and his son Faruq, in power from 1936 until 1952, invoked the power often. Thus, the Wafd party, able to win easily any fair election during the 29 years of monarchical rule, held government power for just seven years. Major policies were ultimately determined by the king or his British "advisers."

The stalemate among civilian political forces was a major factor giving birth to the military coup. Prior to the coup, Nasser and other core Free Officers maintained a clandestine association with the Muslim Brothers, in addition to secret contacts with Wafdists and Marxists. These contacts helped keep those major civilian actors waiting expectantly on the sidelines when the coup occurred. But importantly, at the time of the coup, Nasser possessed no determinative link to any civilian political party or organization, and no master plan for Egypt's development. A few officer-members of the post-coup junta, the so-called Revolutionary Command Council (RCC), possessed links to diverse parties and organizations, but most RCC members and Free Officers in general had no such links; indeed, they had no idea of how they would exercise power when they attained it. However, through discussions with civilian political elites, they confirmed their own doubts about those parties' ability to bury their ideological hatchets and agree upon common reforms. They also correctly perceived the lack of support for the constitutional monarchy. Accordingly, what began as a movement to impose several socioeconomic and military reforms quickly transformed into the officers agreeing upon a lengthier stay in power and the pursuit of grander objectives. In this regard, they came to adopt a position greatly akin to that of the transitional authoritarians. In rather short order, Nasser and his fellow conspirators presented a broad, albeit rather vaguely worded, set of six "revolutionary" principles. These included termination of feudalism and foreign imperialism, an end to monopoly capitalism, construction of a strong military, greater social justice, and a return to parliamentary rule.

With no ideological blueprint in hand, Nasser's regime sought to accomplish these objectives through a process of trial and error, that is, through a readiness to experiment with a variety of policy tools and to employ whichever alternatives appeared to deliver the best results. This approach, as it was played out, manifested the powerful linkages between Egypt's foreign policy and international political alignments, domestic political competition, and the direction of socioeconomic change.

1952-1954: Regime Consolidation

Egypt moved through four different periods following the 1952 military coup, the first of which lasted from 1952 to 1954. Following the coup, the monarch, King Faruq, was removed from power and replaced by a republican, military authoritarian regime under a largely figurehead president, an older, publicly respected general named Muhammad Nagib. Within half a year, the regime sent a tough message to organized labor by harshly suppressing an industrial strike, and all civilian political parties were banned from the political playing field. The political vacuum was weakly filled by the regime-built Liberation Rally organization.

In March 1954, regime opponents made a last-gasp effort to return Egypt to civilian, parliamentary rule, but they were skillfully outmaneuvered by Nasser, who wooed the Muslim Brothers and some trade unionists out of the broad opposition coalition. Later that same year, the Brotherhood itself was outlawed, and its cadres imprisoned or forced into exile, after a failed assassination attempt against Nasser by one of its members on October 26. Nagib, who had come to favor a return to parliamentary rule, was accused of complicity in the assassination and ousted by Nasser and his supporters on November 14. He spent the rest of his life under house arrest.

Regime elites held the view that Egypt's socioeconomic conditions—widespread poverty, absence of a large middle class, high rate of illiteracy—did not provide solid ground for the establishment of liberal democratic rule.[1] They saw the pre-1952 multiparty political game as sterile and socially divisive. Thus, most key elites saw the need for a period of transitional authoritarianism during which the state would promote a socioeconomic transformation to fulfill the aforementioned "prerequisites for democracy."[2] In this opinion, they were supported and abetted by the U.S. government,[3] as well as by many Egyptian civilians. Early on, a land reform policy was implemented in order to encourage economic diversification (especially industrialization), to undercut the political and economic power of Egyptian aristocrats and large landowners, and to improve the fate of Egypt's peasant masses. The educational system was greatly expanded at all levels to reduce illiteracy. Much of the press remained in private hands, although the regime did create new media organs. Most professional organizations retained a significant degree of autonomy.

1954-1960: State-Guided Capitalism

Regime efforts to overcome the legacy of defeat in the 1948 war by strengthening Egypt's military had far-reaching consequences, taking Egypt into a second phase that lasted from 1954 until 1960. Spurned in his initial attempt to acquire Western arms because he refused to sign an anti-Soviet regional defense pact, Nasser turned to the East, procuring Soviet arms under the guise of a 1955 Czech arms deal. Piqued by Nasser's Eastern tilt at the height of the Cold War, the American and British governments tried to punish Nasser by canceling promised aid for construction of the Aswan Dam. In doing so, they engendered a series of tit-for-tat exchanges culminating in the Suez Canal crisis and Suez War of 1956. Although Egypt was handily defeated on the battlefield by the combination of British, French, and Israeli forces, Soviet and American condemnation of the attack on Egypt resulted in the withdrawal of foreign forces. Egypt gained control of the previously foreign-owned Suez Canal and consolidated the Egyptian-Soviet bloc relationship. Nasser's prestige skyrocketed throughout the Arab and Third Worlds, as the Suez War's outcome helped sound the death knell for British imperialism. Regionally, Nasser became the leading figure advocating Arab nationalism and Arab unity. Internationally, his stature underwent a meteoric rise, as he became one of the major spokespersons touting the formal policy of non-alignment vis-à-vis the Cold War's superpowers.

The war also provided a pretext for extensive nationalization of foreign-owned businesses and infrastructure in Egypt. This nationalization fostered a large public sector, and reinforced the growing interest in economic planning and management by the state. Egypt began practicing state-guided capitalism, with an emphasis on industrial development and diversification via import substitution industrialization (ISI).[4] A new mass organization, the National Union, was set up to replace the Liberation Rally and sing the regime's praises. Regime officials became increasingly interventionist in the press and professional syndicate affairs.

1960-1967: Toward an "Arab Application of Scientific Socialism"
Frustration over the inability and unwillingness of Egypt's weak capitalist class to back the regime's industrialization effort, the strengthening of relations with socialist and communist countries in international affairs, and regime endorsement of the new, widespread faith of state economic planning—all these factors led Egypt's rulers to opt for a more clearly socialist path of development beginning in 1960. Widespread nationalization between 1960 and 1964 put ownership and control of much of the economy, especially the industrial, financial, and service sectors, in statist hands. A state-led ISI was embraced by state planners as the principal economic development strategy. A more restrictive land reform policy and additional price and marketing controls affected the agricultural sector.

In domestic politics, the regime replaced the National Union with a new mass organization called the Arab Socialist Union (ASU), and enlisted the support of socialists and communists to develop a new political philosophy—

an Arab application of scientific socialism—to underpin the regime and proselytize to the citizenry. In a deal with Nasser, the Egyptian Communist Party (ECP) formally dissolved itself in 1964 and most of the "ex-communists" assisted the regime. Top regime elites, however, remained steadfastly opposed to communism, wary of Egyptian communists, and keen to leave the regime and ASU's ideological formula open to principles held by transitional authoritarians and cooperative Islamists. Professional syndicates and labor organizations were bound to the ASU, and all major press organizations were nationalized. Ties with the Soviet Union and other Soviet bloc nations increased, much to the chagrin, in general, of most major Western powers. The Israelis, for their part, grew increasingly anxious at the sight of massive Soviet assistance for Egypt's military and economic development.

Egypt witnessed significant industrial development during the 1950s and first half of the 1960s, and the educational system expanded rapidly, lifting citizens' hopes of upward social mobility. In general, among Egypt's broad masses there was great optimism that Nasser was leading the country to a brighter future in building the new socialist society. The regime's ISI strategy, however, required heavy capital and intermediary goods imports, but it did not boost exports and therefore begot serious balance of payments difficulties by 1965. Meanwhile, Nasser's strident anti-Western imperialist foreign policy, which included opposition to conservative pro-Western Arab regimes like Saudi Arabia and Jordan, his support for more radical Arab nationalist regimes and movements in Algeria and Lebanon, Egypt's intervention in the Yemeni civil war, unabashed hostility toward Israel, and support for the Palestine Liberation Organization (PLO)—all elicited a tougher line from U.S. foreign policymakers under President Johnson's administration. In the mid-1960s, U.S. aid to Egypt was cut to punish Egypt and undermine its economic development efforts.

This development was of special significance because Egypt had largely exhausted the large foreign exchange reserves it had held since the end of World War II. Public savings had declined to under two percent of GNP in fiscal 1962-1963, then became negative in 1964-1965 and 1965-1966.[5] Egypt had become increasingly dependent upon foreign assistance for its economic development plan, receiving some $300 million per year from various countries (the Soviet Union, United States, Western European nations, Japan) from 1958 to 1965.[6] The loss of U.S. aid was a serious blow. GNP annual growth fell from 6.4 percent in fiscal 1963-64 to 4.4 percent in 1965-1966, then to 0.3 percent in 1966-67.[7]

Elsewhere, Nasser signed mutual defense arrangements with Syria and other Arab countries. When tensions rose along the Israeli-Syrian border in the spring of 1967, Nasser called for a partial withdrawal of United

Nations (UN) peacekeeping forces in the Sinai peninsula and blocked Israeli shipping through the straits of Tiran. UN Secretary General U Thant surprised Nasser by a total withdrawal of UN forces, and Israel regarded closure of the straits as a *causus belli*. Israeli defense forces proceeded to launch a devastating attack against Egypt, Syria, and Jordan in the Six Day War of June 1967. Egypt's military was crushed, and the country suffered major damage to its industry and infrastructure. The entire Sinai peninsula fell under Israeli occupation, and over one million residents fled their Suez Canal-side homes. Many of these people flocked into Cairo, overwhelming its infrastructural capabilities. All told, the war loss dealt a blow to Nasser's prestige and psyche from which he never fully recovered.

1967–1970: The Travails of Recovery
The 1967 war marked a watershed in Middle East regional history. Many Egyptians had become inebriated listening to Nasser's promises of a brighter, richer, stronger Egypt. For many, these dreams were shattered by the 1967 war loss, as was many Egyptians' confidence both in the socialist path of development and in their Soviet bloc allies. But when Nasser publicly announced his resignation following the defeat, an enormous outpouring of public support led him to renege on his decision and work to deliver Egypt from the depths of destruction.

These developments marked the onset of yet another period, one that lasted from 1967 until Nasser's death in 1970. Egypt's economy was so badly damaged that GNP annual growth hit -3.1 percent for fiscal 1967-68, and the country's economic development effort virtually ceased.[8] The abysmal economy, coupled with the need to rebuild the shattered military, brought a reinforced dependence upon the Soviet bloc. Partially to offset this heightened dependence on the Soviets, however, Nasser led a reorientation of Egypt's regional foreign policy. As suggested earlier, the international Cold War had found its echo in an Arab Cold War that pitted pro-socialist regimes (Egypt, Iraq, Syria, Algeria, Tunisia, People's Democratic Republic of Yemen) against pro-capitalist ones (Jordan, Saudi Arabia, Kuwait, Morocco, pre-1969 Libya). Nasser helped put an end to this conflict and found willing financial help from conservative Arab regimes, including the oil monarchies, to meet the commonly-perceived threat from Israel. Nasser would spend this period working day and night to restore Egypt's military fighting capability, an effort requiring a massive infusion of Soviet assistance and manpower. Meanwhile, diplomatic relations with the United States were severed following the 1967 war, and in general, aid and supplier credits from Western and Far Eastern "more developed countries"

(MDCs)—United States, Western European countries, Japan—dropped to rock bottom, where they remained for seven years.

While the ASU continued as the sole legal political organization, the shock of the 1967 defeat dealt it a serious blow and also engendered a broader societal debate about Egypt's future. That debate helped embolden proponents of Marxist, Islamist, and liberal democratic alternatives to the existing polity. Rival ideological voices were heard with increasing frequency, as the Nasser regime, in an effort to let off steam from the 1967 catastrophe, allowed a slightly greater measure of freedom of expression in the press and professional associations. The massive student-worker demonstrations of 1968, in protest of light sentences handed down to military officers for the 1967 war debacle, gave prove of deep-seated anger and leftist radicalization of certain segments of the citizenry.

Importantly, the hard-strapped government introduced a slight economic liberalization as it sought and received assistance from private entrepreneurs to relieve its postwar burdens and meet the pressing needs of its rapidly growing population. If Yugoslavia's President Tito had helped convince Nasser to go down the public sector path in the 1950s and 1960s, he now encouraged him to modify his strategy. Nasser dispatched one of his economic gurus, Hassan 'Abbas Zaki, to Yugoslavia and Zaki reported back on the need to retain state ownership, but use capitalist administrative and management styles, and make the companies run profitably. At a cabinet meeting, Nasser delivered the message that "The people cannot eat socialism. If they weren't Egyptians, they'd beat me with their shoes. We have to 'hire and fire' [in English]."[9] Thus, under Nasser's watch, potentially important modifications to the economic development strategy were placed on the front burner.

Intra-Regime Competition Under Nasser

Nasser Versus 'Amer

To nearly all outside observers, the post-1954 Egyptian regime gave the appearance of a rather monolithic entity, with Nasser as the undisputed leader charting its destiny. As revealed by subsequent research,[10] this image was inaccurate at various levels. As with most single-party regimes, Egypt's contained several competing factions. Each faction was centered around a powerful elite actor or small group of like-minded elites, and/or anchored in a shared institutional affiliation, ideological interpretation, or set of policy preferences.

In Egypt, at the pinnacle of power, a debilitating rift developed between Nasser and his erstwhile closest personal friend, 'Abd al-Hakim 'Amer. 'Amer, a member of the Free Officers' inner core group, had been appointed in

1953 by then Prime Minister Nasser as his chief of the armed forces and minister of defense, a move that presaged and facilitated Nasser's ouster of Nagib. Following 'Amer's inept handling of the 1956 war, however, Nasser tried to remove 'Amer from office, but was successfully rebuffed. 'Amer, with the clever, albeit corrupt assistance of his office director, Shams Badran, had curried great popularity among his fellow officers and numerous civilian politicians, and had turned the military into his own fiefdom.

A second attempt to remove 'Amer after the secession of Syria from its political unity with Egypt in 1961 also failed. By the 1960s, Nasser, still seen by most external regime observers as omnipotent, was not even able to review his own troops at will. His distrust of 'Amer was reinforced to the point of his consciously pursuing development of the ASU and related institutions as a counterweight to 'Amer's control of the military. Young ASU cadres, albeit nearly all unaware of the actual motivation, were instructed in coup theatre—that is, how to respond to an attempted military coup.

The Nasser–'Amer rift came to a head in 1967, following the 1967 war. Some regime elites go so far as to say that Nasser intentionally took Egypt into the catastrophic conflict in order to provide himself an excuse to remove 'Amer from office. Such claims seem farfetched, but Nasser did call upon key regime actors to orchestrate 'Amer's demise, and their house arrest of 'Amer and several of his closest colleagues led to 'Amer's death. Officially, 'Amer took his own life, but serious doubts remain.[11] Nasser's personality, his inability to trust anyone, was indelibly marked by this long-running, tumultuous clash with his once closest friend. Nasser's distrust of others was nearly total; this had deleterious consequences for regime politics in general.

Ideological and Policy-Based Regime Factions

The Nasser–'Amer rift roughly overlapped with another major source of disagreement and factional competition within the regime, this one anchored in ideological differences and derivative policy orientations. Obviously, this competition had a direct impact on Nasser's attempt to establish his own brand of socialist hegemony within the regime. According to accounts by regime elites, the Nasser regime evolved ideologically over time such that by the 1960s there were three major factions: Leftists, Centrists, and Rightists.[12] Again, to understand politics in Egypt during the Nasser and Sadat periods, it is essential to acquire an understanding of these factions' values and orientations.[13]

Regime Leftists

The Leftist faction grouped individuals of Marxist and/or strong "scientific socialist" orientations. They did not seek to eradicate private property, but they did pursue extensive state ownership and control of the economy, the elimination of antagonistic social class relations, continued close coopera- tion and assistance with the Soviet bloc, a strong anti-Western imperialism posture, and more extensive mobilization of Egypt's masses for political participation via the Arab Socialist Union. Prominent Leftists included for- mer communists and independent Marxists like Isma'il Sabri 'Abullah, Ibrahim Sa'd al-Din, Fuad Mursi, and Lutfi al-Kholi, along with military officers with leftist orientations like core group Free Officers Khalid Muhi al-Din and Kemal Rif'at. (N.B. Throughout this book, I will use the term Leftist to refer to this regime faction. I will use leftist in the lower case in ref- erence to the broad array of left-leaning socialists—as opposed to national socialists—and communists.)

Regime Centrists
Centrists believed in heavy state ownership and control of the economy, and a narrowing of social class differences, albeit not at the expense of the present generation. They strongly supported the special relationship with the Soviet bloc, blended with a strong interest in cultivating the non-align- ment movement, a disdain for U.S. and other Western imperialists' policies, and a commitment to Arab nationalism and Arab unity. Their left-leaning orientation was tempered by a distinct rejection of communism, in part due to their association of communism with atheism, but also because of their readiness to cooperate with national capitalists and all foreign actors willing to assist in Egypt's development. These principles combined to make them adherents to an "Arab application of scientific socialism."

During the 1960s, Centrists held the most important cabinet posts with Nasser's obvious blessing. After 'Amer's removal in 1967, almost all top posts were in Centrist hands. Prominent Centrists included 'Ali Sabri, Sha'rawi Gum'a, Sami Sharaf, Muhammad Fa'iq, Amin Huweidi, and 'Abd al-Muhsin Abu al-Nur, all of whom came from military backgrounds. Non-officer Centrists, like the technocrat 'Aziz Sidqi, also assumed promi- nent positions. Certain Centrists, like 'Ali Sabri, had devoted considerable time to developing political organizations like the ASU's secret Vanguard Organization (VO) and Youth Organization (YO), as well as propagating the regime's philosophy through the Higher Institute for Socialist Studies (HISS).

Regime Rightists
The regime Right was a more ambiguous grouping, embodying individu- als whose commitment to socialism, especially "scientific socialism," was circumspect. Most Rightists were more comfortable with "Arab socialist"

thought. Rightists were dubious of Egypt's association with the Soviet bloc, but for varying reasons. For some Rightists, like core group Free Officers Kemal al-Din Hussein and Hussein al-Shaf'ei, an attachment to a more conservative interpretation of Islam made association with communism and communist regimes a distasteful proposition. Such individuals typically shared a dim view of extensive state ownership and management of economic assets with another subset of Rightists that included core group Free Officers 'Abd al-Latif al-Boghdadi and Zakariyya Muhi al-Din, as well as many prominent technocrats like 'Abd al-Mun'im al-Qaisuni and Sayyid Mar'ei. They saw the nationalizations of 1963 and 1964 as cutting too deep, negatively affecting the interests of too many mid-level and small Egyptian capitalists. Individuals in this group were also more inclined to seek ways to reach out to Western countries so as not to leave Egypt so dependent upon the Soviet bloc. Finally, a third, extremely important sub-grouping of Rightists included individuals who backed extensive state ownership and control of the economy, but were motivated by statist and personal power considerations, not pro-socialist and anti-capitalist beliefs. This camp included 'Abd al-Hakim 'Amer, Shams Badran, and others.

The Rightists' power was great, especially in the military and security apparatuses, but also in the public sector companies and the bureaucracy. Two factors accounted for the Rightists' power in the state: (1) 'Amer and Badran made prodigious efforts to plant retired military officers and their friends and relatives in non-military government posts, and nearly all of these individuals shared a Rightist mindset; and (2) many Egyptian technocrats and bureaucrats were favorably predisposed toward the private sector and capitalism in general given their background and training. Many hoped to emulate either the liberal democratic, pro-free enterprise or "mixed" economy models represented by various Western nations.

Consequences of Intra-Regime Competition and Conflict
As will be amply demonstrated later on, internal personal rivalries often prevented each and every one of these value-based or ideology-based factions from coordinating their efforts and presenting a united front in intra-state wranglings and policy debates. Nonetheless, the importance of the factions' existence was clearly reflected in the blockages, bottlenecks, and confusion that they generated in many key regime policy debates and in attempts to implement crucial government policies. Some students of Egyptian politics, like Migdal,[14] have characterized Egypt as a "weak state," one in which powerful "societal" actors are capable of successfully resisting state-directed development policies. In my opinion, internal regime divisions were every bit as important in explaining the "Egypt as 'weak state'"

phenomenon as any putative strength attributed to so-called "societal" actors. In numerous cases, recalcitrant "societal" actors were directly abetted by state-based elites, a formula that significantly undermined Egypt's largely state-led, economic development effort. To cite just one example, 'Abd al-Hakim 'Amer's ability to control several key posts, including chairmanship of the committee to liquidate feudalism, resulted in a less than uniform application of that committee's efforts throughout the country. Wealthy farmers with connections to 'Amer and his cronies were left largely untouched by that committee's investigations.

All factors considered, at no time during Nasser's presidency did Nasser truly succeed in getting all of Egypt's most powerful actors actively cooperating in the proper implementation of an agreed-upon set of state policies. This was most clearly evidenced in the need to develop ASU cadres to check the power of the military. And, although Centrists occupied almost all key state positions in the period from late 1967 until the time of Nasser's death in 1970, the country's extremely difficult circumstances forced Nasser to choose between leaning more to the Left or the Right. He could opt for a deepening of the socialist experiment by placing more Leftists in positions of greater authority, coupled with concerted popular mobilization behind the socialist message and socialist policies. Or he could call for a slight political and economic liberalization. Nasser chose the latter course, and in so doing, he created greater breathing room for regime Rightists and pro-capitalist societal actors in the final years of his rule.

1970: Egypt's Grim Socioeconomic Picture

From the time of Nasser's 1952 coup until his death in 1970, Egypt underwent numerous, major transformations.[15] Its population had grown from over 21 million to slightly more than 33 million, a 54 percent increase. Education had expanded rapidly at all levels, such that by 1970 there were roughly three times the number of pupils in Egypt's grade schools, and more than three times as many students enrolled in its universities. Meanwhile, although illiteracy had declined by roughly five percent, it remained high at 70.2 percent nationwide. With the economy growing at a very slow pace—the average GDP growth was 3.3 percent per annum between fiscal 1964-65 and 1969-70,[16]—job prospects for the country's burgeoning masses, educated and uneducated alike, were growing increasingly bleak. One palliative was to cram many educated youth into the civil service and public sector companies. Thus, the civil service grew from 325,000 employees in 1952 to an army of 1.2 million in 1970. The government's ability to sustain this policy was dubious, at best. Cairo, a city set up to accommodate the needs of three million, had become home to nearly three times that number. Again, many of its new residents had been driven from their residences in the cities along the Suez Canal due to Israeli occupation of the Sinai peninsula and sporadic fighting along the canal in the 1968–1970 War of Attrition. Consequently, Egypt's housing shortage was acute. Most basic services were strained literally to the breaking point. Water pipes and sewage systems exploded, flooding sections of the city. In homes, water pipes often gurgled and gagged, faucets then spewing out brown water in the homes of those fortunate enough to have domestic plumbing.

The communications system was completely inadequate for reliable use, posing serious handicaps for businesspeople. In making a phone call, one heard metallic clanking sounds after composing the number. A Siemens phone engineer informed me that the system was so antiquated, that what one was hearing was the sounds of metal parts falling into place to complete the connection. So difficult was it to get an open line, and so unreliable were the phones, that some international businesspersons flew to Athens, Greece to make necessary communications.

Cars clogged the streets, and public buses and trams were bursting at the seams. Buses often did not stop; they just slowed down at stops, unloading some passengers and picking up those with the greatest speed and agility. When buses did stop, it often had as much to do with enabling their drivers and ticket collectors to get tea or pick up a quick bite to eat.[17]

Marketplaces were lean. Food and clothing were available at reasonable prices. However, there was little in the way of choice; and there were shortages—within a few years, people would be speaking of a possible "food crisis."[18] Consumer durables were in short supply, generally of poor quality, and beyond most citizens' means. For most people, life was, in a word, difficult.

On top of all this, there was still a war to be fought to liberate the Sinai peninsula and restore Egypt's national pride. The war effort was costing the state some L.E. 700 million ($1.5 billion) in annual military expenditures,[19] more than twice the sum of Egypt's total exports at the turn of the decade.[20] So long as the situation of "no war, no peace" prevailed, Egypt's prospects for socioeconomic development were slim.

Who Was Sadat?

The life history of Muhammad Anwar al-Sadat has been recounted numerous times in great detail. These biographies yield rich insights to Sadat's upbringing, character development, value formation, belief system, and overall personality. Most, however, refeclect distinct pro- or anti-Sadat biases, and many episodes of Sadat's life remain shrouded in mystery.

Sadat must bear responsibility for a fair portion of this problem. His ghostwritten autobiography, *In Search of Identity*,[21] inaccurately inflates his own historical role, while unjustifiably denigrating Nasser's. Among Sadat's admirers, there remains, despite numerous corrections and excellent insights, a penchant to accept Sadat's version of events as accurate despite clear contradictory evidence. To offer just two quick examples, both Finklestone and Israeli attribute the Free Officers' formation to Sadat, as did Sadat in his ghostwritten autobiography.[22] Sadat's claim is simply not true. As was true of several other officers and peers, Sadat did help establish small, clandestine officer groupings to engage in attacks against the British and various Egyptian political opponents. But Nasser alone must be given credit for masterminding the formation of the Free Officers group that conducted the 1952 coup.[23]

Sadat's detractors have also produced flawed biographies. Heikal falls into this category. In a position to write a nearly definitive biography of Sadat's early presidency, Heikal vengefully and unjustifiably trashed Sadat's historical record. For example, he devotes an entire page to the psychological significance of Sadat's failed effort in his teens to become an actor. But he devotes only a few sentences to Sadat's first prison sentence, which lasted from 1942 to 1944, and to the additional year he spent living underground after his escape. Heikal in fact makes it sound as though Sadat suffered no hardships.[24] Heikal's rendition of Sadat's second imprisonment, which lasted from January 1946 until August 1948, portrays Sadat as a privileged ward of the state, devoting much of his time to coordinating the sharing of prisoners' desserts, theatrical events, and rare glimpses of women, while being released occasionally to assist in assassinations of palace foes.[25] As presented, Heikal's account does great injustice to the physical and mental deprivations suffered by Sadat during most of this period, experiences that affected Sadat's health, character, and values for the rest of his life. Indeed, it is almost impossible to imagine the early, impetuously dramatic Sadat having the patience to endure the pejorative, condescending treatment he often experienced during Nasser's presidency, often dished out by Nasser himself, were he not to have recorded his lengthy prison sentences.

Sadat's life certainly merits additional biographical work, but that is not my task. For the purpose of this book, I wish to focus on the more salient value-forming, socialization experiences registered by Sadat from his childhood until Nasser's death in 1970, with an eye to facilitating comprehension of his political behavior before and after he became president.

Sadat's Roots

Sadat was born on December 25, 1918 in the Nile Delta village of Mit Abu al-Kom in the district of Minufiyya. He was the second of four children sired by a modestly paid official, Muhammad Muhammad al-Sadati,[26] through a union with the second of Mr. al-Sadati's eventual many wives, Sitt al-Barrein. Sitt al-Barrein came from a humble Sudanese family. Thus, there was little in Sadat's origins to suggest the heights of national and international stature to which he would one day rise. However, born in a generation in Egypt that was exposed to powerful winds of social, economic, and political change, the environment would prove rich in opportunity for a young man endowed with an imagination as fertile as Sadat's.

Like so many youths of his own generation, Sadat was caught in the maelstrom of forces convulsing a stubbornly traditional society. In the boyhood village where he spent the first six years of his life, Sadat was raised by his doting, loving grandmother, Umm Muhammad. He was left in her care when his mother returned to live with his father, who was performing translation and liaison work for a British medical group in the Sudan. Sadat's grandmother played an extremely important role in his early political socialization. She fed him a steady diet of bold acts by nationalist heroes. Sadat's favorite was that of the fabled Zahran, hanged by British officials in the aftermath of the infamous 1906 incident at Denshaway, a neighboring village. Through this story and others, he developed an intense nationalism, and a sight-unseen hatred of the British.[27] Moreover, so inspired was Sadat by such stories that beginning in his childhood he repeatedly acted out and acted upon dreams of grandeur.

Finally, one cannot overestimate the importance of Sadat's religious training during his childhood. His initial, formal instruction was acquired at the village *kuttab,* or Koranic teaching school. It provided the basis for religious beliefs that would mark many of Sadat's values for the rest of his life.

Mansur Hassan, who would serve as Sadat's information minister, noted that when his own father sent him from his Delta village to Cairo as a boy, it was as if he had been sent to the moon, so radical was the difference in the environments.[28] As Hassan was many years Sadat's junior, one can appreciate just how different rural and urban settings were for the young Sadat, who experienced a similar move at the age of six. Sadat's father had returned to Cairo in 1922 and taken another wife. Two years later he summoned his family in Mit Abu al-Kom to his new home in Kubri al-Qubba, a northern district of greater Cairo. Sadat himself made numerous reference to the difficulty of this transition, often in his typically humorous, self-deprecating style. He depicted himself as a virtual country bumpkin, recalling, for instance, how he threw himself on the floor during his first trip to a cinema in the big city, fearing that the train on the screen was going to run over him.[29]

Anyone who has lived in Cairo in more recent decades, and come to love that city in its present incarnation, can only dream of how intriguing and wondrous the city must have been at the time of Sadat's youth. Certainly the intrigues of the city and the world beyond must have offered focal points far preferable to life at home, where Sadat's mother saw her husband take many additional wives, and where twelve other children vied for their father's attention.[30] In the city beyond the home's walls, there stirred a political effervescence that was irresistible to many in Egypt's small but rapidly expanding corps of educated youth. As noted earlier, from 1923 onward Egypt had entered into a new political era. British imperial representatives maintained great influence over "high politics" with the nominally independent monarchical regime, but there was great political diversity and party activity amid intense opposition to the British occupation.

Sadat himself was caught up in the whirl of political activity over the great issues of the day. Exposure to Egypt's rampant social injustices had a deep impact on his thinking.[31] Later on in his life, one of his own children, a daughter by his first marriage, succumbed to illness and died in part due to his inability to provide proper care for her. Still, Sadat never held the same scorn, revulsion, and even "complex" vis-à-vis the upper class that Nasser did[32] and Sadat's adult life would be rich with friends from all social classes. Rather, the preeminent issue for Sadat was the British occupation, Egyptian subservience, and the loss of Egypt's national sovereignty and dignity.

Thus, in his early youth, Sadat's political consciousness was raised, but not ideologically sharpened. Sadat wrote:

> I cannot say that during the early period of my life my political consciousness had matured or even taken shape. I shared the patriotic feelings of all Egyptians, of course. I took part in the demonstrations, smashing of plates and burning down of trams, and the chanting of slogans calling for the removal of Ismail Sidki Pasha and reactivation of the 1923 Constitution—but I didn't even know what that Constitution really was.
>
>   I can say, however, that a certain feeling had struck root in me by the time I left school—a hatred for all aggressors, and a love and admiration for anyone trying to liberate his land.[33]

Sadat developed a marked propensity for political activism, and experimented with every political party in Egypt.[34] Sadat recalled that as a 12-year-old, upon hearing that "Hitler had marched from Munich to Berlin to wipe out the consequences of Germany's defeat in World War I and rebuild his country [he] gathered [his] friends and told them to follow Hitler's example by marching forth from Mit Abul-Kom [*sic*] to Cairo.

They laughed and went away."[35] Sadat was also deeply taken by Gandhi, who passed through Egypt in 1932, and Sadat took to imitating him in dress and behavior for a brief period.[36] But between Gandhi and Hitler, the latter seems to have made the stronger impression. Sadat, like many other Egyptian youth, was deeply impressed by accounts of the European fascist leaders' rapid empowerment of their countries, and a "true adoration was reserved for what he perceived as the typical Teutonic sense of organization, discipline, precision and obedience to superiors."[37] The depth and breadth of this admiration in Egypt's body politic was manifested by several Egyptian political parties' creation of their own paramilitary organizations, imitating fascist "Brown Shirts" and "Black Shirts" with formations like Misr al-Fatat's "Green Shirts," the Muslim Brothers' "Rovers," and the Wafd's "Blue Shirts." One might also add that in the "Arab world," the expression "The enemy of your enemy is your friend," however hackneyed, represents a maxim. If the Germans could defeat the hated British, many saw good cause in supporting them.

Sadat appeared devoted during his teenage years to overcoming initial difficulties with his schooling, which led him to obtain his secondary school certification from an inferior institution. Beyond his extracurricular political interests, he spent some of his spare time developing a keen, but ultimately disappointing, interest in acting.

Sadat Enters the Military

Sadat's political activism did not truly blossom until he enrolled in the Military Academy in 1937. His decision to pursue a military career seems a natural one, given his longtime attraction to national heroes, and his father's high esteem for military figures like Napoleon Bonaparte and modern Turkey's founder, Kemal Ataturk.[38] Prior to 1936, a person of Sadat's background would not have had the slightest chance of entering the military academy. But in that year, in order to expand rapidly Egypt's armed forces, the government reformed the enrollment requirements by lifting property qualifications, thus allowing children from lower social class backgrounds to apply for admission. However, one still needed to provide proof of one's father's property and income, and sponsorship by a dignitary. Cadets from lower-middle-class backgrounds, like Sadat, Nasser, and Hassan Ibrahim, remained a minority,[39] but could get in with the help of someone who was wellconnected.

Sadat's "reference" came via a British doctor with whom Sadat's father had worked in the Sudan. The former had a rapport with Undersecretary for War (Basha Ibrahim Kheiri), and put in a word on Sadat's behalf. Sadat's encounter with Ibrahim Basha was the first time Sadat set foot in an aris-

tocrat's house. Anecdotally, it is interesting that, despite Sadat's vivid recol-
lection of the Basha's condescending air, decades later Sadat received the
Basha and responded favorably to his special request for assistance.[40] In
contrast, Nasser, who was treated in a similarly patronizing way by his aris-
tocratic "reference," exacted revenge while president by denying the man's
request to go abroad for medical treatment.[41]

As the clouds of war darkened in Europe, cadets in Egypt underwent
accelerated academic programs. So in February 1938, just nine months after
his admission to the military academy, Sadat graduated with the rank of
second lieutenant and was posted to Manqabad in Upper Egypt in the
infantry. It was in Manqabad that Sadat first met Nasser, and was exposed
to Nasser's poignant ruminations about Egypt's plight.[42] Sadat also
befriended Khalid Muhi al-Din in Manqabad.[43] At this time, Khalid was
closer to the Muslim Brothers' thinking; he embraced Marxism in the late
1940s and would retain a leftist orientation for the rest of his life.

Clandestine Political Activity

In 1940, Nasser was posted to the Sudan, while Sadat was sent to Ma'adi,
a leafy residential district just south of Cairo. At this time, Sadat married
his childhood sweetheart, Eqbal 'Afifi, who was the daughter of Mit Abu
al-Kom's village headman (*'umda*). Through his union with Eqbal, Sadat
would have four daughters, one of whom was the child who died in her
infancy. Meanwhile, in Ma'adi, Sadat met other personages who whetted
his appetite for political activism. It was in Ma'adi that Sadat first met and
heard Hassan al-Banna speak. Al-Banna, the charismatic founder of the
Muslim Brotherhood (1928), was then allowed by the palace and the 'Ali
Maher government to speak to military units to build up the Muslim
Brotherhood as a counterweight to the Wafd. Sadat found al-Banna capti-
vating.[44]

Sadat also met Hassan 'Izzat in Ma'adi. 'Izzat belonged to a small group
of Air Force officers formed in late 1939, led by 'Abd al-Latif al-Boghdadi,
that also included Wagih Abaza, Hassan Ibrahim, and Ahmed Sa'udi.[45]
They were in touch with the Muslim Brothers, as well as some small socialist organizations. They also visited and were heavily influenced by the
older, enthralling nationalist figure, Gen. 'Aziz al-Masri, inspector general
of the Egyptian army. All were interested in developing clandestine contacts with the Germans during the war to abet their effort against the
British in exchange for Egyptian independence. Sadat was an attractive
recruit, as his experience with transmitters as a signal corps officer fulfilled
a basic need of the group.

The Boghdadi group engaged in a number of daring episodes. One involved a tragicomic effort to smuggle Gen. 'Aziz al-Masri out of Egypt in an inadequately fueled plane to assist a German-backed coup in Iraq in 1941. In February 1942, with World War II ablaze and Field Marshal Rommel advancing on the Allied forces in North Africa, the British encircled the royal palace with tanks to force King Faruq to drop his pro-Axis prime minister, 'Ali Maher, and replace him with the Wafdist leader, Mustafa al-Nahhas. Egyptian nationalists of various political stripes were doubly incensed: they vehemently denounced Britain's brutish intervention in Egypt's domestic politics and the insult to the Egyptian king; and they decried the complicity of Egypt's most vaunted nationalist party, the Wafd, in this incident. Scores of officers, including Sadat and his confreres in the Boghdadi group, were outraged, and a handful mounted another half-baked plot to remove the British yoke from the king's neck. Sadat spent part of the evening circling the king's palace in a jeep, waiting in futility for others to join him to attack the British.

Prison Time

Through similar pursuits Sadat eventually took up with two German spies who possessed a transmitter and sought to promote German-Egyptian contacts as part of their activities. Discovery of these spies' activities by the British eventuated in Sadat's arrest and first imprisonment from July 1942 until October 1944. This prison term greatly reinforced Sadat's personal hatred of the Wafd party, which was in power by virtue of British support.[46]

Sadat served in three different detention sites (the Aliens' jail in Cairo, al-Maqusa detention center near al-Minya, and al-Zeitoun detention center near Cairo). Sadat, Hassan 'Izzat, and four others managed to escape from al-Zeitoun. One of the four was Musa Sabri, a civilian youth who later served as one of President Sadat's key speechwriters. 'Izzat stayed at large, whereas Sadat, after signing the visitor's book at 'Abdin Palace and advising the king, in writing, not to submit to British dictates, returned himself to detention.[47]

Once the British felt more secure in their wartime position—circa October 1944—the king felt it safe to remove Nahhas as prime minister and replace him with Ahmed Maher, the founder of the Sa'dist party. Ahmed Maher oversaw the release of many opposition elements from prison, including Misr al-Fatat types. Everybody was released, said Sadat, except members of his little group; as a consequence, they planned a successful escape.[48] Sadat spent the next year as a fugitive, assuming a false identity and working as a porter and a truck driver until September 1945, when the war's end brought a lifting of martial law.

With the lifting of martial law, Sadat became a free man, but he reactivated his involvement in various clandestine operations. Specifically, Sadat established contact with Hussein Tewfiq through 'Umar Abu 'Ali. Tewfiq had been shooting at British soldiers in Ma'adi,[49] and Sadat encouraged Tewfiq to focus on higher profile targets.[50] He willingly accompanied Hussein Tewfiq in an attempt to assassinate the Wafdist leader, Mustafa al-Nahhas, on September 6, 1945. Immediately thereafter, this same little band began plotting the assassination of the Wafdist official, Amin 'Uthman, who had earned the opprobrium of many Egyptian nationalists by referring to Egypt's relationship with Great Britain as akin to a Catholic marriage; that is, not accepting a divorce. This effort was successful; 'Uthman was shot to death at short range on January 6, 1946 by Hussein Tewfiq. But when Tewfiq was arrested and confessed, he incriminated his colleagues including Sadat. On January 12, 1946, Sadat was arrested and once again found himself in the Aliens' jail. From there he was soon transferred to Cairo Central Prison, cell 54, where exceptionally harsh living conditions had a profound impact on Sadat's psyche, as he wrote about at length in his autobiography.[51] Sadat remained in this putrid place for eighteen months. (It is interesting to note that Heikal's account of this imprisonment makes no mention of Cairo Central Prison, places emphasis on Sadat's special privileges and lighthearted prison activities, and generally makes it sound as though Sadat suffered few hardships.) [52]

The principals accused in the Amin 'Uthman case were not placed on trial until January 1948. The high-profile trial then lasted until July 1948, followed intently by consumers of the national daily news. In this fashion, Sadat acquired considerable notoriety. Sentencing came in August. Hussein Tewfiq received 15 years in prison, but Sadat was found not guilty, and released. During his final year in prison, Sadat had decided to divorce his wife, Eqbal. Upon his release, he took a flat by himself in Helwan; but his friend, Hassan 'Izzat, soon enticed him to live in Suez City, and it was there that he met and instantly fell in love with the young Jehan Ra'uf. Jehan was immediately smitten by this well-known nationalist figure, whose case she had followed closely.

Sadat's Return to the Military
Sadat took a job briefly with 'Izzat in contracting, then went back to Cairo and took a job as a journalist at al-Hilal that lasted until December 1948. He went back into business with 'Izzat, supervising contracting jobs in Zaqaziq, and lived there with Jehan, whom he had married on May 29, 1949. By fall 1949, however, he had a falling out with 'Izzat over money.[53] This experience soured him on a career in business in general and rekindled a desire to go back to military service to achieve loftier goals.[54] To this end, Sadat sought the assistance of a Dr. Yusuf Rashad in January 1950.[55] Heikal says

Rashad advised Sadat to throw himself at Faruq's mercy, apologize for any wrongdoings and kiss the king's hand, and that Sadat did so.[56] I have not been able to ascertain whether Heikal's details are accurate or not, but clearly Rashad did arrange a meeting for Sadat with Gen. Muhammad Haidar Basha, commander in chief of the armed forces. Haidar gave Sadat a slightly cool reception, but quickly approved his return. Sadat was thus reinstated at the same rank he held at the time of his dismissal—that of captain—on January 15, 1950. His peers had already received two promotions, first to major, then lieutenant colonel.[57]

The Iron Guard

Rashad's past, and Sadat's connection to him, merit closer scrutiny. By chance, Rashad had been on hand to provide medical care to King Faruq following an automobile accident that occurred on November 15, 1943. Faruq took a liking to the suave Rashad, and was at least equally attracted to his beautiful wife, Nahed, whom he made a lady-in-waiting.

In his efforts to find a foil to the Wafd, Faruq eventually called upon Rashad to set up a clandestine group called the Iron Guard. Again, in the early- to mid-1940s, there was enormous sympathy for the king among many Egyptian nationalists. The young king still embodied the nation's symbol; he was widely perceived as personally oppressed and constrained by the British, not as the debauched playboy that he became in subsequent years. Thus, recruiting individuals to support the king was not a difficult task, especially in light of many individuals' (including many officers') hatred of certain civilian politicians. When, exactly, Rashad applied himself to this task is hard to determine.[58] The best guess on the Iron Guard's formation would be sometime during 1944 or 1945.

Sadat had met Rashad while posted in the Mediterranean beach town of al-Garawla near Marsa Matruh in 1941. At that time, Sadat had bent the rules to allow Rashad to use military communications to check on the health of his son. Rashad greatly appreciated Sadat's assistance, and a friendship was established. Sadat says he did not see Rashad after their Garawla days until January 1950,[59] but this seems inaccurate.

The exact date of Sadat's involvement with the Iron Guard, if it happened at all, is as unclear as the date of the group's creation. Heikal's account appears flawed, as he has Hassan 'Izzat recruiting Sadat to the Iron Guard while Sadat was in al-Maqusa,[60] where Sadat was imprisoned from December 1942 until late October or early November 1943[61]—that is, slightly prior to the king's first encounter with Rashad.

Sadat notes that in September 1945, almost immediately after the lifting of martial law, he reestablished contact with an old acquaintance, 'Umar

Abu 'Ali.[62] It was Abu 'Ali who arranged the meeting between Sadat and Hussein Tewfiq, prior to the assassination attempt against Nahhas and the successful assassination of Amin 'Uthman. Tewfiq told the members of his small Egyptian nationalist grouping, one of whom was his cousin Muhammad Ibrahim Kamel (later foreign minister under Sadat), that Abu 'Ali represented an organization that "disposed of superior resources."[63] Kamel gives no name to that organization, although this could have been the Iron Guard.

Muhsin 'Abd al-Khaliq says the Iron Guard started trying to recruit officers after the 1948 war, but success was limited. He claims the following officers were recruited: Anwar Sadat, Hassan al-Tuhami, Kemal Rif'at, Ahmed Yusuf Habib, Hassan Fahmi 'Abd al-Magid, 'Abd al-Ra'uf Nur al-Din, Sayyid Gad Salem, Khalid Fawzi, and Mustafa Kemal Sidqi.[64] Many of the lesser-known officers had previously belonged to a group headed by Mustafa Kemal Sidqi that had plotted the assassination of a senior officer, Atallah Basha, and were arrested in October 1947. Once they were cleared, and Atallah was dumped, Kamel says that they were recruited by Rashad to do the king's secret bidding against his civilian adversaries.[65] Kamel also notes that they moved immediately against their first target, attempting to assassinate Nahhas on April 5, 1948 and again just 20 days later.[66]

Although Sadat does not write at all about participation in these attempts, and Jehan Sadat adamantly rejects Sadat's Iron Guard involvement,[67] he may well have been either directly or indirectly involved with the group. What is certain is that on April 5, alongside 'Abd al-Ra'uf Nur al-Din and Hassan Fahmi 'Abd al-Magid, and on April 25 with Mustafa Kemal Sidqi and 'Abd al-Ra'uf Nur al-Din, Sadat participated in assassination attempts.[68] Sadat himself notes that there was a period during his 1946–1948 imprisonment when he was able to leave prison on several occasions.[69] Heikal claims that Sadat was smuggled out for the assassination attempts.[70] Whichever was the case, Sadat's "availability" seems well-enough established, and he was certainly not lacking in "motive."

Linking Up with the Free Officers

Whatever Sadat's involvement, association, or non-association with the Iron Guard, he was readmitted to the military with Rashad's help. According to Sadat,[71] Nasser and 'Amer were the first to call on him in 1950 to congratulate him when he was readmitted. He implies that resumption of contacts with the leader of the Free Officers group—which had held its first founding committee meeting in October 1949—brought with it his inclusion in the Free Officers' inner group, or Constituent Council.[72] But here, on the basis of my research, Heikal's account is closer to the mark.[73] Many officers, like Muhsin ʿAbd al-Khaliq, were indeed bothered by Sadat's past, because they were convinced he had worked with the Iron Guard.[74] According to my Free Officer sources, Nasser contacted Sadat in 1951, but kept Sadat uninformed about the Free Officers' membership, structure, and activities. Thus, Sadat was given only vague knowledge of a nationalist association that could perhaps use his services, especially his contacts in the palace, to learn what was brewing behind the palace's walls. Sadat was then invited to become a member of the Free Officers in late 1951.[75]

While Sadat's doubters and critics have spilled much ink over his Iron Guard membership, the very success of the military coup in July 1952 stands as testimony to Sadat's loyalty to the Free Officers. Although Sadat was posted in Rafah (in the northern Sinai peninsula) from mid-1951 until the time of the coup, his leaves permitted him numerous opportunities to return to Cairo or Alexandria and meet, separately of course, with both Rashad and Nasser. There were those who believed Sadat worked both sides of the fence,[76] as opposed to providing the Free Officers with information on the palace's maneuverings while planting disinformation at the palace via Rashad, as Sadat himself claimed.[77] But the Free Officers remained intact, untouched, and available to participate in the July 23 overthrow of Faruq. As attested to by several Free Officers, these factors seem ample proof that Sadat did nothing to impair their movement.[78]

Sadat and the Coup

On July 21, Nasser sent Hassan Ibrahim to inform Sadat and others in Gaza to come to Cairo in preparation for the coup. Sadat found no message from Nasser in Cairo, and on the evening of July 22, he took his wife, Jehan, to the movies. He left a note for the doorman to reach him at the cinema if any word came, but the doorman failed to follow Sadat's instructions. When Sadat returned from the cinema, he was belatedly informed that Nasser had left two messages for Sadat to go to ʿAbd al-Hakim ʿAmer's house that evening. Sadat immediately dressed in uniform and left to find his coup-minded colleagues.

This is Sadat's version, and it has been passionately defended by well-informed Free Officers like Hassan Ibrahim, Khalid Muhi al-Din, and Muhsin ʿAbd al-Khaliq.[79] ʿAbd al-Khaliq has studied the coup as carefully as anyone. His viewpoint acquires greater credibility because he openly admits to have been among those who questioned Sadat's subsequent inclusion in the Free Officers due to his Iron Guard past, and to disapprove of much that Sadat did as president.[80] Much of the same can be said of Khalid Muhi al-Din and Hassan Ibrahim, of course. That Sadat may have tried to create an alibi for himself by going to the cinema, and picking a fight there so that he would be noticed, seems perfectly understandable in light of the many years he had already spent in prison for illegal political activity. In addition, as many as 30 to 40 percent of the Free Officers got "cold feet" and failed to show up at all at the time of the coup.[81] By comparison, Sadat's behavior was exemplary. Indeed, he incurred great personal risk on the night of the coup. After donning his uniform, he was temporarily held by security personnel who questioned his presence at one site, and he was at the side of key coup conspirators when initial coup successes were being consolidated. Furthermore, Sadat actually announced the coup. Thus, there can be no doubt that any reversal of the coup-makers' fortune—and there was always the fear that the British might intervene to produce one—would have cost Sadat his neck.

Sadat experienced some of his moments of greatest personal satisfaction in the coup's immediate aftermath. With the coup successfully completed, it was Sadat who was tapped by Nasser to announce the military's seizing of power in the morning radio broadcast. Sadat was, after all, the member of the core group whose name was best known to the public because of the Amin 'Uthman trial; he was also considered to possess an impressive speaking voice. Next, on July 26, 1952, Sadat accompanied Gen. Muhammad Nagib to deliver the ultimatum to King Faruq and Prime Minister 'Ali Maher in Alexandria, and both presided over a dignified sending of Faruq into exile.

Sadat's Post-Coup Performance

Despite Sadat's initially high profile, he did not rise to any position of great power in what became Nasser's regime. And despite the lofty titles he eventually acquired, for example, speaker of the National Assembly, he was not seen as a powerful actor during the Nasser years. Why, one might ask, was this the case? First, Sadat did not aggressively pursue positions of power in the new regime. As he wrote, the 1952 revolution "was the culmination of a lifelong struggle, and, in terms of my own ideals and values, the moment it came off I felt I needed nothing more—nothing else was of any real value to me—and that was why I could then stand easily aside from all squabbles."[82] Second, if he had acted more aggressively, it is highly probable that the heavily calculating Nasser would have sought ways to check Sadat's power aspirations, to nip them in the bud, as he was wont to do with other potential rivals (by assigning them to ambassadorial posts abroad or otherwise distancing them from the locus of power). Third, as discussed more fully below, Sadat was not taken seriously by many of his peers.

Sadat's Regime Friends and Personality Traits
From the early days of the new regime, Sadat developed a warm relationship with Nasser's closest friend, 'Amer. Heikal suggests that Sadat did so as a way to guarantee his own long-term interests.[83] It is even more likely, however, that Sadat grew attached to 'Amer because in 'Amer's bon vivant spirit and kindhearted temperament Sadat found an attractive alternative to the workaholic, often dour, and taciturn Nasser. The friendship between Sadat and 'Amer created an interesting triangular relationship between the three men. Free Officer Wagih Abaza, who knew well all the principals, said that "Sadat's kalaam (talk) was always with Nasser; his behavior put him with the 'Abd al-Hakim 'Amer crowd."[84] As shall be seen, this characterization is simplistic and inaccurate, but does contain an element of truth. Sadat's years of deprivation had not embittered him, but rather left him with a strong joie de vivre. Sadat was more introverted in "mixed" company and certain social situations,[85] but by all reports he loved to sing, dance, and amuse his colleagues with his excellent sense of humor. In fact, he engaged in such activities frequently enough to acquire a reputation among his colleagues for these traits. Some even nicknamed him al-raqqas (the dancer). Regime elites who were more inclined to have fun desired Sadat's presence on social occasions because they knew how pleasant he could make things. Compared to the straightlaced Nasser, Sadat was one of the boys, ready to party.[86] 'Amer and his closest friends, 'Ali Shafiq and Salah Nasr, were known to engage in such behavior to excess.

When Egyptians are describing people, they generally favor someone whose "blood is light" over someone whose "blood is heavy." Indeed, when someone enters an Egyptian's house, the host intones a standard greeting that the guest is "lighting up the house." Sadat had "light blood"; he truly "lit up" his friends' homes. Lacking the keener mind and thirst for information of Nasser, or alternatively, the higher social-class background and connections of 'Amer, Sadat was never seen as a true equal to the two men at the pinnacle of Egypt's power structure. Yet his qualities of friendship, lightheartedness, and affability endeared him to Nasser and 'Amer, keeping Sadat and his family in the hearts of Egypt's highest-ranking elites.

At this juncture, it is important to register two additional points about Sadat's character. First, it seems clear that one should take at face value Sadat's own description of his sentiments at the time of the coup: he was indeed content. After suffering many years in prison, combined with many other years of exhilarating but anxiety-producing nationalistic struggle, he had finally helped to restore Egypt's sense of national pride. Although he continued to play roles in the Nasser regime, and would later resume his risk-taking behavior, at this stage he was in many respects content to rest on his "revolutionary laurels" and enjoy life and the trappings of power. Because, beyond his obviously intense nationalism, he had no ideological axe to grind, and because, without his position in the state, he might well have suffered a serious, at least short-run, status reversal, he proved loathe to take a stand that might put an end to the ride.

Sadat's "EQ"

To end discussion of Sadat's character at this point would be to miss, in my opinion, a second, equally important dimension, one that would manifest itself most clearly only after Sadat assumed the presidency. Recent analyses of an individual's ability to succeed in leadership roles has shown no direct correlation with higher intelligence quotients per se.[87] An individual's success often hinges on his or her "emotional intelligence" or so-called "EQ" as opposed to "IQ." What matters is often one's ability to understand the complexities of interpersonal relations in order to adroitly choose one's course of action. It is perhaps most propitious to view Sadat's track record in light of this new research. Trapped in more conventional conceptualizations of one's abilities, based almost completely on one's intelligence quotient or intellectual prowess, most of Sadat's contemporaries were perhaps too quick in taking their measure of him. As shall be seen, such biased underestimation of Sadat's capabilities would cost some individuals quite dearly in confrontations with Sadat during his presidency.

Sadat was quick to recognize and accept Nasser's position as preeminent leader of the "revolution." He also quickly, and accurately, understood the depth of Nasser's power ambitions and the negative consequences of bucking Nasser's will. Such factors gave him additional reasons to adopt a largely self-abnegating role in the early RCC debates over the country's future. Moreover, because he was predisposed to thinking that authoritarian rulers could accomplish their objectives much more quickly than democratic ones, he also moved quickly to a position of endorsing Nasser's firm grip on power. Accordingly, at one critical juncture, Sadat proposed to all of his colleagues his willingness to step down from power and allow Nasser complete freedom to reconstruct the government as he desired.[88] Although Nasser responded angrily to Sadat's *démarche,* this is without question what Nasser most ardently desired at the time. Sadat not only understood this perfectly well, but was also content to grant Nasser this unlimited authority.

Sadat as Regime Handyman

In brief, Sadat willingly took on regime roles of less importance; but one must also recognize that some of these roles jibed with long-felt extra-military interests and avocations. For example, Sadat had long held a certain fascination with the world of journalism. This interest first manifested itself in his efforts to help cobble together a prison magazine in October 1946, and Sadat worked briefly at *al-Musawwar* in 1948.[89] His flair for the literary was demonstrated in his response to a September 1953 inquiry by *al-Musawwar* magazine as to what one would write to Hitler were he still alive. I quote it here at length because it reveals both Sadat's literary flair and his political beliefs at that time. Sadat wrote:

> My Dear Hitler,
> I admire you from the bottom of my heart. Even if you appear to have been defeated, in reality you are the victor. You have succeeded in creating dissension between the old man Churchill and his allies, the sons of Satan. Germany will triumph because her existence is necessary to preserve the world balance. Germany will be reborn in spite of the Western and Eastern powers. There will be no peace unless Germany again becomes what she was. Both West and East will pay for her rehabilitation, whether they like it or not. Both sides will invest a great deal of money and effort in Germany in order to have her on their side . . . You did some mistakes . . . but our faith in your nation has more than compensated for them. You must be proud to have become an immortal leader of Germany. We will not be surprised if you showed up anew in Germany or if a new Hitler should rise to replace you . . . [90]

Thus, it was not so odd that in December 1953, after resigning from the RCC due to its members' bickering, Sadat founded the regime's new newspaper, *al-Gumhurriyya*. He became its chief editor, and the paper served as the mouthpiece of the RCC and the 1952 "revolution." During 1954, Sadat left *al-Gumhurriyya*, returned to the RCC, and juggled various assignments as a government minister without portfolio. In early 1955, Sadat again resigned from the RCC and returned to *al-Gumhurriyya*, but he did not retain this position very long. An article in which he wrote, rather undiplomatically, about John Foster Dulles' "piggish neck" did not go over well with Nasser, and helped prompt Sadat's removal from that post.[91] All told, Sadat did spend significant time from 1954 to 1956 penning articles, as well as writing several books about Nasser and the 1952 revolution: *Revolt on the Nile, Oh My Son, This is Your Uncle Gamal,* and *Unknown Pages.* As Gordon has astutely observed, through these efforts Sadat not only helped define the official history of the Free Officers and the "revolution," but also played an important agit-prop role, defending the regime against major domestic and foreign challenges.[92]

In his role as a regime handyman of sorts, several of Sadat's assignments were of a religious character. The depth of Sadat's religiosity was clearly marked on his forehead by his *zabib,* the dark "callous" acquired by many Muslims through extensive prayer and friction with the prayer rug. His religious disposition placed him, from a more "ideological" perspective, in proximity to other regime elites like Kemal al-Din Hussein and Hussein al Shaf'ei, although disagreement brought on by other factors, including his "partying," never left Sadat particularly close to these individuals in his personal relations.

Nasser, who was always keen to create special checks and balances, saw the visibly religious Sadat as an excellent candidate to carry the Islamic banner for the regime. After Nasser narrowly escaped an assassination attempt by a Muslim Brother in November 1954, and thousands of MB members were arrested in an effort to crush that organization, Nasser tapped Sadat to serve as a member of the People's Tribunal to try the Muslim Brothers.

Along similar lines, Nasser selected Sadat as Egypt's candidate for the top post in its new Islamic Congress, virtually assuring Sadat's selection as its secretary general in January 1955. In this capacity, Sadat traveled frequently to other predominantly Muslim countries, and worked hard to extend Egypt's influence over issues such as adherence to the Baghdad Pact.[93] The job also provided Sadat the opportunity to establish relations with other figures who would influence his political-economic and social orientations. For example, Sadat met and befriended Kemal Adham, whose sister was married to Prince Feisal. Adham later became head of Saudi intelligence. Sadat was a witness at Adham's 1955 wedding.[94]

Sadat's religious views also influenced his thinking about Israel and "the Jews," the term that most Egyptians used in Sadat's time when talking about Israelis. As one biographer wrote,

> Sadat's pro-German inclinations may also have been subconsciously linked with his deep dislike, distrust and contempt for the Jews. Inevitably his attitudes were influenced by derogatory passages in the Holy Quran rejecting Jews and by Islamic political theory which gave them a well-defined subordinate status within the Abode of Islam . . . Sadat tried to differentiate between Jews, Zionism and Israel, but couldn't help continuing to use the terms interchangeably. Besides his need to dehumanize Jews and Zionists in order to justify his struggle against Israel, his thinking showed residues of European anti-Semitism which could have been drawn from German (probably *Mein Kampf*) and other Western sources. He often invoked standard anti-Semitic arguments about "international conspiracy," "world economic domination" and the "rule of world media." He also accused Zionism of aligning itself with world imperialism, and attacked some "American presi-

dents, notably Lyndon Johnson, for having 'succumbed to Zionist-Jewish pressures.' "[95]

Whether Sadat needed to dehumanize Jews and Zionists "in order to justify his struggle against Israel" is debatable. Nevertheless, Sadat's thinking, especially prior to becoming president, probably differed little from that of other regime notables of a more religious bent, like Kemal al-Din Hussein and Hussein al-Shaf'ei. In independent interviews with each of these men, both inquired whether or not I had read *The Protocols of the Elders of Zion*.[96] Both did so as if to suggest that the book made for enlightening and instructive reading.[97]

Sadat's Other Regime Roles and His View of Regime Policies

In his autobiography, Sadat wrote little about the 1956 Suez Canal crisis and the October 1956 war, events that catapulted Nasser into the stratosphere of popular figures regionally and in the developing world. Sadat spent as much time discussing Nasser's error in giving the Soviets credit for the French, British, and Israelis' withdrawal, while ignoring Eisenhower's pressure for a withdrawal on November 5: "This was absurd because it was the U.S. attitude, as I have said, that turned our defeat into victory. Besides, as a professional politician, Nasser should have seized that chance to consolidate U.S.-Egyptian relations, if only to frustrate the Israeli strategy, which sought the reverse."[98] Here is Sadat, years after the event, belittling Nasser's behavior during what so many Egyptians, Arabs, and others saw as Nasser's greatest moment.

During Egypt's 1958-1961 political unity with Syria, Sadat first served as deputy speaker (1958-1960), then speaker of the joint parliament of the United Arab Republic (UAR). But as lofty as the latter title sounds, especially to individuals coming from more liberal democratic backgrounds, this was not viewed by regime elites as an important post. The parliament's role was largely symbolic; key policy decisions were made by executive officials and brought to parliament to be rubber-stamped, as in so many other authoritarian regimes. Five years after the UAR's dissolution, Sadat was again selected to serve as the speaker of the Egyptian National Assembly. Both stints as parliamentary speaker were of importance to Sadat's long-term career by way of the contact they provided him with Egyptian parliamentarians. As will be seen later, these extensive contacts served Sadat admirably well in a critical showdown with other regime forces.

It was also partly as a result of his position as speaker that Sadat was designated by Nasser to travel to the United States in February 1966. While in Washington, D.C., Sadat met briefly with President Johnson, and had many meetings on Capitol Hill. He exhibited great interest in democratic procedures and how Congress worked.[99] Sadat, accompanied by his wife, also traveled to California, where he met Gov. Pat Brown, and to New York. In New York, pro-Israeli groups engineered a snubbing by Mayor Lindsay. Sadat's escort during this trip was a State Department official, Michael Sterner. Sterner had met Sadat while serving from 1960-1965 in Egypt, having been responsible for covering Egyptian parliamentary affairs. Sadat had noticed Sterner, invited him to tea, and a cordial relationship developed. Although Sterner never received any indication that Sadat was dissatisfied with Egypt's socialism, he found Sadat was "much less of a Nasserite in tonality than the Sabri crowd," all of whose key members he had also met. "They were stiff and always lecturing to us; Sadat, even then, was friendly, humorous, cheerful, open and liked to joke."[100]

This was Sadat's first visit to the United States. Earlier the same year he had accompanied Nasser on a trip to the other superpower, offering Sadat a comparative perspective. According to Jehan Sadat, the trip to the United States made an enormously favorable impression upon her and her husband.[101] "Egypt's Ambassador Kamel confided [to Sterner] that Sadat was so euphoric over his reception in Washington 'it didn't matter what happened the rest of the trip.'"[102] Sterner, too, got an even better measure of Sadat, and was pleasantly surprised by his keen interest in the United States: "It dawned on me he had a different perspective."[103]

During 1962, Sadat had accompanied Field Marshal 'Amer on a fact-finding mission to Yemen. As retaliation for Saudi backing for the Syrian secessionists, and in support of more progressive Yemeni elements, Sadat advocated a limited involvement in the Yemeni civil war. As the war wore on during the 1960s, it turned into an enormous drain on Egypt's military and economic resources, as well as providing opportunities for widespread corruption from which 'Amer and some of his cronies benefited. Sadat described himself as troubled by these developments.[104]

Simultaneously, as chairman of Egypt's Higher Committee for the Liquidation of Feudalism (HCLF), 'Amer oversaw the state's heavy-handed intervention in rural social relations. In his autobiography, Sadat also notes his disapproval of 'Amer's role in the HCLF and its repressive activities,[105] which, by contrast, Centrists regarded as a great success.[106] Sadat's objections had a personal edge. The Sadat family had strong ties with the al-Fiqqi family of Kamshish, a village near Sadat's hometown in Minufiyya. The Fiqqis were the "feudalists" at the center of the biggest de-feudalization case—the 1966 Kamshish affair—which was triggered by the killing of an ASU official who was reporting alleged land reform violations. The Fiqqis, who claimed innocence in the murder, were publicly humiliated and tortured, much to Sadat's deep chagrin; yet Sadat felt he could do nothing to protect them.[107]

Sadat was disturbed by these events, as well as by the secret, debilitating conflict between 'Amer and Nasser. Yet, whatever Sadat's qualms about heavy-handed state activities, improprieties, or regime rifts, he never abandoned ship. While RCC members like 'Abd al-Latif al-Boghdadi and Kemal al-Din Hussein parted ways with the regime in the early 1960s because they disapproved of more extensive nationalization and the socialist deepening, Sadat stayed on. In the early 1960s debate over the new National Charter, Sadat did appear as a primary supporter of more home-grown versions of socialism, opening the door to the juxtaposition of rival formulae. Sadat championed the "Arab socialist" themes presented by regime Rightists, as opposed to more "scientific socialist" and Marxist strains, presented by regime Centrists and Leftists.[108] But his criticism of the socialist deepening in 1963 and 1964 was muted. All regime elites concur that in terms of his formal pronouncements, Sadat remained in lockstep with the official pro-socialist orientation of the regime, that is, an "Arab application of scientific socialism."

Heikal has written that: "As the Yemen war dragged on it had a generally corrupting effect on Egyptian life. It also corrupted Abdel Hakim Amer in various ways, which was to become apparent in his behaviour in June 1967. Sadat saw that Amer's influence was waning, so he once again cultivated a direct relationship with Nasser."[109] In reality, 'Amer's influence and power grew steadily throughout the period leading up to June 1967. Many regime insiders, perhaps Nasser himself, regarded 'Amer as the most powerful man in Egypt.[110] If Sadat began to distance himself politically from 'Amer, it had nothing to do with some perceived loss in 'Amer's power. [111] Moreover, whatever doubts Sadat may have begun to have about 'Amer, Sadat never ceased to meet with him as a friend, and he simultaneously maintained his friendly relationship with Nasser.

Sadat, the "Six Day War," and Its Aftermath

The so-called Six Day War of June 1967, the *naksa* (catastrophe) in the Arab lexicon, produced a psychological shock to the Arab world as a whole. As such, the emotional stresses and strains felt by all responsible Arab elites were enormous. Sadat's behavior, both during and immediately following the war, differed little from that of his fellow elites. The shock was so great that he went home and remained there roughly four days, "dazed and brokenhearted."[112] Interestingly, Jehan Sadat notes that during this period, she would come home from visiting the wounded in the hospitals and find her husband sitting on the balcony at home, with none other than

'Abd al-Hakim 'Amer by his side.[113] Sadat's anger then became so intense as to provoke a return to the more impetuous, foolhardy type of 1942 circling-the-palace-in-his-jeep behavior, with Sadat arming himself with the intention of heading toward the Suez Canal zone to take on the enemy face to face.[114] Cooler minds stopped him from doing so.

Postwar Trials and Tribulations

If Sadat was, in the end, helpless to reverse Israel's occupation of Egyptian territory, he could and did ultimately assist Nasser in his confrontation with 'Amer. Sadat first tried to convince 'Amer that he should accept the vice presidency offered to him by Nasser and step down as commander of the armed forces. But as 'Amer would have none of it, matters rapidly came to a head. On the night that Nasser chose to confront 'Amer, Nasser requested Sadat's presence, as well as that of Zakariyya Muhi al-Din and Hussein al-Shaf'ei. 'Amer, unbending, but now realizing that he had literally fallen into a physical trap set by Nasser, allegedly tried to commit suicide by taking pills in Nasser's house after Nasser had retired upstairs. According to Wagih Abaza, Sadat fished a huge chunk of hashish out of 'Amer's mouth when 'Amer emerged from the bathroom;[115] and 'Amer, seeing Sadat as Brutus, cursed Sadat profusely. Although the friendship between Sadat and 'Amer had never been qualitatively equal to that once joining Nasser and 'Amer, the unraveling of this friendship, and 'Amer's subsequent, alleged suicide, was one that left deep scars in Sadat's psyche as it did in Nasser's. And as shall be seen, it left Sadat extremely cautious in his relationships with Egypt's military commanders during his own presidency.

In the period following the war, Nasser's mental anguish was frequently accompanied by excruciating physical pain. He suffered from hemochromatosis, a disease in which iron accumulates in body tissues, diabetes is attendant, and there is a high occurrence of cardiac arrest. During this period, Sadat's home became a place of welcome relief for Nasser, and the relationship between the two men became closer than ever before.[116] In addition to Sadat's good humor, Mrs. Sadat's grace and charm also helped put the beleaguered Nasser at ease.

Still, Nasser could not shed his workaholic ways, and in September 1969, he suffered a heart attack. Soviet doctors told him that if he did not seek relaxation and refrain from smoking, he ran a high risk of killing himself. Nasser's illness necessitated somewhat lengthy trips for cures in the Soviet Union, and during these periods he left control of the country's matters in the hands of Centrists (Sha'rawi Gum'a, Sami Sharaf, and Amin Huweidi).

In many regards, the seeds for post-Nasserite conflict were sown at this time. Following his successful representation of Egypt's interests at the first

Islamic summit in early December 1969, and prior to Nasser's trip to Morocco for an Arab summit, Sadat was sworn in as vice president at Nasser's insistence. In the meantime, the same trio of Centrists—they called themselves the "Three Musketeers"—continued to handle many affairs of the state behind the scenes.

In June 1970, Nasser was once again in the Soviet Union for discussions relating to arms procurements. While there, to display his pique over Soviet foot-dragging and to offset slightly the Soviets' growing influence, he decided to adopt a peace plan officially proposed by U.S. Secretary of State Rogers on June 19, a plan that included implementation of a ceasefire along the Suez Canal. Back in Cairo, Sadat, uninformed, convened the ASU and, as acting president, rejected the Rogers peace initiative.

Of course, once the Egyptians got their signals straight, Nasser's voice prevailed; but when Nasser returned to Egypt, he was not pleased with Sadat for having issued the rejection statement. In addition, Nasser was also perturbed that Sadat had attempted to use his "executive authority" to engineer the acquisition of a much larger villa located near his own home on the Pyramids Road. The larger home belonged to a Gen. al-Mogi, who was understandably angered by the attempted sequestration.

The psychological stress experienced by Sadat during this period appears to have contributed to Sadat suffering a mild heart attack in July 1970—he had been similarly stricken in 1960. During and after his presidency, Sadat would be criticized as lazy for staying up late at night, sleeping in late, taking lengthy, time-consuming walks in the afternoon, and frequently passing his evenings enjoying a movie. If Musa Sabri's sympathetic account of Sadat's daily routine as president is accurate, then one can deduce that Sadat probably toiled half as much as Nasser.[117] Neglected or forgotten in this criticism, however, is the fact that before Sadat had even turned 51, he had already suffered two heart attacks; before hitting 52, Nasser had worked himself to death. Such factors had a distinct impact on Sadat's calculations regarding his lifestyle.[118]

Primarily because of Sadat's political faux pas, Nasser gave Sadat a "vacation" on September 12, 1970 to think about his misbehavior. But Nasser's anger with Sadat was fleeting. In the end, Nasser seems to have agreed that the Sadat family deserved quarters more befitting a vice president, as he approved their move into the state-sequestrated, Nile-side villa whose owner had been the Jewish-Egyptian millionaire, Castro.[119] The central location of this villa greatly facilitated Nasser's visits. Somewhat ironically, it is located just a stone's throw from what had been the primary residence of 'Abd al-Hakim 'Amer.

Whether Nasser truly intended to pick Sadat as his successor has been the subject of much debate. In one sense, Sadat was a natural choice—he was one of the few remaining members of the Revolutionary Command Council with active involvement in the regime. All the others, except Hussein al-Shaf'ei, and to a lesser extent Zakariyya Muhi al-Din (who removed himself from the political scene following the 1967 debacle),[120] had either died or fallen out of favor with Nasser and or his policies. Al-Shaf'ei was never so close to Nasser because of his excessive Islamic attitudes and Sufistic musings. As Hermann Eilts wrote me regarding al-Shaf'ei, "Already under Nasir [sic] he used to speak of uniting the Islamic world in an anti-Israeli crusade and continued to do so during the period he was vice president under Sadat. Nasir was happy to get any help that he could against the Israelis, but he was too smart to believe in any ideological concept of the Islamic world uniting against Israel or, to put it another way, in military support of Egypt."[121]

As for Sadat as a candidate, he not only was still around, he also now possessed a more intimate rapport with Nasser. Yet for Sadat's detractors, there is no way that Nasser would have ever wanted Sadat to assume the presidential reins. Sami Sharaf, perhaps Nasser's closest aide, notes that Sadat's appointment was, at best, something designed to last for only a relatively brief period to enable Sadat to claim the same, more extensive benefits and pension plan provided to higher-ranking officials after retirement. All the other RCC men whom Nasser cared for had at one time or another served in a capacity that garnered them these benefits.[122] Zakariyya Muhi al-Din recalled: "I was surprised Nasser picked Sadat as vice president. He did so to fill a vacuum. Nasser didn't believe in Sadat's capabilities."[123] Nasser's daughter, Hoda, noted that Nasser and Sadat were indeed friends, but "he couldn't take him very seriously."[124] If her appraisal, as well as that of many others is accurate, it seems highly unlikely that Nasser would have designated Sadat as his successor. But in the end, whether by Nasser's grand design or not, Sadat was left occupying the vice presidency at the time of Nasser's death.

Summing Up Sadat's Ideological Leanings Under Nasser

One other issue warrants scrutiny prior to discussion of Sadat's succession and his presidency: Sadat's ideological predilections. Here, several factors must be kept in mind, such as depth (or shallowness) of ideological conviction, propensity for modifying one's views in an ever-dynamic environment, and short-term tactical positions versus long-term ideals and aspirations.

Like Nasser, Sadat was no ideologue. When Nasser was asked by an Indian journalist, shortly after the 1952 revolution, whether he was a leftist or rightist, Nasser laughed and responded, "Neither. I'm a conspirator."[125] Sadat, too, was first and foremost a conspirator, a plotter. After all, how else would one explain his expressed feelings of being sated, sublimely contented, by the occurrence of the revolution itself, given its clear lack of ideological definition?

But Sadat did have pronounced ideological predilections, or leanings. Fellow officers and civilians of Sadat's generation were attracted by Marxism or Stalinism, by various right-wing authoritarian or fascist models, by liberal democratic regimes, or by al-Banna's Islamic fundamentalist message. Many, like Sadat, experimented with more than one, or even all, of these camps. But it is clear that Sadat, in his youth and early manhood, was most impressed by rightist authoritarian patterns of governance, or at a minimum, saw them as most appropriate for Egypt given its socioeconomic conditions. Sadat was very receptive to al-Banna's call, but he was more impressed by Hitler and other rightwing leaders. This said, it is essential to note that the attraction here was with fascist regimes' success at rapid socioeconomic change, not with their ideals. Sadat was not a fascist.

Perhaps due to the depth of his religious beliefs, and an equating of communism with atheism, Sadat found no allure in communism. Neither did Nasser, who dispatched individuals to study Franco's right-wing regime, as well as Tito's brand of communism. But Nasser harbored a certain resentment, perhaps even a psychological complex, regarding people of great wealth, which helped bring him to a leftist disposition. By contrast, Sadat, coming from a slightly poorer and even lower, lower-middle-class background than Nasser, was attracted to upper-class individuals, and aspired to join their ranks. "He really liked rich people, capitalists, prominent people who could travel to Europe."[126] Thus, Sadat acquired many wealthy friends and acquaintances, Egyptians and foreigners alike.

Sadat's view of liberal democracy was marked by his Egyptian experience. The liberal democratic party of Egypt, the Wafd, had severely disappointed him by its willing cooperation with the hated British during World War II. In addition, Egypt's multiparty politics, in general, with its fractiousness and backstabbing, was as repugnant to Sadat as it was to many of his officer colleagues. Despite this, Sadat knew that liberal democracy elsewhere was not like this; and he retained a sense of appreciation for the rule of law and democratic practice as an ideal type, as a long-term goal for Egypt.

Unsurprisingly, it was Sadat who, in the Revolutionary Command Council's early debates over democracy versus dictatorship, weighed in heavily in favor of the latter because of the greater efficiency (or so he believed) with which such a system could accomplish profound change. Yet, beyond the rightist authoritarian predilections, there was great room for an evolution of Sadat's thinking given his youth at the time of the coup and the dynamic nature of the domestic, regional, and international environments. Sadat's freewheeling spirit made him even more receptive to pragmatic solutions to problems, to trial and error experimentation to discover the most effective policies, than was true of the more serious and stubborn Nasser. And Nasser consciously chose a trial and error policymaking approach. Thus, Sadat practiced considerable policy ambiguity within an ill-defined authoritarianism. And his authoritarianism was conditional; it was a transitional authoritarianism. After all, to the extent that Sadat over time acquired a preference for any particular country's political economy, it was neither the United States nor Soviet Union, but Austria, especially Austria under the rule of Bruno Kreisky's government.[127] Kreisky's government was socialist; but a socialism of the West, set in a liberal democratic framework. Because Egypt's socioeconomic realities did not yet permit it the luxury of such a system, or so went Sadat's thinking, Egypt's regime would need to keep a tight lid on political activity. Its leaders would need to maintain their transitional authoritarian regime until the bulk of the population was literate and enjoyed a significantly higher standard of living, at which time a more permanent, liberal democratic system could be constructed.

Sadat had no rigid left-right ideological viewpoint; he *was,* however, an Egyptian nationalist par excellence. He loathed foreign domination, and sought policies that would enable Egypt to empower and enrich itself; and it is obvious that he thought an authoritarian state most capable of achieving these goals. These sentiments are reflected in his highly positive assessment of the post-1956 war Egyptianization (nationalization) of the extensive, predominantly European foreign assets in Egypt.[128] Egypt's primary concern, from Sadat's perspective, was regaining full political-economic national sovereignty. Once that had been accomplished, he felt it damaging and dangerous that Nasser allowed the country to take such a strong pro-socialist stance as to become mired in the Cold War.

Sadat's rejection of communism was a view shared by all top regime elites, and one that, in many cases, undoubtedly grew out of their high level of religiosity. Sadat was, moreover, particularly wary of Soviet influence and Egypt's extensive military and economic relations with the Eastern bloc. His comparison of standards of living in the Soviet Union and the United States left him far more impressed with the latter country, but again his ideal political-economic regime type fell in between, with countries like Austria.

In summing up, one may describe Sadat, especially the pre-1970 Sadat, as a transitional authoritarian with a certain admiration for the speed with which fascist regimes could accomplish their ends. In other words, Sadat hoped Egypt's future would be a liberal democratic one, in which the state would retain a powerful role in certain areas of the economy. However, to reach that stage—for the purpose of initially realizing profound socioeconomic change—Egypt was best off embracing a rightist authoritarianism akin to certain variants of European fascism. But this rightist authoritarianism was largely shorn of the other trappings of fascism, such as imperialist designs, contempt for humanitarian or democratic ideals, or notions of racial superiority. (Although I will hasten to add that, in light of his political cultural milieu, it would be hard to argue that Sadat did not hold anti-Semitic beliefs for at least much of his early and middle life.) Accordingly, for Sadat, the aforementioned nationalization of foreign businesses, which took Egypt down the path to a large public sector and extensive state ownership and control of the economy, were all positive developments. Like many regime Rightists, however, Sadat disapproved of the more extensive nationalization efforts of the 1960s that signaled a leftist-type socialist deepening, especially those that struck at "more purely Egyptian" interests. In his autobiography, Sadat speaks at length of how these measures, especially the activities of the Higher Committee for the Liquidation of Feudalism, struck at the pride of many honest Egyptians in a debilitating and demoralizing way.[129] "I have always maintained that while the fifties saw the July 23 Revolution realize colossal achievements, the sixties saw it making colossal mistakes."[130]

To reiterate, when the socialist policies of the 1960s were formulated, Sadat voiced no objections, in contrast to individuals like 'Abd al-Latif al-Boghdadi and Kemal al-Din Hussein, who articulated their opposition to the depth of the socialist transformation and left the regime for that reason. By the same token, there is little reason to suspect that Sadat endorsed the regime's new socialist path out of genuine ideological conviction. And it is worth noting that, during the ideological debates of the 1960s, Sadat was a proponent of "Arab socialist" theses. As Boghdadi recalled, "It always seemed obvious to me that Sadat was just being hypocritical with Nasser. Sadat wasn't a Nasserite, but he aimed to please Nasser, to show zealous support, and to execute his orders. Sadat always said, *"ana ma'a al-mu'allim"* ("I'm with the boss").[131] Or again, to repeat Wagih Abaza's assessment, Sadat may have been with Nasser in his *kalam* (rhetoric), but he was with the 'Amer crowd in terms of much of his behavior. Other regime elites sensed this as well, and all felt that Sadat, if they had to categorize him, merited placement among the regime's Rightists.

Sadat's Decision-making Style
Finally, one must add that Sadat, in his decision-making style, was enigmatic. Those who knew him best never really knew exactly what he was thinking, or exactly where he was going. Their confusion derived, in part,

from Sadat's ability and desire to engage in skillful deception and dissembling, and to listen to others' advice without revealing his own preferences and long-range plans. As his daughter Camelia recounted, "He . . . urged me to pull back from matters in order to see them more clearly. 'Envision things and calculate them,' he urged me; 'understand a goal and then plan how to reach it.' He envisioned and planned, but he did not overwhelm people with his insights and strength. He preferred to keep his views to himself. He never showed his power. This was a response to his environment growing up, an environment in which showing power often invited confrontation."[132] And as Camelia also noted, her father also preached that one should "Never show you are weak—your weakness."[133] Tactical thinking guided much of Sadat's behavior, and therefore must be kept in mind when evaluating his public statements and his assessments of factors motivating his decisions. Such caution is all the more necessary because we heard only from Sadat the power holder and power practitioner, not Sadat the retiree, at arm's length from the world of politics.

No one, then, ever really knew what Sadat was thinking or plotting. He made his calculations alone, silently, as if he were once again sitting in his prison cell plotting an escape. As Sayyid Mar'ei said, "There were always five to seven persons counseling Sadat, but no one person was ever told the overall picture and overall strategy. He would put one point here, then one point there, and ultimately connect the points to make the picture. 'Why put this point there?' someone would ask him, and he might explain, but he never gave the total picture that was in his head; he never revealed his overall strategy."[134]

Nasser's Death

On September 28, 1970, Nasser went into cardiac arrest: an attack that proved fatal. Sadat was overtaken with genuine grief and emotion. He fainted during Nasser's funeral procession and had to be taken away to recover. Michael Sterner, who saw Sadat during this period, describes him as "shattered by Nasser's death; his face was ashen."[135] No one in Egypt could imagine Sadat, or any other regime figure for that matter, filling the giant's shoes. Yet within eight months of Nasser's death, Sadat's elite rivals would discover just how calculating Sadat could be. In October 1973, Sadat would stun the whole world with the strength of his cunning in war, and later, equally amaze that world with his ardent desire and courageous effort to make peace.

2

Sadat's Consolidation of Power

At the time of Nasser's death, Sadat occupied, at best, a formal position of *primus inter pares* in Egypt's governing elite. In less than eight months, he was in sole possession of power. As this transition unfolded, most observers, including many Egyptian elites, saw it as nothing more than a power struggle at the pinnacle of the state. But in reality, this struggle was of far greater significance, for its protagonists privately held divergent ideological orientations, as well as profoundly different preferences regarding Egypt's tactical and strategic political options.

Determining Nasser's Successor

Sizing Up the Candidates

Immediately following Nasser's death, members of the Arab Socialist Union's Supreme Executive Committee (SEC), top government ministers and key advisers held a series of meetings to select Nasser's successor. From a constitutional point of view, Sadat, as vice president, represented the most likely candidate. Moreover, as a former Revolutionary Command Council member and the man who had publicly announced the 1952 revolution, his selection would symbolize regime continuity. Sadat's only remaining "in-house" competitor in this regard was Hussein al-Shaf'ei. All other RCC members had either died or become distanced from power. Shaf'ei wanted the presidency, had been an RCC member, and probably saw himself as more qualified than Sadat; but as will be discussed shortly, Shaf'ei had several strikes against him.

Although Sadat's occupation of the vice presidency gave him a slight advantage, no one regarded constitutional provisions as binding, and SEC members and ministerial officials had considerable leeway to determine the succession. The Centrists were best-placed to shape this decision. 'Ali Sabri (ex-prime minister and current minister of state for air defense), Sha'rawi Gum'a (minister of interior), Sami Sharaf (minister of state for presidential affairs), Muhammad Fawzi (minister of war and commander of the armed forces), Amin Huweidi (minister of state), Labib Shuqeir (speaker of the parliament), 'Abd al-Muhsin Abu al-Nur (ASU secretary general), Muhammad Fa'iq (minister of information), and others not only occupied key government posts, but also constituted a majority in the ASU's Supreme Executive Committee, and by extension controlled the ASU Central Committee (CC). In brief, from all appearances, the government, regime party, armed forces, police, and intelligence forces were firmly in Centrist hands.

As noted earlier, during periods of Nasser's absence from power due to acute illness, the "Three Musketeers" (Gum'a, Sharaf and Huweidi) had ruled the country, with Sadat, Heikal, and Muhammad Fawzi looking in. In terms of brute strength, Gum'a, as minister of interior, controlled the police, Mabahith Amn al-Dawla (State Security Investigations), and Amn al-Markizi (Central Security Forces). Sharaf controlled the president's armored division—the Republican Guard—with 300 tanks in Dashhur (just south of Cairo), and was seen by some as the most physically powerful man inside Egypt. Huweidi controlled a major portion of the intelligence services; and General Muhammad Fawzi, of course, commanded the armed forces.

Yet several problems prevented the most prominent Centrists from staking a claim to the presidency. To begin, Centrists felt somewhat constrained because neither Sabri, Gum'a, nor Sharaf, the three most powerful Centrist-faction members, enjoyed a favorable public image. Sabri, whom Nasser had cast in the role of Moscow's man in Egypt, had been "burned" by a scandal. In July 1969, he was caught trying to bring in tens of trunks filled with carpets, crystal, jewels, and other valuables from the Soviet Union. Because Nasser had wanted to clip Sabri's wings and take an indirect slap at the Soviets, he passed on this news to Sabri's nemesis, Heikal, who gladly published it in September of that year. Furthermore, anti-Sabri sentiment ran so deep among many high-ranking officers that some, it is rumored, threatened a coup in the event he was made president.[1]

Gum'a was second in importance after Sabri, but as Ahmed Beha al-Din put it, he was important "in his post" and had no real "name" among the citizenry.[2] To the extent that he had a public image, it was largely negative. As minister of interior, Gum'a had earned the hatred of broad sectors of the public through his association with state repression, especially in putting down the mass student-worker demonstrations of 1968.

As for Sharaf, he was virtually unknown to the general public. In Fuad Mattar's words, "For eighteen years hardly anyone ever saw a picture of Sami Sharaf, although everyone had heard about him."[3] And again, what they had heard about him gave rise to concern because he was associated by many with intelligence-gathering activities that had often been put to repressive ends.

No leading Centrist possessed Sadat's generally positive public image, and each had powerful detractors in elite circles as well. In contrast to Sadat's longtime aversion to rocking the political boat,[4] both Sabri and Gum'a had locked horns with numerous political adversaries and created a long list of enemies in the regime. Sabri, one of the more cosmopolitan members of the regime, fluent in a handful of languages, was seen as a real statesman by some,[5] but he was greatly disliked by many for his supercilious, ultra-abrasive personality. His archenemy, the highly influential Heikal, was intent on deterring any presidential power grab by Sabri. Moreover, there was no love lost between principal Centrists themselves; rather, they were split into loose sub-factions. Sabri, Muhammad Fa'iq, and Dia al-Din Dawud clustered together in one subgrouping, Gum'a and Sharaf in another, and there were additional sub-factions as well. The principal Centrists were at odds because Gum'a and Sharaf had reservations about the vibrant mass organizations, like the Youth Organization (YO), that Sabri had constructed,[6] and because they saw Sabri as "stiff, stubborn, and lacking in tact."[7] These animosities were an impediment to agreement over a Centrist presidential candidate.

Key Centrists feared that Sadat was not fully committed to their conception of Nasser's ideals. They had always seen Sadat as a Rightist, much closer to the 'Amer crowd throughout the 1950s and 1960s than to ASU Centrists or Leftists. Sadat's lifestyle, aspirations and ambitions, his well-known appreciation for Western versus Eastern countries' standards of living, and his friendships with wealthy Arabs, all indicated a Rightist orientation; so had his advocacy of a Rightist, Arab socialism. Still, Sadat had stood by Nasser through thick and thin and had consistently mouthed the regime's socialist line; and prominent Centrists were unaware of any special links Sadat had with pro-Western Arabs like the Saudi intelligence director, Kemal Adham, or perhaps with the United States.[8]

Shaf'ei's loyalty to Nasser had also been unshakable, but he had no real coterie of supporters, was given to religious mysticism, and was even closer to religious regime Rightists than Sadat. Moreover, Shaf'ei had earned Nasser's disapproval by complaining that the 1967 defeat was due, in part, to the *hirasa* (sequestration) of many Egyptians' properties,[9] and he reached out to regime Rightists after Nasser's death. Finally, Sadat had enjoyed a much closer personal relationship with Nasser than Shaf'ei, and Nasser had designated Sadat as vice president, even if no one had seen this as having long-term implications in Nasser's mind.

The only other potentially serious candidate for the position was former Vice President Zakariyya Muhi al-Din, who had largely withdrawn from the political field immediately following the 1967 Six Day War. At Nasser's funeral, Egyptian television cameras focused on Muhi al-Din more than anyone else, a clue to some that he was favored by regime influentials, like Heikal, as was indeed the case. Muhi al-Din had been tapped by Nasser as his successor at the time of his post-June 1967 war resignation; now Heikal floated a rumor that Nasser had again tapped Muhi al-Din on his deathbed. Muhi al-Din's big disadvantage, however, was that he was readily perceived by Centrists as the most formidable Rightist; he was bright and strong-willed, possessed great integrity to go along with his powerful connections in the military and intelligence apparatuses, and had squared off against Sabri repeatedly in the 1960s over major economic and foreign policy issues. His candidacy was also opposed by the Soviets, who saw him as too pro-American and feared he might behave like another Dubcek.[10] Compared to Muhi al-Din, Sadat was much easier for Centrists to chew, and much safer.

Finally, Centrists preferred Sadat to potential extra-regime challengers with RCC credentials, like 'Abd al-Latif al-Boghdadi or Kemal al-Din Hussein,[11] who had opposed a "deepening" of socialism. Following Nasser's death, these individuals joined Zakariyya Muhi al-Din, Hussein al-Shaf'ei, Hassan Ibrahim, and others in signing a memorandum, circulated among top regime elites, that called for setting up a six-month National Security Council to oversee creation of a National Council. The latter council's members would draft a constitution and call for a presidential election to be supervised by an independent judiciary.[12] The memorandum disturbed many top officials, including Sadat, who saw in it a bid by old RCC members to regain regime control. Years after these events, Kemal al-Din Hussein described Sadat's perception as erroneous, noting that the former RCC members were not insisting on any role for themselves in these transitional organizations.[13] But at the time, key elite actors indeed felt threatened.

Setting Terms to Succession: Agreement on "Collective Leadership"
All of the aforementioned considerations weighed heavily in the Centrists' decision to approve Sadat's ascension to the presidency, but their approval ultimately hinged upon Sadat's formal acceptance of five conditions: (1) there would no longer be individual rule, as experienced under Nasser; (2)

the ASU's SEC and CC members were to study all key issues and adopt motions by a majority vote; (3) the Maglis al-Umma was to vote on all major issues; (4) the president was not to assume the duties of the prime minister; and (5) ministers were to take decisions in their own areas of administration.[14]

When the Centrists sat down with Sadat, Heikal, and other elite actors to discuss the succession, all present, including Sadat, agreed that no single individual could possibly assume the superhuman responsibilities that Nasser had carried; nor would it be advisable for anyone to do so.[15] Nasser's death at the age of 52 seemed ample proof of this, it was believed. Sadat's agreement to these conditions, tantamount to a commitment on his part to collective leadership, allayed Centrist apprehensions that any real harm might come from a Sadat presidency. Through collective leadership, Centrists could outvote Sadat on any crucial issue. Moreover, agreement that ministerial officials, ASU leaders and other regime leaders would now possess greater decision-making autonomy in their positions carried special significance. Because Centrists controlled nearly all vital state apparatuses, they felt assured that Sadat could not possibly impose his will. When journalist Mahmud al-Sa'dani complained to Sharaf that his Vanguard Organization (VO) cell in Giza opposed a Sadat presidency, and warned that Sadat would dump them all after three or four months, Sharaf responded that there was no reason to worry, and added that if Sadat deviated from Nasser's path, "I'll shoot him."[16]

Earlier commentators asserted that Centrists' endorsement of Sadat derived from his reputation as Nasser's "poodle" or *"bikbashi sahh"* ("Colonel Yes")—a "yes-man" who could be easily manipulated behind the scenes while still casting a favorable public image.[17] For example, in what would emerge as a well-known joke about Sadat, one was asked to explain how he got the *zabib* on his forehead. A response to the effect that Sadat got it from praying was quickly rebutted by the questioner, who then went on to say, "No, you see, in Nasser's day, whenever Sadat tried to speak out at a cabinet meeting, Nasser would poke him in the forehead and shout, 'Shut up, you.'" Again, there was substance to the joke; Sadat was not widely respected by his peers; Leftists, Centrists, and Rightists alike.[18] Virtually all regime elites saw the posts Sadat had held (including, obviously, that of parliamentary speaker) as of secondary importance. Many insiders, including prominent Rightists, described Sadat as the court jester, cracking jokes and acting the clown to amuse his colleagues, and as being a genuinely likeable person, but ultimately one who had failed to earn their respect.[19]

Still, elites involved in picking Sadat for the presidency discard the notion that his selection was determined by perceptions of his being weak and easily manipulated. Rather, his choice was predicated on his agreement to collective leadership.[20] Under Nasser, SEC meetings were characterized by members asking Nasser his opinion on the issues of the day, with little input originating from other members. With Sadat as president, there was to be free-flowing discussion by all, followed by a vote to decide which option to pursue. Centrists fully expected to carry the vote on all important issues.

On the basis of this agreement, the SEC voted unanimously for Sadat to become president. On October 8, the Maglis al-Umma voted approval of Sadat's candidacy; and on October 15 Sadat was officially elected president, receiving more than 90.4 percent of the vote in a nationwide plebiscite marked by a low turnout. (This figure should not be taken at face value, of course, primarily because it was fabricated. But even as a contrived number it was designed to reflect Sadat's "weakness" compared to the "five nines"—99.999 percent—that Nasser had "garnered" at the polls.) In his inaugural address, Sadat declared that he was following "in Nasser's path"; and in an act that offended some Muslims' sensitivities because it smacked of idol worship, he bowed before a statue of Nasser when exiting the Maglis al-Umma. These actions offered further reassurances to dubious Centrists, as did the composition of Sadat's first cabinet, presented on November 18. Beyond some objections (by Sabri, *inter alia*) to the selection of Mahmud Fawzi, a moderate, foreign policy technocrat, to fill the post of prime minister, Centrists remained in firm control of the coercive apparatuses, information, and almost all other key positions.

Sadat's Showdown with the Centrists

Building Bases of Support

From September 1970 until January 1971, Sadat respected the collective leadership principle.[21] But to most of his peers' surprise and chagrin, Sadat began demonstrating an unwillingness to accept the conditions that made him a nominal president. For 18 years, he had served Nasser in a totally self-abnegating fashion. Nasser had shown little regard for collective leadership despite a very brief initial flirtation with its practice.[22] When Nasser, in the early stages of the revolution, called for debate over democracy versus dictatorship, Sadat joined others in touting the efficacy of one-man rule, even though he would not be the direct beneficiary. Perhaps unsurprisingly, within months of assuming the presidency, Sadat began expecting the same unconditional acceptance of his autocratic rule that he had so readily granted to Nasser.

In addition to these factors, Sadat, like many others who had been inner core members of the "revolution," was no great admirer of Sabri, Gum'a, and others. He saw them more as "opportunists" who had usurped RCC core members' rightful place at the pinnacle of power. All top elites recalled how irate Sadat had been when the results of CC voting for SEC members were announced in 1968 and he finished fourth in the voting, behind several prominent Centrists. Sadat was convinced that Centrists like Sabri and Gum'a rigged the vote to his detriment and embarrassment.

Sadat also sensed, from the earliest days of his presidency, that Sabri and others were treating him with disdain, felt he could be easily controlled, and were ignoring his orders. Hamdi Fuad, longtime chief foreign correspondent with *al-Ahram,* recounted that:

> on one occasion, in Sadat's absence, 'Ali Sabri was having tea with Soviet President Nikolai Podgornoy during his visit to Egypt. Someone spoke of the president [Sadat] and Sabri said, jokingly, "What president?" Murad Ghalib and I were sitting there. So Sadat knew that he had to get rid of them. He also knew that they only represented a minority of the people. I think that from the very beginning he was thinking of which direction he was headed in, namely, toward the West. I think that even before he became president he was thinking along such lines and calculating. Every year he took a step in that direction. He knew that kicking out the Sabri crowd would please the Arabs, the United States, and most Egyptians.[23]

Because Sadat's relationship with Nasser had been more intimate than that of Nasser to Sabri or others, Sadat had ample reason to see himself as one of Nasser's equals. Also, it was he who had languished for years in prison due to his revolutionary activities in the 1940s, not the "opportunists" like Sabri and Gum'a. To feel constrained by former "second string" officers who couldn't begin to match his revolutionary historical record was now irksome to Sadat the president, to say the least.

During his first months in power, Sadat quietly and effectively used his formal and informal powers as president to build his own bases of support. In doing so, he would show that, first, he had far greater cunning than his rivals ever began to imagine, and second, that he had learned far more from his Machiavellian master's experiences than had the putative Nasserites themselves. It was, after all, Sadat who had given Nasser a copy of Machiavelli's *The Prince,* a book Nasser read some 17 times,[24] and from which Sadat himself, as he would prove, had clearly derived many important political lessons.

Courting the Military

Lesson number one in the authoritarian political jungle was to safeguard backing by those controlling the major coercive apparatuses, the military and police. Again, Centrists thought that with Fawzi and Gum'a in command of the military and police, respectively, and with Sharaf basically in control of the Republican Guard, their interests were covered. They failed to appreciate two factors: (1) the propensity of subordinates in an authoritarian setting to obey the formal authority, namely, the president; and (2) the deep repository of discontent, especially in the armed forces, created by (a) the 1967 war loss, (b) the blame heaped upon military commanders in general for that loss, (c) Field Marshal 'Amer's suicide, and (d) the increased influence of Soviet officers. Sadat, by contrast, retained a sound understanding of military and police officers' sentiments, and cleverly curried favor with individuals whom he knew to be closer to his own "closet"-Rightist predilections. He also knew much of the aforementioned discontent had translated into a hatred for the likes of Sabri, and he played upon this hatred to the hilt.

To secure support in the military, Sadat focused his attention on Lt. Gen. Muhammad Sadiq. Sadiq was already military chief of staff, second in command behind General Muhammad Fawzi. Sadat nurtured Sadiq's appetite for assuming the top post. Sadiq, who came from a large landowning family, and had spent many years as a military attaché in West Germany, was accurately pegged as a Rightist in elite circles. In private, he held strongly negative views of Egyptian dependence upon the Soviets, views shaped by his class background, anti-communist sentiments, loathsome appraisal of life in the Soviet Union, and exposure to Soviet officials' derogatory comments about the Arabs' military capabilities. In contrast to the Centrist General Fawzi, Sadiq disapproved of the Soviets' influence throughout the Egyptian command structure.

While Soviet officials may not have known of Sadiq's sentiments early on, many Egyptian officers knew that he hated the Soviets. Nasser knew this as well.[25] Because Nasser loved to make political balances, he had appointed Sadiq as director of Military Intelligence in June 1967, obviously wanting an anti-Soviet man in that crucial position. Once there, Sadiq made sure that Intelligence remained without Soviet advisers, the only department in the army with that distinction. Nasser went on to appoint Sadiq as military chief of staff at the time of the Sabri import scandal.[26] In the early 1970s, under Sadat's watch, Sadiq again made his position crystal clear, threatening resignation if Soviets were brought into his department.

Sadat also knew that Sadiq was not alone in his dislike of the Soviets and Soviet-oriented Centrists. Most officers were still chafing from the harsh treatment and embarrassment they suffered following the 1967 defeat. The military's rapid reconstruction after that defeat owed much to the Soviets' massive support, both in materiel and training. But therein lay the crux of a new problem; for now, almost 20 years after the "revolution," many people felt Egypt had fallen under the tutelage of a new imperial power. Nowhere was this sentiment stronger than among military offi-cers.[27] With some 15,000 to 20,000 Soviet military and technical person-nel in Egypt,[28] many Egyptian officers rankled under the efficacious but often overbearing supervision of their new taskmasters. The Soviets were present in a supervisory capacity at all important levels of the command structure. In those positions they were known to keep close tabs on the professional performance and personal lives of the Egyptian officers.[29] Some Egyptian officers felt a loss of personal freedom. From Egyptians' stereotypic accounts, one concludes that the gregarious, jocular Egyptians felt ill at ease with the cold, aloof, miserly Soviet counterparts. And when the Soviets let their hair down on various national holidays, some Egyp-tians were alienated by the Soviets' stubborn efforts to get them to cele-brate by consuming alcohol. Such factors combined to strain many Egyptian officers' relations with their Soviet guests.[30]

As time elapsed following the war, more officers learned that it had been Nasser's decision, based in international political considerations, to have Egypt suffer the first strike by the Israelis despite the deep reservations of the commander of the armed forces, 'Abd al-Hakim 'Amer, and Air Force commander Sidqi Mahmud. Many officers simply regretted 'Amer's demise, for he had won their affection through his amiable personality, as well as his office's largesse in providing public sector jobs, apartments, cars, and easier travel opportunities to them and their families. In contrast, other officers, like Gen. Kemal Hassan 'Ali, had expressed to Sadat their sense of betrayal by the high military command, and especially by 'Amer. Yet the post-*naksa* blanket condemnation of military officers infuriated them. Fol-lowing the 1967 debacle, the government imprisoned over 1,000 officers for malfeasance even though they had had no power over what had hap-pened in the war. In addition, reports that their Soviet advisers were insist-ing not only on placing officers on trial, but having them shot for incompetence, outraged most officers.[31] One might safely say, therefore, that most officers held a dim view of Centrists' arguments, that blame for the 1967 catastrophe should be borne first and foremost by the officer corps in general.

Sadat was well aware of these sentiments, and shared most of them him-self. To the extent that officers had an ideological disposition, it was predominantly Rightist, primarily because of 'Amer's decade and a half of pampering. This Rightist disposition would represent a continued source of insurance to Sadat against any attacks from the Center and Left. To protect that insurance, Sadat cultivated good will among the officers and sought to remove their post-*naksa* sense of shame. He made a huge step in this direction by restoring most of the 1,000 cashiered officers to the military during 1971.[32]

Meanwhile, General Fawzi, though respected, was not well-liked in the military. Insiders recalled that Fawzi was among the officers who allegedly got "cold feet" on the night of the July 22, 1952 coup—hardly a trait designed to earn respect among his peers. Some believed (incorrectly) that he had obtained his lofty position because of his family relationship to Sami Sharaf, the silent but powerful insider. When I interviewed General Fawzi at his home, I found an old, frail, very polite, sweet, and soft-spoken man who actually wept at the end of the interview as he discussed how difficult his life had been made, first by 'Amer, then by Sadat. But while in command, Fawzi, although a very effective taskmaster for overseeing the military's reconstruction, projected a stern personality that left many fellow officers cool to him and made him, in the estimation of some, less well-equipped to boost morale and lead the armed forces into battle.

Pleasing the Police

Sadat also needed to curry favor in the Ministry of Interior, that is, among Egypt's police forces. Again, Gum'a had overseen much regime repression, election-rigging, and deception, including the forwarding of false reports to Nasser that whitewashed coercive excesses and/or provided Nasser with deniability. Distaste for Gum'a afforded Sadat a layer of potential support among some more "professionally-oriented" police officials. Perhaps more important, however, was Sadat's recognition that police officials generally desired greater autonomy from the armed forces, and wished to be led by one of their own rather than by a military officer, as had always been the case under Nasser.

Appeals to Other Regime Elites

Sadat's efforts to shore up his bases of support extended beyond the coercive apparatuses. Among top echelon regime elites, there were many, like Heikal and 'Aziz Sidqi, who disliked Sabri and other prominent Centrists, even though their views on many issues of importance were often quite concordant. In brief, Sadat benefited from personality splits and power rivalries within the Centrist faction. In what would prove a recurring gambit, Sadat began wooing those who disliked Sabri, Gum'a, Sharaf, and others to his side. He also began ideologically outflanking his Centrist foes by recruiting prominent Marxists; for example, he made Lutfi al-Kholi and Muhammad al-Khafif members of the ASU Central Committee. Like Sadat, but with perhaps greater cause, many Leftists disliked the Centrist principals because they believed the latter had rigged ASU elections in 1968 and had cheated them out of a golden opportunity to make a major advance within that organization.[33] More generally, Sadat also sought the assistance of many elite actors whom Nasser had mistreated, abused, belittled, or otherwise antagonized.

As has been extensively discussed by Binder,[34] Ansari,[35] Waterbury,[36] and Sadowski,[37] Sadat sought solid backing from the rural middle class and rural elites. In the Maglis al-Umma, Sadat kept in contact with Rightist parliamentarians whose friendship he had made through long years of work with the Maglis and as Maglis president, particularly more conservative representatives from the Sa'id (areas south of Cairo), Beheira, and his home province of Minufiyya. Sadat also cultivated new friendships with influential citizens who had been harmed under the Nasser regime, such as those whose properties had been sequestrated.[38] His brother-in-law, Mahmud Abu Wafia, came from a large landowning family, and Abu Wafia both encouraged and assisted Sadat in his cultivation of these relationships. Upper-class landowners like Sayyid Mar'ei (with family roots in Sharqiyya) and Muhammad Hamed Mahmud (from Beheira) played comparable roles. Mar'ei,[39] whose political resilience and agricultural expertise had enabled him to hold positions of influence under Nasser, had been named one of the deputy prime ministers in the November 18, 1970 cabinet. Thus, although the Centrists had a formidable lock on the formal positions of power, Sadat began building his own support base by whetting the appetites of Rightists, anti-Sabri and anti-Musketeer types, as well as anti-Nasserites, in various state arenas and social strata. Most dramatic in the latter regard was Sadat's December 20, 1970 decree reinvigorating a 1969 decision by Nasser to terminate property sequestration and allow owners to regain control of their land.

The Heightening of Intra-Regime Conflict

It took Sadat just four months to begin publicly demonstrating a proclivity for autonomous decision-making, thereby transgressing the collective leadership principle. The developments leading him down this path were momentous because at their heart was the issue of the resumption of warfare with Israel. To recap, U.S. Secretary of State William Rogers had launched a peace initiative in December 1969, then restated it in greater detail at a press conference on June 25, 1970. Nasser, angered by Soviet defeatism vis-à-vis Egypt and foot-dragging on arms deliveries, had signaled willingness to accept the Rogers proposal in his annual anniversary-of-the-revolution speech on July 23, 1970, and a 90-day ceasefire began on August 8, 1970. Nasser may have been engaging in artful deception, as well. According to General Fawzi,[40] Nasser had informed him that the battle of liberation would begin at the end of the 90-day ceasefire, that is, on or slightly after November 7, 1970. Nasser's death had led all to agree on a ninety day extension of the ceasefire, but during SEC discussions in December 1970 and January 1971, it was decided, with Sadat's approval, that the ceasefire would not be renewed[41] and Egypt would go to war not long thereafter. To prepare for war, a National Defense Council was set up in December; its members included Sadat (chair), Gum'a, Sharaf, Fawzi, Fa'iq, Abu al-Nur, Mahmud Riyad, and Ahmed Kamel (director of General Intelligence).

All Centrists were convinced that the Egyptian military's reconstruction had been completed and a resumption of hostilities with Israel was the first order of business. Special emissaries were sent abroad during this period to mobilize international support for the view that Egypt had exhausted all means for finding a peaceful solution to the conflict with Israel. Among these emissaries were Lutfi al-Kholi and Muhammad al-Khafif, who were sent to the Soviet Union, France, Italy, and elsewhere to drum up support for Egypt's foreign policy position, and also to deliver the message that Sadat was to be trusted because he intended no fundamental policy changes.[42]

Unbeknownst to nearly everyone, Sadat was already seeing matters differently with regard to the conflict with Israel. Sadat's calculations were anchored in his belief that the United States alone held the key to the conflict's resolution because the United States, in his estimation, was the only true superpower.

Sadat's Relationship with the United States

What produced Sadat's favorable views of the United States? By all accounts,[43] Sadat's first trip to the U.S. in 1966 made an indelible mark on his thinking about both superpowers. Given his own personal tastes and preferences, as well as his aspirations for Egypt, Sadat was inclined to evaluate a country's political-economic system in terms of consumer durables and technology, and here the Soviet Union was simply no match for the U.S.

Sadat's Centrist and Leftist opponents, most notably Sami Sharaf, would later allege that from roughly this time forward, Sadat was on the receiving end of funds from the U.S. Central Intelligence Agency (CIA).[44] In making these allegations, Sadat's foes consistently refer to an article by Jim Hoagland that appeared in the *Washington Post* on February 22, 1977.[45] While this article revealed CIA assistance to Jordan's King Hussein, it made no mention of Sadat being a direct recipient of CIA funds. It did note, however, that while vice president, Sadat received "a steady private income" from Kemal Adham, and that Adham was a conduit of CIA funds for various Middle East leaders.[46] As head of Saudi intelligence, Adham certainly had assets of his own as well, so Sadat may or may not have know its source, whatever that source actually was.

Whether or not Sadat had private direct contacts with the CIA during the 1960s and very early 1970s was impossible for this author to establish. Efforts to elicit responses from two CIA agents operating in Egypt in the 1960s and early 1970s came to naught. Furthermore, to the best of my knowledge, no relevant CIA documents have been declassified. Until these sources or comparable ones elsewhere "open up," there is no way of ascertaining whether a direct Sadat–CIA relationship existed. Finally, even if such a relationship did exist—and it would appear plausible that one developed in the early 1970s—one cannot conclude that Sadat had "sold out" to the Americans.

On the basis of my research, I can only offer the following comments. First, there is no indication from declassified, Freedom of Information Act records,[47] nor from recently declassified U.S. State Department cables,[48] of any special treatment for Sadat or direct relationship with him. Second, no formerly well-placed State Department officials whom I have interviewed ever heard of any such relationship, although they admit that a CIA connection could have existed without their having known of it.[49] Third, declassified State Department documents reflect clearly the surprise of key State Department officials and National Security Council advisers when Sadat began signaling to them his interest in warmer ties shortly after he became president. Admittedly, their surprise cannot be taken as proof of no CIA–Sadat relationship because the CIA could easily have kept Sadat as a contact or placed him on the CIA payroll for several years running without informing the State Department. Fourth, if Sadat did have a CIA relationship, either directly or through Adham, it is possible that this was done with Nasser's approval. There is no reason to believe that Nasser questioned Sadat's patriotism, and he kept very close tabs on everyone; therefore, in Nasser's mind, Sadat would have made an attractive candidate for making secret contacts with an adversary. After all, Nasser had successfully cast Sadat in such a role before the 1952 coup. One former, very knowledgeable Free Officer, who wished to remain anonymous on this point, told me that Sadat had established a CIA connection in the 1960s with Nasser's blessing. Sami Sharaf rejected the possibility that this might have been the case,[50] but Nasser's extremely close-to-the-chest machinations could have left room for such an arrangement. Heikal clearly played such a role for Nasser and Sadat with the U.S.,[51] just as Heikal's early mentor turned nemesis, Mustafa Amin, had.[52] And Amin's demise in this capacity—he was tried and convicted on pro-U.S. espionage charges in 1965—coincided interestingly with the putative development of a Sadat connection. Also, Amin and Heikal could not have been Nasser's only CIA go-betweens. But again, I am most inclined to throw cold water on conjecture about any direct Sadat–CIA connection during the 1960s in light of State Department officials' behavior toward Sadat in the 1960s and early 1970s, and I find no supporting evidence for the notion that Sadat had secretly "sold out" to the Americans.

What is certain is that Sadat kept the company of many individuals with interesting links to official U.S. representatives, and a distinct preference for the West. During the 1960s, due to his own religiosity and through his chairmanship of the Islamic Conference Organization, Sadat had established friendly relations with numerous elites from conservative, oil-rich Gulf nations, as had an old CIA Egyptian contact, Hassan al-Tuhami, who ran in these same circles.[53] Sadat and his wife developed a close personal relationship with Kuwaiti Prince 'Abdullah al-Mubarak al-Sabah and his wife Su'ad al-Sabah in the latter 1960s, and the prince was rumored to be a CIA go-between with Arab leaders.[54] Sadat presented his friend Muhammad Hafez Mahmud to the prince as a financial adviser.

Perhaps more importantly, during 1970 and 1971, Kemal Adham made frequent trips to Egypt and became one of Sadat's principal advisers.[55] Sadat also conferred often with Saudi Ambassador Hisham al-Nathir; and a special transmitter linked Sadat with King Feisal. These individuals all encouraged Sadat to improve ties with the United States, as did the shah of Iran, whose connections with the CIA were well-known, and with whom Sadat was totally enthralled.

Political deaths and private diplomacy provided the backdrop to Sadat's personal efforts to improve relations with the United States. Sadat recounts that when he regained consciousness after fainting at Nasser's funeral, the first person he saw was Eliot Richardson, who had headed the U.S. funeral delegation. Sadat told Richardson to inform President Nixon that "All I want is peace . . . I am prepared to go to any lengths to achieve it."[56] Unfortunately for Sadat, nothing came of this because Richardson returned to the U.S., reporting that Sadat wouldn't last more than four to six weeks in power.[57]

Egypt and the United States had maintained diplomatic contacts with one another despite the severance of formal diplomatic relations. Ashraf

Ghorbal, a Harvard Ph.D., had been slated to become deputy chief of mission in Washington, D.C. just before the 1967 war, but did not assume his post because of the war. However, six months after it he became the chief of Egypt's interests section to deal with U.S. relations. His American counterpart was Donald Bergus, who worked out of the U.S. Interests Section in the Spanish embassy in Cairo. Cables from Bergus were equally pessimistic about Sadat's tenure. In late September, Bergus opined: "Acting President Sadat will not emerge as permanent leader."[58]

Also perceiving Sadat as weak, former Free Officer 'Abd al-Mun'im Amin opted to approach Sadat with advice and assistance. In particular, Amin suggested that Sadat rethink Nasser's anti-American position. Sadat sent Amin to put out feelers with the American interests section personnel regarding the Americans' view of Sadat, and Amin received word from Nixon that he was happy to engage in "side contacts" with Sadat.[59] Amin believes this was the real beginning of Sadat's closer relations with the United States.[60]

American officials in Cairo underwent a rapid change in their perceptions of Sadat. Bergus met Sadat on October 3, 1970, and cabled the State Department as follows:

Personally I was much more impressed by Sadat's performance than I had expected to be. I found it hard to believe that this was the same man who had indulged in so much plain anti-American rabble-rousing in public meetings throughout Egypt during first six months of this year. Perhaps his new responsibilities have made some change."

Throughout conversation Sadat stressed his and UAR's feeling of friendship towards America. We can talk about very difficult matters and as friends, and that Israel problem [is the] only real obstacle to close relations between two governments.[61]

Of course, such changes in official Americans' perceptions of Sadat translated into greater warmth and receptivity toward Sadat and his emissaries, and provided positive reinforcement for Sadat's flirtations.

Sadat's assumption of the presidency had indeed affected his political thinking and behavior. Sadat sent Nixon a letter dated November 23, 1970, thanking Nixon for his kind message of October 14, the Richardson delegation's attendance at Nasser's funeral, and most importantly, expressing a desire for good relations with the United States.[62] But this letter was preceded by numerous private contacts during October and November marked by expressions of the desire for warmer relations between the U.S. and Egypt. These took the form of private encounters in Cairo between

Bergus and, alternately, Heikal, Prime Minister Fawzi, and Sadat. Reporting on a November 9 private meeting with Heikal, Bergus noted that Sadat had a strong interest in increasing and strengthening a U.S.-UAR dialogue. Bergus described Heikal as "the most dovish he has ever been," said that Heikal quoted Nasser on the impossibility of a military solution to the conflict, for either side, and noted that Heikal, for the first time, envisioned a Palestinian solution in terms of King Hussein's abdication, and the creation of a Palestinian state comprising both the East and West banks of the Jordan and the Gaza Strip.[63]

For several months, these contacts and communications with Americans were so private as to leave almost all other top Egyptian elites in the dark. No real indications of a change in Sadat's orientations, or his willingness to activate latent political desires, came until the end of the year. In December 1970, Israel's Moshe Dayan floated the idea of a partial (30–40 km.) withdrawal of Israeli forces in the Sinai peninsula in exchange for a clearing and reopening of the Suez Canal to international navigation. Although Sadat rejected this overture in an ASU Central Committee meeting held on December 16, it was clear to a few keen observers that he was affected by the idea.[64] This was indeed the case.

On December 24, Sadat received a letter from President Nixon, thanking Sadat for sending an Egyptian delegation to President Eisenhower's funeral. Sadat seized the opportunity, and had Sami Sharaf's office summon Bergus to meet Sadat at the Barrages rest house. According to Bergus' cable, Sadat said that in this "unofficial" meeting, "he wanted to open his heart to me in the hope that I would pass his innermost feelings on to President Nixon." Reviewing the history of Soviet–Egyptian relations, Sadat asserted that the Soviet presence was necessitated by the conflict with Israel and the pro-Israeli position held by the United States, but that Egypt took no orders from the Soviets and had no stake in the Cold War. He added, however, that Egypt would never abandon efforts to restore its full national sovereignty.

> "Egyptians are a simple people," went on Sadat, "but there are two issues which make them want to fight to the death: land and dignity. In an Egyptian village bloody feuds over a meter of land sometimes last for fifty years." "My conclusion is this," said Sadat, "we will never reach the day when Egypt will surrender to either the East or the West. At the same time we are open-minded and ready to understand and discuss and to do what must be done for peace. I am willing," said Sadat, "to go anyplace in the world if it would save one Egyptian casualty, wounded or killed, but we won't surrender our land or our dignity. We say this after all the United States has done to us, the United States, not the Israelis."

Bergus ended his report with the following comment:

I think Department will agree that this was a reasonably interesting experience. I think it possible that with plenty of patience and a dash of style and finesse we can do business with this guy. He is so obviously reaching out for some kind of encouragement from President Nixon, despite much of what he says. I will be reflecting about this conversation over my Christmas turkey...[65]

At the end of their meeting, Sadat gave Bergus the following letter to send to Nixon:

To begin with, I had sent you a message with Ambassador Richardson who visited Egypt to offer condolences on Nasser's death, but you never replied to it.* You have, meanwhile, supported Israel's claim that Egypt violated the terms of the Rogers Plan although you know very well that the territory east and west of the Canal is Egyptian.

Now that you have sent a letter of thanks to our prime minister and wanted it conveyed to me, I am writing you to confirm the contents of the message I sent you with Ambassador Richardson and to add a few things. You would be mistaken to think that we are in the sphere of Soviet influence: we are not in the Soviet sphere of influence nor, for that matter, anybody's sphere of influence. I'd like you to know, furthermore, that nobody could claim to be Egypt's tutelar [sic] power. So, if you wish to talk about anything concerning Egypt, the venue will be Cairo and the talks will be with me, not with any other party [by which I clearly meant—as I explained to the diplomat looking after U.S. interests in Egypt—the Soviet Union, which wanted to act as our master, a "right" Nasser had granted the Soviets at one time]. I'd like you also to know that we take our own decisions freely and independently, so that if you prove friendly to us, we shall be ten times as friendly; if hostile, we shall be ten times as hostile. As it is the law of nature for each action to have a reaction, a good move by you will be met by a dozen good moves by us, and vice versa.[66]

*N.B. Sadat's autobiographical version ignores his November letter to Nixon.

Sadat claimed to have received a response from Nixon within 48 hours, in which the latter urged Sadat to consider pursuing a peaceful resolution of the conflict with Israel.[67] And regime elites have concurred that Nixon's letter also had its impact on Sadat's thinking.[68] So much is true, but while the substance of Sadat's account is fairly accurate, its details are interestingly erroneous. Declassified State Department documents show that on January 4, 1971, Heikal paid yet another visit to Bergus, asking when a reply to Sadat's Christmas eve message to Nixon would be forthcoming. Heikal told Bergus that he was "one of the few who knew of Sadat's decision to open this channel" of direct communications to Nixon, and also noted that he had persuaded Sadat to write his November letter to Nixon against heavy opposition from many around Sadat.[69] In addition, a Department of State telegram drafted by M. Sterner and W. B. Smith II on January 19, 1971 contained the makings of a reply to Sadat, stating that the "President [Nixon] is appreciative of Sadat's desire to open private dialogue with him, and we do not believe we should close door[s] on any channel which might improve US-UAR relations and thus contribute to our efforts to achieve peaceful settlement."[70] But the declassified documents highlight the fact that paralleling Egypt's public, conflict-oriented diplomatic offensive, there were secretive, peace-oriented contacts between Sadat and U.S. officials.[71] And it was precisely the secrecy of these contacts and Sadat's private diplomacy that produced deep resentment and turmoil in the Egyptian elite.

In an interview with me, General Fawzi alleged that:

in the beginning of 1971, these contacts with the U.S. administration became known to us, that is, Washington-Anwar Sadat contacts; not Washington-Cairo contacts. It is okay for contacts to occur within a framework, but not outside the framework. The diplomatic tradition—any president can talk within the framework of the policy, but if he gets outside the framework, it is wrong. The official written policy of the Foreign Affairs department was this—we had broken off diplomatic relations with the United States and were engaging in the Rogers initiative; that's all. Sadat wanted to make other contacts, for example, the February initiative. Sadat was telling Kemal Adham, who tells Washington, D.C., "I'll make a February initiative, then the Israelis can move troops away from the canal and I'll get the Russians out." How did we learn of these contacts? We discovered a direct line to Washington, D.C. from Sadat's house. A president can do this, yes, but not outside the policy that's set. I was making security measures for Cairo and I discovered a signal being sent out of Cairo to the outside world. I ordered a triangulation study and the report came that the apparatus was above Sadat's house. The report came in January 1971. I sent the report to Sadat about the transmitter at his Giza house. Sadat responded: "How do you know?"

I said: "It's our work to know such things."

Sadat said: "Shame on you. This isn't right."

Fawzi: "Why did you get rid of the Intelligence services? This is their job."

Sadat: "What's your advice?"

Fawzi: "Take it out of your house."

I took it away. He put it in his secretary's house and didn't use it any more. You judge, Dr. Kirk, what does this suggest to you? So he was working behind everybody's back, making his own private foreign policy. Why did he want to do this privately?! This was the beginning of our showdown with him.[72]

Sadat's February 4 Suez Canal Initiative

Having received no clear signal from the Americans in response to his plea to Nixon, Sadat sought a means to impress upon the Americans the sincerity of his overture. On February 2, as the February 5 expiration date for the ceasefire once again drew near, Sadat called a meeting of the National Defense Council, with SEC members and several cabinet officials also in attendance. At that meeting, during which all the principal actors, except Prime Minister Fawzi, expressed their readiness and willingness to resume warfare, and saw the moment as propitious, Sadat informed his colleagues that he had the opportunity to embarrass Egypt's adversaries by announcing a peace project. He would call for a final 30-day extension of the ceasefire to give one last chance to the great powers to promote peace.[73] But when Sadat made his February 4 speech before the Maglis al-Umma, he went well beyond his February 2 statements, and publicly announced his willingness to clear the Suez Canal and resume its normal operation, as well as extend the ceasefire for an additional six months, if Israeli troops withdrew from their positions east of the canal, and allowed Egyptian forces to fill the void. In essence, Sadat's bid paralleled Dayan's earlier proposal. It was made without his having received any additional overtures by American officials, who still questioned Sadat's ability to remain in office.[74]

Importantly, Sadat's February 4 initiative was undertaken without any prior discussion or consent from the collective leadership. Only Heikal, Sharaf and Prime Minister Fawzi knew of the initiative in advance of its announcement.[75] In fact, many regime leaders first learned of the initiative by reading about it in the newspapers. [76] This development infuriated Centrists and set in motion a power clash with major implications for Egypt's political-economic future.

Centrists were all the more alarmed because Sadat's initiative came amidst a growing propensity among certain other regime elites either to speak of a peaceful resolution of the conflict with Israel, or to question Egypt's military preparedness. No one had dared speak of peace while Nasser was still alive.[77] Now Sayyid Mar'ei, Mustafa Khalil, and to some extent 'Abd al-'Aziz Higazi and other technocrats were warming to this idea. Sadat himself not only shared this thinking, but also was displaying a new willingness to initiate policy changes along these lines without prior discussion with his SEC colleagues.

Simultaneously, debate developed outside the SEC and in the press over whether or not the military was adequately prepared for war. The press debate pitted Heikal—whom many saw as parroting Sadat's privately-held views, if not planting them in his head—against a number of ASU heavy-weights, most prominent among whom figured SEC member Dia al-Din Dawud and ASU Secretariat member 'Abd al-Hadi Nassef. According to Heikal, Egypt could not hope to defeat Israel without first altering the U.S. relationship with Israel. He wrote on March 19, "the aim of Egyptian foreign policy must be to reduce the scope of the military and political support to Israel, and the major source of this support is the United States."[78] This commentary came on the heels of Heikal's highly provocative editorial columns of March 5 and 12. In the March 5 column, entitled "Nasser is Not a Legend,"[79] Heikal argued that Nasser's final policies were not cast in bronze, that the military was unprepared for war, and that the United States should not be considered Egypt's enemy. In the March 12 column, entitled "Salute to the Men"[80] [of the military], Heikal presented so poignant and detailed a description of Israel's formidable defense as to demoralize the Egyptian forces charged with the task of destroying it. These articles, combined with charges by Heikal, which appeared in *Newsweek*'s January 12 issue,[81] that "the ASU was killing political life in Egypt," were more than Centrists could tolerate, as evidenced by the vehemence of their responses in *al-Gumhurriyya.* [82] The Lebanese magazine *al-Hawadith* reported on March 26 that some ASU members were so incensed that they wanted Heikal brought to trial. [83] Obviously support for such a move would have been far greater if the ASU types had known to what extent Heikal was involved in behind the scenes efforts to further relations with the United States.

Termination of the Ceasefire: Preparing for War?

Because Sadat's February initiative elicited no strongly positive response from either the Israelis or the Americans, Sadat had decided on March 6 not to renew the ceasefire. Egypt had returned to the tenuous position of "no war, no peace" with Israel, but Centrists were relieved to see Sadat moving ahead, from all appearances in great earnest, with plans for the battle. Sadat quietly reformed a Committee to Prepare the State for War, headed by Vice President Shaf'ei and including numerous top civilian officials, which met twice between March 19 and March 22.[84] From March 17 to March 25 Sadat personally reviewed battle plans with all top military commanders. At no time, according to Fawzi, did he voice any reservations about the military's preparedness.[85] To Fawzi, Egypt was just a stroke of Sadat's pen on battle orders away from war.

Were the Egyptian forces indeed ready? General Fawzi certainly thought so, but high-ranking officers who went on to fill key positions in

Sadat's regime felt differently. Sadiq had serious reservations, as did Gen. Muhammad 'Abd al-Ghani al-Gamassi and Gen. Kemal Hassan 'Ali. [86] The latter two countered Fawzi's assertions by stating that there was no offensive plan under Nasser for the simple reason that the rearming of the military wasn't completed until after Nasser's death. [87] General 'Ali notes that after becoming second in command of the Artillery in mid-May 1971, it was clear to him that Artillery officers were eager for the battle "but not before preparation with the necessary arms."[88]

So what was going on? Perhaps the clearest answer has been provided by Lt. Gen. Saad al-Din el Shazly. Shazly wrote:

> "The truth is that when I became Chief of Staff on May 16, 1971, we had no offensive plan. There was a defensive plan code-named Operation 200 and a more aggressive one called Granite. But although Granite incorporated raids into Sinai, it too fell far short of being a true offensive plan."[89]

One may deduce that Centrists had either a renewal of the War of Attrition or some other form of limited warfare in mind, although political machinations may have been behind Centrists' calculations as well. Ahmed Kamel, director of General Intelligence, later testified in court as follows: Centrists thought that if Egypt went to war and scored a partial victory crossing the canal, their jobs would be all the more secure at home. If the war was lost, Sadat would be blamed by the public and they'd still be safe. Asked if the Centrists intended to make Sadat lose his position by going to war prematurely, Kamel responded that the basic goal was for them to keep their jobs whether Sadat got booted or not; and if Sadat got out of line, they'd try to dump him.[90]

The Arab Unity Debate

By late February, Sadat had already started to follow up on another initiative that rapidly acquired its own importance and ultimately ran counter to any undivided focus on a war effort: Sadat's call for political union by Egypt, Libya, and Syria. High-level meetings ensued, culminating in a joint announcement in Libya by Sadat, Libya's Colonel Qaddafi and Syria's President Assad on April 17, 1971 of agreement to form a new Union of Arab Republics. This announcement was a complete surprise to most SEC members; once again collective decision-making had been ignored.

As with Sadat's February peace initiative, the Arab unity bid was perceived by most SEC members as a serious distraction from the war effort, and as yet another matter providing Sadat with an excuse for postponing warfare to play other foreign policy cards. In Sha'rawi Gum'a's words, "We weren't against unity in principle, but we didn't want anything to postpone the battle. After Nasser's death, getting the Jews out of Sinai was one of our primary objectives. The Sudan, Sadat, and the Syrians pressured Qaddafi to make unity, which Qaddafi didn't really want then."[91]

Sadat told Hermann Eilts that while Sadat had issued the invitation, it was Qaddafi who had pushed for a unity scheme. Sadat "went along with it" because he needed Libyan financial help, but ensured the "looseness" of the ensuing "confederation." Eilts's comments about the confederation's track record are revealing. He noted that Sadat's statements:

> may have been posturing to the American ambassador, but when one looked at how totally unused the tripartite confederation was—with its prime minister and cabinet members in the Heliopolis Hotel doing nothing, pitifully having to ask the American media and other embassies for basic information because they could not get it from the Egyptian government—one could not help but conclude that Sadat attached no great importance to the organization. And this was already obvious in early 1974 and was not simply a product of subsequent Egyptian-Libyan tensions because of the peace process.[92]

Sadat was indeed posturing before Eilts. Sadat wanted the "confederation," but he wanted it most to pick a fight with the Centrists.

Centrists had good reasons to fear that this was not the only goal Sadat might accomplish behind the political union with Syria and Libya. They recognized that a new union would provide the pretext for reorganizing the political system, a transformation that could be exploited by Sadat to dissolve the ASU and undermine other institutional bases of Centrist power. Most Centrists believed in hindsight that Sadat's unity scheme was a ploy designed to pick a fight over an issue where they would be viewed as contradicting pan-Arabist ideals. Whether a ploy or not, Sabri and Sadat openly clashed when Sabri spoke out against the union during discussions with the Libyan leadership in March.

From a Centrist perspective, indications that Sadat was getting out of line grew dramatically in March and April. General Intelligence operatives had bugged the house of Donald Bergus, and recorded conversations between Bergus and Sadat's secret emissaries as well as Bergus's conversations with American colleagues, like Michael Sterner.[93] As events unfolded from March into early May, the tapes revealed Sadat's intention to fire or distance those opposed to his February peace initiative, his wish to alter the domestic political establishment, his desire for Bergus to tell Dayan that he hoped Dayan would assume the prime ministership of Israel, and his long-run hopes for peace with Israel.[94] The tapes were passed on by Ahmed Kamel, and held in confidence by a small group including Gum'a, Sharaf, Muhammad Fawzi, and 'Ali Sabri. Also, on April 3, former Free Officer Magdi Hassanein, then serving as ambassador to Czechoslovakia, had a private conversation with Sadat, during which Sadat indicated that he would drop Sabri and dissolve the ASU. Hassanein quickly warned Sabri and Gum'a that "Sadat will do to you what Muhammad 'Ali did to the mamluks"—which is to say, Sadat would slaughter them.[95]

For these reasons, the confrontation reached a new level of severity following the April 17 unity announcement, and more specifically, when Sadat decided to force the unity issue at an April 21 SEC meeting. At that meeting, Sadat refused to adhere to the accepted practice of working toward unanimous decisions via lengthy discussion. Instead, he repeatedly insisted on a quick vote, perhaps to discern which members would stand against him. In this vote, Sabri, Dawud, Shuqeir, and Abu Nur voted against Sadat's union idea, with Sadat, Shaf'ei, and Fawzi voting for it. (Stino was absent; Gum'a was in attendance, but had no vote.)

Angered by this loss, Sadat vowed to take the matter before the Central Committee. Dawud recalls that the SEC members tried to calm Sadat by suggesting further discussions, but Sadat refused and a CC meeting was scheduled for April 25.[96] Centrists now feared that Sadat might appear quickly before the CC and try to win its support in an abbreviated debate, with Sadat presenting himself as the defender of Arab unity. Consequently, the Centrists decided to beat Sadat to the punch by presenting their views on the issue to CC members before Sadat spoke to them. Each of the key group members met CC representatives in groups of 10 to 15 in their offices to explain the situation. Sadat later heard of these meetings, and it was his interpretation of their content that, in part, led him to believe that a coup conspiracy was being mounted against him.[97]

Part of Sadat's paranoia was clearly self-induced, for while the Centrists were holding their behind-closed-door sessions, Sadat was carrying on his own clandestine activities. Despite the cool reception by Americans and Israelis to his February peace initiative, Sadat had not abandoned the peace ship. Secret contacts with Americans continued, and Sadat's entreaties resulted in a visit to Egypt by State Department official Michael Sterner. On April 22, Sterner and Bergus met with Sadat for two hours at the Barrages rest house for what—to their surprise—turned out to be serious discussions about an interim peace arrangement. Sterner said, "We could see that he wanted to negotiate peace. He was serious. This was important stuff. But what we didn't know was whether he was going to be dumped."[98]

Once again, Centrists acquired information about this meeting from Egyptian intelligence, having secretly taped conversations between Bergus and Sterner in Bergus' home. According to some reports, these conversations included Sadat's idea of dumping 'Ali Sabri prior to the visit by Secretary of State Rogers.[99] Sterner does not recall any discussion of such internal political matters,[100] and Bergus' cable corroborates his claim.[101] Plenty was said, however, about Sadat's peace overture; this explains why Sharaf and others were convinced by mid-to-late April of Sadat's intentions to perhaps seek a separate peace with Israel.[102] Elsewhere, General Fawzi noted that on April 23—the day after Sadat met Sterner and Bergus—Sadat secretly informed the Soviets of his intention to dump 'Ali Sabri, hoping that by making them privy he might allay their suspicions of his long-run intentions when he ousted "their man in Cairo."[103]

The May 1971 Clash

Far above the view of the general public, the domestic political stage was now set for a major showdown. With CC members forewarned of Sadat's "true objectives" regarding the unity scheme, and with many of those members already predisposed to back Centrists given both the Centrist-dominated process by which they had been selected[104] and Sadat's neglect of the CC over the previous two months, Sadat's attempt to bring the union issue to a CC vote on April 25 proved even more embarrassing than the SEC vote. For starters, Sadat's supporters felt compelled to present a point of order to prevent Sabri from revealing the secret discussion that had occurred among the Arab heads of state, an effort that produced much foot-stomping by outraged Centrists. Beyond the Centrist bias, most CC members were simply curious and wanted to capitalize on the rare opportunity to hear what the summit leaders had discussed. Therefore, only four of the 150 committee members—Mar'ei, Heikal, Ahmed Sayyid Darwish, and Mustafa Abu Zeid Fahmi—sided with Sadat on this point of order. Sabri was thus permitted to detail Sadat's lone-wolf efforts to arm-twist Qaddafi and Assad into a unity agreement, and he did so using exceptionally condescending language with Sadat.

To surmount this acrimony, a compromise motion was approved to review Sadat's proposal and to revise the text on the unity treaty. Sami Sharaf and another Egyptian envoy were dispatched to Syria and Libya to secure approval for revisions. Despite Sadat's effort to characterize these changes as trivial in a speech on March 14, the modifications included dropping the notion of forming a united state, rather than forming a confederation, and requiring unanimity among the three heads of state to approve major policies in place of a two-thirds majority vote. Approval of these modifications was gained by April 29. The CC met that day and its members accepted the revised confederation proposal, as did the Maglis al-Umma. The revised proposal effectively sustained Sabri's major objections.[105]

But now the confrontation's climax was at hand. On May 1, in the traditional May Day speech to workers in Helwan, Sadat again found himself facing a hostile assembly. Centrists and workers occupied the front rows, and persisted in chanting pro-Nasser slogans and holding up pictures of Nasser at every opportunity, thereby intentionally slighting Sadat. Greatly perturbed, but not intimidated, Sadat departed from his prepared speech and attacked what he described as nefarious "power centers" (individuals who led factions that controlled state institutions to serve their factions' interests), saying he wouldn't allow such elements to impose their will. In the car, leaving the site of the speech, an infuriated Sadat told Hafez Isma'il, "I'll hang them!" Isma'il responded wanly, "Please don't."[106]

Sadat had not named names during his speech, but the very next day all major newspapers carried the news that Sabri had been stripped of his vice presidency. On May 3, Sabri wrote and submitted his resignation from the SEC and remained at home. Some observers saw Sabri's demise as a present for Secretary of State Rogers, who arrived in Cairo on May 5 for two days of discussions with Egyptian officials, including a meeting with Sadat on May 6.[107] The Rogers visit was extraordinary; it represented the first visit by an American secretary of state since 1953, and it came despite the continued absence of formal diplomatic relations between Egypt and the United States.

Following his ouster, Sabri did not sit idly at home, but rather called Gum'a daily, beseeching him not to fear Sadat and to move quickly. But most Centrists did not perceive Sabri's demise as a "first blow against all of us,"[108] and the absence of strong personal bonds between Sabri and others weighed against a rapid, collective show of solidarity on Sabri's behalf.[109]

Key Centrists also found solace from less obvious sources. The night of Sabri's dismissal, Sharaf insisted there was nothing to worry about because "Nasser is with us. We know Nasser's advice."[110] General Fawzi had brought a professor named Sheikh Mubarak, well known in elite circles as a medium, to summon Nasser's spirit, and through this medium Nasser had delivered his message. Sha'rawi Gum'a was also among those present and similarly felt reassured. On another occasion, Gum'a had told Mahmud Amin al-'Alim, "You communists don't understand these spiritual matters. Five years ago Sheikh Mubarak correctly predicted I'd become governor."[111] Thus, for various reasons, Gum'a answered Sabri with pleas for patience, saying he was preparing to do something.[112]

During this crucial period, Centrists felt hamstrung by their belief that the battle with Israel was imminent. Why? General Fawzi had gone to

Sadat's Giza home on April 26, 1971 and Sadat set May 20 as a tentative date for implementing the "Granite" battle plans.[113] On May 9, Fawzi returned to Sadat's Giza home and Sadat said that warfare would commence on June 2. Fawzi was told to arrange meetings between Sadat and half of the military officer corps on May 11, and the other half on May 12, as part of his final war preparations.[114] During this meeting, Sadat turned his focus to troubling aspects of the domestic political scene, suggesting to General Fawzi that there were about 100 individuals he'd be getting rid of in a week or two, by which Fawzi assumed he was referring to Sadat's Central Committee opponents.[115]

After Sadat and General Fawzi concluded their meeting, Sadat steered Fawzi into a second, highly secretive meeting at Sadat's home that included Sadat, Prime Minister Fawzi, Foreign Minister Riyad, and Ashraf Ghorbal, along with Joseph Sisco, Undersecretary of State for the Near East, Donald Bergus, and Roy Atherton, also of the U.S. State Department. Sisco outlined the Israelis' response to Sadat's interim peace overture. General Fawzi not only heard the stringent conditions demanded by the Israelis for an interim agreement,[116] but observed firsthand Sadat's near total faith in the Americans to work out a partial settlement.[117]

Immediately following this meeting, Sadat held a two-hour private discussion with Sisco in which Sadat confided a great deal. Beyond talk of interim peace arrangements, he noted that General Fawzi and the military were "very negative" and opposed any interim settlement unless it allowed a movement of troops across the canal. He also informed Sisco that Foreign Minister Riyad didn't really want to do anything to improve relations with the United States, not out of any anti-American sentiment, but because he found it fruitless. By contrast, said Sadat, Prime Minister Fawzi "likes Americans," and therefore Sadat had decided to rely more on the prime minister than Riyad for foreign affairs. It was during this session that Sadat, having been told repeatedly by his American interlocutors that Dayan was proving the most flexible among key Israelis, noted that he "prays to God in hopes that Dayan will become prime minister." And finally, he told Sisco that he was "going to the people," and would be meeting the ASU tomorrow to arrange for top to bottom elections "since about 100 out 150 [CC members] are against him."[118]

On May 10, Sadat called a SEC meeting, refusing to invite Dia Dawud and Sabri—who had submitted his resignation anyway—because, said Sadat, "this meeting is in my house, and neither of them has the right to sit on any chair here."[119] Their absence also helped stack the SEC deck in Sadat's favor. The very next morning, Sadat met with Gum'a and informed him that he intended to call for the ASU's dissolution, with new base-to-summit elections to be held at month's end. Gum'a then went off to share this bombshell with other Centrists and wheels were set spinning as to how to respond to Sadat's decision to overhaul the party.

Did the Centrists then plot a coup to oust Sadat? On the basis of my research, I have concluded that there was no coup conspiracy by principal Centrists as alleged by Sadat and others. No Centrist, even years after the events, and after years in prison, has admitted to any such plan. Sha'rawi Gum'a stated: "There was no conspiracy from our part—we had all powers in our hands. If we had planned a conspiracy, we could have won, *mish kida* (right)?"[120] Well, not necessarily, as shall be seen. But while I find the disavowals of a coup by Gum'a and all the other principals as truthful, I also find them disingenuous. While all undoubtedly desired dumping Sadat at this juncture, at a minimum they wished to rein him in. Accordingly, Centrist behavior was easily perceived as coup-oriented; and in the "eat, or be eaten" environment that they had helped create, one can easily understand Sadat's "counter-coup" behavior. Equally understandable is how any putative coup attempt was used to justify Sadat's ridding the regime of his major Centrist opponents.

Why do I arrive at these conclusions? Sabri's demise, and the plans to reorganize the ASU, caused regime elites in general to exchange views on what would come next, with many Centrists and their sympathizers discussing what should be done to bring Sadat back into line. Individuals whose allegiance to Sadat or preference for his orientations outweighed that of their association with his Centrist opponents—people like Heikal and others—had been signaling Sadat to be on guard. Heikal warned Jehan Sadat that her husband's life was in danger.[121]

Another warning came from Mustafa Kamel Murad. Murad was an erstwhile amorous suitor of Jehan Sadat, and a former Free Officer. He had become chairman of the board of the Eastern Cotton Company, a public-sector firm in Alexandria. Murad had started to get wind of elite turmoil through conversations with Sami Sharaf, who several years earlier had recruited Murad to his secret Vanguard Organization cell. In April 1971, Sharaf had tried to get Murad to attack Sadat in parliament as an American agent, saying he could prove the accusation. But Murad did not believe Sadat had sold out to the Americans, and he had grown sick of the socialist system. After mulling over his conversations with Sharaf, Murad decided to recount them to Sadat. Shortly thereafter, Sharaf contacted Murad and the following exchange ensued, according to Murad:

Sharaf: So, you went to see Sadat last night. When did you go?
Murad: About 10:00.

Sharaf: No, you went at 7 minutes before 10:00. When did you leave?
Murad: About 12:00.
Sharaf: No, you left at 12:13.

Sharaf then presented a typewritten transcript of the entire conversation between Sadat and Murad from that evening, and "ordered" Murad not to meet Sadat again. Sharaf said, "Either you are with us or against us. This is your last warning." Murad responded, "Then I am against you." Sharaf said, "Why? This clown. This Abyssinian. He's a liar, an actor. He can't make democracy work in Egypt!"

Murad then went immediately to Sadat's house; the date was May 10. He led Sadat out into the garden and told him that his house was bugged, and that he must move quickly to protect himself.[122]

At approximately 1:00 A.M. on May 11, three intelligence officers (Col. Muhammad Mu'awad Gad—from the Administration of Officer Affairs, Armed Forces; Hassan Rashwan Sul'iman—from GIA; and Taha Zaki—from General Investigations) had a tape delivered to Sadat's secretary at Sadat's Giza home.[123] Sadat and his wife listened to the tape, as did Heikal, who was called from his home nearby. It contained a conversation between Farid 'Abd al-Karim, ASU secretary-general for the Giza governorate, and journalist Mahmud al-Sa'dani, both Centrists. Besides Sa'dani's profanely disparaging comments about Mrs. Sadat, the conversation included a query and comments as to whether Fawzi was "ready." This was interpreted by Sadat and his fellow listeners as meaning that Fawzi was ready to move against Sadat. 'Abd al-Karim has always maintained that he was talking about Fawzi being ready for "the battle" against Israel.[124] Sharaf notes that both he and Gum'a had been given the tape and listened to it four days before it was taken to Sadat and attached no significance to it.[125] But Sadat and his confidants concluded that Sadat was facing an imminent coup and they took measures to prevent it from unfolding.

Sadat responded to these menacing developments with moves to ensure support from the coercive apparatuses. Sadat had continued to meet with Sadiq and other military officers throughout March and April,[126] and by late April he already had an understanding with Sadiq that the latter would do his utmost to guarantee the military's backing. Sadat kept his Fawzi-arranged meetings and spoke to army unit commanders on May 11, then addressed air force commanders on May 12. Sadat spoke to the officers in a manner to ensure their support. He told the officers that there was a 99 percent chance that warfare would begin soon, and only a 1 percent chance that his peace initiative would succeed, but that he would be sending a special envoy to Washington, D.C. in 15 days to get the Americans' final position. He also informed the officers that he had dumped Sabri because he represented a power center and because he had stood in the way of unity with Libya and Syria, which all of the Central Committee had supported.[127] With a pained-looking General Fawzi standing nearby, he announced that he would "grind to pieces" any elements trying to establish "power centers" that "threatened national unity."[128] On both occasions, the officers responded to Sadat's pronouncements with strong—and for Sadat, reassuring—applause.

Fawzi writes that during this period he tried in vain to get Sadat to sign battle orders, enabling Fawzi to initiate warfare. While riding to Sadat's May 12 meeting with the air force officers, Sadat told General Fawzi, "I think they [his Centrist opponents] want it [war] so that when we win, they'll say 'we won' —No. Never."[129] Only then, says Fawzi, did it become crystal clear that all Sadat's talk about the battle was just designed to deceive him and the other officers, that is, to distract and contain the military while Sadat went after his domestic opponents.[130] So Fawzi decided to draft a letter of resignation.

Some ASU activists were contemplating a more offensive reaction to Sadat's threatened dissolution of the organization. In as close a recognition of coup-like behavior made by anyone, Mahmud Amin al-'Alim, a well-known "ex-communist," noted that, "In our last ASU Vanguard Secretariat meeting, we decided that there is no hope with Sadat. We planned to use the legal organs of government to make a change. Labib Shuqeir was in our group; the CC was controlled by all of us, so we thought this possible. We met on the twelfth [of May]. Our meeting may have caused Sadat to think there was a coup."[131]

Even without knowledge of such discussions, one would have expected Sadat to fear that the ASU's secret Vanguard Organization was undoubtedly being mobilized, or mobilizing itself, in defense of Gum'a, Sharaf, and other leaders. Sadat, like all other RCC members, had been intentionally excluded from the organization by Nasser; therefore, he could not easily assess its capabilities or disposition.

On May 13, Mamduh Salem arrived in Sadat's home, having been summoned from Alexandria by Sadat, and was promptly sworn in as minister of the interior by Prime Minister Fawzi. Salem, the governor of Alexandria, was a former high-ranking officer in the *Mabahith Amn al-Dawla* (State Security Investigations) department. He had often accompanied Nasser on foreign trips to provide security. Salem immediately contacted his friend, Gen. Sayyid Fahmi, head of the *Mabahith* in Alexandria, and appointed him director of the *Mabahith* at the national level, replacing Gen. Hassan Tal'at. (Tal'at and his second in command, General Zuhdi, were subsequently arrested under orders from Sadat.) [132] Salem's selection to head the Min-

istry of Interior was astute. Again, Nasser had consistently filled the position with military officers, offending policemen's sensitivities. The appointment of a career police officer, Salem, boosted police morale and earned
Sadat precious support.

While awaiting Salem's arrival from Alexandria, Sadat had called Gen.
al-Leithi Nassef, the formal commander of the Presidential Guard, to tell
him to get ready because "the battle" would begin as soon as Salem was in
place. Nassef assured him that his plan to repel any intervention by the
Central Security forces (under Gum'a) or the armed forces (under Fawzi)
had been ready for two months.[133] Nassef had a very close personal relationship with Sharaf, and Sharaf had oversight of the Republican Guard;
but Sharaf, in what he later described as one of his biggest mistakes, had
told Nassef on May 12 that he should respect the authorities and the chain
of command in his professional conduct.[134]

On May 13, Sadat also summoned Sami Sharaf to inform Gum'a that
he should submit his resignation, and that his successor had already been
sworn in. (Sharaf and Salem were actually in different rooms of the house
at the same time.) Even at this stage Sadat provided Sharaf the opportunity
to break with the Centrists, but Sharaf chose another destiny. After leaving
Sadat's house, he joined Gum'a, who was at General Headquarters with
General Fawzi, Muhammad Fa'iq, and Sa'd Zayyid. Zayyid, a former Free
Officer and incumbent governor of Cairo, was well known for his cavalier
declaration in the 1960s that "the law is on vacation." While at headquarters, Sa'd Zayyid suggested taking five soldiers and a tank to go get Sadat—
yet another threatening statement that undoubtedly got back to Sadat—but
Zayyid's idea was dismissed and most of the group proceeded to Gum'a's
house.[135]

On the afternoon of May 13, General Fawzi called General Sadiq, Gen.
Muhammad 'Ali Fahmi, and Gen. Ahmed Zaki to his office to apprise
them of Sadat's position and of his decision to resign because Sadat was
"placing all his confidence in the Americans."[136] Sadiq asked, "You mean,
he's selling the country to the Americans?" To which Fawzi responded in
the affirmative, telling Sadiq that Sadat was selling the country to the
Americans *mafrusha* (fully furnished). According to the Sadat crowd, Fawzi
instructed Sadiq to place the army on alert because he feared there might
be street protests against the resignations of several high officials when the
mosques let out after the Friday noon sermons the next day, but Sadiq and
the others refused on the grounds that the army should stay out of politics.[137] They urged Fawzi to reconsider his decision to resign. When Fawzi
told them his mind was made up, Sadiq said he should at least wait another
24 hours to think things through.[138]

According to Fawzi, once he had discerned Sadat's true intentions, he told Sadiq on May 13 that if Sadat was not planning on going to war, and was selling the country *mafrusha* to the Americans, then his responsibilities were over. Sadiq feigned approval of Fawzi's position, then reported these words to Sadat posthaste. Said Fawzi, "Because of these words, Sadat sentenced me to 15 years in prison. But the real reason for my arrest [in the wee hours of the morning on May 14] was that he didn't want to make the battle at that time." Now in tears during the interview, Fawzi continued, "I accepted to go to prison rather than say the real reason because if the people of Egypt knew that he refused the battle, he would be in a very awkward position. Also, I didn't want Israel to know. I had no connection to the May group except one thing: We all belonged to Nasser and his personality and politics and principles. There was no agreement concerning getting rid of Sadat at all."[139]

Faced with Sadat's dismissal of Gum'a and Fawzi's decision to resign, high-ranking Centrists gathered at the homes of Gum'a and 'Abd al-Muhsin Abu al-Nur. At Gum'a's home, they decided to resign en masse rather than give Sadat the time to defeat them one by one.[140] Gum'a had phoned General Fawzi and told him to come to his house. When he arrived there, Gum'a had already been joined by Sharaf, Zayyid, Fa'iq, and Hilmi al-Sa'id. Also present was Ashraf Marwan, husband of Nasser's younger daughter, Mona, who worked in Sami Sharaf's office. Marwan was tapped to carry letters of resignation from Gum'a, Sharaf, Fawzi, Shuqeir, Dia al-Din Dawud, and Fa'iq to Sadat's house, arriving there just prior to their resignations' announcement on the last evening news broadcast at 11:00 P.M. on May 13.[141] 'Abd al-Muhsin Abu al-Nur made his way to Gum'a's house after 11:00 P.M. "I heard the resignations announced on the radio; they said on the radio that I'd resigned, too, but I hadn't. If it was a coup, why would anyone resign?"[142]

By their simultaneous resignations, Centrists hoped to acutely embarrass Sadat and force him to respect the institutions of government. As one member put it, "We wanted to show him that he did not and could not have a free hand in the exercise of power. Our intent was not to make a coup d'etat."[143] All felt certain that had they not resigned, Sadat's plan was to eliminate them one-by-one. Some expressed the belief that had they not resigned collectively, they might have been spared imprisonment and accusations of sedition,[144] but their ouster from power was still certain. Dawud says the Centrists opted against 'Abd al-Ghaffar Shukr's suggestion of responding to Sadat's challenge by orchestrating a show of force.[145] For days, Centrists had been contemplating whether they had it in them to make a coup or not. In the end, given the country's precarious position—

being on the brink of war—they decided to respect legal means to display their displeasure with Sadat and simply resigned.

From the perspective of Sadat and his backers, there was much cause for feeling imperiled. How could they be certain that top Centrists would forego coup suggestions and opt for protest resignations alone? And more importantly, what reaction might their resignations bring? According to Sadat's backers, the Centrist plan was for the mass cabinet resignations to trigger an outpouring of popular support on Friday, with Nasser's 1967 postwar resignation as a model in mind. Vanguard Organization types would spring into action, mobilizing fellow members in the professional syndicates, labor organizations, and peasants. General Fawzi would then be justified in calling the army into the streets to restore order, and an extraordinary session of parliament, whose president was the Centrist Labib Shuqeir, would be called at which Sadat would be dumped.

Somehow, from the Sadat camp's perspective, Sadat had to out-trump the mass resignation card being played by the Centrists. With his young son, Gamal, standing guard with a shotgun at the front door, and his own gun at his side, from roughly 12:00 midnight on, Sadat tried to manage the crisis, huddled in his Giza house with his wife Jehan, Muhammad Hassanein Heikal, Sayyid Mar'ei, Muhammad 'Abd al-Salam al-Zayyat, Hussein al-Shaf'ei, Mustafa Kamel Murad, 'Aziz Sidqi, and others. Jehan Sadat, herself panic-stricken, recalled that her husband remained completely calm. "I was afraid he was so calm and so deliberate that he'd move too slowly to catch them." And when Ashraf Marwan arrived with the news of the collective resignations, the president's response was, "Well, they've made it easier for me now."[146]

Sadat's reliance on and support from the coercive apparatuses was crucial. Sadiq had gone to Sadat's house around 8:30 P.M. on May 13 to inform him of Fawzi's intentions. Sadat had made Sadiq minister of defense on the spot, and told Sadiq to contact the chiefs of staff of the various military branches. None of the latter offered any opposition to the change in command and no forces were mobilized in support of the Centrists. Gen. Ahmed Isma'il went to Sadat's house, and Sadat named him director of the General Intelligence Agency, replacing Ahemd Kamel.

Republican Guard commander Nassef was contacted almost immediately following the 11:00 P.M. news broadcast on May 13. By the next morning, the Guard and the military had placed nearly all top Centrists under house arrest, and by the following day, they had detained a total of some 90 high-ranking officials with no resistance. General Fawzi was already under house arrest by 2:00 A.M. on May 14.

Over the next 24 hours, a number of additional factors combined to seal the Centrists' fate. First, whatever Centrists may have hoped to provoke or elicit in the way of a popular outpouring on their behalf simply did not materialize beyond several minor demonstrations, one of which began from a mosque on Gumhurriyya Street in Cairo on Friday. 'Aziz Sidqi, a Centrist who had clashed personally with Sabri to the point of despising him, was instrumental in issuing strong statements denouncing those who resigned, as well as in mobilizing public sector workers and security personnel for demonstrations against them. Through Sidqi's efforts, the streets were politically neutralized.

Second, many cabinet members, including Prime Minister Mahmud Fawzi, refused to resign along with the Centrists. In addition, Nasser's children, as well as his close confidant, Heikal, all showed solidarity with Sadat during the crisis, although most of them later regretted having done so. Collectively, their behavior greatly abetted Sadat in the court of public opinion, as they created a strong perception of continuity with Nasser's line.

Third, Sadat's influence in the Maglis al-Umma proved extremely beneficial. In early April, Sadat had appointed 'Abd al-Salam al-Zayyat, an ostensibly committed socialist and speech writer for Sadat, as minister of state for Maglis al-Umma Affairs. This innocuous-looking appointment proved fortuitous in the ensuing events. Zayyat had served as Maglis secretary for years and had established close ties with many parliamentarians. He helped Sadat engineer an extraordinary session of the Maglis al-Umma, which was held on Friday, May 14. Although the Maglis was in session during this period, many parliamentarians were away from Cairo because Friday is the Muslims' religious day of rest. From 1:00 A.M. onward, the task fell to Zayyat, Mar'ei, Mustafa Kamel Murad,[147] and others to muster as many parliamentarians as possible for the session, whose proceedings were to begin at 8:00 P.M. Other deputies who assisted included 'Azmi Rashed al-Mikawi of Giza, Yusuf Makadi from Minya, Ahmed 'Abd al-Akher and Muhammad Mazhar Abu Krishah from Sohag, Muhammad 'Uthman Isma'il from Assiut, and Muhammad Hamed Mahmud from Beheira.[148] All were eventually rewarded by Sadat, at least in the short-term, with governorships and other political appointments.

The parliamentary session was a far cry from any exemplary model of democratic behavior. The Umma's speaker, Shuqeir, and deputy speaker, Kemal al-Hinawi (Centrist), were both thrown out of the assembly, and other deputies, like Ahmed Taha (Leftist), were excluded as well. Early in the proceedings, al-Hinawi asked, "Would you call this a democratic system?" To which Murad responded, no irony intended, "Whether it's democratic or not, you have to go. This is a coup. There's no democracy in a coup."[149]

The remaining parliamentarians listened to speeches by Murad and others who denounced the resigning ministerial officials as a "power center," declared the Maglis's solidarity with President Sadat, and voted the censure and removal of 18 members of parliament with strong Centrist ties, including the Centrist speaker, Labib Shuqeir. Just one day earlier, Sadat had gone to a hospital to visit Shuqeir's son, who'd had an operation. Sadat took flowers and sat with the boy in the hospital; on the next day, he had Shuqeir arrested.[150]

The parliamentarians unanimously called upon Murad to serve as the new speaker, but he declined, saying that he knew Sadat wanted Hafez Badawi to assume the post.[151] The parliamentary session's outcome was then exploited fully by Sadat as a vote of confidence in his authority and used to justify the arrest of Centrist officials.

Centrists have claimed that the actual number in attendance at the Maglis session was far less than the officially recorded number of 263. They say only individuals known by Zayyat to be loyal to Sadat, their estimates range from 52 to 70 or so,[152] were actually assembled in the short time available. This figure is close to that provided by Murad as the number of deputies they phoned (60), but Murad noted that by 3:00 P.M. there were already about 150 deputies assembled in the chamber, and by 6:00 P.M. they were 250 to 260, well over the desired two-thirds majority.[153] Other parliamentarians' names were allegedly forged on the final declaration issued by the Maglis to create the appearance of a quorum.[154] For example, the record shows Dia al-Din Dawud's brother-in-law, Samir al-'Alaya, as present and voting to dump Dawud and company, yet the relative was not present and never would have agreed to sign.[155] Also, many Aswan deputies were recorded as present, but their presence has been contested.[156]

But Zayyat, who later became one of Sadat's staunchest critcs, nevertheless maintained that a genuine quorum was attained.[157] He stated that there were no more than five or six falsified signatures. Zayyat chalked up Sadat's success in the Maglis to the following factors: "One: Sabri and company were not well-liked by many Maglis members. Two: When there is a struggle between two factions in Egypt, people will side with the ruler. Three: There was no conspiracy, so there was no Centrist mobilization of Maglis members. Centrist officials had only agreed upon resigning, nothing else."[158]

It remains uncertain how the Maglis might have voted with all members in attendance. Sadat certainly had greater influence in the Maglis than in any other state institution because regime Rightists, liberals, and other conservatives had proven difficult to dislodge from that body. Nevertheless, it seems noteworthy that some 200 Maglis members failed to return to their seats when the following Maglis was elected. Most losers were either blocked from nominating themselves or otherwise defeated because of alleged Centrist ties.[159] As Mahmud Amin al-'Alim noted—basically confirming Zayyat's third point—Sabri and Gum'a could have just as easily used the Umma to take a position against Sadat, if they had simply gotten their acts together.[160]

Sadat's May Victory: A Summing Up

Many reasons were forwarded by elite respondents to explain the ease with which Sadat pushed aside his opponents, some of which have already been discussed. Primary among these explanations is the long-term cost to the Centrists of introducing police-state activities to Egyptian politics on an unprecedented level of sophistication. Sadat knew that ASU chieftains like Sabri, Gum'a, and their colleagues were seen by many Egyptians as ruthless, political sharks. They had alienated important sectors of the broad political elite by the ASU's association with wiretapping, the "knock on the door" by the infamous *zuwwar al-fagr* (dawn visitors, the security operatives who often arrested political dissidents at dawn), the torture of political prisoners, and other repressive activities. Many Centrists, including Sabri, perhaps did not warrant association with these activities as much as those in charge of internal security and intelligence services or the military police during the 1960s. Still, largely in contrast to Sadat, Centrists were widely perceived as closely associated with those involved in these oppressive acts, and certainly were directly involved in the defeudalization committee's heavy-handed treatment of large landowners. Given this perception, Sadat correctly surmised that there existed a large pool of anti-Centrists—all those throughout the media, syndicates, the military, and the bureaucracy who had suffered at their hands, combined with those who disapproved of the Centrists' close association with the Soviets. In brief, Sadat knew he could exploit their unpopularity to help secure his own supremacy.

Second, much of the Centrists' power derived from proximity to their former patron, Nasser. When Nasser died, the public was likely to examine with a more critical eye those who had pretensions of being his successor and find some unworthy of their support. Third, relations among Centrists reflected a fair level of distrust. In the Centrist faction, there were rumors of Sharaf plotting against Sabri and antagonism between Sabri and Gum'a. The friction among Centrists was debilitating. Fourth, most officers did not personally like General Fawzi. Fifth, the Centrists' strength instilled in them a sense of security, a belief that Sadat was incapable of any serious threat to their control. When the crisis reached its peak, Sabri alone feared Sadat wanted to "make a coup."[161] Sixth, some Centrists' sense of security was based on seances in which they communicated with Nasser's spirit, not on more rational calculations. Unfortunately for them, Nasser's spirit proved as deceptive as Nasser could be incarnate. Thus, when the actual confrontation came, Centrists were caught with no plan of counterattack.

By contrast, Sadat is depicted as knowing from his first day as president that he wanted to dislodge the Centrists from power, and immediately began investing much time and effort to put the pieces in place to achieve that objective. In the economical words of the distinguished Leftist, Hussein 'Abd al-Razzaq, "Sadat had a plan; they [Centrists] didn't."[162] Again, Military Intelligence, following Sadat's order to Sadiq, tracked Fawzi and Sharaf's every move for several months; Nassef's plan was also carefully prepared. An enthusiastic reception of Sadat by peasant masses in Beheira on May 13, arranged by Sayyid Mar'ei without ASU involvement, helped offset the embarrassing May 1 reception Sadat received from workers at Helwan. Elsewhere, Tewfiq 'Awida arranged for Sadat to speak at the Hussein mosque on the Prophet's birthday on May 6, providing Sadat the opportunity to display his support for and backing by the Sufi sects.[163]

Also helping Sadat was most ASU Vanguard members' inability to assess the full significance of this intra-elite struggle. In his speeches, Sadat sounded every bit as socialist and anti-American as others, even more than Nasser on occasion, to those who did not know him more intimately. Therefore, although the ideological diversity that had crept into even the Vanguard Organization, not to mention the ASU, meant that some Vanguardists would have backed Sadat, Sadat also benefited from the fact that most Vanguardists were only familiar with his public pro-socialism persona and rhetoric. Moreover, misperceptions persisted because many of Sadat's post-May cabinets were replete with former Vanguard members.[164] Even someone as close to Sadat as Zayyat admits to having been fooled as to Sadat's long-run intentions. Thus, misperceptions and a lack of information, even in broader elite circles, led regime actors to view the Sadat-Centrist confrontation as one of "personal politics" or a power struggle among individuals, not a confrontation between actors holding different ideological positions. Accordingly, many felt it best to simply avoid entanglement.

Finally, Sadat skillfully added to this ideological confusion. His newly-appointed government, formally announced on May 13, returned many of its previous members; it also included Isma'il Sabri 'Abdullah, a prominent "ex-communist," as deputy minister for planning, the first time that a Marxist was appointed to a cabinet post. Similarly, on May 17 Fuad Mursi, another Marxist luminary, was among those appointed to the new ASU provisional secretariat. Meanwhile, Sadat met with Marxist Lutfi al-Kholi and other Leftists, then packed them off to convince Soviet officials not to worry about the May group's downfall.[165]

All of these moves gave Marxists and regime Leftists in general the impression that, on balance, the demise of the Centrists was a portent of beneficial change. Most individuals in this camp had no love for the likes of Sabri, Gum'a, and Fa'iq; they saw them as "hypocrites; socialists in public and capitalists at home."[166] And again, regime Leftists and Marxists also saw Centrists as the ones who had cheated them out of CC and SEC posts by rigging the 1968 ASU elections.

As for Sadat, Leftists had him "pegged as a Rightist among the July 23 types, but not as a reactionary."[167] Besides, here too there was a lack of information. Isma'il Sabri 'Abdallah recalled that:

> People knew little about Sadat, Sabri, Gum'a, and others because they had been so overshadowed by Nasser. There was no way to distinguish who was good or bad. I was in Moscow at the time of my selection for the cabinet, and my first reaction was that of complete dismay. I stayed an extra week in Moscow, and I contacted Khalid Muhi al-Din, who was in Budapest. All comrades asked me to accept. Why? First, we weren't responsible for the existing mess. Second, we had suffered under Nasser more than anybody else. Third, we had to prevent an openly anti-socialist attitude. Fourth, we had in mind a deadline, that is, the war with Israel; and there was no wish to divert attention from the battle or cause internal disunity. So, in the spirit of a national front, we decided to accept Sadat's offer.[168]

The Leftists' positive response to Sadat's overture was significant. Equally important, Leftist leaders' views matched those held by organized labor and urban workers. Posusney has shown that most senior union leaders opposed the dominant Centrists for having curtailed union democracy; "the majority of union leaders and activist workers at all levels welcomed the corrective revolution."[169] As one longtime worker-activist told Posusney, "The workers didn't like Sadat but we *hated* Sha'rawi Gum'a, 'Ali Sabri, etc., who acted like they and only they understood socialism and spoke for all the people."[170] In brief, this was payback time for Gum'a's orders to police to shoot at worker and student demonstrators in 1968. Such attitudes deprived Centrists of potential bases of mass support during the critical period immediately following Sadat's moves to consolidate power.

Sadat's principal adversaries were placed on trial in September 1971, with three well-known regime Rightists—Hassan al-Tuhami (counselor to the president), Badawi Hamuda (Supreme Court chairman), and Hafez al-Badawi (new speaker of the Maglis al-Umma)—serving as their judges.

They were, of course, handpicked by Sadat. All the principals were found guilty and received sentences of varying lengths and severity. Zayyat says Sadat insisted upon the court sentencing Sabri, Sharaf, and Farid 'Abd al-Karim to death. Tuhami approved the death sentence, but Zayyat intervened behind closed doors to say there was no conspiracy, therefore they shouldn't be killed. Zayyat says he just wanted them placed under house arrest. But Badawi Hamuda seems to have played the critical role in determining these three men's fate; he rejected the death sentence and told Hafez al-Badawi that he would sign the death sentence only on Sadat's promise to lighten their sentences, barring which he would commit suicide from the Qasr al-Nil bridge.[171] The deal was struck, and Sabri, Sharaf, and 'Abd al-Karim were issued death sentences that were immediately commuted to life in prison by Sadat. The verdict was announced on December 9, 1971.

General Fawzi was sentenced to life imprisonment (commuted to 15 years by Sadat) by a separate military tribunal. Abu al-Nur received 15 years in prison, Dia al-Din Dawud and Muhammad Fa'iq, 10 years each; Ahmed Kamel, seven years. All told, 67 other individuals received sentences of five years or less; 14 were acquitted. Beyond this, several hundred individuals—mostly Centrists who were either related to the principals or known as strong sympathizers—were purged from government posts.[172]

The Impact of the Corrective Revolution

When Sadat's car came to the fork in the road, his chauffeur asked him which way to turn, left or right? He asked the chauffeur which direction Nasser would take, and was told he would turn to the left. Sadat thought, then told the driver, "Okay, then signal left and turn to the right." Well-known joke during Sadat's presidency.

Sadat's New Cabinet

Sadat's new "May 13" cabinet saw new faces in places previously occupied by prominent Centrist foes—Sadiq replacing Fawzi as minister of war, Salem for Gum'a at interior, and 'Abd al-Qader Hatem replacing Fa'iq at information. 'Aziz Sidqi was promoted to deputy premier. Still, there was considerable continuity, even in key posts, with Mahmud Fawzi remaining premier, Muhammad 'Abdullah Marziban still minister of the economy, and Ahmed Bultia heading the Ministry of Labor. The absence of change in these posts reinforced perceptions of regime continuity with respect to its fundamental economic policies, although this would be misleading in many respects.

Regarding regime relations with extra-governmental political currents, no real change appeared in the offing. Not long after Sadat's victory over the Centrists, Mustafa Kamel Murad, still exuberant, engaged Sadat in a conversation over the regime's future:

> Murad asked: "So what's next? What about the other political currents?"
> Sadat said: "Like what?"
> Murad: "Like the Muslim Brothers, communists, and so forth."
> Sadat: "You mean you want to bring them back—to have political parties?"
> Murad: "I'm not bringing them back; they exist already. Just make them legal."
> Sadat: "Then let's postpone the whole idea."
> Murad continued, "'Aziz Sidqi and Zayyat told Sadat that Murad is crazy. The country is boiling, and political parties will make it boil all the more. Let's just keep the ASU and kick out some people. So Sadat kicked me out and kept Sidqi and Zayyat."[173]

In keeping with Sidqi and Zayyat's thinking, Sadat's initial success against his Centrist rivals paved the way to a deeper purge of Centrist rivals throughout the regime. This effort, combined with Sadat's public pledges of abolishing police-state practices, affording greater protection of individual liberties and liberalizing the political system, was later dubbed the "Corrective Revolution" by Sadatists.

As the "corrective" adjective suggested, Sadat's purge was undertaken in Nasser's name, and indeed actively abetted by people like 'Aziz Sidqi, who could not readily discern Sadat's political stripes, and had abandoned their ideological confreres. After decreeing the ASU's dissolution on May 20 as a prelude to new ASU elections, as well as freezing ASU assets, Sadat defended the move by claiming that Nasser himself had intended to do as much (as secret documents allegedly stolen by Sami Sharaf from the safe in Nasser's home would have proven, said Sadat).[174] Nasser, Sadat asserted, had wanted to correct two errors, both left unachieved due to his premature death.[175] One was to reform the ASU by removing it from the grasp of the "power centers." The other was to hold new elections for the Maglis al-Umma, where previous elections had been too heavily engineered by those "power centers." In pursuing these objectives, Sadat would merely fulfill the wishes of his predecessor. In a sense, Sadat's rendition of Nasser's intentions was accurate.[176] The major difference, of course, was that Sadat would use these changes to eliminate Centrist voices in a manner Nasser may have never envisioned. Regime types like Sidqi, even Heikal, were unwittingly digging political graves for themselves and many of their principles.

The ASU's short-term dissolution permitted a major purge of Centrist elements. Zayyat, a self-described Leftist, replaced Abu al-Nur as the temporary ASU secretary general. ASU provincial secretaries general were then dumped and replaced with provisional secretaries, Vanguardists were ordered to cease activities, and syndicate organizations experienced purges, as shall be examined.

Sadat's move to remake the ASU was facilitated by post-May criticisms of that organization by disgruntled Leftists and Marxists. Ahmed 'Abbas Salih, editor of *al-Katib,* went so far as to issue the first public call to restructure the ASU to permit more meaningful representation and debate.[177] His views were echoed by Marxists alienated by Centrists' control and misuse of the ASU.[178] Thus, leftist forces in general supported Sadat's expressed desire to make the ASU a more democratic and representative institution, and many were heartened by Zayyat's choice as acting secretary general.

On June 2, Sadat announced that the new ASU elections would be free, that is, unhindered or controlled by ASU leaders, as had been standard practice. This was not to be misinterpreted to mean absolute freedom, of course, as Sadat reminded the nation on June 10 in declaring that "elements of reaction and the enemies of socialism" would be excluded from those elections, but hope was kindled of a new democratic centralism invigorating the ASU ranks.

Sadat's New Policymaking Dilemma

On June 10, the ASU issued a new Plan for National Action, which laid out Egypt's socioeconomic development goals for the next 20 years. The plan was drafted by Zayyat and Sidqi, with the assistance of Marxists Fuad Mursi, Isma'il Sabri 'Abdullah and Muhammad 'Ali al-Khafif. It spelled out the Sadat regime's post-May commitment to cherished "Nasserite" principles: the certainty of the socialist path, the notion that socioeconomic freedom precedes political freedom, the vanguard role of the working class in the "coalition of working forces," the preeminent role of the public sector and heavy industry in economic development, Egypt's commitment to Palestinian rights and her inseparability from the Arab nation, friendship with the Soviet Union as a matter of principle, and the equating of U.S. support for Israel with U.S. occupation of Egyptian territory. The declaration also stressed the importance of governmental institutions and the sovereignty of law.[179] Such pronouncements were greatly heartening to the broad spectrum of leftist forces in Egypt. Ironically, they echoed much of the standard Centrist lexicon.

Indeed, a new difficulty facing Sadat was that in coopting anti-Sabri Centrists like Sidqi, and a boatload of Leftists, these individuals acquired

ASU and governmental posts that they then used to safeguard the advancement of their own policy preferences, such as those emblazoned in the Plan for National Action. While Sadat publicly expressed satisfaction with every detail of this plan, he tried to pigeonhole this largely Leftist master plan for Egypt's future. Yet, despite his sleight of hand, the new ASU National Congress proceeded to wholeheartedly endorse the program. Zayyat opines that this may have resolved Sadat to the need for a long-range plan to eliminate the ASU.[180]

Remaking the Arab Socialist Union

On July 1, voting took place to elect members for the 5,720 basic units (10 members per unit), followed by elections for provincial committees. These elections were disconcerting to Sadat, as many known Centrist sympathizers were victorious.[181] These results necessitated greater regime "attention" to the outcome of elections for higher ASU posts. On July 21, elections for the secretaries general of the governorates were held and only four incumbents were returned alongside 17 new secretaries general.[182] When delegates were elected to the National Congress level, some 1500 individuals, mostly sympathizers of the imprisoned Centrists, had been purged. The purge was overseen by Sidqi and Zayyat.[183]

From July 23 to 26, the ASU National Congress met to elect 200 Central Committee members, with Sadat appointing an additional 30. Elections to the Central Committee were "very controlled."[184] Unsurprisingly, the new CC membership reflected considerable turnover; only about 20 of its 150 "full" (versus the 50 "provisional") members were present in the 1968 CC, and of these 20, half were top government and technocratic officials. Many prominent repeaters, like Sayyid Mar'ei, Kemal Ramzi al-Stino, Mahmud Fawzi, Hafez al-Badawi, and Ahmed Darwish, were Rightists or apolitical technocrats. New Rightists included Mahmud Abu Wafia (Sadat's brother-in-law), Ibrahim Shukri, and Sayyid 'Ali Roston; the latter two both had strong historical ties to the pre-revolutionary, quasi-fascist Misr al-Fatat party.

The high turnover and preeminence of Rightist notables was deceiving. First, some of the new CC members were not Rightists, for example, the Centrist 'Aziz Sidqi, whose keen dislike of Sabri had caused him to side with Sadat. Second, there was also the self-described Leftist, Muhammad al-Zayyat, who backed Sadat because he "was convinced that Sadat could implement real liberal democracy in Egypt and that conditions were ripe to do so."[185] Third, the new CC also included more "big name" Marxists than before, as Sadat appointed Lutfi al-Kholi, Fuad Mursi, and Muhammad al-Khafif as members. Their appointments flattered Marxists and assuaged fears that they and Soviet officials had of Sadat, much to Sadat's benefit, although it held the risk of granting them greater influence. Fourth, a great number of the "rank-and-file" members were Centrists or Centrist sympathizers, leaving the CC "unsafe" from Sadat's perspective.[186]

A new ASU general secretariat was announced on August 12. Its leadership ostensibly marked a return to greater ideological diversity. Its members included the "ex-communist" Mursi, the former Muslim Brother Kemal Abu al-Magd, former Misr al-Fatat member Ibrahim Shukri, Salah Gharib (a Sidqi protégé), and 'Abd al-Hakim Musa (Centrist). Zayyat was named First Secretary on August 13, a reward for his May travails, but also an apparent boon to Leftists. Of the 21 provincial secretaries who had served under 'Ali Sabri, only four were re-elected.[187]

Yet, despite Sadat's partial control of the CC election and the turnover in the secretariat, he retained doubts about the ASU leadership's ideological coloration. Accordingly, he balked at completing the ASU's electoral overhaul, postponing SEC elections until October 1971 "to give CC members a chance to better know one another."[188] October would pass without the election being held, however, and by mid-February 1972 Sadat was still claiming that CC members didn't know each other well enough, adding that "I don't want to go back to the style of the power centers," and asking rhetorically "Should we use a list?" (to "nominate" some candidates as Nasser had).[189] Through this reluctance, Sadat revealed his doubts about the CC's membership, and showed his reluctance to make the SEC a potentially powerful institutional rival—one which, if conquered by opponents, might place him back in the bind of collective leadership. In the end, Sadat simply announced that the SEC election would be postponed until after "the battle" (against Israel); but ultimately, no SEC election was ever held. Leftists were disgruntled. They were hoping to build a strong mobilizational party with a potent SEC and powerful Vanguard Organization, but their voices were drowned out by Rightists, who were happy to see the party's apparatuses atrophy.[190]

Perhaps most telling was the selection of the prominent regime Rightist, Sayyid Mar'ei, as new ASU secretary general. Mar'ei replaced Zayyat on January 17, 1972. In typical fashion, this move was "balanced" by Sadat's simultaneous appointment of the Centrist 'Aziz Sidqi to replace Mahmud Fawzi as head of a new government. Nevertheless, the Arab Socialist Union was now headed by an individual issued from the rural bourgeoisie.

Mar'ei's selection did not mean all was lost in the minds of other ideological currents' leaders. In Mar'ei's first speech as the ASU's leader, he declared: "I do not think that the ASU represents the people" and called for changes to take place to get real representation and real opposition *within* the ASU.[191] This speech was regarded as radical at the time.[192] His call was the precursor to the establishment of nine committees, out of which came the Political Futures Committee, and on which there was strong representation from diverse ideological currents—communists, one or two Muslim Brothers, regime Leftists, the Sheikh al-Azhar, and others.[193]

Importantly, Mar'ei's call echoed ideas forwarded by regime Leftists and independent Marxists to establish *minabir* (plural of *minbar,* that is, pulpits, platforms, or forums) within the CC to afford real representation of various social forces and as a desired step toward a multiparty system.[194] Also, Muhammad al-Khafif, a Marxist, was placed in charge of the Higher Institute for Socialist Studies (HISS), the highest-level, predominantly socialist training institution during the Nasser regime, when it reopened a few months following the turmoil of May 1971.

If the broad political left had room for optimism, so did religious conservatives. It was announced on May 25, 1971 that the Youth Organization would undergo a reorganization to be completed by November 1972. On June 6, 1971, Kemal Abu al-Magd, a lawyer with know Muslim Brotherhood family ties and sympathies, was selected to serve as the provisional director of the Youth Organization, replacing the Centrist, Mufid Shihab. On August 19, 1971, Abu al-Magd was appointed to the full-time position of general secretary of the Youth Organization. His directorship augured well for some degree of Islamization of that organization's curriculum and activities. This heightened the likelihood of Egyptian youth receiving a new type of political socialization—one with a much heavier religious coloration. Over time, these modifications would cause Sadat enormous difficulties.

Adjusting Regime-Civilian Relations

A Little Liberalization Here, A Little More Control There

After the ASU's "reconstruction," Sadat took other measures to consolidate his power and augment his popularity. He met with student representatives on August 17 and told them that the state would no longer interfere in student activities.[195] On August 20, Interior Minister Mamduh Salem said that 134 of a total 380 political prisoners, most of them MB members, would be released from prison. Salem also announced that "political isolation" would automatically be lifted in 1972 from the 13,000 individuals included in that category.[196]

Sadat's reconciliation with the Muslim Brethren grew out of his own sympathies for religious Rightist, not to mention those of his vice presi-

dent, Hussein al-Shaf'ei; but there were other factors involved. Sadat's contacts with the Saudis undoubtedly brought requests to take a more benign
view of the Brethren, and as early as February 1971 Sadat had received a
former Egyptian MB member, Kemal Nagi, who had been living in exile
in Qatar. Nagi, who was allowed to stay in Cairo for over one week, came
bearing a letter from other MB exiles that stated that while they harbored
a desire for vengeance against the likes of Gum'a, Sharaf, and other Centrists,
they held no animosity for Sadat.[197] As Sadat went on to wage war against
his regime opponents, he did not ignore the potential benefit of shoring
up alternative bases of civilian support. Indeed, Ahmed Gami'a asserts that
"after eliminating the power centers, he [Sadat] thought of calling upon
the Brothers' leaders who had fled abroad to return to Egypt, and they were
ready to cooperate with him. Among those leaders that I went and met at
Sadat's request were Dr. Yusuf al-Qardawi, Dr. Ahmed al-'Asal, Eng. 'Abd
al-Ra'uf Mashhur, Eng. 'Abd al-Mun'im Mashhur and Dr. Salim Nigm."[198]
Similar calculations were behind Sadat's release of prominent Brothers like
Salih Abu Raqiq and 'Abd al-Qader Hilmi from Egyptian prisons.[199]

Meantime, in response to workers' disturbances during August, believed
to be inspired by Centrist elements, some ASU units were disbanded in
those locales. Several radio and television personnel suspected of Centrist
sympathies were also dismissed,[200] and government control of these media
organs was tightened, prompting the media director, Mustafa Khalil, to
resign.[201]

A New Name for Egypt and Parliament, and a New Constitution

On September 2, 1971, in an interesting reassertion of Egyptian independence, the country's name was changed from the United Arab Republic
and became the Arab Republic of Egypt. The Maglis al-Umma was dissolved on September 8. Its name was changed to the Maglis al-Sha'b (People's Assembly), and elections were scheduled for November.

On September 11, a new, permanent constitution was submitted to a
public referendum and received a 99.98 percent yes vote. The constitution
embodied most of the organizational provisions and precepts of the 1968
National Charter—the document from which it explicitly drew its inspiration. It ensured the predominance of presidential power, including the
power to rule by decree, and retained the notion of the government being
founded on "an alliance of the working people," which is embodied in the
ASU. It also specified that 50 percent of the People's Assembly members
be workers and peasants. However, the new constitution also included special provisions safeguarding the freedoms of speech, assembly, and religious
belief and guaranteeing against unauthorized searches and seizures. And it

strengthened parliamentary autonomy, strengthened parliament's power of interpellation, and enhanced the independence of the judiciary. Article 2 stipulated Islam as a major source of legislation; but Article 3 stated that sovereignty belongs "to the people," which as Rutherford points out, was at odds with the Islamists' notion that only God is sovereign.[202] At a minimum, these articles looked good to most citizens on paper and reinforced the image Sadat sought to create of a turn to the sovereignty of the law and rule through institutions.

Ironically, many "liberalizing" articles allegedly owed their inclusion to Prime Minister Mahmud Fawzi and others' objections to Sadat's attempt, inspired by his counselor Mustafa Abu Zeid Fahmi, to establish the ubiquitously supreme formal power of the presidency.[203] Still, Sadat endorsed the changes, and he needed not worry too much anyway, as the constitution fell well short of articulating independent and powerful legislative and judicial branches of government.[204] Other authoritarian measures and mechanisms also remained effective, such as Law 32 of 1964, which gave the state extensive powers to intervene in the affairs of civil society groups and associations.[205]

In declaring this constitution to be permanent, Sadat departed from Nasser's practice of regarding the existing institutions as transitional, as Sadat expressed his intention to shift out of the "revolutionary mode" and into a "state of institutions."[206] The slogan designed to highlight the basic values and underpinnings of this new system was introduced on September 20, just one day after Sadat formed a new (albeit largely unchanged) government. The new state, said Sadat, would be based on "science and faith."[207] In pronouncing this slogan, Sadat departed from Nasser's "Arab application of scientific socialism" and moved toward a position that prescribed a greater role for religion in societal affairs. The former, provisional constitution had designated Islam as the religion of the state. Again, Article 2 of the new constitution gave teeth to Sadat's "science and faith" slogan by adding that Islam was a major source of legislation.[208]

Other Liberalization Measures

As noted before, Sadat's decision to release many political prisoners (excluding Centrists) meant the freeing of most Muslim Brothers, a development that reinforced early perceptions of Sadat as courting the support of the religious right. However, Sadat also showed in October that his quest for new bases of support went beyond courting Islamists and was associated with a more widespread reorientation of the political economy. On October 23, news came that the 119 "reactionary" judges removed in 1969, a move dubbed the "massacre of the judiciary," and for which Sadat bore some responsibility, would be reinstated.[209] Just six days later, newspapers announced that some 5,000 landowners affected by the 1969 land reform would receive compensation from the state over the following ten years. Sadat also personally presided over publicly burning tapes of thousands of wiretapped conversations, and spoke repeatedly to Egypt's citizenry of the need for political liberalization.

Freeing Up the Lawyers' Syndicate

Pro-Nasser elements in the Lawyers' Syndicate were affiliated with all three regime factions. Rightist and Leftist lawyers were unopposed to the May 1971 "Corrective Revolution," while Centrist lawyers were impugned and weakened by the assault on Centrist leaders. A notable casualty in this latter regard was Ahmed al-Khawaga, the former Vanguard member and naqib (council chairperson), who was blocked from competing in the 1971 syndicate elections because of his ASU Vanguard and Centrist ties.[210] Khawaga had served as naqib from 1966 to 1971. Significantly, his position was filled by the 1971 election of Mustafa al-Barad'ei, a staunch believer in parliamentary democracy and a well-known sympathizer of the Wafd.

All lawyers who had been jailed after 1952 due to associations with banned political organizations—Muslim Brothers, Wafdists, communists—were granted new life when Sadat published a law lifting their political isolation. The traditionally strong Wafdist contingent in the bar syndicate was heartened by Sadat's liberalization measures and wistfully accepted those measures at face value when they were first issued.[211] Islamist lawyers, basking in the newfound freedom bestowed upon them by Sadat, responded equally favorably.[212] Many lawyers were also very pleased with the boost to private, legal practice that accompanied the revival of the private sector under Sadat.

In sum, by reopening the door to previously excluded or constrained societal interests and political currents—especially capitalists and the religious right, but even many leftists and liberal democrats as well—Sadat sought to demonstrate that his regime's legitimacy would be based on, at least in part, the defense of individual rights and liberties and a partial resuscitation of liberal-democratic principles.

Beating the ASU with the Maglis Stick

An integral part of Sadat's move to restructure power in the political system was to bolster the Maglis al-Sha'b while he weakened the ASU. For starters, the ASU membership requirement for candidacy in Maglis elections was dropped. Also, on October 3, the ASU Central Committee barred individuals implicated in the May "coup conspiracy" from standing in the parliamentary elections. When elections were finally held in early November 1971, this decree discouraged some Centrists from competing for Maglis seats. Nevertheless, according to most observers a minority of Centrists still won election to the new assembly, and this was disconcerting to Sadat.[213] Overall, the renewed strength of Rightists in the Maglis was capped off by Hafez al-Badawi's election as its president.

Sadat's efforts to have the People's Assembly supplant the ASU in importance were transparent. For example, in accordance with a November 9 presidential decree, any CC members who lost in the Maglis elections would be given "open vacations"; that is, relieved of their duties with pay. The same fate was reserved for any ASU secretaries of the central, district, and village levels who were defeated. Conversely, all who won Maglis seats and weren't members of lower-level ASU committees would be added to those committees. In addition, all Maglis members would acquire the right to attend organizational meetings of the ASU Governorate Committees. Because Rightists had always fared relatively well at winning Maglis seats even under Nasser,[214] the above provisions were likely to infuse a greater degree of Rightist supervision and influence throughout the ASU's hierarchy.

The change of direction being engineered by Sadat was made explicit in his November 11 speech to the newly elected Maglis, in which he proclaimed:

> We are approaching the stage of transition from democracy for the people to democracy by the people.
>
> For me, as I understood Gamal 'Abd al-Nasser, the 23 July revolution's objectives and all the rectification operations which arose to correct and reguide the course—the latest of which were the outcries of the masses on 9 and 10 June 1967 and on 14 and 15 May 1971—have many meanings and values: (1) that democracy is the voice and movement of the people without trusteeship; (2) that socialism is the course of the people's working forces and that it is no longer necessary for anyone to force them to it; (3) that the state is an instrument serving the public interest, not a supreme authority above it; (4) that free and serious dialogue among the political, constitutional and executive establishments is the means of arriving at the right decision. . . . ; (5) man is the homeland; democracy begins with him and socialism should be in his interest; the state is at his service and decisions are taken to promote his everyday life. Therefore, we must reject any abstract logic.[215]

Sadat's ideological "orientations" were partially revealed in this speech. In Sadat's opinion, state ownership and control of the major means of production provided a sufficient basis for the practice of socialism. This conception of socialism ruled out building a political, educational, and social system to underlie a socialist economy along Eastern European lines. As long as Sadat held power, he would exercise it to block the development of any class-based, single-party socialist system. Whether he would be able to escape his deeply ingrained authoritarian "orientations" to deliver on his lofty democratic promises was another matter.

Foreign Reactions to Sadat's Domestic Politics

Placating the Soviets

In general, foreign diplomats, observers, and policy analysts had difficulty discerning the political signals emanating from Cairo in May 1971. The Soviets, who had invested so heavily in Nasser's Egypt, were understandably alarmed and confused by Sadat's May shake-up. Nasser had cast Sabri in the role of Moscow's man in Egypt back in 1964, and the Soviets had dealt with him accordingly from that time forward. General Fawzi had cooperated effectively with Soviet military personnel, whereas General Sadiq was suspect at best. By some reports, Sami Sharaf was in the Soviets' employ[216]; this strikes me as completely ludicrous, although it is possible that Nasser had him acting as a double agent. Whatever the case with Sharaf, the Soviets had most of their eggs in the Centrist basket, and were disturbed by Sadat's May victory.

Sadat sought to assuage Soviet fears during the May events. Again, he informed the Soviet ambassador of the action he intended to take against Sabri so that the latter would feel it was not taken from an anti-Soviet position. Immediately after the "corrective movement," Sadat gave Egyptian Marxists their first government portfolios as well. But the Soviets were taking no chances. Soviet President Podgornoy paid a quick visit to Cairo and pressured Sadat, whom they did not trust, to sign immediately a friendship treaty, thereby establishing the strategic nature of the Egyptian-Soviet relationship.[217] This treaty, signed on May 27, raised the status of relations to a level steadfastly rejected by Nasser, who had remained staunchly averse to communism and wary of Soviet domination. When Hafez Isma'il asked Yugoslavia's President Tito why the Soviets had pressed so hard for the treaty, he responded, "Because they need a *bumaga* (paper or document in Russian) to feel more comfortable."[218] For his part, Sadat felt compelled to sign the *bumaga,* fearing that if he refused, the Soviets would deprive him of essential aid and arms,[219] weakening his domestic political position as well as Egypt's as a whole.

The Soviets may have been relieved by Sadat's public display of friendship; certainly, many Egyptian Marxists were pleased. But from all appearances, the Soviets reserved doubts about Sadat, undoubtedly planted by earlier conversations with Centrists. During his visit to Cairo, Soviet CC Secretary Ponamarev was taken on an evening Nile cruise. He told Zayyat that "the Nile's water had started to flow in the opposite direction."[220] As the boat passed alongside the Nile's bank near the fashionable southern Cairo neighborhood of Ma'adi, the sounds of party revelers carried out across the water. According to Kemal Abu al-Magd, Ponamarev intoned, "Listen to that! Does that sound like a people that is preparing itself for war?!"[221] But the word from Brezhnev was that the Soviets were ready to help Egypt to the fullest "provided this is what Sadat himself wants."[222]

The Soviets knew that through their control of arms and materiel supplies to Egypt, they could make life very difficult for Sadat. Soviet surface-to-air missiles (SAMs) protected Egypt's skies from deep penetration bombing by Israel's air force. In addition, Egypt's military remained in need of reinforcing that air defense system, and was desperate for long-range aircraft, bridging equipment for a Suez Canal crossing, and other items.

Sadat's Personal Diplomacy with the United States

Soviet doubts about Sadat were well warranted. As has been demonstrated, from early on Sadat made foreign policy his sole preserve, conducting totally clandestine foreign contacts, and often leaving his own foreign ministry in the dark as to his intentions and activities. His February 4 initiative and the unity talks came entirely out of the blue as far as most principal decision-makers were concerned.

There are fascinating parallels here between Sadat's lone-wolf, clandestine policy-making behavior, and that of the paramount "back-channel" communicator, National Security Council Adviser Henry Kissinger, who was leaving U.S. State Department officials in the dark as well. Certainly, Sadat must have seen in Kissinger a kindred spirit in this regard, and their communication styles effectively reinforced one another at this historical juncture. (Here, one must not forget Sadat's historical track record, his Signal Corps training, and his fateful encounter with German Nazi agents in Egypt who had their own secret transmitter.) In addition, Nixon himself was the master of the grand coup—the opening to China, détente with the Soviet Union. Nixon also believed that "Unpredictability is a leader's greatest weapon."[223] Thus, there was much in Nixon's behavior to reinforce and/or inspire Sadat's own penchant for bold and unexpected moves, and for Sadat to feel attracted to Nixon as well.

Although the Americans had serious doubts about Sadat's longevity in power, by mid-November 1970 the State Department was proposing that Nixon undertake several steps, however modest, to improve U.S.–Egyptian relations.[224] A number of other countries' diplomats encouraged the

Americans down this path. Egypt's interests section chief Ashraf Ghorbal noted, "Bergus and I were in practical terms ambassadors, and from January 1968 to 1972 we were very active."[225] Ghorbal remained a reliable interlocutor, but as a declassified State Department document of March 12, 1971 reveals, Ghorbal was "never a central figure" in U.S.–Egyptian discussions over the conflict, because the Americans preferred Bergus' direct "access to high Egyptian officials."[226]

Following the 1967 war, the Egyptian foreign ministry's appraisal had been that the United States would accept nothing less than a Pax Americana in the Middle East—a "settlement" that placed U.S. and Israeli considerations above those of all other parties. Years later, the official appraisal had changed little, and Egypt's Foreign Minister Mahmud Riyad presented a report to Sadat to this effect on April 13, 1971, prior to U.S. Secretary of State Rogers' May visit to Egypt.[227] Most Foreign Ministry officials and others concluded that Egypt should focus on preparations for the battle, and this view remained predominant in the foreign ministry both before and long after the events of May.

Sadat, by contrast, and largely in private, deduced that if the United States held all the cards to a solution, then approaching the United States to drive a wedge between the Americans and Israelis constituted a more pragmatic and constructive approach. Ahmed Beha al-Din characterized Sadat's position even more starkly: "What was Sadat's vision? He wanted to be completely in the American camp, a member of the Western defense system. His idol was the shah [of Iran], from the point of view that the shah was totally with the Americans. Sadat saw the U.S. as the only superpower; the U.S. alone could help Egypt economically, or in its dealings with Israel. The U.S. alone could solve all of Egypt's problems. So, how to get the support of the United States was what guided his thinking. The Soviet Union was just a 'second rate power.'"[228]

Again, from the onset of his presidency, Sadat used intelligence and foreign ministry channels to establish direct contact with President Nixon. By late December 1970, he had taken Bergus into his confidence and his direct and indirect (usually through Heikal) contacts with Bergus and other Americans increased in frequency in early 1971. Through his February 4 initiative, he was already following up on proposals that his Israeli enemy, Moshe Dayan, had suggested just months earlier.

Sadat received a reply from Nixon on March 4, transmitted through Bergus and Heikal, which stressed "the need for patience and an extension of the ceasefire without deadline, to give time for the Israelis fully to grasp the importance of the change in the UAR's position."[229] In Sadat's eyes, this meant that the United States would not exert effective pressure on

Israel to comply with the United Nations Jarring proposal of February 8. Jarring's proposal was based on U.N. Resolution 242; it called upon the Israelis to withdraw to the June 5, pre-1967 war positions, and Egypt had responded positively to its conditions on February 16. For all intents and purposes, the Israelis had rejected it.

After receiving Nixon's response, Sadat summoned Bergus to the Barrages rest house on March 5 to inform him that he would not extend the ceasefire. He told Bergus that he had just returned from a secret visit to Moscow on March 1 and 2, where he found the Soviets much keener on peace than President Nixon. He noted that Israel, in its refusal to comply with the Jarring proposal "was challenging him directly. Israel apparently thought he 'had no guts.' He would show the world that he had guts."[230] He gave an eight-page letter to Bergus to send to Nixon on March 5, in which Sadat made most of these same substantive points. Sadat also noted that Nixon, as former vice president, must certainly recall Israel's compliance with President Eisenhower's call for a withdrawal of forces during the 1956 war.[231] But Nixon's response to Sadat on March 31 was once again a call for more time to study Sadat's February 5 initiative and the Israelis' reaction.[232]

On April 22, Sadat took another strong step toward the Americans. He met for two hours with Michael Sterner, who had become head of the Egypt desk at the U.S. State Department, and Donald Bergus, on the lawn at the Barrages rest house outside Cairo. At that meeting, according to Sterner, Sadat "got down to business, pulling out a huge map of the Sinai and pointing to the lines he was willing to withdraw to. We picked up our ears. We got the full presentation on that occasion—he talked about how this would relate to an overall peace agreement, length of a ceasefire, the Jarring agreement . . . This was pretty much of a bombshell in Washington."[233] Unfortunately, Sadat's proposal didn't fly. Sterner says Moshe Dayan and Abba Eban were interested, but Golda Meir remained suspicious and Israeli officials in general ridiculed the State Department officials who took Sadat seriously; Nixon and Kissinger didn't seem really interested, and the whole idea just ran into the sand.[234]

In May, Sadat eliminated the key officials with the closest ties to the Soviet Union, beginning with Sabri. Again, as Sterner notes, "We received no clue in our April meeting with Sadat about any plan to dump Sabri."[235] Still, from Sadat's perspective, Sabri's demise was also seen as a nice present for Rogers, who visited on May 5. But the meeting with Rogers brought a stark new reality to American-Egyptian relations, as Rogers stated in no uncertain terms that as long as the Soviet Union was in Egypt, it would be very difficult for the United States to change the situation in the Middle

East.[236] Without wishing to imply any causal connection here, Sadat next took another step in that direction by outwitting the other high-ranking, pro-Soviet Centrists with his "Corrective Revolution." In Cairo and Washington, analysts found difficulty understanding this development. "A thwarted coup by Gomaa, or a planned maneuver by Sadat?," cabled Bergus, who worried that "Sadat remains vulnerable to a public which could easily turn hostile when found with a continued impasse over a negotiated settlement with Israel, or a settlement whose form it regards as capitulatory."[237] Sterner recalled, "There was no surprise that this happened, but there also would have been no surprise if it had happened the other way."[238]

The May 27 Soviet–Egyptian friendship treaty also caused some consternation in Washington. American officials hoped for reassurances through a visit by Prime Minister Fawzi that Sadat had promised, and remained baffled by his failure to show up. They sent word to Sadat through Heikal that "an interim settlement involving partial Israeli withdrawal and the opening of the Suez Canal to all international traffic could serve the interests of both sides and facilitate ongoing efforts and progress in negotiations for a final and comprehensive peace agreement."[239]

On July 6, in Cairo, Bergus and Sterner met with Sadat and Heikal for discussions over an interim plan for reopening the Suez Canal. Sadat was irritated by U.S. officials' doubts over whether or not his previous offer still stood in the aftermath of his treaty with the Soviet Union, stating that the treaty changed "absolutely nothing." He declared himself ready to resume diplomatic relations with the United States if an interim accord was reached, just as an accord would prompt him to ask Soviet military and officers—but not the advisers—to leave Egypt. Sadat complained bitterly about U.S. arms deliveries to Israel, adding that Egypt was not receiving anything from the Soviets that would enable them to stand up to the Phantom aircraft provided Israel.[240] When Sterner and Bergus expressed concern over the lines of communication with Sadat, and the "friction" this caused in their interaction with the Egyptian foreign ministry, Sadat dismissed their objections with a wave of the hand, and "was definitive in stating his wish that we continue to use Heykal as channel to him."[241]

During the same month, Sadat sent troops to back Sudan's Numeiri against a communist workers-inspired coup attempt. (One astute observer of Egyptian politics recalled that Sadat, with his Sudanese maternal roots in mind, was very excited about prospects for unity with the Sudan;[242] however, little ever came of this dream.) Sadat's support to Numeiri caused friction between Sadat and the Egyptian left, as well as Egyptian trade unionists, leading to Sadat's first intervention in syndicate affairs.[243] It also offended the Soviets, but while it may have scored some points with U.S. officials, they remained intent on backing the interim agreement proposals. When Sadat made his first official (non-secret) visit to the Soviet Union in October 1971, he went via Kuwait and Iran.[244] According to Hafez Isma'il, the Saudi foreign minister had made it clear that his government was interested in forming a Teheran–Riyadh-Cairo regional axis, and Sadat was immediately interested.[245] Muhammad 'Abd al-Salam al-Zayyat, who was very close to Sadat at this juncture, also notes that Sadat was enchanted with the shah of Iran's role in U.S. imperial strategy, and desired something comparable.[246]

Somewhat paradoxically, Sadat's public visit to the Soviet Union, had unintended consequences. The Americans had held off on increasingly demanding requests by Israelis for additional weapons.[247] But when the Soviets declared in October that they would strengthen Egypt's military capabilities, the Americans acceded to the Israelis' request, and the Egyptians were miffed.

By year's end, December 18, it was announced that the Yale and Harvard crew teams had been officially invited to compete against Egyptian and British crews in races to be held on the Nile. As the time, it was hard to miss the parallels with the "ping-pong diplomacy" that had ushered in the thaw in U.S.-China relations in April of the same year.[248] Whether the Nile was beginning to flow in another direction or not, at a minimum, its waters had been stilled in a manner making it far easier for "American rowers" to compete. But to Sadat's chagrin, the Israelis showed no inclination to respond to his initiatives; and the American scull was all but dead in the water. On December 30, Bergus reported from Cairo that Sadat "said unless U.S. can produce Israeli acceptance of Jarring February 8 memo, Egypt had no interest in continuing efforts to reach interim settlement. If we can pass him any indication at all of flexibility in Israeli position, I believe Sadat will quickly resume his interest."[249]

Conclusion

The collective decision-making agreement instituted with Sadat's ascension to the presidency seemed to guarantee Egypt's continued movement down a Centrist path. But Sadat's Rightist orientations surfaced within months of assuming the presidency, and his policy and process disagreements with Centrists resulted in the "Corrective Revolution." Removal of most key Centrists from power in the events of May 1971 broadened Sadat's policy-making latitude, and in light of Sadat's "orientations," enhanced prospects of his charting a new political economic course for Egypt. Signs of political liberalization pleased Leftists and Rightists alike, as did Sadat's post–May 1971 political appointments.

If regime Rightists and Leftists were happy, the same could be said for various civil societal elements. Organized labor was happy to be rid of the May group types, while Sadat's promises of an end to the police state and his property de-sequestrations were heartening to a broad range of civilian political and economic interests in urban and rural areas alike.

In the foreign affairs arena, signing of the friendship treaty did much to reduce Soviets fears. Meanwhile, unbeknownst to nearly everyone, Sadat initiated and developed important contacts through various channels with the United States, laying the basis for a potentially huge shift in Egypt's foreign policy. But as the record would clearly show, even if Sadat sought to place himself in the American camp, he was not willing to do so at any price.

3

A Renewal of Civil Society

In his public addresses, Sadat linked his "Corrective Revolution" to a termination of police state activities, a return of the rule of law, and a restoration of basic civil liberties. In nearly all sectors of Egyptian society, individuals and corporate bodies desiring greater political and economic freedom were quick to test the limits of Sadat's commitment to liberalization. For the purposes of this study, I shall limit my examination to a handful of arenas: Egypt's universities, religious institutions, specific sociocultural domains, the lawyers' association, the print media, and the journalists' syndicate. In those arenas, as in others, civilian forces of various political ideological colors sought to establish their own influence and control, competing against their ideological rivals and representatives of the state.

The Universities: A New Generation of Student and Youth Activists

Generations of Egyptian university students have sustained a tradition of political activism.[1] For most of the early decades of this century, the universities remained the preserve of young men and women from upper-middle- and upper-class families. They engaged in primarily anti-British, Egyptian nationalist demonstrations and related activities. In a sense, university student activists had been upstaged in the early 1950s; the dashing young officers who made the "revolution" had become the darlings of Egyptian popular society. By 1970, however, enough time had elapsed to produce an entire new generation of students, and in the nearly two decades that had elapsed since the "revolution," the university student body's social profile was radically altered by an unfettered expansion of free public education at all levels.

Table 1: Expansion in University Student Enrollment

Year	Men	Women	Total
1970/1971	131,890	46,065	177,955
1971/1972	146,124	52,950	199,074
1972/1973	164,620	64,114	228,734
1973/1974	195,637	80,426	276,063
1974/1975	224,799	95,301	320,100
1975/1976	296,650	124,934	421,584
1976/1977	317,519	136,131	453,650
1977/1978	334,701	141,835	476,536
1978/1979	336,707	149,071	485,778
1979/1980	350,683	159,576	510,259
1980/1981	384,218	174,309	558,527

Sources: CAPMAS, Statistical Yearbook (Cairo: The Central Agency for Public Mobilization and Statistics, 1975)(in Arabic); CAPMAS, Statistical Yearbook (Cairo: The Central Agency for Public Mobilization and Statistics, 1981); and United Nations, Statistical Abstract of the Region of the Economic and Social Commission for Western Asia, 1981-1990 (Amman, Jordan: United Nations Publications, 1992).

In contrast to the 1950s and early 1960s, universities in the 1970s admitted far more students from rural and provincial areas, and were less discriminatory against students from lower social class backgrounds. As Erlich notes, "Sadat, in contrast [to Nasser] conceived of higher education in populist Egyptian rather than elitist pan-Arabist terms, and initiated its opening to the urban lower classes and to the rural and provincial population."[2] Thus, in early 1971, Sadat ordered a lowering of admissions criteria, permitting practically all secondary school graduates to benefit from higher education. This new generation of students carried with them their families' hopes and dreams that they might achieve a tangible measure of upward social mobility. Poor peasants and destitute urban dwellers notwithstanding, university students now represented much more of a microcosm of Egyptian society. Although a heavy gender imbalance remained, each class saw a great increase in the number of women. While university enrollment of men almost tripled from 1970 to 1981, enrollment of women quadrupled.

Causes of Student Unrest
A Woeful Economy
The period from 1967 to 1974 was one of serious economic stresses and strains. The priority placed on rebuilding the military meant massive defense expenditures representing 15 percent of GNP, with economic

investment falling off to an all-time low of 9.1 percent during this period.[3] Trade and aid from OECD countries hit rock bottom; and the country's citizenry even experienced an increase in health problems caused by deficiencies in caloric intake.[4]

The rhetoric of the Nasser regime, along with its policy of guaranteed state employment to all secondary school and university graduates, had greatly raised the expectations of Egypt's youth—a foreboding harvest of expectations that Sadat's regime now reaped. The harsh realities of postwar Egypt—the overcrowding of Cairo and Alexandria, severe housing shortages, and reduced prospects of gainful employment in the already bloated state bureaucracy—created an environment ripe with frustration. University graduates hired by the state earned beginning salaries of L.E. 17 per month, which, despite additional benefits, was nowhere near enough to live comfortably. And because of rapid population growth, it was now becoming impossible to provide gainful employment to Egypt's youth in general. According to one estimate, some L.E. 750 million per year in investment was needed to meet employment demand, whereas the 1971-72 budget envisioned investment of only L.E. 350 million.[5]

The economy was not growing rapidly enough to create new high level jobs of any significant number. As Moore discovered, for Egypt's students in engineering—among Egypt's best and brightest—"the chances of promotion into the bourgeoisie were dramatically declining."[6]

The economy's weakness also translated into fewer funds for education. Despite significant expansion of higher education in the 1970s, Sadat's more liberal admissions policy still meant more bodies crammed into university classrooms. Students often had to stand for lectures, and there were shortages of essential class material. The quality of education declined accordingly.[7]

The War Psychosis
Greatly aggravating the depressing economic situation was a stressful war psychosis, induced by the unbearable situation of "no war, no peace." Regime officials, media voices: all constantly echoed calls of preparation for war via the slogan "No voice higher than that of the battle," but it had begun to feel as if the battle would never come.[8] The youth, including university students, experienced immeasurable anxiety, because post-*naksa* efforts to rebuild the military depended on a newly instituted mandatory drafting of better-educated youth.

A New Breath of Freedom
One of Sadat's principal weapons for disarming Centrist adversaries and garnering support for reorganizing the political system was his promise to

terminate police-state activities, that is, close the internment camps, end wiretapping, put an end to political isolation, and guarantee greater respect for individual liberties. As part of this campaign, Sadat issued personal assurances to university student representatives that domestic security agencies would not meddle in their activities, and he ordered the release of 65 students still being held for their participation in the Mansura-Alexandria student demonstrations of November 1968.[9] Students were pleased by Sadat's promises of greater freedom of expression. Taking him at his word, they began organizing political activities with a degree of independence and insouciance largely unknown during the Nasser era.

The late 1960s and early 1970s were a time of great social and political ferment around the world. Egyptian youth, well attuned to the growing social ferment and radical political activism in Europe and North America, were not lacking issues that lent themselves to student mobilization. Furthermore, many older students had considerable practical experience; they had participated in the massive demonstrations of February 1968. Repressed by Egyptian security forces, the resultant psychological scars constituted a major source of student animosity toward Sha'rawi Gum'a and other Centrists.

The 1968 repression had long begged the question of students' broader personal freedoms. Writing in *Rose al-Yusuf,* 'Abd al-Sitar al-Tawila noted that university campus life made most students feel as though they'd never left home; there was the same lack of freedom to dress or act—whether in political or amorous relationships—as they wished, and students experienced the same generational conflict with many of their parents in loci, their professors and administrators. Al-Tawila concluded that "The new generation of students wants freedom."[10] In short, many of the moral and political concerns of Egyptian youth and students in the early 1970s matched those of Western youth. Egypt even witnessed the appearance of hippies, albeit a very small number. Egyptian students, like their American counterparts, had their own concerns about war, but most of them also had much more pressing economic difficulties confronting them. Theirs was no "post-materialist" environment. Under these circumstances, many students sought to articulate their anxieties and concerns.

Political Competition on University Campuses

Mobilizational Competition Among New Currents and Groupings
From a more purely political perspective, leftist students were far and away dominant on Egyptian campuses, followed by more diffuse, liberal-oriented elements. This is not to say that Islamist students were totally absent. The first references that I found to "sightings" of female students wearing long dresses

and head veils—that is, to women dressing in conformity with the *ziyy al-islami* (Islamic dress code)—were to a handful of students attending the College of Applied Arts and the Higher Institute for Technical Education, both in Cairo, in April 1971.[11] As will be seen shortly, religious organizations began to emerge in the late 1960s and early 1970s, but religious elements remained a distinct minority. The university campus scene was completely different from its stridently religious mode of less than one decade later.

Among political activists, Egyptian universities started to burgeon with activity after the June 1967 defeat, although much of that activity had remained sub rosa because of the ubiquity of state informers. A number of political discussion groups, called *usrat* (families), had emerged and generated a great deal of debate. There were religious and leftist *usrat* alike; but the leftist *usrat* were much larger and more numerous.

Leftist *usrat* were often public or "front" organizations for illegal communist organizations that were still in formation. The largest communist grouping was composed of individuals disillusioned by their cooperation with the Nasser regime. They disapproved of Nasser's postwar retreat from a greater socialist deepening, and his failure to harness the energy exhibited by the student and worker demonstrators of 1968. This group, *al-Gama'a bila Ism* (the Group Without a Name), was the most important secret organization on university campuses in the late 1960s; its front organization was the Followers of the Palestinian Revolution. *Wahdat al-Shuyu'iyin* (Unity of the Communists), commonly referred to by its acronym, *wow sheen,* also figured prominently. It was formed by communists who had disapproved of the Communist Party's voluntary dissolution in 1965. Its members formed two "families" on campuses: *Usrat Misr* (Egypt's Family) and *Usrat al-Qanat* (the Canal's Family). A third secret organization, the Revolutionary Current, did not become well known until circa 1971; its front organization was the *Gama'iyyat Kuttab al-Ghadd* (Cooperative of Tomorrow's Writers). This group assembled a number of Marxist intellectuals, but was less inclined to engage in street action than the aforementioned groups. Other political groups included "The Society of Political Studies and Abd al-Hakam al-Garrahi Family at Cairo University Faculty of Economics; . . . al Salam [Peace] Family at Ain Shams Faculty of Engineering; [and] Zuhur al-Salam [Flowers of Peace] Family at Ain Shams Faculty of Law, among others."[12]

Formal Student Politics and the Youth Organization (YO)
Paraphrasing al-Tawila, at the onset of the Sadat presidency, formal student political life was dormant; the student union was only heard from at the time of elections or sponsored trips, and its elections were contested by

shillal (blocs of friends) or personalities in which even the ASU had no real role.[13] ASU and YO committees were present, but few students wanted anything to do with them, because they represented little more than organizations for "snitches." According to one anonymous appraisal,[14] in the heyday of Centrist control, the YO had an "Organization Committee" whose members kept tabs on YO, Student Union, and student ASU members. YO campus leaders were selected by ASU higher-ups, and the Organization Committee possessed the power to remove "undesirable" students' names from student union election ballots, thereby stifling these potentially democratic forums.

The YO had atrophied during the 1968-1970 period. Centrist efforts to resuscitate the YO by a new YO secretary, Mufid Shihab, were in the works by spring 1971, but the "Corrective Revolution" brought their suspension. Despite Sadat's pronouncements of greater liberalization, and an August 1971 decision to remove police guards from university campuses for the first time ever, security surveillance of students was maintained. But by publicly espousing a more liberal stance, and allowing the YO to lapse temporarily into inactivity, Sadat created two new realities: (1) a situation in which regime interference in student political activities would constitute a violation of his own ground rules, thereby undermining a major basis of his regime's claim to legitimacy, and (2) a letting down of the regime's guard, enabling alternative political organization to occur. Sadat's liberal pronouncements, however successful in garnering societal support in the short run, were pregnant with risks, especially given his short-run, less-than-fully democratic intentions.

New Student Activism
During the 1970-1971 academic year, leftists made the first attempt to politicize the student university elections when a candidate at the Economics Faculty, Magdi Hussein, introduced an explicitly political platform.[15] Students at Cairo's Veterinary Medicine Faculty staged a sit-in at the beginning of the 1971-1972 academic year over post-graduation salaries, and in late 1971, one of the more visible signs of increased political activism occurred through the appearance of political wall-posters and political magazines, written by leftists and liberals, on university campuses.[16]

Elsewhere, despite Sadat's efforts to shift power away from the ASU and affiliated organizations, the YO remained in place and offered an arena for interest articulation and the expression of grievances by university students and young people in general. Because so many YO activists were die-hard Centrists, many of whom had cut their political teeth under 'Ali Sabri's tutelage, their continued influence left Sadat ill at ease. But because Sadat was still keeping his ideological cards close to his chest in the post-May period, and despite calls by Rightists to silence the YO's "communists," he gave in to Centrist and Leftist calls to allow youth to express their frustration in YO forums.[17]

Sadat's concession was important because, to repeat, the clear-cut leaders of student and youth activity in the early 1970s were Marxists and self-proclaimed "Nasserites." (The latter term, disliked by Nasser himself, had no currency during Nasser's life.[18] Individuals closest to the Centrist faction, as well as some Leftists, now assumed this label.) In September 1971, these elements organized a symposium at 'Ain Shams University on the political, social, and economic thought of Gamal 'Abd al-Nasser, seeking to answer the question "What is the future of Nasserism in Egypt?" General agreement was reached between both Marxists and Nasserites over the value of the Nasserite experience, while disagreement arose over such issues as the ASU's fate. Marxists seemed intent on seeing each of the ASU's "coalition of popular working forces" (i.e., the workers, peasants, national capitalists, professional syndicalists, etc.) acquire more distinct roles within the ASU, along with greater freedom of movement and organization outside it (such as the right to have their own newspapers). They did not wish to see the ASU dismantled; they merely hoped to invigorate it through greater democracy and liberalization within the existing system. For their part, Nasserite students were, on the whole, reluctant to accept such changes in the ASU's internal structure, even though they agreed with the need to invigorate the ASU through a new emphasis on developing its mobilizational capabilities.[19]

Late in December 1971, a "Palestine Week" was organized at Cairo University's Faculty of Engineering. Despite Sadat's public pronouncement to the effect that 1971 would be the "Year of Decision," the year had now all but expired without the nation going to war, thus prompting the symposium to discuss this failure. The symposium revealed the presence of two currents: (1) those who supported Sadat's position on the war's postponement, and (2) those who opposed it.[20] Opponents included both Marxists and Nasserites who sought regime compliance with the following demands: (1) organization of a militarily-trained student militia to serve as a rear-guard force backing up the regular military in the event of war; (2) a commitment to abandon all peaceful initiatives to resolve the conflict in "light of their futility"[21]; (3) movement toward a war economy; and (4) greater freedom of expression at the universities.[22]

Sadat's "Fog" and Student Protests

Responding to the students, Sadat delivered a speech on January 13, 1972 in which he argued that "the battle" had not been fought in 1971 because of the international "fog" caused by the Indo-Pakistani War. Soviet arms shipments intended for Egypt were indeed re-routed to India, but many Egyptian students were unconvinced. In response to Sadat's ostensibly feeble excuse, the most prominent student group, the Followers of the Palestinian Revolution, initiated a series of political discussions at Cairo Polytechnic that produced a sit-in that began on the night of January 15-16. The same group called for a new meeting at Cairo University on January 17. This group employed its strength and organization (as well as bully tactics) to dominate the meeting,[23] and the students drafted a declaration based on the aforementioned demands. At the Polytechnic sit-in on January 19, participants drafted a call to university students from all faculties to meet at Cairo University on January 20 to present a common front. Thousands of students turned up at this meeting. They formed a Higher National Committee of Cairo University Students (HNCCUS), issued a message calling upon Sadat to come to the university to respond to their concerns, and threatened a sit-in if he did not comply. When Sadat didn't show, about 1,000 students began a sit-in in Cairo University's main hall.[24]

In an effort to reassert itself, the official Student Union held an assembly on January 22 attended by representatives of all major ideological currents.[25] At this meeting, Marxist students were in a minority, but maintained an active role. The declaration produced at this meeting called for: (1) a full explanation of the meaning of the "fog" expression; (2) rejection of any Soviet efforts to impose a "peaceful solution," because only war could produce results; (3) acknowledgement that if the United States is the enemy, its interests in Egypt and throughout the Arab world should be attacked; (4) the necessity of a war economy; and (5) military training for students. More generally, the students expressed a desire for greater freedom at the university, freedom of speech, and greater democracy; although, once again, most were calling for the latter changes to occur *within* the ASU's structures, not for movement toward a liberal democracy.

Government officials met student leaders from both the HNCCUS and the Student Union. HNCCUS representatives agreed to a deal whereby they sent about 200 delegates to the People's Assembly on January 23 and presented their views. In addition, a proclamation they drafted was to be published in the major daily newspapers (still government-controlled) the next day, in exchange for which they would end their sit-in. But late on January 23, Sadat's emissary, Gamal al-'Uteifi, reported back to the students that Sadat had nixed publication of the proclamation, in part because a second group of students—the Student Union representatives—had come to parliament after the HNCCUS delegates and had presented a different set of views.[26]

The sit-in was broken up by a police raid at dawn on January 24, 1972;

Ghazali, and gradually introduced religious slogans, fasting, and collective "breakfasts" on university campuses—all during Nasser's days.[37]

Under Sadat, the regime began to take a special interest in these groups. Following the events of May 1971, a plan was conceived by Muhammad 'Uthman Isma'il (presidential adviser and, eventually, ASU secretary for Organizational Affairs) and 'Uthman Ahmed 'Uthman (a wealthy entrepreneur and close friend of Sadat, who had longstanding ties with the Muslim Brotherhood). They convinced Sadat that the regime should encourage the growth of these fledgling Islamic groupings on university campuses, enabling them to become a countervailing ideological force against the Marxists and Nasserites.[38] This included permitting new Islamist groups to set up religious camps on university campuses during the summer months, as well as eventually clandestinely arming some Islamist group students with light weapons.[39] Ironically, Isma'il's clandestine organizational activities were "cloaked" by his simultaneous public appeals in the name of "national unity," that is, warning against an American-Zionist conspiracy to incite Muslim-Christian tension, and sponsorship of People's Assembly legislation allowing the death penalty to anyone attempting to destroy "national unity."[40]

Third, the Youth Organization was given a new orientation with greater emphasis on religion. This metamorphosis was initiated when Sadat appointed Kemal Abu al-Magd as YO provisional secretary on June 10, 1971, then as full-time YO secretary on August 19, 1971. Again, Abu al-Magd was a lawyer and religiously devout man. His ties to the Muslim Brotherhood included a family dimension—he was the brother-in-law of MB Supreme Guide, Hassan al-Hudeibi.[41] Abu al-Magd saw his task as one of reorienting the YO "by highlighting Islam as a tool or means of progress, advancement, renaissance and motivation; in short, by presenting a new Arab-Islamic identity."[42]

During his first year in office, Abu al-Magd got off to a slow start, as he had to coordinate the YO's organizational activities and its curriculum's design with others, many of whom were Leftists. Reorganization of the YO, first mentioned in an *al-Ahram* article on May 25, 1971,[43] was not formally announced until September 23. The actual work did not begin until February 1972, and the training of new cadres finally got underway in March.[44] At first, Abu al-Magd was assisted by a mix of prominent leftists (Fuad Mursi, Isma'il Sabri 'Abdullah, *inter alia*) and a fellow religious Rightist ('Abd al-'Aziz Kamel). The same mixing of ideological minds to determine the YO's philosophy had occurred within the YO during Nasser's days, when the objective had been to forge a regime philosophy, or hegemonic doctrine, from a blend of scientific socialist, Arab nationalist, and

Islamic ideals.[45] But by summer 1972, when the Soviet military personnel were expelled from Egypt, Abu al-Magd had obtained greater control, leftist influences were on the wane, and religious ones were waxing.

The New Ideological Mix

The significance of this shift deserves elaboration. In providing explanations for the radicalization of Islamist movements in the post-1952 period, Carré offers four, but it is the first of his four explanations that is most relevant here:

> First, there is no doubt that the Taymiyyan [reference to Ibn Taymiyya's philosophy] atmosphere that has dominated the official post-Reformist teaching since the 1930s contributed to the spread of extremist vocabularism and prepared a potential audience to radicalism. Even the obligatory "Islamic teaching" textbooks in the Nasserite schools were, surprisingly enough, Muslim Brethren-oriented in many subjects and generally Taymiyyan in their approach. What was originally propagated and taught as a religious cliché finally became accepted as an operational prophetic slogan. Thus, neo-Hanbalite tradition, originally marginal, has in our times become the dominant influence.[46]

Explication of Carré's text is in order. To begin, Ibn Taymiyya (1268–1328), perhaps the greatest Islamic thinker of his time, wrote when Muslim lands were under the domination of foreign Tatar rulers. The Tatars had formally embraced Islam, but fell far short of ruling by Islam in practice. Ibn Taymiyya asserted that is was justified for Sunni Muslims to revolt against rulers who failed to rule in accordance with Islamic law. His puritanical rigor, or "fundamentalist" thought, provided the basis for the neo-Hanbalite school, which has persisted into modern times. Neo-Hanbalite principles served to inspire the Wahhabis, who provided the theological basis of the conservative Islamic system of contemporary Saudi Arabia; it also inspired the political-religious ideals of certain Muslim Brothers, including Sayyid Qutb. Thus, the irony to which Carré alludes, is that under Nasser texts were utilized that derived from the neo-Hanbalite tradition.

In fact, use of Muslim Brethren-oriented textbooks in the Nasser era was "surprising" only in terms of the fate of MB members who would not bend to cooperate with the Nasser's regime. Their imprisonment, torture, or exile has led many to believe that Nasser had declared war not only on the Brothers but on all of their ideals; this was far from the truth. For his part, Nasser sought to incorporate Islamic ideals in the political philosophy being drafted by the regime's intellectuals, and many of those ideals were taken carte blanche from the Brethren. In fact, as part of Nasser's "*politique des intellectuels*" (referred to in the preface), he recruited "former" Brethren like Kemal Abu al-Magd and 'Abd al-'Aziz Kamel to inject an Islamic component to his regime's political philosophy, or hegemonic doctrine.

Under Nasser, those Islamic ideals remained part of a larger package. Accordingly, they were tempered by scientific socialist and Arab nationalist principles, as well as by the presence of "former" communists and Arab nationalists in the YO, the Higher Institute for Socialist Studies, and the ASU in general. Under Sadat, by contrast, the special relationship with the Soviet Union was altered in the summer of 1972, and between 1972 and 1975, regime proponents of first "scientific socialist," then "Arab nationalist" ideals, were removed from or quit their regime posts. These changes affected the regime's ideological mix, leaving Islamic ideals in the ascendant, and largely unrivaled by other political philosophical influences. Even though regime leaders paid lip service to liberalization and democratization as new ideals, they made no real effort to re-socialize Egyptian youth with democratic ideals because they had no intention of fulfilling truly democratic aspirations, at least not in the short run.

In an August 1972 interview,[47] Abu al-Magd described his goal as that of rallying youth within a framework of philosophical unity, but this new framework was greatly shorn of its previous scientific socialist content. His two phase plan called for setting up organizational activities during phase one (April 1972-March 1973) to arrive at membership of 30,000 (including targets of 10,000 workers, 5,000 peasants, 4,000 university and higher institute students, and 6,000 secondary students), and in phase two, to complete the YO's reorganization and attain a total membership of 75,000. The Student Federation was expected to work with the YO—that is, the YO would serve as the main youth organization and would be "entering" the universities. Interestingly, in this same interview, Abu al-Magd stated that he was often approached by people and asked why he didn't use the YO to remove leftist elements among the youth. His response implied that he had no intention of doing so, and that the organization was not used in this manner. But in the end, of course, he knew that others, like Muhammad 'Uthman Isma'il, were already seeing to countering the leftists by means of their own, whether Abu al-Magd fundamentally approved or disapproved of those activities.

The YO was allegedly used as a conduit for channeling money to Mabahith students and/or religious organizations. But it seems that the YO may not have been directly involved in such activities, rather Muhammad 'Uthman Isma'il and others undertook them independently. Abu al-Magd disapproved of using Islamists to balance the Marxists, but acquiesced to Sadat, who bought the idea as a way of countering the Marxists. Abu al-Magd said, "Of course, Sadat was very hostile to Marxists and feared Soviet influence. The Soviets had been crude enough to express dissatisfaction over the removal of the Sabri group."[48]

Isma'il's ability to engage in clandestine assistance to Islamists was strengthened when he was named director of the ASU's Organizational Affairs committee in the new ASU General Secretariat announced by Sayyid Mar'ei on July 31, 1972. In that new secretariat, 'Abd al-'Aziz Kamel was named to direct the ASU's Committee on Propaganda, Thought, and Religious Affairs, while Abu al-Magd retained the YO directorship. Ibrahim Shukri, also sympathetic to Islamist ideals, was appointed director of the Professional Associations Secretariat. No prominent leftists figured in the new General Secretariat.

Appearance of the Gama'aat

During this period, the seeds were sown that grew just months later into the first new Islamic political organizations of the 1970s. The *Gama'at Shabab al-Islam* (literally, the Youth of Islam Group, or GSI), received official approval for its creation at the Conference of University Student Federations in Mansura on October 12, 1972.[49] The first GSI branch was then set up at Cairo University's Faculty of Engineering on October 21.[50] The GSI was led by 'Essam al-Ghazali. Ahmed Gami'a asserts that Muhammad 'Uthman Isma'il was responsible for setting up the GSI with Sadat's approval,[51] but three kinds of GSI branches came into existence: some GSI branches were established autonomously; some were autonomous, then came to cooperate with the regime; others were fostered by the regime itself.

The words of Wa'il 'Uthman, a founding member of this branch, are indicative of the general sentiments that attracted individuals to the original, autonomous GSI: "The Soviets had been kicked out of Egypt because they defended us with words only. The United States backed Israel to the hilt, and the Europeans were incapable of helping us. Therefore, the only alternatives were either to give in to the peaceful solution or to defend ourselves and depend upon ourselves by returning to God."[52]

Wa'il 'Uthman observes that during the first GSI meetings, pronouncements were made to the effect that due to Egypt's continued dependence upon the Soviets for military assistance, the Sadat regime was unable to intervene to stop the spread of communism at the universities; this task therefore fell on the students' shoulders. From his perspective, because student Mabahith representatives voiced no objections to such appraisals at these meetings, GSI members felt reassured about the regime's position and the accuracy of their assessment.[53] At a minimum, the regime would present no obstacles to the emergence of anti-Marxist and anti-Nasserite religious groups. And the religious groups' messages obviously struck a responsive chord among students; the GSI organization recruited some 600 members on the first day of its formation and its membership rapidly climbed to 1,000.[54] Wa'il 'Uthman perhaps did not or could not fully appreciate to what extent individuals such as himself were serving the ends of new regime elements like Muhammad 'Uthman Isma'il.

During roughly the same time frame, independent of regime efforts, a second group, or more precisely set of groupings called *al-Gama'aat al-Islamiyya* (Islamic groupings, or GI) emerged following a colloquium featuring Sheikh al-Sha'rawi at Cairo University.[55] Among those associated with its activities were Dr. 'Essam al-'Aryan, Dr. 'Abd al-Mun'im Abu al-Futuh, Dr. Hilmi al-Gazzar, and Eng. Abu al-'Ala Madi.[56] They were seen as very close to the Muslim Brotherhood in its early years, and unlike the GSI, kept their distance from political scuffles on the university campuses. According to Hala Mustafa, the GI grew out of an *usrat* which had gone under the name of the Religious Committee, and had initially limited its concerns to social, cultural, sports, and other recreational activities.[57] Its publications dealt with issues of morality and general behavior, a pet issue being that of the need to separate men and women in university classrooms. Out of this relatively insignificant, apolitical club emerged the GI, which would come to dominate campus political life in just a matter of years.[58] By the end of the decade, more radical GI elements would coalesce to form *al-Gama'at al-Islamiyya* (the Islamic Group, IG). The IG would represent one of the regime's greatest challengers from the late 1970s into the 1990s.

Other Factors Stimulating the Islamist Resurgence

Several other important religious and sociocultural developments of the early 1970s were of equal if not greater weight as factors boosting the membership in Islamist groups. One related to a sense of competition generated by the appearance of a new, activist pope leading the Coptic Community; a second derived from a new women's rights agenda; a third derived from the growth of Islam, Islamic education, and the emergence of strong new Islamic personalities in Egyptian society.

The New Coptic Pope and Papal Activism

When I was elected to the patriarchy, and I visited Sadat, he welcomed me too [very] much and he said to me: "I know quite well the history of 'my church' and I want it to return to its glory." But when I tried to do so, he didn't give me the chance. [The pope chuckled.] I am sorry to say this. Pope Shenouda III[59]

Sociocultural and religious developments in Egypt were of equal if not greater concern to many who joined the GSI or similar groupings at this time. 1971 had proven a momentous year for Egypt's second largest religious community—the Coptic Christians. Kirollos VI, elected as Coptic Christian pope in 1959, died and was succeeded in November 1971 by a relatively young (47-year-old) former war hero. Kirollos VI had been a completely spiritual figure; he actively refrained from a politicization of issues. By contrast, the new pope, Pope Shenouda III, had cut his political teeth as a youth in the *Kutla* (Bloc), a splinter from the Wafdist party led by Egypt's most politically illustrious Copt, Makram 'Ebeid. As a priest, Shenouda was part of the new generation of "modernizers" annoyed by the church's lack of dynamism under "traditionalists" like Kirollos VI.[60] One should note that Coptic clergy must have been tracking the reforms introduced by the Vatican that grew out of the Second Vatican Council (1962-1965) and the Medellin conference (1968). Efforts to reinvigorate the Roman Catholic church brought a Marxist-inspired radicalization of church doctrine in many countries, and on balance, produced comparable tensions between "traditionalists" and "modernizers."[61]

In Egypt, Marxist influence within the clergy was nil, but the "traditionalists" versus "modernizers" rift in the clergy and in the broader Coptic community would persist throughout the Sadat presidency. The "modernizers" movement had been established by Father Matta al-Maskin. Upset by Shenouda's prominence, Maskin crossed over to the "traditionalists'" camp.[62] Initially, Sadat made a pitch to draw Shenouda into a cooperative posture. But as events unfolded, bringing increasing distance between Sadat and Shenouda, traditionalists would hook up with Copts from the lay community who had special ties to the Sadat regime, for example, people like Musa Sabri, the journalist, to show their disapproval of Shenouda's policies.

Papa Shenouda, as he is affectionately referred to, wasted no time parting with his predecessors' ways and presenting himself as a relatively aggressive defender of the Coptic community, and he undertook a number of reforms to strengthen the Coptic church. As the Pope saw it, Egypt's rapid population growth meant that the Coptic community was growing as well, therefore more churches and clergymen were needed to service their spiritual needs.[63] Shenouda rose to this challenge, creating new seminaries throughout Egypt and abroad to add to the lone one that was in Cairo at the time he assumed the papacy. He then boosted the number of metropolitans, bishops, priests, and monks; for example, the number of metropolitans tripled over a 25-year period. He chopped up large dioceses to create smaller ones to improve church services, held weekly Friday-night lectures followed by question and answer sessions attended by thousands, drew upon his professional journalism skills to write and publish dozens of books, shepherded the publication of a monthly magazine called *al-Karaza*, and oversaw the construction of new churches.

Shenouda's activism did not go unnoticed. In March 1972, pamphlets were circulated in Alexandria claiming that the new pope had launched a campaign to convert Muslims to Christianity.[64] In the summer of 1972, a Coptic priest in Alexandria gained a reputation for miraculous faith-healing, thereby allegedly managing to convert some 300 Muslims to Christianity.[65] *Tabshir,* "conversion" to Christianity from Islam, is banned by Egyptian law. For Muslims, conversion to another religion is apostasy, a sacrilege punishable by death; so some Muslims were outraged by news of the conversions. According to another report, Coptic–Muslim clashes began when a professor at Alexandria University, who had earned his doctorate in the United States, succeeded in converting some students to Christianity. He had befriended the students by coaching them for exams. One of the students who converted was killed by his outraged brother; and Egyptian authorities filed a report, submitted to Sadat, claiming they had proof that the CIA had given money to the professor to cause sectarian strife in Egypt.[66] The upshot of all this was that the summer of 1972 was marred by several Coptic-Muslim disturbances.

But the issue providing the spark to ignite deeper Coptic–Muslim tensions was a longstanding, potentially contentious one: that of church construction. In keeping with an 1856 Ottoman decree that was still in force, non-Islamic faiths in Egypt were tolerated but were not to be given freedom to expand. Government licenses were required for a new church's construction, and the Sadat government, perhaps due to Sadat's religious Rightist leanings, demonstrated less forbearance of the law in issuing permits than did Nasser's. Shenouda's response was to give tacit approval for illegal construction, but illegal construction raised the ire of not just Islamists but also government officials, exacerbating Coptic-Muslim tension. To cite but one example, the aforementioned Muhammad 'Uthman Isma'il held a position of considerable influence in the ASU General Secretariat, and went on to serve as governor of Assiut. According to very credible sources, Isma'il was wont to opine in Muslim company that "Copts, Israelis, and Jews are our enemies; we must cut the throats of Christians to get to the Jews."[67]

The first, serious incident under Sadat's watch came on November 5, 1972 over an illegally-constructed church in al-Khanqa, a town 12 miles northeast of Cairo. When the church bells were rung during Ramadan prayers, unknown Muslims, presumably Islamists, took it as a provocation and burned the church.

This was by no means the first church-burning episode in Egypt's long history, although the Nasser era had been relatively incident-free. What made this case unique was that in the past, church officials had typically responded by turning the other cheek. Following this incident, Shenouda ordered 50 priests to rally on the outskirts of al-Khanqa; they collectively marched to the burned church site and prayed. Local Muslims responded with a counter-demonstration, a Copt allegedly fired shots in the air, and this led to the burning of several Copts' shops and homes.[68]

Sadat blew up when he learned of Shenouda's move.[69] Sadat's thinking, in part, was that with Israeli troops still sitting on the banks of the Suez Canal, any display of internal disunity was not to be taken lightly. Sadat was apparently so angry that he threatened to go to the People's Assembly to have Shenouda stripped of his papal title; only skillful stalling by Muhammad Hassanein Heikal purchased enough time for Sadat to calm down and reconsider the frightful implications of that move.[70]

Still, this wasn't the end. Shenouda initiated a personal fast that lasted from the latter part of November until the last week of December. This finally prompted a visit by Sadat during which the following exchange occurred, as recounted by Shenouda:

Sadat: "You've been building churches illegally."
Shenouda: "Yes, because we can't build them legally."
Sadat: "How many churches do you need? You tell me and I'll give you ten more."
Shenouda said this question caught him off guard; he didn't know how many to say for fear it might be too much.
Sadat: "Why are you silent?"
Shenouda: "I don't want you to get attacked by Muslims."
Sadat: "Don't worry; just tell me."
Shenouda: "Well, there are twenty provinces, each with all of its villages, cities, etc. If I ask for just two per year per province, that makes forty."
Sadat: "Fine, you can build fifty per year then."[71]

Shenouda says he was most pleased by this exchange, and he ended his fast.[72] Sadat went on to set up a parliamentary investigative committee on the Khanqa incident; and he went to the Supreme Islamic Council, headed by one of Egypt's top religious authorities, the Sheikh of al-Azhar, and got its members to call for good relations between Muslims and Copts.[73] On December 12, both the Sheikh al-Azhar and Shenouda issued statements condemning the Khanqa violence. However, the long-term practical impact of this encounter would prove far from satisfactory from both parties' perspectives, as shall be discussed later. And Sadat's problems with

Shenouda simply provided grist for general Coptic-Muslim discord. One of the committee's findings was that of 1,442 Coptic churches, only some 500 had permits.[74] Some Muslim students—who do not appear to have had any direct role in the Khanqa incident, or in another in which Copts were stoned in Damanhur—may have been spurred on by such developments and revelations to rally to Islamist organizations.

The Push for Women's Rights

Yet another factor contributing to a religious/conservative backlash was the new push for women's rights. Egypt was among the first countries in the region to produce women's rights activists in the late 1910s and 1920s. In the 1970s, a new generation of Egyptians was plugging into the worldwide feminist movement. Though few in number, womens' rights advocates were split by ideological affinities. First, there were leftists who engaged in numerous discussions, as well as gave speeches and wrote about women's issues. However, they did not create a formal association until after Sadat's death, when Nawal Sa'dawi and others founded the Arab Women's Solidarity Committee. Second, and more significant, was an informal "establishment" group of women's rights advocates, among whom was the president's wife, Jehan. These women were aided, over time, by the Egyptian Women's Organization and the Cairo Family Planning Association.

From the earliest days of Sadat's presidency, Jehan Sadat let it be known that she would not emulate the traditional, cloistered behavior of Nasser's wife. Long before acquiring her status as wife of the president, Jehan Sadat had assumed an activist role, whether by encouraging her husband to push legislation to improve women's social conditions in the late 1950s, or actively attending to the needs of wounded and disabled military personnel in the 1960s. In the early 1970s, Mrs. Sadat had chalked up numerous run-ins with the likes of Sami Sharaf and others, who felt she was carving out too powerful a role for herself and exceeding the bounds of propriety for a president's wife.[75] The wives of Egypt's presidents had never been referred to as al-sayyida al-ula (the First Lady). Jehan Sadat enjoyed the reference, and relished the opportunity to use the role to heighten concern for women's issues and advance women's rights.

Dovetailing with Mrs. Sadat's activism was that of Dr. 'Aisha Ratib. Ratib graduated from Cairo University Faculty of Law in 1949, earned her doctorate in 1954 after a year and a half stay in Paris, and worked her way up to become chair of the International Law department at Cairo University. A self-described "apolitical" professor, "with neither socialist nor capitalist leanings,"[76] she was asked to present herself for ASU CC elections in 1971 and won, finishing second in the overall voting. In January 1972, she was appointed minister of social affairs, and became the only woman in the cabinet.

Ratib's appointment took her completely by surprise.[77] When she received the call from the Ministry of Interior's office to present herself for what turned out to be the government appointment, she thought she was being called in to be chastised for a recent lecture at Cairo University Law School in which she asserted that the Arabs should have accepted the 1947 partition of Palestine in order to gain a sovereign foothold and raise a flag. Whether or not Sadat got wind of these comments is unknown; Ratib was told by Sadat on a later occasion that he chose her because of her comments in a CC meeting, attended by Sadat, about the need for limits to the president's powers.[78]

Well aware of poverty's disproportionately heavy impact on women, and the discriminatory impact on women of Egypt's conservative sociocultural mores, Ratib set about trying to do something to ameliorate Egyptian women's lot in life. In an interview, Ratib said: "I saw poverty and knew well the conditions of women before becoming minister. As minister, I immediately began trying to do something. I made a committee in 1972; it included a *mufti* [religious authority capable of issuing a *fatwa,* or religious ruling] and Sheikh Muhammad al-Khafif, as well as several open-minded religious *shuyukh* [plural of *sheikh,* or authority], among others. We worked on the changes at the Magma'at al-Buhuth al-Islamiyya [Islamic Research Institute]. I told Mrs. Sadat and President Sadat about it; both backed me fully."[79] This effort centered on reform of Egypt's personal status laws, namely, laws pertaining to marriage, divorce, and other proceedings. To some extent, Ratib had to undo or circumvent Article 11 of the new 1971 constitution, which proclaimed that "The state pledges its support for women in reconciling their duties to the family and work in society. It also guarantees women's equality to men in political, social, and cultural arenas *provided this does not contradict the rules of Islamic law* [emphasis added]."[80] From early 1972 onward, this team began work at the Islamic Research Institute, "with the full backing of both President and Mrs. Sadat."[81] Their work began to bear fruit in the form of numerous proposals, including raising of the legal marriage age, requiring a judge's permission for polygamous marriages, and requiring divorces to take place only in a judge's presence and after the judge attempted reconciliation.[82] Public discussions of these proposed reforms caused rumblings that crescendoed into a strong backlash from conservative Muslims and Islamists in the press, and to an initially lesser extent, in the streets. Consequently, Sadat decided to quash the effort at this time.

Another important factor affecting gender issues was the rapid increase in women obtaining higher levels of education and entering the work force. As seen in Table 1, female enrollments in Egypt's universities rose dramatically under Nasser and Sadat; this increase was even greater at the preparatory and secondary levels of education. Accordingly, more and more women also graduated and went on to compete against men in traditional male bastions like the bureaucracy, public sector companies and professional areas. Many conservative Muslim men, young and old alike, were bothered by the mere presence, or close proximity, of non-family women.[83] Women sitting next to men in large, crowded classrooms; women sitting or standing next to men in crowded buses, engendering physical contact; women wearing skirts, using the same staircases as men— all of these situations created emotional stress for conservative-minded individuals of both sexes. These social problems were, in turn, politicized.

During the 1970s, these social problems were exacerbated by the university system's expansion in more provincial areas, including the traditionally more conservative South (*al-Sa'id*). New universities included Zagazig, Helwan, Canal, Minufiyya, Mansura, Tanta, and Assiut; and all saw rapid growth in male and female enrollments.[84] There was also an increased presence of provincially-minded students at urban universities. This phenomenon was well-documented in a study by Sa'd al-Din Ibrahim, who went on to demonstrate how students from provincial backgrounds made up a disproportionate percentage of the members of radical Islamist organizations.[85] Again, their political behavior was in part determined by a conservative backlash against pushes for improving women's rights.

Meanwhile, from 1974–1975 to 1979–80, the number of pupils in the Azharite religious educational system grew rapidly; al-Azhar primary, preparatory, and secondary schools doubled, almost tripled, and septupled, respectively.[86] Al-Azhar University's women enrollments jumped six-fold between 1969–1970 and 1979–1980.[87]

Reappearance of Islamist Elements Beyond the Universities

Increase in the Islamic Faithful

Egypt's population growth translated into growth in the size of the Islamic faithful. Here, there were no laws hindering the construction of new mosques, and the number of mosques mushroomed.

As evidenced by this table, the state was slow to place new mosques under its wings. In addition, because the 1950s and 1960s had been a relatively "secularized" moment in Egypt's history, and the number of young men training to become preachers was lower, the state failed to place official preachers in many of the newly constructed mosques. Finally, over the same period, many new mosques were constructed by individuals who desired autonomy from the state.

Table 2: Growth in the Number of Mosques

Year	Total Mosques	State-Annexed	With Official Preacher
1952	15,800	1,706	85%
1962	17,224	3,006	71%
1975	28,738	5,163	47%
1979	34,000	5,600	45%

Sources: Morroe Berger, Islam in Egypt Today, 1970; Patrick D. Gaffney, "Shaykh, Khutba and Masjid: The Role of the Local Islamic Preacher in Upper Egypt," Ph.D. thesis, University of Chicago, 1982; and especially Francis Cabrini Mullaney, "The Role of Islam in the Hegemonic Strategy of Egypt's Military Rulers (1952-1990, Ph.D. thesis, Harvard University, 1992, 175.

The politicization of religion in Egypt had interesting parallels in numerous Latin American countries. There, during the same time frame, shortages of priests combined with rightist authoritarian regimes' circumscription of political space, rapid population growth and the spread of literacy, and yielded a proliferation of new religious groupings, such as the ecclesiastical base communities (CEBs). These groupings and related religio-political factors proved crucial, even determinative, of political change in Latin American in the 1970s and 1980s.[88] Egyptian politics would also be heavily affected by the rapid proliferation of religio-political groupings.

Return of Muslim Brothers

Elsewhere, Sadat's relaxed attitude toward religious conservatives gave new life to previously banned, excluded or exiled religious preachers and activists. The Muslim Brotherhood had suffered two intense waves of repression under Nasser in 1954 and again in 1965-1966. Legions of its members had been imprisoned, with many subjected to torture. A significant number had also managed to leave Egypt; most took haven in Saudi Arabia or other religiously conservative Arab countries, while smaller numbers took up residence in Europe or the United States. As noted earlier, after the events of May 1971, Sadat began a gradual releasing of MB members from prison; such as 'Umar al-Tilmesani (who became the MB's supreme guide upon Hassan al-Hudeibi's death in 1973) and Shukri Mustafa (who would become the leader of the Takfir wa-l-Higra group), with the final MB prisoners freed on March 22, 1975.[89] These releases encouraged exiles to return to Egypt. In addition, because some of the latter had experienced financial success while abroad, their assets facilitated the mounting of new business and sociocultural activities in Egypt.

The attendant difficulty for Sadat was simple—whether these elements felt any sense of gratitude to Sadat for their newfound freedom or not, many were no more inclined to remain silent than were the students. Because much of their initial political commentary targeted the Nasser regime and their treatment while in prison, Sadat was not initially bothered; indeed, their criticism helped counterbalance Nasserite voices and the impact of May 1971. Still armed with the same ideological sword, and now further impelled by a vindictiveness that ran deep, these former Brothers, including Supreme Guide Hassan al-Hudeibi, not only refused to pledge allegiance to Sadat,[90] but slowly and surely turned on him. As Carré writes, "Between 1957 and 1971 (even 1974), the Muslim Brethren and their friends, sometimes their families too, were the specific and constant victims of . . . political repression. After the oral confessions and printed testimonies of both victims and executioners were made public in the period from 1972 to 1980, it was no longer possible to deny the repressive essence of Nasser's regime from March 1954 on, a repression that continued even for some time after his death. Violence generated violence, and repression in turn generated terrorism."[91] Of course, the MB effectively renounced the use of violence against the state throughout the Sadat era and well beyond, but the organization could not prevent individual members from acting on their own or forming radical offshoots.[92]

The Appearance of Outspoken Preachers
Also benefiting from Sadat's greater tolerance for Islamist elements was a number of preachers, many of whom adopted critical postures vis-à-vis Sadat's regime. Perhaps the best known of these was Sheikh 'Abd al-Hamid Kishk, a blind preacher schooled at al-Azhar, who had been imprisoned in 1966 as a suspected Muslim Brother and who had also been tortured. Released in 1968, Kishk was subjected to additional stints in prison.

A fire-and-brimstone preacher who mixed Koranic verses with popular curses, Kishk rapidly acquired massive turnouts for his Friday sermons at the Source of Life mosque near 'Abbasiyya. As Gilles Kepel noted,

> Sheikh Kishk was a sensation in contemporary Egyptian Islam. His popular, down-market eloquence won him considerable success. But since he had tasted the Nasserist concentration camps early in life, he never placed his talent at the government's disposal, and cast himself instead as the censor of mores and attitudes which, whether in morals or social and political life, ran counter to Islam as he understood it. The sweep of Kishk's reprobation is vast, and he fears nothing and no one, or so his admirers believe. He thus came to be seen as a Muslim Robin Hood for whom "commanding the

Good and forbidding Evil" was not just a matter of style, but a law of life itself. This brought him even greater success, as his popularity swept the entire Arab world, making him untouchable except in periods of sharpest crisis, as in the month that preceded Sadat's death."[93]

Kishk spared no one, be it Sadat or his wife, from the opprobrium of his sermons, and new means of communication were exploited to spread his word. Cassette players were all the rage in the 1970s, a potent means for the diffusion of information in a semi-literate public. The distribution of Kishk's cassettes began circa 1972,[94] and just as the use of tapes and photocopies became the bane of the shah of Iran's existence, the tapes of Kishk and other critical Islamist preachers gave impetus to the Islamist resurgence in Egypt and came to haunt Sadat.

Assertiveness by Establishment Figures

Finally, there were important developments among "establishment" Muslim preachers. The position of Egypt's preeminent religious authority, the Sheikh al-Azhar, was filled by Sheikh ʿAbd al-Halim Mahmud (1973-1978). Although Mahmud was very supportive of Sadat's efforts against the communists and leftists in general, he also was altogether too outspoken and aggressive in pushing for the implementation of Islamic law from Sadat's perspective. Mahmud's behavior was matched by that of other prominent "establishment" *shuyukh,* like Sheikhs Mahalawi, Ghazali, ʿEid, al-Badri, Abu Ismaʾil, Salama, and ʿAshur. All made life more difficult for Sadat.

Regime-Leftist Confrontation: Round Two

Clashes on the Nation's Campuses

Islamist elements were reappearing on university campuses and gaining strength, but Marxists and Nasserites still ruled the roost. However, the summer 1972 ejection of Soviet personnel and the GSI's rapid growth presented new opportunities and challenges to leftist students.

Reasserting their political presence and strength from the outset of the new academic year, a second anniversary symposium on Nasser's thought was held at ʿAin Shams University in September 1972. It was again primarily attended by Marxists and Nasserites, but this time those elements castigated the regime for having deserted Nasser's path and accused its leaders of being anti-Nasserite. They based their accusation on an assessment of Nasser's personal philosophy as Marxist-inspired, that is, nearest to the thinking of the regime Left of the 1960s.[95] The students concluded that Sadat had departed from Nasser's line and adopted a "defeatist solution."

They issued demands for both a war economy and greater freedom.[96]

This symposium was a mere prelude to events planned for mid-December 1972, when Marxist students discovered a cause célèbre in the case of three medical students who were disciplined for violating new regulations against the hanging of political wall-posters. The Marxists' protest rally held on December 19 took on an entirely unexpected dimension, however, when Marxist and Nasserite students in attendance were attacked by a group claiming to represent the GSI branch from the Cairo University Law School. In actuality, no GSI branch yet existed at the law school, and it was later discovered that the attackers had been dispatched from the office of the ASU's Secretary for Organizational Affairs—Muhammad 'Uthman Isma'il.[97] The GSI absolved themselves of any responsibility for the attack and denounced it in principle,[98] but at the time the incident was widely perceived as setting a precedent for leftist-Islamic student confrontation.

As an outgrowth of these incidents, and in response to regime policies in general—particularly the failure to go to war—a conference was planned by Marxists for January 1, 1973 at which they intended to withdraw confidence from the Student Federation and form a National Democratic Union of Students. To prevent this plan from unfolding, security forces arrested 45 Marxists, including the 1971 student movement's leader, as well as a GSI founding member, on December 29.[99] Hundreds of students demonstrated against these arrests on December 30-31 at Cairo University, and the first week in January was marked by clashes with police at 'Ain Shams University and elsewhere. Leftist students staged protests and sit-ins at all five universities in which thousands of students participated.[100] The GSI called a sit-in and hunger strike at Cairo University in which some 35 to 60 members participated.[101] All told, some 120 students were arrested, along with 21 supporters.[102] The universities were closed and did not re-open until February 3.

The Islamist Cavalry to the Regime's Rescue

Intriguingly, during the universities' closure, GSI members suddenly found themselves being courted by the regime.[103] They met with government officials, People's Assembly representatives, the ASU's first secretary, the ASU's secretary of Organizational Affairs, and Mabahith representatives. Regime authorities attempted to elicit background information from them and, more importantly, went to great lengths to demonstrate regime respect for Islamic thought and their willingness to assist the group financially or by other means. The commonality of interests in opposing "communist" organizations was highlighted.

GSI members' first impressions of the authorities were very favorable. Wa'il 'Uthman recalls, with evident surprise, " . . . the truth is we found them to have a rare faith, with their offices decorated with Korans . . . even in the Mabahith Amn al-Dawla! . . . ASU members were calling one another 'hagg' (one who has made the pilgrimage to Mecca) after it had been 'rafiq' (comrade) during the 'Ali Sabri era!"[104]

Although Wa'il 'Uthman insists that the GSI rejected offers of regime assistance, his observations suggest that his organization was not the only religious grouping on the receiving end of regime flirtations.[105] Moreover, that some regime officials did succeed in either co-opting another group's support or creating groups of their own through the Mabahith is evident from elite interviews.[106] In fact, all that remains doubtful is the exact nature of Sadat's role in encouraging these Islamist student groupings. In an interview, Mar'ei told me the groupings were primarily the "brainchild" of the ASU's secretary of Organizational Affairs, Muhammad 'Uthman Isma'il, and that Sadat was greatly angered when he learned of Isma'il's undertaking.[107] But Sufi Abu Talib, at greater historical distance from these events, averred that Sadat okayed the plan.[108] Another Sadat intimate, Ahmed Gami'a, attributes a more proactive role to Sadat, claiming that Sadat instructed his aides to "create an Islamic *tayyar* [movement]."[109] A former intelligence officer, Fuad Hussein, informed me that Sadat gave the green light to the Mukhabarat and Mabahith to leave alone the GSI and GI to make a balance against the Marxists and Nasserites, and furthermore, that Sadat continued to leave them alone until about 1979-1980.[110]

Whatever Sadat's exact role in their creation and/or sustenance, the campus presence of religious groupings gave the regime an effective means to disguise part of its attack on the Marxists and Nasserites. Throughout the months of February and March 1973, the universities gave witness to brutish struggles pitting leftists against a mix of Mabahith elements and religious group members. This anti-Marxist campaign spread well beyond the confines of university campuses and inflicted serious setbacks to the Marxist current in Egypt in particular. Thus, with regard to the disposition of forces at the universities, Marxists were placed on the defensive by developments in early 1973, while the Islamists' "star" began to pass into the ascendant. During the 1973 summer vacation, Islamist students were allowed to organize their first big summer camp at Cairo University.

Finally, it might be noted that Islamist fortunes in general were further buttressed by the 1973 appointment of the new sheikh al-Azhar, 'Abd al-Hamid Mahmud. Again, Mahmud would retain that prominent post until 1978; to the regime's discomfort, he would prove an ardent advocate of various Islamist causes, including reasserting the independence and vitality of al-Azhar and the rapid implementation of Islamic law.[111] His presence was greatly encouraging to Islamist students.

Sadat's Difficulties with the Press Corps and Other Syndicates

Sadat's Problems with the Press

Regime friction with Nasserite-Leftist forces on university campuses was damaging to regime relations with the press corps and other professional syndicates. There was irony here in that of all the professions beyond the military, Sadat knew journalists best because he had worked briefly as a journalist himself.[112] Moreover, in contrast to Nasser's clear preference to work with and through Heikal, Sadat made a conscious effort early on to be on good terms with most journalists. But though he knew the press corps quite well, what friends he had there were either Rightists or apolitical, whereas most journalists were to Sadat's left. Over time the number of well-known writers with whom he could work on a regular, productive basis was whittled down to a handful.

In keeping with the transformation to be wrought by the May "Corrective Revolution," elections were to be held in all syndicates. These elections were observed with great interest by regime officials, who hoped to see the fortunes of Centrist-Vanguard types reversed. In the June 1971 Journalists' Syndicate election, the major contenders for the post of *naqib* (council chairperson), were Musa Sabri and 'Ali Hamdi al-Gamal. Sabri, a Rightist and a Copt, was one of Sadat's few, longstanding friends in the press corps; their relationship stretched all the way back to time shared in prison under the British. Sabri, like Muhammad Hassanein Heikal, came from a relatively humble social class background and had made his mark in the Amin brothers' stable of journalists. Due to writings that angered Nasser, he had been transferred away from his mentors at *Akhbar al-Yom* to work at *al-Gumhurriyya,* and was basically barred from writing about politics while Nasser remained in power. Gamal was also a Rightist, hailing from one of the powerful families of Damietta, but Centrists turned Nasserites and some Leftists latched on to Gamal's candidacy because of Musa Sabri's tight relationship with Sadat and their desire to make an anti-Corrective Revolution point.[113] Gamal's victory, combined with the poor showing of other Sadatist-Rightist candidates competing for syndicate council seats, greatly angered Sadat and marked the first in a series of clashes between the regime and the Journalists' Syndicate.[114]

Throughout 1971 the directorships of the major press organs were changed to remove Centrist and Leftist types and replace them with individuals more amenable to Sadat's policies. In the new government of May 13, the staunch anti-Marxist, 'Abd al-Qader Hatem, had been made deputy premier and returned to his old post of minister of information, an agency he had helped to build from the ground up. (Hatem was a former Free Officer who had acquired influential posts during the Nasser regime, but whose relations with Nasser, it was well known, were marked by tension. By the late 1960s, he had been removed from positions of influence due to competition with Heikal and his less-than-enthusiastic attitude toward socialism.)

Fathi Ghanim (who was more known as a literary figure than a political man, but who had served as 'Ali Sabri's mouthpiece at one time) had been dismissed from his position as editor of *al-Gumhurriyya* in May and replaced by Mustafa Bahgat Badawi, a Rightist. Ihsan 'Abd al-Quddus, another longtime personal friend of Sadat, was appointed president of the board of directors of *al-Akhbar* in July, with Musa Sabri as editor. Heikal remained editor of *al-Ahram;* he had played a crucial role supporting Sadat during the May crisis, and was intimately involved in secret Egyptian–American contacts. According to Musa Sabri, these major editorial board changes were made by Sadat, without Sadat having either solicited the opinion of or informed Heikal beforehand. In this manner, Sadat signaled to all Marxist and Nasserite journalists that Heikal was powerless to protect them.[115]

Of course, these changes did not eliminate Marxist and Arab revolutionary currents from the print media, as evidenced by the continued publication of *al-Tali'a* and *al-Katib* by the same editorial boards. Nor were Marxist or Left and Center-Nasserite journalists any less active in the media on the whole; so there remained ample room for confrontations between these journalists and Sadat's government.

Clashing With the Journalists
The most important confrontations between journalists and the regime developed out of the 1972-1973 student disturbances. When students demonstrated in January 1972, they drew some heavy fire in the press;[116] nonetheless, the Journalists' Syndicate issued a formal declaration of support for the students, echoing their call for an end to the situation of "no war, no peace" and asking for greater freedom of the press.[117] Distribution of the declaration caused Sadat to reprimand several writers, although Sadat promised greater press freedom in a private meeting with journalists in February.[118]

Far more serious was the sense of outrage felt by many journalists during the latter months of 1972 when they began to learn that the regime was responsible for arming those "Islamist group" students who were beating and stabbing Marxists on the university campuses. In an extremely heated meeting at syndicate headquarters in December, many journalists denounced the regime's policies, and this animosity was sustained by the student disturbances and related arrests of late December and January.[119]

On January 8, 1973, three of Egypt's most prominent writers, Tewfiq al-Hakim, Louis 'Awad and Nagib Mahfuz (later of Nobel laureate fame) penned a letter defending the students protesting regime policies.[120] The following day, this letter appeared in the Lebanese daily, *al-Anwar*, which suggested that its message would have fallen victim to Egyptian censors. In response, Sadat summoned Egyptian press directors on January 10 and scolded them for their "negligence."[121] On January 11, Minister of Information Hatem brought Hakim, Mahfuz, and 'Awad into his office for questioning.[122] Then on January 31, Sadat gave a speech in which he threatened to dismiss all dissidents—all those who were "exploiting democracy" to denigrate the regime.[123]

Purging Leftist Opponents
On February 3, 1973, Sadat made good on his promises to crack down on regime detractors. Although the purging action targeted journalists most heavily, it was also designed to expunge other regime Marxists. For example, not long after Sadat appointed Egyptian Trade Unions Federation (ETUF) President Salah Gharib as minister of labor in January 1972, Gharib squared off against communists, Nasserites, and other leftist elements to consolidate government control of top union posts. In March 1973, Gharib called an ETUF executive committee meeting and dumped its three communist board members. Nasserites played payback for the way communists had treated them during and after the May 1971 crisis, refusing to support communists' efforts to defy Gharib's moves.[124]

To carry out the broad, yet selective, purge of leftists, an ASU Disciplinary Committee was created. Its members included Hafez al-Badawi, Muhammad Hamed Mahmud, Ahmed 'Abd al-Akher, Kemal Abu al-Magd, Yusuf Makadi, and Muhammad 'Uthman Isma'il. All were Rightists, many hailed from rural provincial backgrounds, and at least two of them (e.g., Abu al-Magd and Isma'il) had past and present links with Islamist organizations.

During February, this committee stripped some 111 writers and journalists of their ASU memberships, a move that entailed an automatic loss of jobs for those in journalistic careers. Among those axed in what became dubbed the "massacre of the press" were nearly all prominent Marxist, Leftist, and Centrist writers, including such luminaries as Yusuf Idriss, Muhammad 'Awda, Ahmed Beha al-Din, Michel Kamel, Mahmud al-Maraghi, Lutfi al-Kholi, and Makram Muhammad Ahmed. All were accused of either directing or abetting student demonstrators in their clash with the regime.[125]

The regime's assault split the press corps' ranks.[126] On the one hand, there were some writers like Tewfiq al-Hakim, Nagib Mahfuz, and others with whom Sadat reconciled, and who subsequently worked in concert with his regime. On the other, a significant group of writers and intellectuals opted out of the system altogether rather than accept new job assignments in public sector companies. For example, Ahmed Beha al-Din, who had written speeches for Sadat and was one of Egypt's most celebrated writers, found himself assigned to an administrative position with the public sector Beta Shoe Company.[127] Many of the purged writers, Beha al-Din included, quickly took up journalistic careers in neighboring Arab countries. Beha al-Din would return, and even re-establish a working relationship with Sadat; others became and remained an unending source of biting commentary on Sadat's regime as journalists working abroad.

The "disciplinary" action struck at the very heart of Marxist and Nasserite influence in the ASU and the media. But in the case of the Journalists' Syndicate, at least, these forces proved far more resilient than anyone expected. Since the dismissals had caused six individuals to be dropped from the syndicate's council, keen attention became focused on the June 1973 syndicate elections. Here, regime expectations were clearly unfulfilled; all seats previously held by Marxists and Nasserites were recaptured by journalists of similar ideological identities.

Table 3: Journalists' Syndicate Council Elections

Year	1971	1973	1975	1977	1980	1981
Partisan Identity						
Independent liberal	2	3	1			
Wafdist					1	
Right–Sadatist	1	1	2	4	3	5
Center–Nasserite	5	4	7	5	6	5
Leftist		1	1		1	2
Nat'l-Indep. Left	1	2	1	1	2	1
Islamists/MB						
Chameleons	2					
Professional syndic.	2	2	1	1		
None			1	1		
Unknown						
TOTAL	13	13	13	13	13	13

The new naqib, 'Abd al-Mun'im al-Sawi, was elected on the basis of his campaign promise to convince regime officials to return the 100-plus journalists to their previous posts.

The Regime Extends an Olive Branch

Sometime after the elections, Ashraf Ghorbal, the aforementioned diplomat, was presented by the regime as a mediator to resolve its conflict with the journalists. Discussions mediated by Ghorbal lasted until September 28,

1973, at which time the conflict was finally settled by Sadat's announcement that 104 journalists were to be reinstated.[128]

At the same time, Sadat amnestied students who had been arrested during the demonstrations. Both acts of clemency did much to restore a semblance of harmony on the domestic front. Only a handful of people knew that these moves were concessions designed to pave the way for a much grander undertaking—the launching of the October 1973 war.[129]

The Rocky Road of War Preparations

The Troubled Relationship with the Soviet Union
Again, a great source of disagreement between the May group Centrists versus Sadat and his backers hinged on whether or not the military was prepared for warfare, as well as whether or not Egypt had fully exhausted diplomatic alternatives. Centrists had answered both questions in the affirmative; Sadat and his supporters disagreed. Importantly, General Sadiq was among those insisting on obtaining materiel sufficient to liberate the Sinai, at least up to its strategic Mitla and Gidi passes.

During the second half of 1971, while Sadat carried on with his secret diplomacy with the Americans, Egypt's foreign ministry maintained its hawkish posture, and the Egyptian military pursued war preparations. But during this period, the Soviets began to drag their feet with respect to arms supplies. Their lethargy persisted, despite an agreement to boost supplies made during Sadat's October 1971 visit to Moscow.[130] For example, Hafez Isma'il says Egypt asked for a deterrent force in October; the Soviets responded that they'd ask their scientists if they could put a conventional warhead on an MRBM, but nothing really came of this.[131]

Soviet foot-dragging may have derived from doubts about Sadat's post-May 1971 intentions, but safer money rides on the inclusion of this factor in a multivariate explanation. First, the Soviets already had their obligations and entanglements in Vietnam. Second, during much of 1971 the Soviets *were* preoccupied by their Indian client's needs in the major build-up to the Indo-Pakistani War, which began on December 8, 1971.[132] Third, involvement in the two preceding conflicts would have made a third, Middle East war difficult to manage. The Soviets did not want the Egyptians or other Arab clients to initiate hostilities with Israel at this juncture.[133] They were, as Sadat had told the Americans, "keen" on peace. Fourth, the Soviets were reluctant to provide Egypt with offensive weapons in light of their poor 1967 performance.[134] And fifth, they were in the early phases of a momentous development—movement toward U.S.–Soviet détente.

When Soviet military supply shipments were suddenly sent on to India, passing through Egypt on their way, Sadat was infuriated. The Soviets told Sadat that India appeared more prepared for war than Egypt, so the equipment had been sent there. Sadat had to eat humble pie during the February 1-2, 1972 meetings in Moscow. After Sadat pointedly asked who had given the order to send the equipment to India, Brezhnev responded that he, himself, had done so.[135] Sadat came away from this meeting extremely disappointed. The Soviets offered the Egyptians nothing in the way of offensive weapons, only defensive ones; and the post -summit communique "pointedly reiterated the Soviets' aim of a peaceful settlement within the ambit of U.N. Resolution 242."[136] Yet another summit in Moscow in late April brought similar results, although following their May 1972 summit with the Americans, the Soviets promised to move quickly to consolidate Egypt's military capabilities.[137]

But superpower détente, consecrated in the Nixon-Brezhnev May 29 summit, seriously strained Egyptian-Soviet relations. Egypt's military officers, preparing earnestly for the imminent "battle of liberation," were greatly importuned and angered by delays in Soviet arms shipments, and the unwillingness to provide offensive weapons. Following the American-Soviet summit, influential civilian foreign policy advisers shared their pique. Along with détente, the superpower summit had brought a call for "a military relaxation in the Middle East." These developments prompted a seminar discussion at al-Ahram's Center for Stragegic Studies during which the value of the Soviet friendship, in light of détente, was questioned.[138] During the same month, a petition signed by former Free Officers 'Abd al-Latif al-Boghdadi, Zakariyya Muhi al-Din, Kemal al-Din Hussein, and Hassan Ibrahim, as well as former Cairo governor, Salah Dessouki, (all of them Rightists), heavily criticized the nature of Soviet assistance.[139] Heikal, Hussein al-Shaf'ei, Mustafa Khalil, and Isma'il Fahmi also joined this chorus.[140]

In the military, General Sadiq was so frustrated by Soviet weapons delays that he accused Soviet personnel of a systematic effort to deplete Egypt's gold reserves—a claim that was grossly exaggerated[141]—and he issued an order for Soviet personnel to be taxed on all objects taken out of Egypt. Anti-Soviet sentiment mounted until, according to press reports, Sadiq issued an ultimatum to Sadat to rectify the situation.[142]

That Sadat needed an ultimatum seems doubtful. According to another insider, Soviet ambassador Vinogradov had tapes of Sadiq telling his officers to pose problems for the Soviet experts, and he played them for Sadat. Sadat told Vinogradov he'd tell Sadiq to stop, but instead Sadat told Sadiq to keep it up.[143] By June and early July, Sadiq was so fed up with the

Soviets that in meetings with Gerhard Mertins of the West Germany Merex Corporation, he asked Mertins to contact American officials to see if they could help if the Soviets were expelled, and expressed an interest in purchasing the company's bridging equipment.[144]

Sadat's personal doubts about the long-run value of Egypt's relationship with the Soviet Union were sealed by U.S.-Soviet détente. For Sadat, the joint U.S.-Soviet communiqué urging a "military relaxation" was a critical turning point.[145] By mid-June, Sadat sent Brezhnev a seven-point questionnaire to find out what the Soviets intended to do to help Egypt militarily and diplomatically. The July 8 reply included no response to Sadat's questions, despite Sadat's cover note warning that Egypt's relations with the Soviets depended on the answers.[146] Sadat was angered. After discussions with only Sadiq and Prime Minister Fawzi,[147] Sadat told Vinogradov that the Soviet military personnel, having accomplished their task in Egypt, should leave the country within nine days. By July 17, the Soviets had packed their bags, just prior to public announcement of their expulsion.

"My father was a very patient man," said Sadat's daughter, Noha. "He tried all channels; but when he came to the end of his patience, he would close the door and that was it. The expulsion of the Soviets was an example of this. He wasn't a bargaining man at all."[148] Said Sayyid Mar'ei, "No one knew he would kick out the Soviets. The most important factor was that he was fed up with them; although a secondary reason was the idea of kicking out the Soviets so they wouldn't be involved in any war."[149] Regarding the latter point, Hafez Isma'il, Sadat's special foreign affairs adviser, noted that Soviet troops were to have departed by July 1970 before warfare was resumed under Nasser's watch, but that Nasser had asked for a six-month extension, and no one had returned to review the issue after his death.[150] General Gamassi asserted that Sadat had confided that "it is necessary to get the Soviets out before we go to war because if we win, they'll take the credit. If we lose, they'll blame the Egyptian officers. Sadat also wanted to send a message that he wasn't the Soviets' man in the region."[151]

Restoring Fruitful Ties with the Soviets

In the months that followed the Soviet troops' eviction, Sadat repeatedly spoke of the Soviet Union in public in friendly terms.[152] Hafez Isma'il avers that relations with the Soviets actually remained quite cordial following their troops' expulsion.[153] Isma'il's kind words cannot obfuscate the Soviets' genuine anger over their unceremonious dismissal; but significantly, Soviet-Egyptian relations quickly evolved toward a tense, yet productive, status.

On August 29, Sadat sent a letter to the Soviets informing them that they had until October 1972 to prove their commitment to Egypt's defense needs. No meeting of importance occurred until October 16, when Prime Minister 'Aziz Sidqi, traveled to Moscow. Sidqi gained a strong sense of how angered the Soviets were because of their expulsion,[154] but Sidqi's visit represented a turning point in efforts to patch up Egyptian–Soviet relations.[155] The Soviets had invested too heavily in Egypt to simply burn all their bridges. Moreover, as previously noted, they already had stayed in Egypt longer than might have been the case had Nasser not died when he did. So the Soviets continued to entertain their client's entreaties, using their strong bargaining position to chalk up their own concessions. As for the Egyptians, as long as the U.S. could engineer no change in the conflict's status quo, Soviet assistance remained indispensable.

Shortly after 'Aziz Sidqi's visit, General Sadiq was relieved of his command post. Ostensibly, Sadat fired Sadiq after an October 28 Supreme Council of the Armed Forces meeting revealed that: (1) Sadiq had not followed Sadat's orders to prepare for battle by November 1972; (2) commanders stated that their troops were not prepared for war, again partly because they lacked essential material;[156] and (3) some commanders displayed a personal reluctance to go to war.

Noha Sadat, without offering any detailed explanation, simply portrayed Sadiq as someone who had "betrayed my father's trust."[157]

But there was certainly more to Sadiq's ouster than this. From Nasser's tragic relationship with Field Marshal 'Amer, Sadat had learned at least one major lesson, to wit, that any president might pay an extremely heavy price on both the domestic and international political ledgers if the military's commander grew too powerful to be brought to heel. Sadiq was clearly acquiring such strength and becoming too demanding for Sadat's liking. Hamdi Fuad, *al-Ahram's* principal foreign affairs reporter during the Sadat presidency, noted that "When Sadat kicked out the Soviets, he then kicked out Sadiq because he had become so influential and Sadat didn't want him to get credit for removing the Soviets from Egypt."[158] General Gamassi even went so far as to accuse Sadiq of "trying to become like 'Amer. He tried to offer services like 'Amer. So Sadat got rid of him for these reasons. Also, a secondary reason was that it wasn't in Sadat's character to keep strong people around him."[159] Finally, Sadiq was opposed to Sadat's desire for a very limited war.[160] He preferred to wait until Egypt had enough men and materiel to be able to retake a greater portion, or even all, of the entire Sinai.

Still, dumping Sadiq pleased the Soviets and helped clear the path for renewed dealings. According to Gamassi, the Soviets knew that Sadiq "complained often and openly about the Soviet Union, and had tried to woo him. They invited him to the Soviet Union and gave him the red carpet treatment, but Sadiq was unchanged. He still said, they don't want to give us weapons . . ."[161]

Sadiq was replaced by Maj. Gen. Ahmed Isma'il and relations with the Soviets improved rapidly.[162] While not seen as terribly impressive, General Isma'il was politically safe—Nasser had named him military chief-of-staff in 1969, then dumped him later that same year, after an embarrassing raid by Israelis netted an entire Egyptian radar station. By February 1973, Isma'il's team met Soviet officials in Moscow, the Soviets okayed several requests for an upgrading of Egypt's military capabilities (T-62 tanks, mobile SAM missiles, Scuds, anti-aircraft artillery, TU-123 light bombers, etc.), and timely deliveries soon ensued. Sadat accurately labeled this the largest arms deal ever concluded between the two countries.[163] Gen. Kemal Hassan 'Ali notes that more arms came pouring into Egypt after Sadat dumped the Soviets than at any time before.[164]

Relations with the Americans—Dreaming of a "Surprise Tree"

> Isma'il referred to a story in Egyptian folklore which involved a "surprise tree." If a person climbed into the "surprise tree" in Cairo he might come down in Alexandria or Port Said. Egypt wanted to climb the "surprise tree" and descend at her international boundaries and a final peace settlement.[165]

From late 1970 throughout 1971, Sadat was searching for the "surprise tree." He never found it, and by early 1972 his sense of disappointment in American officials was enormous. In a February 1972 public address, he attacked the United States and Secretary of State Rogers in the harshest of terms. In Sadat's mind, U.S.–Egyptian relations had reached a new low.[166] Sadat told *Newsweek* editor Arnaud de Borchgrave that proximity talks over an interim agreement were a "dead horse." "I did the politically unthinkable a year ago. Where did it get me? Nowhere."[167] The lack of progress, combined with the fresh military supplies to Israel, caused Sadat to toughen his position in early 1972. He would only enter proximity talks if the Israelis gave the Americans a prior commitment that they would withdraw to the pre-June war Egyptian border in a final peace settlement.[168]

Interestingly, American diplomats had grown so accustomed to the disparity between Sadat's private diplomacy and Egypt's public foreign policy that they did not give Sadat's February fulminations their just due. Instead, they sat around waiting for the next installment in private diplomacy.

In a frank review of U.S.–Egyptian relations in May, Ashraf Ghorbal made the following comments to Assistant Secretary of State Joseph Sisco:

[T]ime after time Egypt had agreed to some form of negotiations with Israel only to find Israel backing off when real issues faced in these negotiations. This had happened with Jarring's February 8 memorandum, which everybody knows was taken from [the] US October 1969 paper, and it happened again on interim agreement last year. Between October, when Egypt had viewed favorably US proximity talks proposal, and February, when [the] US told Cairo of Israeli acceptance, situation in Cairo's eyes had radically changed. Sisco had, according to press reports, seen [Israel's] Amb Rabin 30 times. Result of these sessions had been while Egypt received words of praise Israel received arms. Cairo could only interpret this as USG [U.S. government] acquiescence in and tacit support for Israeli intransigence on the substantive aspects of a peace settlement.[169]

In this same meeting, Sisco reminded Ghorbal that for the Israelis, withdrawal to any line would be less satisfactory than the line Israel was currently holding. Therefore, the Egyptians should be happy that the Americans, in exchange for the weapons they had shipped Israel in late 1971, had managed to enlist Israeli support for interim settlement talks.[170] The Egyptians were not convinced.

Just two months later, however, Sadat decided to drop yet another bomb—his expulsion of the Soviet forces in Egypt. Despite continued contacts with Egyptians, American officials were dumbfounded by Sadat's move. Kissinger had signaled the Egyptians that so long as Soviet forces remained in Egypt there was no hope for peace in the area. During Secretary of State Rogers' May 1971 visit to Egypt, Rogers had more explicitly stated that it would be difficult to alter the status quo if Soviet troops remained in place. But what the Americans could not understand was why the Soviets' eviction had not been held out in exchange for some meaningful American concession.[171]

According to Sayyid Mar'ei, Sadat told him, "If I'm going to kick out the Russians or make some decision, I'm going to do it because it is the right thing to do and best for Egypt, not just to please someone or get something in exchange for it."[172] But Sadat undoubtedly hoped and expected to gain some reward from U.S. officials.

The Americans' failure to understand Sadat's move could be chalked up to cultural differences. In Egypt, where the rules of the bazaar make bargaining commonplace, it is often considered distasteful and caddy to haggle over some matters. Good deeds or noble acts are performed unilaterally, but it is expected in such circumstances that the beneficiary will respond by rendering a service of commensurate magnitude.

Sadat's dramatic move did beget a response, but it was far less than Sadat might have hoped for. Sadat[173] said Kissinger contacted the Egyptians within one week after the expulsion to ask for a high level meeting. Kissinger has recorded that within one month of the expulsion, Sadat "had reactivated the direct channel to the White House."[174] But little came of these contacts. U.S. Interests Section personnel in Cairo saw the expulsion as motivated by Sadat's desire "to stabilize internal Egyptian politics and his own decision-making base," that is, one may assume, to placate the military.[175] Otherwise, they saw Sadat as having "no clear concept of where to try to take issues of war and peace next."[176] In Washington, the expulsion did not inspire a more generous position. When Egypt's foreign minister came fishing for U.S. views after the Soviets' eviction, U.S. personnel in Cairo were instructed to give a reply that:

> makes clear we intend to hold to our present position. Our strategy is to bring home to Cairo that the only negotiating option open to it is that of entering proximity talks under U.S. auspices on an interim Suez Canal agreement, on which we remain available to help if the Egyptians wish to pick up this option as the Israelis have done. This is also the course which Israel wants us to pursue.[177]

American and Israeli positions were very close. Israel's Deputy Prime Minister Yigal Allon told American officials in Tel Aviv that Sadat's expulsion of the Soviets proved "Egypt could not get its territory back by war," and that the Americans and Europeans just need to "stand fast and offer no further opportunities for Sadat to think, mistakenly, that others will pull his chestnuts out of the fire."[178]

The U.S. channel was kept open. It was decided that Kissinger and Hafez Isma'il would confer in either September or October; but U.S.-Vietnamese negotiations caused this meeting to be delayed until February 1973. When the top-secret meeting, held in a New York suburb, finally occurred on February 25-26, Isma'il expressed Egypt's desire for movement during 1973 toward agreement over the fundamental principals of a comprehensive settlement. For his part, Kissinger merely chose to impress upon Isma'il that only a change in the status quo might provide the impetus for conflict resolution. Despite Kissinger's explicit warning, Isma'il concluded from Kissinger's remarks that Egypt would have to go to war to alter the status quo.[179] A declassified, "Eyes Only" State Department document sheds additional light on the Kissinger–Hafez Isma'il meeting. It recounts a conversation between Kemal Adham and a Cairo-U.S. Interests Section official named Greene. According to Adham, Kissinger asked Isma'il whether Egypt accepted Israel's permanence as a state, and Isma'il said that Egypt's recognition of U.N. Resolution 242 provided a sufficient response.

Kissinger then spoke of a 5–7 year transition period, during which Israel would retain control of Sharm al-Sheikh in the Sinai peninsula, to be followed by the establishment of an international regime. The rest of the Sinai would be demilitarized. According to Greene's report, Adham continued, "Hafez Isma'il had demurred with the point that this would leave Sinai open for Israel to re-enter and quickly get back to the canal, to which Dr. Kissinger had replied several times that since Israeli forces are already at the canal, problem is to get them to move. Adham said that the question 'How do you get them to move?' had been hard for the soldier in Ismail to swallow."[180]

In his public addresses, such as the traditional May 1 speech, Sadat delivered a tough message. "Partial and interim solutions were to be rejected," he said, adding, "What has been taken by force can only be regained by force." But despite the tough talk, Sadat went on to reaffirm that Egypt would continue to make diplomatic efforts, and he was again seen by official American analysts as lacking any feasible plan of action.[181]

Kissinger and Isma'il met again secretly on May 20, 1973 at a provincial farmhouse between Chartres and Paris. However, Kissinger found Egypt's position was unchanged from the one proposed since February 1971, namely, the call for a comprehensive peace in one go, with no interest in interim agreements. Kissinger commented that in retrospect, Isma'il knew by then that because Kissinger had nothing new to offer, Egypt was definitely heading to war.[182] For the Egyptians, the American position constituted, in essence, a confirmation of the view held by the now powerless Centrists. The Americans would do nothing meaningful to drag the Israelis toward peace unless forced to deal with a new, harsher reality.[183]

In his July 23, 1973 anniversary of the revolution address, Sadat called the United States a "big gangster," reiterating his negative attitude toward U.S.–supported diplomatic efforts and the idea of negotiations with Israel. He also mentioned the potential for future Arab leverage on the United States growing out of the world "energy" and "monetary" crises; and announced there would be no postponement of "the battle."[184] No one in Washington was buying it. A State Department Bureau of Intelligence and Research report of August 8, 1973 began, "While his threats of military action ring increasingly hollow, a mounting payments deficit is jeopardizing urgent domestic needs."[185] The same report noted that Sadat appeared to be receiving crucial assistance from the Saudis, "but this won't solve Sadat's basic problem of dislodging Israel from the Sinai."[186]

Finally, whether the Egyptians realized it fully or not, other developments in Washington boded ill for their diplomatic efforts by the end of the summer in 1973. First, the Watergate scandal began to distract top

American officials from all but the most pressing foreign policy concerns, and the Middle East was not on the front burner. Second, on August 22, 1973, Nixon nominated National Security Council adviser Henry Kissinger to become secretary of state, and on September 22, 1973, Kissinger was sworn in. As Quandt has written:

> In the absence of acute crises, American policymakers paid comparatively little attention to the area [the Middle East]. The basic frame of reference, set by Nixon and Kissinger, emphasized the U.S.–Soviet rivalry and the need to maintain the balance of power in Israel's favor. Periodically the State Department tried to launch a new initiative—the Jarring talks, the interim canal settlement, proximity talks—but the White House was only mildly supportive at best, and on occasion distinctly negative. Bureaucratic rivalries became personalized in the Rogers–Kissinger quarrel. On the whole, Nixon sided with Kissinger.[187]

For all intents and purposes, Kissinger's appointment as secretary of state ended prospects of the United States leading Israel into negotiations on terms acceptable to the Egyptians.

Deciding on War

The Soviets' expulsion was not rewarded by any significant modification in U.S. policy, and Kissinger's retrospective appraisal of Egyptian calculations was on target. Hafez Isma'il had met Sadat and Ahmed Isma'il in the Barrages presidential rest house in early March 1973 for a debriefing. As Isma'il recalls, Sadat listened pensively, then abruptly sat back as if struck by some epiphany. In that early March meeting, Sadat had asked Hafez Isma'il to replace 'Aziz Sidqi as prime minister in a new government. But when Isma'il returned one week later, on March 15, to discuss this issue with Sadat, Sadat informed him that he would head the new government himself, much to Isma'il's relief. Hafez Isma'il feels certain that Sadat had, in the interim, taken the decision to go to war, and that the new military commander, Ahmed Isma'il, had requested a six-month delay to allow for arrival and assimilation of the military equipment promised by the Soviets in February 1973.[188] Other cabinet members, like 'Aisha Ratib, also felt certain that the decision to go to war had been made in March, although she and her colleagues had no idea when exactly the first blow would be delivered.[189] Actual plans for the war were drawn up by Gamassi, director of Military Operations, and shown to Syrian President Hafez al-Assad when he visited Egypt secretly and met with Sadat at Borg al-'Arab in April 1973.[190] At that meeting, Sadat and Assad agreed on October 1973 as the most propitious moment to strike.[191] Sadat's broad intentions were then revealed to his government ministers in a long cabinet meeting on April 25, 1973, when the principle of a war to liberate Egypt was reconfirmed. (On the same day, Sadat received a note from President Nixon, thanking Sadat for the beautiful silver service set delivered to the Nixons by Hafez Isma'il.) [192]

The Soviets' expulsion led Israelis and Americans to believe that the likelihood of war had decreased, whereas Sadat saw the Soviets' removal as a necessary prelude to war. Indeed, Sadat says that he began to prepare for the battle in July 1972, immediately after the Soviets' departure.[193] The Egyptians would not have been able to wage war with the Israelis with such a large Soviet presence because the probability of the war escalating to include direct American involvement was too great. With the Soviets gone, warfare became "thinkable" and could be waged under conditions whereby a victory would be viewed as a purely Egyptian accomplishment.[194]

Pending the initiation of hostilities, Egyptian diplomats ardently plied their trade, successfully selling the image of exhausting all peaceful means for conflict resolution, and thereby creating a more sympathetic international environment for Egypt, as Heikal had recommended.

Finally, coinciding with the aforementioned developments was a further consolidation of Arab unity for the sake of the "battle." Through diplomatic channels, an excellent rapport was established between Egypt and the major confrontation states—Syria and Jordan—as well as major Arab financial supporters, Saudi Arabia, Libya, and Kuwait. The release of Muslim Brothers from Egyptian prisons, the eviction of the Soviets, the movement away from an "Arab application of scientific socialism"—all of these developments had won approval from the Saudis and Libyans, enhancing Egypt's strategic depth prior to "the battle."

Alongside these preparations, considerable forethought was given to prepare for use of the "oil weapon" in an unprecedented manner. Specifically, Mustafa Khalil, who conceived the "oil weapon" idea, was entrusted with the duty of drafting a plan of action that could be agreed upon by major Arab oil exporters.[195] The plan would impose an oil embargo upon Israel's supporters, shaking the energy base of the Western capitalist economy.

Interestingly, Sadat's intentions had been placed on full display at the end of March 1972. In an interview with Arnaud de Borchgrave that appeared in *Newsweek,* Sadat noted that negotiations had now completely failed; "[e]verything in this country is now being mobilized in earnest for the resumption of the battle—which is now inevitable."[196] "The irony was that, at the time, virtually nobody believed him."[197]

Conclusion

Going into the autumn of 1973, Sadat's position left a great deal to be desired. The domestic political situation was ripe with potential for great instability. Sadat had moved away from a system of tight political control by the ASU and promised greater protection of individual liberties. But while having greatly undermined the ASU, he had not built a strong institutional alternative. Once rival political forces began to exploit greater opportunities to express themselves, they did so largely outside the existing institutions, thereby posing a more serious threat to the regime.

Throughout 1972-1973, both students and workers—primarily led by Marxist and Nasserite elements—demonstrated with increasing frequency, expressing their unwillingness to tolerate any further postponement of "the battle." Efforts to construct an Islamist counter-force were undertaken, and this made a political difference on university campuses, but leftists' remonstrations were strong enough that the regime could not easily ignore or combat them. With the new 1973-1974 academic year approaching, another cycle of conflict and repression was in the offing unless their grievances were somehow addressed. Beyond the psychological duress produced by unceasing preparation for "the battle," the economy was on the brink of collapse due to the weight of military reconstruction and forced neglect of infrastructural development during the six-year period following the 1967 *naksa*. As Sadat admitted several times in speeches after the war, the public treasury was virtually empty when the war was at long last fought.[198] At a National Security Council meeting held on September 30, 1973, Sadat told its members that "our economy has fallen below zero. We have commitments (to the banks, and so on) which we should but cannot meet by the end of the year. In three months' time, say, by 1974, we shan't have enough bread in the pantry! I cannot ask the Arabs for a single dollar more; they say they have been paying us the aid in lieu of the lost Canal revenue, although we didn't, or wouldn't, fight."[199] Regime leaders had few alternatives but to put "the battle" behind them so they could begin to confront the country's other pressing needs.

Sadat had attempted to initiate a dialogue with the Israelis and their American supporters through the February 1971 overture and other diplomatic initiatives. He persisted in this effort, despite great political risk, throughout 1972 and into 1973, but his effort yielded no acceptable outcome. For the principal Egyptian decision-maker, the only answer therefore seemed to reside in a new war—a war that, it was hoped, would extract Sadat and Egypt from the quicksand into which they were so rapidly sinking.

4

The October 1973 War
and Its Impact

"You have to change the *status quo,* the situation that you're in; but I'm not
inviting Sadat to change the situation militarily. If he tries that, Israel will
win another time by an even greater measure than she won in June 1967."
—Henry Kissinger's warning to Sadat as recounted by Hafez Isma'il.[1]

Kissinger was wrong. Before October 6, 1973, Egypt was confronted by a
seemingly invincible foreign power occupying a large chunk of its national
territory. Only a miracle, it was widely believed, could dislodge the Israelis
from the heavily-fortified, sand bank emplacements along the Suez Canal
that constituted the Bar Lev line. Therefore, the successful crossing of the
canal and penetration of Israel's line of defense, a brilliant military achieve-
ment indeed, wrought feelings of exaltation among the Egyptian populace.

True, at the war's end, the Israeli Defense Forces were on the verge of
crushing Egypt's Third Army, the road to Cairo was open before them, and
only the superpowers' intervention prevented a rout. Thus, Israelis and their
supporters still view Egypt's annual celebrations of the October War with
a mixture of surprise and derision. But the average Egyptian, to this day,
remains convinced that victory was Egypt's; and if the converse of Clause-
witz's adage is true, that the end of warfare is politics, then it is difficult to
challenge the Egyptians' point of view. From the Egyptian leaders' perspective, there had been, after all, "no thought of being able to crush the
IDF and enter Israel; only a limited war was envisioned, one that would
show Nixon and Kissinger that we wouldn't accept the status quo."[2] In fact,
Sadat was wary of Kissinger's prophecy: "Sadat feared the Egyptian military
being crushed again; so he set a very modest goal of advancing 10–15 kilo-
meters east of the canal and stopping."[3] The bottom line is that despite the

war's military outcome, the Egyptians accomplished their objective or providing an impetus for political negotiations that ultimately brought the return of their lost land.

So, in most Egyptians' eyes, it seemed that after years of bitterness and despair following the catastrophic June 1967 defeat, God had finally bestowed His blessings on Egypt's soldiers and guided their incredible crossing of the canal. After all, some soldiers had even seen angels riding on the shoulders of their comrades as the miraculous canal crossing unfolded.[4]

Sadat's Window of Opportunity

The principal beneficiary of this victory could be none other than Sadat. Long maligned as fearing to engage in "the battle," Sadat now became the strategic genius who had patiently and surreptitiously crafted the surprise attack and victory. He became, in short, the *buttal al-'ubur* (the hero of the crossing). His popularity soared to an all-time high, creating a political situation comparable to the one Nasser enjoyed following the 1956 Suez Canal War, in which Nasser had snatched political victory from the jaws of military defeat. Public confidence in Sadat was so strong as to enable him to chart the nation's destiny according to his own political-economic vision. Of course, he would quickly discover, as had Nasser before him, that getting the bulk of Egyptian society and key international interests to respond in keeping with his government's development plans was an altogether different matter.

Given his Rightist, pro-Western orientations, and emboldened by his popularity, Sadat seized the opportunity to reorient Egypt's major policies. Postwar conditions reinforced Sadat's belief that a distinct Western shift in Egypt's international political alignment, coupled with economic and political liberalization, offered the only way to bail his country out of its woeful socioeconomic situation.

As Sadat now began repeating, the world was no longer the same after the October War.[5] His claim was not without foundation. As a result of the October War, the accompanying oil embargo, the quadrupling of oil prices and the enormous wealth acquired by Middle East and North African (MENA) oil-producers, the entire world was thrust into a new era, in which numerous nations had to cope with Middle Easterners' extensive control of world energy supplies. In fact, more than two decades later, this massive restructuring of energy costs was recognized as perhaps the principal factor to have shaken the foundations of Western Europe's welfare states.[6] Most oil-producing nations had excellent cause for rejoicing, and the Egyptians were justified in believing they could tap into this euphoria.

After all, the Egyptians played a crucial role in the early determination of MENA oil policy. Sadat had instructed Mustafa Khalil, Sayyid Mar'ei, Prime Minister Fawzi, and Muhammad Hassanein Heikal to prepare a memo, which Sadat read and okayed, to convince the Saudis and others to treat oil as a strategic commodity. Mar'ei was sent to the Gulf to discuss financial support from the Arabs. Khalil was sent to present the oil-as-weapon threat, and events unfolded, in his words, as follows: "If you [the West] support Israel militarily, we can reduce oil output. We reduced oil output by five percent to send a message that the Arabs could play along. The Arabs also wanted a fifteen cent increase per barrel. Oil was at $3.30 per barrel. I said we could raise it to $10 per barrel; this won't displease U.S. producers. After December 1973, prices went even higher, but I wasn't responsible for this."[7]

Due to the level of coordination experienced by Arab nations during the war, Sadat now mused over the Arab world's emergence as the "sixth world power."[8] Oil-rich Arabs, it was expected, would show their gratitude for Egypt's role in the victory, and with their financial support, Egypt might at last pull itself out of its deep economic rut. Also, having gained the respect of the Western powers through their display of military might and orchestration of Arab (oil) solidarity, Egypt would be afforded new possibilities to establish a more constructive relationship with those nations, including the United States, and to capture Western and Far Eastern direct investment.

Reorienting the Egyptian Economy

For Sadat, transformations in the international environment created conditions under which Egypt's political-economic development could be reoriented and accelerated. If Sadat had already concluded before the October War that the ASU-socialist format of the 1960's was a failure, he saw even more justifications and possibilities for altering that format now. Besides, he could argue, wouldn't this be in keeping with the "trial and error" logic held by Nasser himself?

Again, Nasser had already taken some moves to liberalize the economy in the 1968-1970 period. In addition, Eastern European socialist countries had already initiated economic openings to the West in the early 1970s. As 'Abd al-'Aziz Higazi noted, "One of the main motivations for our opening was the fact that Eastern European countries themselves were doing so. Even the Soviet Union was opening up to West German and U.S. capital."[9] Communist Poland was on its way to becoming one of the world's biggest manufacturers of golf carts.

But there were powerful demonstration effects from non-communist countries as well. From 1967 to 1973, Brazil's "economic miracle" attracted international attention, and South Korea's export-led growth strategy was providing impressive results. In both countries, right-wing military authoritarian regimes were overseeing this rapid economic growth.

In Egypt, policymakers had introduced Law 65 of 1971 to attract greater Arab and multinational corporation (MNC) investment; but it had elicited no strong response. Now the opportunity to make a more concerted effort presented itself. Still, any economic rapprochement with the capitalist world would be tempered by the fact that within the regime itself, support for state ownership and control of important sectors of the economy was great. Consequently, key regime economic elites were more inclined to search for less-than-radical means to stimulate the economy. In Fuad Sultan's words, "The general trend and feeling of many cabinet members was in favor of state ownership; they did not believe in the private sector and market forces. They saw the lack of foreign exchange as the major problem. So opening up to this foreign money became a good option to them."[10]

The absence of foreign currency, severe since the late 1960s, was seen as the principal motivation for partial economic liberalization. Through the burdens of war and an unhealthy economy, by the spring of 1974 Egypt had racked up a $15 billion foreign debt, primarily owed to the Soviet Union. Equal to six years of export earnings, this debt caused some observers to conclude that Egypt was in the Soviet Union's pocket,[11] although the threat of unilateral debt repudiation must have caused some concern in the Kremlin. At any rate, regime elites now held high hopes that petrodollar rich Arab cousins and Iranians would want both to reward Sadat and Egypt for the war performance and to entice Egypt down the capitalist road. It was time for dreaming grandiose dreams. With Iranians, Saudis, Kuwaitis, Qataris, and Emirate sheikhs showering hundreds of millions of dollars in assistance upon their Egyptian brothers, Western and Far Eastern governments and MNCs would smell great opportunities for extending aid and supplier credits to assist Egyptian development efforts. And petrodollars could be recycled back into their national economies if Egypt would open its economic door. Egypt's capital accumulation problems were soon to end, or so it was envisioned.

Sadat went with his personal predilections, and the contours of his new strategy for Egyptian development formed quickly. As technocrats like Khalil noted, "the economic opening was very closely related to the new surplus of capital in the Arab world. Here came the change in my thinking. I was not a socialist in the 1960s; I was just really concerned with the public sector projects' success. As long as we had a budget deficit, we couldn't make the public sector work. So we had to open the door."[12] To revive the stagnant economy, Egypt would seek massive economic support from its Arab brothers and Iran, as well as large infusions of capital and transfers of technology from Western and Far Eastern governments and MNCs.

A model for such cooperation had been worked out in September and October 1973, and formally signed on December 14, whereby a mixture of Arab-American financing was arranged for construction of the SUMED (Gulf of Suez to Mediterranean Sea) pipeline, to be built by Bechtel. Such a project had been discussed since 1968; but in over five years, it had gone nowhere. Now, the *International Herald Tribune* trumpeted this deal as the first major U.S. economic involvement in Egypt since Secretary of State Dulles decided against financing the Aswan High Dam in 1956.[13]

On January 10, 1974, the U.S. Export-Import Bank approved a direct loan guarantee of $100 million for SUMED's construction, the first such loan by the bank to Egypt in ten years.[14] This was followed by news in February that Chase Manhattan would lend $80 million for the SUMED project, as well as open a branch in Cairo—the first direct American bank activity in Egypt since 1956.[15]

Although the initial SUMED deal collapsed, it was resuscitated by other interested parties, and the SUMED project remained emblematic of what many Egyptian policymakers hoped was in store for their economy. New ties were being forged that clearly affected their thinking. For example, Chase's director, David Rockefeller, who had already established a relationship with Sadat,[16] encouraged Sadat's movement down a more capitalist path.

Further promotion of foreign investment necessitated new legislation providing strong incentives and guarantees to foreign capital. As already noted, a precedent for such legislation had been set through the provisions embodied in Law 65 of September 1971. Egypt had also signed an agreement with the International Bank for Reconstruction and Development (IBRD, or World Bank) in October 1971, endorsing its principles. However, between 1971 and June 1974, only 50 out of 250 projects had been approved, and not a single one had started up.[17]

The new push to attract foreign investment came during the first half of 1974. On February 11, Sadat set up the Agency for Arab and International Cooperation for this purpose. By May, in keeping with the April announcement of the "October Paper," the government approved a draft law exempting foreign investors from import duties, granting five-to-eight year tax holidays, permitting repatriation of 50 percent of profits, and providing guarantees against sequestration or nationalization. Then, in June 1974, Law 43 for Arab and Foreign Investment reinforced the thrust of Law 65 (1971), endorsing the provision of the draft law, opening up previously protected areas of the economy to foreign investment, and allowing the entry of foreign banks.[18] Arab investors were allowed additional privileges, including the ability to purchase urban real estate and housing. All Law 43 approved projects (including those involving public sector firms) were exempted from the labor laws, compulsory labor representation on company boards, and salary and profit-sharing schemes that applied to public sector companies.[19] These policies constituted the basis of Egypt's new economic development strategy, dubbed by the regime as *al-infitah* (literally, "the opening").

How Deep Was the Shift? Movement Toward a "Mixed" Economy

The intent of these economic reforms was not to dismantle the large public sector, as had been made clear in a March 5, 1974 statement issued by the ASU. But because these changes coincided with important shifts away from the previous pro-Soviet, pro-socialist policy line and heavy Eastern bloc trade, and Sadat's "orientations" were known to many elites, the ASU statement was not taken at face value. Many people, regardless of their ideological preferences, assumed that these changes marked the beginning of a wholesale abandonment of socialism and a turn to capitalism. Leftists, Egyptian and foreign alike, perceived a headlong rush toward capitalism and a dismantling of the public sector via privatization. But regime leaders, including Sadat, had a more nuanced strategy and "mixed" economic outcome in mind.

There were regime voices calling for privatization. "The Egyptian economist Fuad Sultan proposed publicly, even before the 1973 war, that the government shed failing public sector enterprises. Then, in December of that year, the parliament's Plan and Budget committee recommended partial privatization of successful parastatals."[20] But these developments did not constitute part of a powerful push for privatization by regime elites. As Mustafa Khalil said, "We didn't think about privatization at all. This idea [privatization] took root with Thatcher's success; later came Gorbachev and the collapse of the Soviet Union."[21] (One will recall that Thatcher assumed power in 1979; Gorbachev came to power in 1985, and the Soviet Union's collapse came in 1991.) And in Hassan 'Abbas Zaki's words, "No one in the 1970s really spoke of elimination of price supports or subsidies or of privatization. Not until Gorbachev's book[22] [in 1987] did people become convinced of the need for privatization. Sadat was surrounded by socialists. All of the ministers of planning were pro-socialist—Gaballah, Ganzuri. He called for an open door policy, but he didn't say privatization or liberalization."[23]

In the eyes of staunchly pro-capitalist elements, that is, those who would have preferred a "shock therapy" shift, nowhere near enough was done to provide the economy with a proper reorientation. Fuad Sultan, for example, would have preferred a capitalist "cold turkey." As Sultan later lamented,

Sadat knew little to zero about economics, so he left the economic details to the administrators, who did little to scrutinize and change Nasser era laws in depth. Sadat said, "Okay, let's open up"; but he stayed dependent upon the same team to draft the economic plan; so Isma'il Sabri 'Abdullah and Fuad Mursi [both Marxists] helped draft the "October Paper."

The "October Paper" was the name given to the new postwar economic policy introduced in April 1974. Sabri 'Abdullah actually chaired the writing of the October Paper.[24] Other key architects of the plan, 'Abdullah Marziban and Sherif Lutfi, held more positive views of the private sector's potential contribution. But as Sultan noted, "Almost all key state economic decision-makers, with the exception of a few like myself, were in favor of the public sector at this time; the general trend and feeling was pro-state ownership, with little faith in the private sector and market forces. They saw the lack of foreign exchange as the biggest obstacle to development, so opening up to foreign capital became an attractive option to them; but there was no talk of privatization. Privatization was still a dirty word to most state planners."[25]

Great credence is lent to Sultan's view by Isma'il Sabri 'Abdullah. Sabri 'Abdullah had been contacted by Higazi, whom Sadat had tapped as prime minister, and was told that Higazi "wanted me because we're at a critical juncture and I need you. You will be second in command of the whole economy. So I accepted, telling Higazi, "We'll see what happens." Our economic strategy was: (1) to increase production; to help anybody to do this—private and public sector alike; (2) to secure Arab investment or loans, and direct or indirect savings or remittances of Egyptians; (3) to give an opportunity to Egyptians and Arabs with money to invest; a belief in Arab economic integration."[26] Of course, Sabri 'Abdullah had no faith in Western capital. During our interview, he cited 1971 statistics that showed that 75 percent of world FDI was cross-invested by MDCs; and that of the remaining 25 percent invested in LDCs, 18 percent was in oil ventures. Sabri 'Abdullah said, "I told them, 'They will never come. Running after Western FDI is a mirage. We must mobilize local resources and get Arab integration.'"[27] Still, Sabri 'Abdullah helped draft and endorsed the overall strategy, and despite his negative outlook about Western FDI, he clearly hoped the new plan's broad appeal to foreign capital would garner significant Arab investment in Egypt.

From Sultan's perspective, however, the legislation accompanying *infitah* still bore too much of the ideological imprint of its numerous leftist hand-maidens, and therefore remained woefully inadequate. Sultan asserts that "all anti-private sector regulations continued under Sadat."[28] For instance, the labor law, the foreign exchange law, the capital markets law (prohibiting foreign commodities from being traded on the stock exchange), laws governing international trade, export procedures, limitations on indirect ownership—all remained "hostile" from an Egyptian private sector—especially national capital—perspective. Indeed, the first conference to review all of these laws did not come until 1982, under President Mubarak.[29]

Khalil, Zaki, and Sultan's characterization of attitudes toward privatization are somewhat exaggerated, but generally accurate. There were voices in high and influential places calling for privatization, even before infitah.[30] However, regime voices publicly calling for privatization were lonely, and even if Sadat wanted a significant measure of privatization, as shall be discussed shortly, he, too, refrained from uttering the "p" word in public. Also, highly indicative of regime elites' views at this time is the fact that little to nothing was done to help small and medium-size Egyptian manufacturers. This was particularly shortsighted because this sector accounted for between one-quarter and one-third of all industrial output during the 1970s, and over half of industrial employment.[31] With Law 86 of 1974, local currency Egyptian investors acquired parity with Law 43 foreign currency Egyptian and foreign investors, but this parity was conditional. The government had to judge local currency capitalists' projects as being in accordance with the state's five-year plan,[32] and this created numerous bureaucratic obstacles to real parity. Moreover, according to Wahba, it wasn't until Law 159 of November 1981, after Sadat's death, that July 1961 ceilings for annual salaries and profits were dropped.[33] For most Egyptian capitalists, high rates of taxation, mandatory percentage payouts to workers, mandatory representation of workers and employees on company boards, and frequent bureaucratic interventions all remained in place throughout Sadat's presidency.[34] Under Sadat, the "switch to capitalism" ignored the most numerous set of urban capitalists and their responsiveness to capitalism's most basic ingredients, beginning with profit motivation.

While the regime failed to lift the hopes of many urban, "productive" capitalists, it did "open the door" to importers and a comprador bourgeoisie. Through introduction of the "own-exchange" import system in June 1974, the importation of foreign goods was greatly facilitated; importers were allowed to acquire necessary foreign exchange without going through government banks. The government's hope was to ease the acquisition of raw materials, and intermediary and capital goods to boost local production; the outcome would be quite different.

Sadat also created new opportunities for rural capitalists who had provided a strong base of support for Sadat against his Nasserite Centrist opponents. The agricultural sector had remained largely in private hands, but state intervention was extensive; the state determined crop rotations and controlled rural incomes through monopoly control of farm inputs and compulsory marketing of crops. The long-time net effect had been high effective taxation of that sector and a rural-to-urban transfer of wealth. Under Sadat, this situation began to change, albeit slowly until the mid-1970s. Already in 1973, the government offered broad-based tax and customs exemptions to all farmers, and the rapid increase in the number of crop rotation violations between 1973 and 1975 was indicative of greater laissez-faire.[35] In 1974, government purchasing prices for crops were raised, and after 1975, the government began to move away from compulsory marketing and pricing.[36] A law introduced in June 1975 also enabled landowners greater leverage against their peasant tenants.[37] Nevertheless, compulsory cropping, marketing, and pricing remained in place for many agricultural products during Sadat's presidency.

On balance, Sadat's long-term objective was a "mixed economy," not some pure capitalist's paradise. His strategy for economic change was gradualist, and he provided strong backing for many statist policies.

There was a powerful political calculus behind Sadat's new "mixed" economic policy. As Sufi Abu Talib explained:

Sadat wanted gradual change because most people were accustomed to the ancient regime (Nasser period). Many workers and peasants were in the People's Assembly by virtue of the 50 percent representation rule; they wanted to keep their posts. Sadat didn't want to alienate such elements needlessly, so he wanted to reverse nationalization efforts gradually and begin privatizations, but not under that name, because privatization sounded bad at that time. His policy was not to confront the workers and their leaders; so he left the public sector companies alone and created new joint ventures alongside them, believing that over time the new joint ventures would replace the public sector without people being able to say he had canceled the public sector. We [Sadat and Abu Talib] had discussed all this after the 1973 war and were likeminded. We also agreed that strategic industries must remain in government hands, that is, Mahalla [textiles], Helwan [iron and steel], defense, electricity, etc. There was no country to be imitated; just democratic principles.[38]

Thus, for Sadat and nearly all key regime elites, certain industries were seen as sacrosanct: textiles, iron and steel, aluminum, weapons production, and pharmaceuticals. The public sector companies in these strategic industries were among Egypt's largest. Beyond these "sacrosanct" companies, entry into joint venture arrangements was seen as an attractive, middling ground of privatization for other public sector companies, one that averted the dirty "p" word. But, as will be seen, Sultan's characterization of Egypt's legal investment environment was accurate, that is, it remained unattractive to most major foreign investors. Foreign banks entered Egypt, as did several "foot loose" companies in the late 1970s, but no serious joint venture projects in manufacturing appeared until 1980-1981.

Defending State Ownership and Control

Sadat had no desire to undo the entire public sector, and even if he had, he was well aware that the public sector had so many well-entrenched defenders that he couldn't have taken them all on. Workers, peasants, and their leaders were not the only defenders of Nasser-era "socialist gains" and the public sector because, at one level, everyone living in the country—rich or poor, Egyptian or foreigner—typically benefited from heavy subsidies and price controls on a wide range of products and services. These included basic foodstuffs, electricity, rent, medicine, gas for cooking, petroleum products, and much more. Yet, for those actually employed by the state, there were other pro-socialist or pro-statist motivations.

Pro-Socialist Biases of "Statist" Regime Elements

Elites and Their Progeny

As already seen, all of Sadat's closest advisers were committed to maintaining a sizeable public sector and many other socialist practices. Jeswald Salacuse, who was at the Ford Foundation in Cairo from 1967 until 1976, was involved in helping draft economic liberalization legislation. He noted that most Egyptian officials during this period were deeply affected by nearly two decades of socialist practice and were highly distrustful of Western capital. Moreover, Salacuse found many of those officials dealing with Law 43 project proposals as lacking the knowledge to deal with them effectively, and as coming from backgrounds like the Central Bank where they had grown used to saying "No." To top it off, many were reluctant to pursue *infitah* too avidly because "they didn't know how long it would last."[39] In other words, and as will be demonstrated, it wasn't until the latter 1970s that those Egyptian authorities most directly involved in overseeing *infitah* policies started to feel more comfortable with the thrust of *infitah* and actually believed in its value and long-run viability. Such factors clearly had a hugely detrimental impact on *infitah* in its infancy. In discussing a failed effort to privatize two small public companies in 1975, Posusney notes, "It is not clear to what extent union leaders serving in parliament, as opposed to other forces, were responsible for this modification. The prolonged nature of the controversy over privatization does suggest that opposition to the scheme existed outside the labor movement as well, and extended into the government in spite of Sadat's personal support for it."[40] Indeed it did.

For close to two decades, but especially between 1958 and 1968, hundreds of military officers had been provided positions on public sector companies' boards of direction, and other regime friends and family members had been similarly pampered by the politically powerful. To offer just one example,[41] at Salon Vert, a department store nationalized in 1962, there had been two accountants in the early 1960s. By 1968, there were 36 accountants. Meanwhile, during the 1960s, Salon Vert's board of directors had been stuffed with retired military officers who "took the biggest paying positions, then brought in their friends and relatives."[42] In the 1960s, 25 percent of the public sector company managers were from the military.[43] Zaki guesstimated that by the early 1970s, over 50 percent of company directors were officers, "but it was hidden. They could say engineer, but not mention *liwa* (military general). Many were not qualified."[44]

By the early 1970s, the military-created regime had been in place for a full generation, and therefore had already started to provide for its own children. Many regime elites—the term "state capitalists" comes readily to mind, but "state socialists" is perhaps more fitting—were Nasserite-era Rightists. They approved many of Sadat's major economic and political reorientations, but obviously opposed any change that would challenge the privileged positions they had acquired in the state and the attendant social status. While many grew increasingly attracted by the opportunities to link up with foreign capital through joint ventures, they neither sought nor desired changes that would undercut their continued ability to appropriate state assets. As Fa'iqa 'Abd al-Rahman noted, "Most public sector managers were technocrats, but because of the benefits and privileges they obtained, committee member stipends, prestige and influence, they became supporters of socialism for their own vested interests."[45] In essence, many "state capitalists" were pro-socialism, and therefore might be labeled as "state socialists." But to label them capitalists or socialists would seem an affront to either economic philosophy; therefore they are perhaps best labeled as "statists"—individuals who preferred continued, extensive, state ownership and control of the economy.

Public Sector Workers

In addition to reckoning with these "statist" elements, Sadat and other economic planners had to deal with other serious socioeconomic forces.

According to 'Adil Gazarin,[46] CEO of Nasr Automotive (Egypt's auto and truck manufacturer), the state's effort to fight unemployment by forcing public sector companies to hire unneeded labor had been going on since 1964. This had led to 40 percent labor redundancy in his firm. And of course, the practice was widespread. This, along with the government's freezing of prices for public sector products despite increases in input costs, were cited by Gazarin as the two principal factors plaguing public sector companies.

As regarded the labor issue, it was feared that any rapid move toward privatization would produce massive layoffs of redundant laborers in Egypt's public sector firms, and this would cause a serious political backlash. Despite some initial conflict, Nasser had earned high marks from organized labor. Any hint of reorienting the economy away from socialism ran the risk of alienating this support, and putting organized labor in a new position of confrontation with Sadat's regime. Posusney is right on target, pointing out that with the onset of *infitah*, "workers' "socialist gains" were widely perceived as under attack... [and that] these threats served to revitalize the labor movement, restoring a sense of purpose that many unionists felt had been lost during the Nasir years."[47] Debate in the Egyptian Trade Unions Federation and elsewhere gave regime officials clear signals that they might have a real fight on their hands if they tried to "dismantle" the public sector.

State Parasites

Beyond the factory workers, there was an army of parasitic economic actors, such as the *shallalin* (carriers), who carried, stockpiled, and redistributed government-subsidized products for resale at black market prices, usually under the supervision of corrupt government officials of varying stature. The state, whale-like behemoth that it had become, had attracted enormous schools of parasitic pilot fish in nearly all areas of its activities. More inclined to conduct business in the shadows, these individuals were also capable of various forms of resistance, from subterfuge to public disturbances, if their collective interests were threatened by government reforms.

State Bureaucrats

The behemoth of all socialism-spawned behemoths was the state bureaucracy. Under Sadat's turn to capitalism, the number of state bureaucratic employees would actually grow from 1,200,000 in 1970 to 1,900,000 in 1978, and 2,135,000 in 1980.[48] The number of civil servants was nearly double that of public sector company workers, 1,080,000, in 1980.[49] Any truly cold embrace of capitalism and government downsizing would have led to the jettisoning of huge numbers of civil servants, most of whom could not have been absorbed by the private sector given its rate of growth. Sadat knew as well as anybody that this huge corps of civil servants had the potential to create a fearsome backlash to any crude shift to capitalism.

Private Sector State Subcontractors
Finally, as Sadowski has cogently argued, and as Sadat knew perfectly well, most Egyptian capitalists did not want the state to disappear from the economic scene:

> Egyptian businessmen and economic reformers . . . tend to endorse the idea of liberalization. They want freedom from state controls and regulations, and they want the government to stop mandating and supervising what they produce and for which markets. Yet businessmen and reformers, even the most liberal ones, resist the idea of cutting the state's budget and reducing its centrality in the economy. They believe that the private sector is still too weak to prosper on its own and that it requires massive government support and public investment to develop; . . . these groups are not étatists (they believe that businessmen and the market should define the direction of economic policy rather than technocrats or officers), but they remain *dirigistes* (who believe that economic development requires the support of a strong state).[50]

Such thinking was perhaps also true of many private sector workers. The wages, benefits, and job security that came with public sector blue-collar jobs made such positions attractive to a sizeable percentage of private sector workers,[51] and many hoped that one day they might acquire a public sector job.

In Sum
With these factors and forces in mind, the intent of Sadat's new economic policymakers was not to dismantle completely the existing system. Rather, the hope was to attract foreign capital, and allow foreign aid and private FDI to create new employment opportunities in foreign companies and joint ventures. Public sector firms entering into joint ventures would be invigorated by new technologies, capital, management techniques, and a more competitive edge. All public sector companies were granted greater decision-making autonomy from the state, although strategic industries — the list was not short—were kept firmly in state hands. Incentives were offered to induce Egyptian capitalists to contribute to economic development and address existing commodity shortages as well, and rural capitalists were given somewhat greater freedom of movement.

Infitah: The Foreign Policy Dimension

For *infitah* to succeed, relations with those countries viewed as potential sources of foreign capital had to be placed on a sound footing. Improved relations with petrol-rich MENA countries would help Egypt obtain increased donor aid and private investment from those sources, as would better relations with the "more developed countries" (MDCs) of the West and Far East.

For these policies to work, prospective foreign investors would have to be convinced not just of their investments' profitability, but of their safety, not only from nationalization, but from destruction in another Middle East war. Thus, the decision to pursue economic development with significant MDC capital participation portended a linkage between economic development and Middle East peace. In consequence, the potential contradiction between a foreign policy conceived to achieve economic development and a policy whose priority was an honorable resolution of the conflict with Israel was placed in relief.

Sadat thought it possible to surmount this contradiction through the leverage provided by the Arab oil weapon; that weapon now presented MDCs with new incentives for overseeing the conflict's resolution on terms acceptable to Arabs, moving several Western countries from their pro-Israeli bias. Moreover, MENA bankrolling of Egyptian economic development would attract Western and Far Eastern businesses. But alongside these considerations, Sadat was also becoming convinced, through Saudi urging and contact with American officials, that the latter alone were ready and able to obtain peace from Israel. This belief set him all the more firmly on his course to improve formal relations with the United States. In doing so, he ran the acceptable risk of leaving his Soviet "friends" in the lurch. More problematic was the risk that peace with Israel might jeopardize his relations with other Arab nations. Finally, both outcomes might produce negative reverberations on the domestic political front.

To repeat, for Ahmed Beha al-Din, one of Sadat's foreign policy critics, Sadat's long-run vision for Egypt boiled down to a desire to "place himself and Egypt entirely in the American camp. For Sadat, the Soviet Union was a second-rate power with poor technology. The United States was the *only* superpower, the only country capable of helping him to solve both his economic problems and achieve peace with Israel. How to attain U.S. support therefore guided his thinking."[52] Beha al-Din's comments make for an interesting comparison when juxtaposed with those of Ashraf Ghorbal, one of Sadat's longstanding foreign policy advisers, because they are nearly identical. For Ghorbal, "Sadat's grand vision was to put an end to the war with Israel. How was Egypt to get peace? By placing his trust in Kissinger, and getting close to the United States, but knowing how to insist on the minimum acceptable conditions for peace."[53] Similarly, General Gamassi noted that "Sadat was completely impressed by Kissinger. I think Sadat put all his cards on the table for the United States to deliver the goods from Israel. Sadat was sure the United States could get Israel to leave through peaceful means."[54]

By late October 1973, the Americans were chaperoning disengagement talks between Egypt and Israel in the Sinai no-man's land occupied by United Nations forces at Kilometer 101. On November 7, at the end of Kissinger's first visit to Egypt, it was announced that both Egypt and the United States would elevate their respective interest sections to ambassadorial level. That Sadat was favorably disposed to yet greater cooperation with the United States was fully confirmed during his first meetings with Kissinger in November and December 1973.[55] Kissinger was quick to reinforce the notion, also planted in Sadat's mind by the Saudis, that only the Americans could deliver peace with Israel; yet it was Sadat himself who insisted that the two set aside discussions of the disengagement issue to sketch out a more grandiose plan for future American–Egyptian relations.[56]

When Sadat met again with Kissinger and his aides at Aswan on January 12, 1974, it was Sadat who talked his new friend Henry into remaining in the area, engage in shuttle diplomacy, and move forward the peace process.[57] What resulted from this was the first Egyptian—Israeli Sinai Disengagement Agreement, supervised by American and United Nations officials, signed on January 18, 1974. Again, the October Paper was introduced in April 1974, followed by Law 43 in June 1974. Thus, by mid-1974, a grander political-economic framework was already coming into focus. U.S. Public Law (PL) 480 wheat and wheat-flour aid assistance and World Bank development assistance were flowing to Egypt, and this assistance was reinforced by the provision of aid and supplier credits from a host of MDCs. Whether this was just the tip of the new economic iceberg, as Sadat hoped, remained to be seen.

In June 1974, a Watergate-beleaguered President Nixon was invited to Egypt and was afforded an exuberant, morale-boosting welcome by the Egyptian masses. He, too, promised American aid. But as Hermann Eilts pointed out, ". . . . the Congress did not act on this until just before Christmas 1974, and aid did not really begin until the following year. The year 1974 was a difficult one for Egypt, economically: the Soviets had practically stopped their aid because of unhappiness over Sadat's allowing the U.S. to act unilaterally in the peace process, and no appreciable American aid having been approved by Congress."[58] The American–Egyptian relationship was far from problem-free, but there was no mistaking the Egyptian leader's aspirations for that relationship.

Impact of the Policy Changes— A Deepening of Societal Cleavages

Sadat was significantly altering Egypt's development strategy. Conducted in the afterglow of the October War, moves to consolidate his new foreign policy and economic strategies went largely unopposed on the domestic front when first introduced. As one observer said, "Marxists and Nasserites saw Sadat was going down the U.S. path immediately after the October War, but they couldn't speak out against Sadat because everyone was chanting, "*intasarna!*" [We won!]"[59] However, as shall be seen, Sadat's honeymoon was brief.

A number of factors helped create the initial, postwar sense of optimism. First, the influx of Arab, Iranian, Japanese, and Western aid, and the appearance of new "first world" products in a formerly Spartan marketplace, counted a great deal. By 1975, for the first time in some eight years, the size of aid disbursements exceeded debt amortization payments, and did so by an impressive $1.8 billion.[60] Second, Egypt recovered its Sinai oil fields, and moved from a net outflow to a net inflow of funds from oil transactions between 1975 and 1976. Optimism here was underscored by an announcement that Egypt was floating on a sea of oil.[61] Third, the Suez Canal was cleared and reopened to traffic by mid-1975, earning hundreds of millions of dollars for the state. Fourth, improved relations with the Gulf countries also allowed for a more massive outflow of Egyptian labor; the 34,000 Egyptians working abroad in 1973 would grow to over two million by 1982.[62] Their labor netted a rapid, huge increase in foreign remittances. From 1973 until 1979, official foreign remittances more than doubled every two years, passing from $116 million in 1973 to $2,445 million in 1979 (See Appendix B),[63] and official figures were undoubtedly low given the amount of money transferred by illegal market mechanisms. Fifth, growth in tourism expanded at a dizzying pace, with highly affluent Arab and Western tourists entering Egypt in record numbers. Annual revenues from tourism rose rapidly, also bringing hundreds of millions of dollars in revenues. Finally, growth rates leaped to new heights, rising from a pathetic 2.7 percent in 1974 to above 10 percent for both 1975 and 1976 and averaging roughly 8 percent for the balance of the decade.[64]

On May 12, major Cairo papers carried translations of a *Business Week* article describing Egypt as on the verge of an economic boom.[65] However, this optimism was partly illusory, as well as premature. Much optimism and apparent growth was built on the inflow of "rents" from the Suez Canal and other sources, as opposed to increased production. Foreign remittances were improperly factored into calculations of the GDP growth rates to inflate those figures. Optimism was also built, noted 'Abd al-Razzaq 'Abd al-Magid, on "the disastrous policy of borrowing via supplier credits, which began in 1974, and saw Egyptian borrowing leap from $70 to $80 million annually to $1.4 billion in 1974. When the crunch for liquidity came, Egypt had to go borrow from the Arabs. It was the era of recycling petrodollars."[66]

Egypt had registered a small balance of trade surplus in 1973 ($222 million), but with the flood of imports, this changed to deficits of $833 million deficit by 1974 and $3,166 million by 1976.[67] Meanwhile, the cost of government subsidies would sail from $175 million in 1972 to $1,700 million in 1976.[68]

Another enormous difficulty was that capital accumulation did not necessarily mean reinvestment in productive capacity in Egypt. Prospering Egyptian capitalists were still more inclined to keep cash reserves in "safer" foreign banks. An estimated $20 billion was held abroad by Egyptians in the 1960s; this amount was estimated to have doubled in the 1970s.[69] Meanwhile, many small and medium private capitalists were suffering; the shifting foreign policy winds meant they lost their most important foreign markets in the Eastern bloc, while Western markets were disinterested given the generally low quality of Egyptian manufactured goods, and "own-exchange" imports created formidable competition in the domestic market.

Within a span of just two years, from 1973 to 1975, these abrupt socioeconomic changes began to expose Egypt to a set of powerful, potentially explosive, issues along nearly all of its major societal fault lines.

New Social Class Actors and Heightened Class Conflict

When Sadat was told that some people were getting exceptionally rich, not a few through less-than-honest business deals, his response was: "What do you expect? They have been living in tents for such a long time. Let them be." Hassan Mar'ei[70]

The Emergence of the "Fat Cats"

The new economic policies combined with outright corruption as well as serious deficiencies in the regulation of public and private-sector business practices and tax collection to create numerous opportunities for amassing fortunes in a short time span. Although the successor regime of Husni

Mubarak eventually provided great opportunities for personal enrichment, for years after Sadat's death it was said in Egypt that "if you didn't get rich when Sadat was president, you could forget about it." Most of the nouveau riche acquired their wealth through import schemes, government sub-contracting, exchanging money, or representing foreign business interests. There were "fat fellahin" as well: that is, farmers also cashed in on economic liberalization, although just how many there were was harder to establish.[71] But in a country where most citizens were poor and the regime still called itself socialist, the appearance of many new conspicuous consumers, dubbed "fat cats," was odious to citizens who favored a more egalitarian society. By the end of 1975, a People's Assembly report showed there were already some 500 millionaires in Egypt—"fat cat" products of *infitah*.[72]

The most visibly fat of the fat cats was none other than 'Uthman Ahmed 'Uthman, close personal friend and confidant of President Sadat. As a young contractor, 'Uthman had left Egypt to find fortune in the construction game in the Arabian peninsula and elsewhere in the region. His first major business coup in Egypt came with acceptance of his bid for the Aswan Dam project in 1956. Although his company fell victim to the state's turn to socialism and was nationalized in 1961, 'Uthman stayed on as the company's director and was granted a special exemption from the state to run the company according to more capitalist criteria regarding hiring, firing, and worker incentives. 'Uthman's was the only company in the 1960s with no workers on its board of directors. In part, 'Uthman acquired this special status through the relationship he cultivated with 'Abd al-Hakim 'Amer. Among 'Amer's numerous divertissements was a passion for soccer; he was an ardent supporter of the Zamalek Club. 'Uthman would sit next to 'Amer at Zamalek Club games, and according to his nephew and employee, Isma'il 'Uthman, 'Uthman "sponsored the Isma'iliyya club to get to talk to 'Amer."[73]

Having survived the trials and tribulations of Nasser's socialist experiment, 'Uthman's clear-cut preference for free enterprise was rejuvenated under Sadat. During most of the Nasser era, Sadat was 'Uthman's neighbor. Over time, the two men became friends and spent long hours, several times per week, walking and chatting with one another about the Egyptian political economy. Isma'il 'Uthman noted that "From 1973 on, Sadat and 'Uthman would walk for two hours . . . almost every day."[74] Such "access" enabled 'Uthman to reinforce Sadat's doubts about socialism and the damage done to Egypt's economy under the socialist experiment, as well as nurture his pro-capitalist leanings. Yet here again, with Egypt's quintessential capitalist as with Sadat, there was an expressed admission that "there are a number of areas in which it is acceptable, even necessary, to have public ownership, such as the iron and steel industry, the military, railroads, public utilities, etc."[75]

Under Sadat, 'Uthman's company, the Arab Contractors, flourished. To quote Baker, "Net company profits rose steadily from L.E. 1.6 million in 1972 to L.E. 22.4 million in 1981–1982. Fixed company assets in land, buildings, and equipment increased in value from L.E. 16.5 million to a stunning L.E. 1,990 million. In 1981 the Arab Contractors group comprised 33 companies and four consortia, involved in construction, food production, banking and insurance, hotel and medical care facilities, and engineering services in addition to construction."[76] In most people's estimation, 'Uthman became the richest man in Egypt, with personal wealth exceeding $1 billion by the 1980s,[77] and his political economic influence with Sadat seemed commensurate with his wealth. 'Uthman became Sadat's economic *wunderkind,* entrusted over time with major national projects such as reconstruction of the canal cities, development of new military sites, or oversight of the national food security program. And as demonstrated by his support for certain Islamists, 'Uthman's political weight grew both behind the scenes as well as with his assumption of formal government responsibilities. The tightness of 'Uthman's relationship with Sadat was highlighted by the marriage of his son to the younger of Sadat's daughters by Jehan in 1975. It was rumored that 'Uthman paid a L.E. 1 million dowry on his son's behalf.[78]

'Uthman was not alone in finding fortune in Sadat's Egypt. The April 1974 issue of *al-Tali'a* claimed that unnamed sources in the Ministry of Finance believed there were 187 millionaires in Egypt.[79] And as previously mentioned, this figure had jumped to some 500 millionaires by the end of 1975.[80] To Sadat's ultimate embarrassment, many fortunes were made via illicit activities or through bilking the government. In elite circles, 'Uthman was notorious for his alleged skimming off government projects.[81] According to one high-ranking official, 'Uthman's company submitted a L.E. 60–70 million revision to the bill for costs incurred in the Suez Canal tunnel construction due to modifications requested by the military. When General Gamassi was asked about the increase, he denied having asked for any change.[82]

Sadat's brother, 'Esmat, went from being a poor truck driver to a wealthy smuggler of contraband, and was convicted. Sadat's wife, Jehan, was widely suspected of having accumulated a fortune through various endeavors, including her Waqf wa-l-Amal charitable foundation, and a land development scheme,[83] although Mrs. Sadat has been ardently defended against such allegations by otherwise strong critics of her husband's policies.[84] To some observers, the 1974 marriage of Jehan's daughter, Noha, to Sayyid Mar'ei's son, Hassan, had also purveyed the image of regime cronyism given the Mar'ei family's wealth and political connections. Ashraf Marwan, who sided with Sadat in May 1971, became director of a new Arab Military Industrial Organization, and allegedly parlayed that role and excellent connections to the Saudis into kickbacks and a considerable fortune. Stories of regime corruption—whether substantiated or not—were known to everyone throughout Egypt; they did much damage to the Sadat regime's reputation.

A final important point is in order: "fat cat" wealth knew no specific ideological orientation. 'Uthman was not alone among individuals with a pro-Islamist orientation who were enriched in Egypt's new economy. Many Muslim Brothers and other Islamists made or augmented their fortunes in this environment, just as did other entrepreneurs with liberal democratic or "statist" orientations. The significance of this point will be discussed more fully at a later point.

Public Versus Private Sector Income Disparities in Urban Areas
With *infitah,* many Egyptians became troubled by the disparities in earnings that derived from the development of a dual—public versus private sector—economy. Data on public versus private blue collar wages and wage ratios show a public sector wage advantage being retained throughout the 1970-1981 period, although that advantage comes close to disappearing completely over the course of the decade. For example, while public sector blue collar wages increased from L.E. 4.19 to L.E. 12.89 between 1970 and 1980, private sector blue collar wages increased from L.E. 2.81 to L.E. 12.04.[85] However, public sector employment brought additional benefits and job security unmatched by most private sector jobs. On balance, the data suggest that public sector jobs appeared relatively attractive to many, perhaps most, blue collar workers.

While it is hard to argue with the data, it is important to place it in perspective by disaggregating it. One may begin by noting that as private businesses and banks multiplied in Egypt, and as the presence of foreign businesspersons and tourists increased, important differences in public versus private sector income developed. By the mid-1970s, among workers, low-skilled work might yield L.E. 10 per month in the private sector versus L.E. 6-7 per month in the public sector. Perhaps more importantly, higher-skilled private sector jobs often paid as much as L.E. 150 per month versus a L.E. 60 per month rate in the public sector. At the management level, the disparity was even greater; private sector jobs paid some L.E. 600-700 per month, compared to a meager L.E. 200 per month in the public sector.[86] Assaad and Commander's research shows the impact of *infitah* on wages, with 1975 as the last year that the real wage index was more favorable for the public sector.[87] At the time (circa 1976) Sa'd al-Din Ibrahim estimated than an urban family needed L.E. 350 per annum (L.E. 27.50 per month) to keep above the poverty line.[88]

Sadat urged regular increases in public sector employees' salaries and other benefits during the 1970s, fueling consumption and inflation. University and high school graduates, as well as factory workers, were receiving paychecks in the late 1970s that were at least two times more than their paychecks of the early 1970s. However, public sector workers' wage increases came in slower response to inflation, estimated at 25-50 percent,[89] and from 1975 to 1976 onward, private sector wages always kept ahead.[90] True, many public sector workers remained loath to leave their jobs because of job security, benefits, and uncertainty about long-run economic change.[91] Many of these workers, however, knew they could retain their public sector jobs while illegally moonlighting in the private sector.

While many workers preferred to retain their public sector jobs, legions of state employees grew increasingly demoralized and, in one form or another, opted out. As Ayubi noted,

> Sadat's newly revitalized private sector created a new economic class receiving wages several times higher than the corresponding wages received by government employees. A typical Egyptian teacher, to put the situation in perspective, receives the equivalent of approximately $40 per month. The lowest rung on the government pay scale is a meager $20 per month. A taxi driver, with luck, can earn several times that amount in a single week. Under the Nasser regime, the economic rules, with some exceptions, were more or less equal for everyone. Salaries were low and there were few luxury goods to purchase with the monies received. Rent controls and subsidized food compensated for the low wages and ensured government employees a minimally adequate standard of living. Under Sadat's open door policy, by contrast, the Egyptian market was flooded with luxury items, most of which were well beyond the reach of the average government employee. Many government employees with marketable skills either deserted government service for the private sector or accepted extremely lucrative positions in the Gulf. No less than one-third of the respondents in the *Al-Ahram* survey, by way of illustration, were primed to seek positions in either the private sector or the Gulf. Yet another one-third were weighing the possibilities of such a move."[92]

Most public sector employees either experienced status reversals or resorted to moonlighting and/or corruption to preserve if not enhance their previous standard of living. Half the cab drivers in Cairo, it seemed, were government functionaries, public school teachers, or public sector company employees, even though all government employees were legally barred from moonlighting. Schoolteachers also entered into the questionable, but widespread, practice of offering costly private lessons to enhance pupils' chances of passing their examinations. From top to bottom, the system became replete with some form of cheating to enhance one's income.

Private versus public sector income disparities facilitated private sector raiding of public sector talent at many levels of the employment hierarchy. It seems safe to deduce, moreover, that such raiding enhanced private sector productivity at the public sector's expense.

Rural-Urban Disparities; Gains in Rural Income
In the countryside, the level of income and government subsidies received by the average peasant remained inferior to that of poorly-paid urban laborers. For instance, peasants who migrated to Cairo could earn three times as much per day carrying bricks than as a rural laborer in the 1970s.[93] That said, a number of factors brought an improved standard of living for most peasants during the 1970s. To begin, peasants realized larger incomes due to stronger urban demand for agricultural products and the liberalization of marketing mechanisms, especially for non-government regulated crops. Second, Egyptian peasants working in Libya, Iraq, Saudi Arabia, and elsewhere constituted almost half of the Egyptian labor force abroad, and earned 300 to700 percent more than Egyptian salaries for skilled and unskilled workers.[94] Of the massive remittances that flowed to Egypt after 1973, some 20 to40 percent went directly to rural households.[95] Adams writes that these factors combined to produce a 25 percent increase in real agricultural wages in some districts between 1973 and 1980, and caused "the number of rural families living in poverty to decline precipitously . . ."[96] Government controls on the agricultural sector had been designed to milk its surplus to rebuild the shattered military and economy after 1967, such that by the end of the 1967–1973 period, 60 percent of all rural families were living beneath the poverty line compared to just 24 percent in 1964-1965.[97] By 1982, under 18 percent of rural households were living under the poverty line[98]; and one must note that peasant labor constituted roughly 40 percent of the total Egyptian labor force during the 1970s.

The Expatriate Factor, and its Impact on Egyptians
The influx of Westerners and outflow of East Europeans brought its own important changes to Egypt's economy and society. Most East Europeans had kept a paranoiac distance from Egyptians as well as Western expatriates. For example, East Germans who came to know West Germans and

socialized with them in private would often ignore them in public. Soviet citizens would take the steps in a building rather than ride up an elevator with strangers; all for fear that someone might report them for anti-Soviet behavior if they were seen "meeting in private" with non-Soviets or non-communists.[99]

Most East Europeans were more practiced at exploiting the cooperative networks, and simply did not have the wherewithal to be strong consumers, not to mention spendthrifts. There were dozens of stories of Soviet soldiers and sailors sharing a soft drink or sharing a cigarette because they couldn't afford otherwise. One friend recounted being in a Zamalek shop when a Russian woman painstakingly selected a few eggs, making sure each one displayed not the slightest hint of a crack. After she exited, the shop owner shook his head and exclaimed to all present, "feen al-ingleez, feen ayyam al-ingleez." ("Where are the English? Where are the days of the English?")[100] In short, the East Europeans generally left many Egyptians reflecting wistfully on the days when the British were in Egypt.

The postwar influx of Arab, Western and Far East businesspersons and tourists altered the economic scene, as their combined presence created a new class stratum of sorts in Cairo and major tourist destinations. Between 1970 and 1973, the number of official "tourist nights" registered by Europeans and Americans roughly doubled, and by 1977 that figure had nearly doubled again.[101] (See Table 3). Growth in Arab "tourist nights" was equally dramatic in absolute values.[102] Arab and Western tourists spent lavishly by Egyptian standards, and created a demand for more upscale goods. Their consumption patterns provided a glimmer of "what might be" to some, but a strong dose of relative deprivation to many others.

Expatriate residents benefited materially from other Egyptian policies. The fixed rates for housing rents that had been applied during the Nasser era remained in place throughout Sadat's presidency. Those rates held steady whether they were applied to a one-room hovel accommodating a large family, or a luxury apartment or villa. In consequence, Egypt could and did offer luxury housing to expatriate employees of foreign firms with a lengthy presence, for under $10 or $20 per month. The same held true for Egyptians who either maintained or acquired such housing during the Nasser period. However, for the burgeoning population of Egyptian citizens seeking new housing, and facing an acute housing shortage, there were major negative consequences associated with this pricing policy. To begin, it created strong disincentives to the expansion of housing construction for some builders. Beyond this, those builders who took the plunge anyway felt compelled to seek a profit illegally in the form of demanding "key money," a huge lump sum payment made by the lessee to move into an apartment, for which the lessee then paid the government-determined monthly rent rate. Most Egyptians found it impossible to come up with the requisite funds for "key money" payments. In many cases, this literally meant delayed marriages. By contrast, the superior purchasing power of MDC expatriates meant fewer problems in obtaining housing even when they had to search in the open market.

Interesting anomalies developed out of the enlarged expatriate/tourist presence. Egyptians employed in either the private sector and/or catering to the needs of foreigners were likely to earn significantly higher incomes than those employed in public sector companies and banks. Private maids, cooks, apartment brokers, doormen, and many others working for Arabs or Westerners now often earned more money or enjoyed other benefits than university graduates or skilled workers employed in the government bureaucracy or public sector companies.

Growth of the Black Market; or "Changa Money"

For most foreigners residing in Egypt during the *infitah* era, it was nearly impossible to walk any distance in downtown Cairo without being approached by someone who asked, in mildly mangled but perfectly comprehensible English, if you wished to change money. The increase in foreign tourists and businesspersons, and the increase in business transactions with representatives of hard currency countries, portended increased opportunities for black market currency exchanges. As Fa'iqa al-Rifa'i explained, "a formal foreign exchange market was almost non-existent. Egyptian banks were seriously undercapitalized, and there was a strong need to get Egyptian money back to Egypt."[103] Thus, black market opportunities abounded, given Egypt's fixed exchange rates.

The black market in currencies had first appeared in 1968. Following the war, the Egyptian government freed up out-migration, enabling many Egyptians to go work in the Arabian peninsula, Iraq, and Libya. As noted earlier, this labor migration accelerated rapidly in the 1970s, giving rise to an even stronger search for ways to most profitably remit foreign earnings to Egypt. This stimulus to black market money activity was greatly reinforced by introduction of the "own-exchange system" in June 1974. This system allowed private sector importers to acquire or convert foreign exchange without any official record, and without having to go through public sector banks.[104] To acquire precious foreign exchange for itself, the Egyptian government did free up the banking system in 1974 so that all four public sector banks could do business in all economic areas. Previously, the National Bank of Egypt held a monopoly on foreign trade transactions. The Egyptian government also offered Egyptians a premium of 22 piasters over the official exchange rate of 43 piasters to the American dollar. Government banks failed, however, to match black marketeers' ability to meet local foreign currency demands.

Egyptian businesspersons were developing a voracious appetite for dollars. As Yusuf Mansur, director of Mansur Chevrolet (founded in 1974) put it, "In an inflationary climate, the dollar's steady appreciation was our biggest problem since we were buying in dollars and selling in Egyptian pounds. If you're not careful, all your profits get eaten up by devaluation of the pound. So, we put dollar deposits in country. Our balance sheet was in dollars. We had regular repurchasing of L.E. profits into dollars."[105]

Black marketeers, well aware of Egyptian businesspersons' hard currency needs to import goods or keep money in dollar accounts, offered consistently higher exchange rates than the government. In addition, bigger black marketeers could deliver or exchange huge sums of cash within very short time spans compared to the official banks. In Cairo's fashionable Zamalek district, at a small candy and trinket shop run by a man whose name, fittingly enough, was pronounced as "Dahab," which translates as "gold," individuals appeared with briefcases or large bags filled with cash and their currency exchanges were finalized with great efficiency. In similar fashion, individuals like Sami 'Ali Hassan, Ashraf Sa'd, Ahmed Gamal, Salah al-Dab'a, al-Rayyan, and others acquired fortunes as black marketeers. Sami 'Ali Hassan was the king; his wealth was estimated by some at $3 billion, exceeding that of 'Uthman Ahmed 'Uthman. He used some of his earnings to purchase a yacht that he named *Lord*.

Government officials basically closed their eyes to these black market activities. Indeed, by the latter 1970s, government officials literally were calling certain black marketeers on a regular basis to get the exchange rate.[106]

The Upshot With Regard to Class Conflict

These factors, and many related developments, resulted in increasing signs of class antagonisms. In the countryside, there were increasing disparities in income, but many middle-level peasants were experiencing more rapid gains than richer peasants and farmers,[107] and overall standards of living were improving. Thus, from a materialist perspective, the countryside remained relatively quiet. However, continued expansion of educational opportunities, including the opening of several provincial universities, combined with rural-to-urban migration, out-migration to work abroad, and the attendant breaking up of families—all represented social mobilizational variables with their own unsettling impact on rural life. To many, these changes produced interesting challenges to their traditional values, and thereby created new issues in the realm of politics.

In urban areas, "fat cat" conspicuous consumption, income disparities, and status reversals were glaring. The most disgruntled elements were bureaucrats and public sector factory workers who had been relatively pampered and protected under the Nasser regime, but many small and medium-sized capitalists were unhappy as well. All urban residents witnessed firsthand the appearance of new shops, such as those along Shawarbi Street in central Cairo, chock-a-block with imported consumer goods. Large groups of individuals would form in front of shops' display windows, suddenly being introduced to the riches of the "First World." They stood staring at items, from new shoes to stereo equipment, that hardly any of them could afford. At the same time, Egypt quickly made its way toward distinction as the world's largest importer of Mercedes Benz, and sleek foreign imports competed with donkey-drawn carts in Cairo's incredibly crowded streets. Foreign-based fast food restaurants like Wimpy's and Kentucky Fried Chicken appeared on the scene, but only foreigners and Egyptian elites could afford to eat there. In Cairo, major Western hotels proliferated and were used by Egypt's nouveau riche to fete their children's weddings; sumptuous parties were thrown with tabs running into the tens of thousands of Egyptian pounds. Remember, at the same time, better paid public sector workers were making L.E. 20 per month, while the minimum salary for industrial workers was pegged at L.E. 12 per month. At L.E. 1.5 per kilo of meat, or L.E. 6 for shoes, most urban working class Egyptians and many bureaucrats were having great trouble making ends meet.

Many citizens, especially those who had taken socialism and its message of egalitarianism to heart, reacted negatively to the abrupt departure from the political economy of the 1960s. Confronted with the seemingly enormous disparity in the material fecundity and distributive aspects of the two systems (capitalism versus socialism), some citizens demonstrated their dissatisfaction through strikes or other forms of protest. The first signs of worker unrest came in fall 1974, with four moderate-sized protests.[108] Then, on January 1, 1975, over 1,000 Helwan steel mill workers demonstrated against the rising cost of living and clashed with police. With inflation running at 25 to 50 percent, it was especially difficult for workers on fixed incomes to adjust to the market's vagaries.[109] Demonstrators chanted "feen al-futur, ya battal al-'ubur?" ("Where is our breakfast, oh hero of the crossing?") and ("Where is Nasser?"). Fifty-four workers were arrested. Even more important, another 250 to 400 Marxists, Nasserites, and others were arrested after being blamed by Sadat for having "exploited the climate of freedom" and instigating the workers' demonstration.[110]

Two days after these arrests, on January 4 the Interior Ministry announced that a communist organization allegedly involved in the workers' demonstration had been discovered.[111] Although it was not admitted to at the time, communists were indeed behind the workers' industrial action. *Al-gama'at bila ism* (the Group With No Name), which had a clandestine publication entitled *Ahmed 'Urabi al-Misri,* was later credited with this activity.[112] Particularly unsettling to regime authorities was the show of solidarity for the workers by students, primarily Marxists and Nasserites, who mobilized for demonstrations on January 2, 4, 6, and 9. Nearly every month of 1975 and 1976 brought reports of labor unrest. There were major disturbances in March 1975 at the Mahalla al-Kubra textile factories, forcing the plant to be closed for four days. There were also large strikes in Cairo, Alexandria, Damietta, and Mahalla al-Kubra in March 1976; and major strikes in August and September 1976 in 'Amiriyya produced clashes with the police. These events brought campaigns to arrest clandestine communist organizations' members in July and August 1975, and March, April, May, and September 1976.

Sadat blamed all labor-related disturbances on communist subversives, although when Sadat or other regime officials spoke of "communists" they were either using the term very loosely or to purposefully confuse the public. In essence, the term was applied to just about everyone on the political left.

The Egyptian Communist Party had reconstructed itself clandestinely on May 1, 1975 by "The Group with No Name" members who had managed to avoid arrest.[113] Although government accusations that the ECP or other leftists were behind most of the labor unrest fell on deaf ears, this was indeed the case. While the strikes had clear economic motivations, most were arranged by workers who were close to or directly associated with leftist organizations. For example, the 1975 Helwan strike was led by one Rashad al-Gabali, who went on to become an important member in the leftist National Progressive Unionist Grouping (NPUG, or Tagamu'a).[114] The 1976 textile factory strikes in Alexandria were directed by Abu al-'Izz al-Hariri, who later became a member of the NPUG Secretariat.[115] Nevertheless, Sadat's accusations were perceived by most citizens as an attempt to discredit workers' legitimate grievances by passing them off as communist-inspired.

Religious–Secular Strife, Challenges to the Old Moral Order
Foreign "Challenges"
Another societal cleavage, the fault line separating Islamists from more secularized Muslims, rapidly deepened during the mid- to late-1970s. A host of factors contributed to this phenomenon. To begin, Egypt was not immune to changes ushering in a new morality in the rest of the world:

the emergence of the women's liberation movement and feminism, the advent of birth control pills and sexual liberation, the drug culture, environmentalism, changes wrought by Vatican II (1962-1965) and Medellin (1968), liberation theology, Christian fundamentalism, the slow but steady growth of Jewish fundamentalism following the 1967 war, the expansion of telecommunications, and the expanded presentation of Western movies and television programs. In Egypt, such changes either stimulated interest and adherents to new social movements, or triggered conservative backlashes, some of which were religiously inspired.

The veritable explosion of foreign tourists (Arab, Western, and Japanese), and great increase in the number of expatriate businesspersons and their families was of great importance here, again, because these individuals often represented agents of behavioral change and an alternative morality. Public displays of affection, mini-skirted tourists, bra-less visitors, nudity at the Megawish Club Med on the Red Sea—all represented discrete events touching Egyptians' social and moral consciences. As phenomena associated with local reporting on the social and moral decadence and decline of the West, they quickly shaped Egyptians' thinking, bringing a great variety of reactions. Some took to Western liberalism with a vengeance, others reacted in abject horror, finding the strongest line of defense in conservative interpretations and practices of their religion.

Table 3: Tourist Nights According to Origin   (000)

Year	Arab	Europe	American	Other	Total
1970	221	66	35	36	358
1971	260	95	30	43	428
1972	314	132	44	51	541
1973	332	119	43	43	535
1974	412	152	56	56	676
1975	3621	1410	426	397	5854
1976	4081	1768	502	445	6796
1977	3592	1748	593	469	6339
1978	3717	2085	840	495	7137
1979	3408	2377	955	364	7104
1980	3595	2865	1043	581	8084

Sources: CAPMAS, Statistical Yearbook, 1975; and CAPMAS, Statistical Yearbook, 1981.

The oil boom, with its great boon to the welfare of Arabian peninsula residents and Libyans, made its own contribution in this area. Saudis, Kuwaitis, and Libyans, banned from alcohol consumption and gambling in their own countries, flocked to Egypt in increasingly large numbers to engage in Islamically forbidden pursuits. Although government approval for gambling was first approved by the Nasser administration, the first casino contract, for the Nile Hilton, was signed on April 29, 1970; thus, the casino's operation coincided roughly with Sadat's arrival in office and was associated with his regime. Egyptian citizens were barred entry, a ban that continues to this day, but by the mid-1970s, the casinos at the Nile Hilton and Sheraton Giza hotels were replete with white gown and checkered *kefiyya*-clad Arab men, guzzling their Johnny Walker scotches and testing their gambling luck against Allah's will. By 1976-1977, Gulf Arabs' numbers were augmented by a heavy influx of wealthy Lebanese, fleeing the civil war at home.

Elsewhere, in the same hotels or in the nightclubs along Pyramids Avenue, other Arab Muslims were quaffing drinks in between deluging their favorite belly dancers with American greenbacks. By night's end, a good number of these fellows were primed to seek the company of the ladies of the night, boosting fortunes in the prostitution industry. Some Arab men ventured into poor areas of Egypt to buy brides from downtrodden, unprincipled Egyptian fathers. Meanwhile, hashish and other drug trafficking was similarly driven up by the purchasing power of Arabs and Westerners, all of whom partied much more conspicuously, if not prodigiously, than had the East Europeans.

Ironically, at the same time that Gulf Arab and Libyan men were contributing to concerns over Egypt's moral decline, their governments and independent compatriots used their massive oil earnings to assist Islamist students and Islamist organizations. Clandestine funding was provided, permitting Islamist students the luxury of offering cheap copies of textbooks and cheap clothing that conformed with the Islamic dress code. Given the multitude of poor students at Egyptian schools and universities, such assistance endeared many recipients to their benefactors. In this manner, the number of women students conforming with the *ziyy al-islami* (Islamic dress code), grew very slowly but steadily in the mid-1970s.

Indigenous Contributions to Religious-Secular Tension
As already seen, Sadat's regime abetted the reemergence of Islamists and Islamic groupings in the early 1970s. Former Muslim Brothers living in exile, whether self-imposed or not, felt it safe to return to Egypt, where they were greeted by Brothers who had recently been released from Egyptian prisons. Some of these Brothers began to resume political activity, covertly in the beginning, and the fact that many Brothers had experienced considerable material success while residing in Saudi Arabia or elsewhere helped grease the wheels of their political pursuits.

Simultaneously—due to the increased number of Egyptians working in the conservative Gulf countries and Libya, as well as the increase in affluence and permission to travel allowing more Egyptians to perform the *hajj* (pilgrimage to Mecca) and *'umra* (off-season pilgrimage) than in earlier years—more Egyptians were exposed to conservative Islamic systems. They returned with their Islamic ideals and values reconfirmed and solidified, and some desired Egypt's transformation in this direction. Meanwhile, some Egyptians who went to Western countries had a "Qutb-like" negative experience.[116] They returned to Egypt not wishing to emulate the Western model, but publicly condemn it; they were all the more intent on reinforcing their Islamic faith and values to fend off the "corruption" and racism they witnessed in the West.

Conservative Islamic Influences on Sadat
For his part, Sadat, who had made his regime's slogan, "Science and Faith," went to great lengths to demonstrate that his personal religiosity was as marked as the *zabib*[117] on his forehead. Two simple examples were manifested in early formal references to Sadat as *al-ra'is al-mu'min* (the believer president), and as Muhammad Anwar al-Sadat (Muhammad, of course, being the prophet of the Islamic faith). The October War was cloaked in religious symbolism; the war was launched during the holy month of Ramadan, and its code-name was Operation Badr, the name given by the prophet Muhammad to a war fought against infidels.

Sadat appointed former Muslim Brothers and other Islamist sympathizers to significant regime posts, encouraging non-regime-linked Brothers to become more assertive. He also played the Sufi card, providing government financial backing for festive events engaged in by the popular Sufi sects. And one will recall that Hussein al-Shaf'ei, Sadat's vice president, was a devoutly religious man given to Sufistic musings.[118] Shaf'ei remained in office until 1975, when he was replaced by the young Air Force commander, Husni Mubarak, who had distinguished himself during the October War.

While 'Uthman Ahmed 'Uthman's influence on economic matters has been widely discussed, the depth of his influence with regard to the Islamic resurgence begs closer scrutiny, and has undoubtedly been underestimated to date. 'Uthman hailed from the same city, Isma'iliyya, as the founding father of the Muslim Brotherhood, Hassan al-Banna. In his autobiography, 'Uthman is crystal clear in his admiration of al-Banna, and the impact he and the Brotherhood had on his life. 'Uthman writes:

> I was a full member of the Muslim Brotherhood group in Isma'iliyya . . . I never left it except after my graduation from university . . . my work kept me busy . . . and started to take up all my time, springing from Allah's . . . words . . . " And He said Work, and Allah and His prophet and the believers

will see your work." But my relationship with the group remained a spiritual connection on the one hand, and a material connection via regular dues payments on the other . . . I split from them as an organization, but as far as the principles are concerned, and values, I remained linked to them and followed their program from those days until today.[119]

Whether during the 1950s or 1960s, facing severe repression, or during the more auspicious environment of the 1970s, 'Uthman's principal company—the Arab Contractors—discriminated in favor of Muslim Brethren in its hiring policies. 'Uthman saw in Muslim Brethren the hardworking, honest individuals that could help make his company a success. Through his overseas operations, in Saudi Arabia, Kuwait, and Libya, 'Uthman also maintained close contacts with religiously conservative elements of the Brotherhood's kind.

Given 'Uthman's special access to Sadat, it is essential to keep 'Uthman's values in mind in assessing Sadat's decision-making regarding moderate Islamists and their margin of political maneuver. 'Uthman's influence visà-vis the Islamist card in the universities in the early 1970s has already been discussed. Just as the frequency of his walks with Sadat increased after the 1973 war, so did his ability to persuade Sadat that moderate Islamists were to be trusted and allowed greater involvement in government and more freedom of political and economic movement. Such advice was crucial to Sadat's laissez-faire attitude with regard to GI growth on university campuses into the late 1970s. Finally, 'Uthman's influence cut both ways, therefore he remained politically useful to Sadat. For example, one very high-ranking government minister, whose identity I will not reveal, spoke about 'Uthman's ability to profit from cost overruns, identified Credit Suisse as the bank used by 'Uthman to launder his money, and guesstimated that 'Uthman held at least $2 billion in foreign banks. He then added, "'Uthman controls the Muslims; that's why Sadat didn't do anything."

Liberal Influences on Sadat
But while Sadat often wrapped himself in a religious cloak, and saw himself as a devout Muslim, the pro-secular, pro-Western dimension to his personality, combined with his wife's similar pre-disposition, compelled him to condone actions that Islamists saw as unacceptable or even outrageous. For one, he made no serious attempt to keep his wife, Jehan, out of the public eye. She steadfastly emerged in the postwar period as a highly visible figure in international conferences on women's rights issues alongside Iran's Princess Farah and the Philippine's Imelda Marcos. Jehan Sadat "pushed very hard for women's rights. She pushed very hard to get women in pol-

itics and regarding the *ahwal al-shakhsiyya* (personal status law). As her daughter Noha asserted, "My mother was very active; she likes to work; and she has a strong revulsion to *bait al-ta'a* (the house of obedience)."[120] Alongside reporting on Jehan's activism, a few pictures of Sadat's daughters, clad in bikinis ("Look at little Jehan! She's naked!" many exclaimed when they saw the photos) also made their way into popular magazines. Islamists saw all such behavior as entirely inappropriate, and mother Jehan as blameworthy. Imam has noted that in the trial of Sadat's radical Islamic assassins, the defense repeatedly pointed to his daughter Jehan's behavior as providing partial justification for their act.[121]

Second, in contrast to Nasser's calculated, persistent avoidance of the issue,[122] Sadat's liberalism, reinforced by strong encouragement from his wife, engendered efforts by Social Affairs Minister 'Aisha Ratib to draft legislation to modify the personal status laws. Although drafted with the careful assistance of Azhari officials, this legislation, which sought to curtail the widespread practice of polygamy as well as strengthen women's rights in divorce and inheritance cases, was greeted by a good deal of public opprobrium. In a street demonstration, Azhar University students castigated Ratib for her role in these reforms. Thus, when the bill was presented to Sadat, he asked Ratib to withdraw it. "The bill was sent to the cabinet and it was put in the refrigerator. It was later revived and modified by Amal 'Uthman."[123] But despite the bill's short-run quashing, Jehan Sadat, Sayyid Mar'ei, and Sadat himself were all seen as proponents of this legislation. This constituted a major cause for their becoming objects of conservative Muslims' wrath during the mid-1970s, and that animus would return with even greater force when this bill was taken out of the refrigerator and turned into law in 1979. Islamists would refer to the legislation as "Jehan's law."

The Military Technical Academy Incident

Tension along the religious-secular fault line manifested itself on April 18, 1974 with the Kulliyyat al-Fanniyya al-'Askarriyya (Military Technical College) incident. Members of a theretofore unknown group led by Salih Sirriyya (a Palestinian Jordanian), dubbed by state officials and the press as the Fanniyya 'Askariyya group, perpetrated the first attempt to overthrow the Egyptian government to establish an Islamic state. They did so by attacking the college in Heliopolis to arm themselves, then assassinate Sadat, who was scheduled to hold a high-level ASU CC meeting to discuss the October Paper. The revolt never succeeded in moving beyond the school's grounds due to successful resistance offered by its guards, but it left 11 dead and 28 wounded. In retrospect, it marked the dawn of a new era in Egyptian political history.

Sirriyya was a Palestinian, born near Jaffa in 1933, and forced into exile along with his family during the 1948 war. He acquired Jordanian citizenship, studied in Cairo, and went to the Military Academy in Iraq.[124] According to Hala Mustafa, he was among the founding members of Yasir Arafat's Palestinian group, Fatah, and one of those responsible for its military operations.[125] He belonged to the Muslim Brotherhood organization in Jordan, joined the more radical Islamic Liberation Party following the 1967 war, and fled to Iraq following the 1970 Black September clash between King Hussein's army and armed Palestinian groups. His religio-political affiliations resulted in his being forced to leave Iraq as well. He arrived in Egypt in late 1971, and frequented prominent Muslim Brothers, including MB Supreme Guide Hudeibi prior to his death in 1973, and Zaynab al-Ghazali, Egypt's most prominent "Sister."[126] Sirriyya drew political philosophical inspiration from Hassan al-Banna, Sayyid Qutb, the Pakistani Abu al-A'la al-Mawdudi, and the Iranian 'Ali Shari'ati.

What the public knew as the Fanniyya 'Askariyya group was known to its members as the *Gama'at Shabab Muhammad* (Muhammad's Youth Group, and also called the Islamic Liberation Party (ILP). To create this organization, Sirriyya recruited primarily among students in Cairo and Alexandria, including some students at the Technical College. Indeed, these recruitment sites formed the basis for three subgroupings within Sirriyya's organization: (1) the Cairo subgroup, with Talal al-Ansari as its prince; (2) the Alexandria grouping, with Hassan al-Halawi as prince; and (3) the Military Technical College subgroup, with Karim al-Anaduli as prince. Most members were from middle- and lower-middle-class backgrounds, and from rural or first generation urban families. The group's core principles included a strong enmity toward the West along political and civilizational lines. They saw Sadat's regime as *kafir* (non-believing; therefore condemnable) and rejected its Western dependency; they also denounced socialism and capitalism, embracing an Islamic alternative, and viewed the Arab-Israeli conflict as a religious conflict and principal axis of confrontation with the West.[127]

Some 92 individuals stood trial in the Fanniyya 'Askariyya case. Sirriyya and his top aide were executed in November 1976; 29 others were given prison sentences. Sirriyya was gone, and his group fell apart, but this was not the last to be heard from other members.

In June 1974, 90 people were detained for distributing pamphlets that called for a return to rule by an Islamic caliph.[128] No specific Islamic group identity was attributed to those detained. Meanwhile, greater regime vigilance against radical Islamist groups following the Fanniyya 'Askariyya incident netted other members of that group in February 1975, as well as members of small, relatively unknown groups: they targeted a group that state officials called al-Takfir w-al-Higra (Denunciation and Holy Flight) in May 1975, arrested Taha al-Samawi group members in June 1975, and arrested additional Takfir w-al-Higra members in November 1976.[129]

Disagreements Based in Regime-Type and Ideological Preferences

Sadat's political, economic, and sociocultural reforms brought renewed debate over which ideals should underpin Egypt's political regime. While Sadat had been quick to speak in terms of a new era guaranteeing individual rights and freedoms and the sovereignty of law, he was much slower to deliver on a specific conception of what political institutions could, would, and should safeguard those rights. The October Paper was introduced in April 1974 and "endorsed" by national referendum on May 15, 1974, the third anniversary of the Corrective Revolution. It was presented as a sequel to Nasser's National Charter and March 30 Program. In the October Paper, Sadat expressed his rejection of the "theory of the single party," but he also registered his opposition to calls for a multiparty system. He labeled multipartism as too divisive to national unity under Egypt's "present circumstances," the old refrain referring to the confrontation with Israel. Sadat may have been dreaming of an Austrian political-economic model, but he still saw himself as mired in Egyptian realities.

Sadat's short-term solution was to maintain the ASU's "coalition of the working forces" as a sound framework for preserving national unity, while enhancing prospects for greater expression of divergent interests within that coalition. The role for an opposition within the ASU was discussed by Mustafa Kamel Murad in April 1974.[130] Greater tolerance of ideological diversity also began to manifest itself during 1974 in the form of a series of televised debates over Egypt's political future that featured representatives of diverse ideological currents. While few Nasserites were in evidence, Marxists like Isma'il Sabri 'Abdullah and Khalid Muhi al-Din participated alongside Islamist-leaning regime elites or friends like Kemal Abu al-Magd, Sufi Abu Talib, and Sheikh Sha'rawi. 'Aisha Ratib and others weighed in with a more secular, regime viewpoint.

Near the end of 1974, Sadat set up a Committee for Formulating the Future Political System in Egypt. The committee, presided over by Mustafa Khalil, had some 140 members. Khalil reported that only eight members wanted an outright change to a multiparty system, over 30 advocated keeping the ASU as it was, while the rest were in favor of opening the ASU to permit the appearance of *minabir* (platforms or forums; plural of *minbar)* as a transitional phase toward legalization of multiparty politics. The thoughts of those in the majority camp were affected by the desire for a gradual change away from the ASU. Some were also reacting negatively to the political liberalization unfolding in Portugal, where dozens of parties had appeared suddenly, creating a chaotic political scene. Finally, it was also felt that if there were to be a gradual change away from the ASU, then Sadat would a new party to support him.[131]

Forging a Regime Political Philosophy; Sufi Abu Talib's Role

Sadat's long-run preference ran in the direction of scrapping the existing political regime and replacing it with a hybrid model, one reflecting Egypt's transition from a soft single-party authoritarianism toward some new liberal-Islamic regime. Sadat tapped a legal scholar, Sufi Abu Talib, to develop and delineate a new political philosophical basis for the Egyptian regime.

Abu Talib graduated from Cairo University's Law School in 1946, then spent several years studying on scholarships in France and Italy. He returned to Egypt in 1952 with an assistant professorship at his alma mater and eventually became department chairman. During the 1950s and 1960s, Abu Talib had bent with the prevailing ideological wind, joining the regime-backed political organizations. As an ASU member, Abu Talib came in first place in a 1968 base unit election and thereby became assistant secretary of the university ASU; but his electoral success was a mixed blessing. In the "100 Flowers Blossom" atmosphere engendered by Nasser's March 30 (1968) Program, which aimed at political reform and some element of internal democratization, Abu Talib spoke out against the prevailing ideology of Egyptian socialism. In our interview, he characterized the majority view under Nasser as one holding that Egypt's regime reflected an application of Soviet socialism. He had opposed this, he said, arguing that Egypt should have "a compromise between Muslim values and the social welfare system and democratic socialism found in Scandinavia."[132] He had forwarded these ideas in a book entitled *The Arab Society*[133] in 1965, in which he criticized communism and systems adopting communist ideals. His repeated articulation of these views had brought a clash with Centrists and Leftists, prompting his friends to fear for his well-being and advise him to leave Egypt. Abu Talib went to the University of Beirut in 1969 and stayed there until 1972.

Like so many others with histories of antagonistic relations with Centrists, Abu Talib's credentials and ideological disposition made him a good fit in Sadat's regime. His first meeting of substance with Sadat came when he was nominated vice president of Cairo University in 1973. One day after assuming the university vice-presidency, Abu Talib's office phone rang and he was informed that Sadat wanted to meet him. They met for one to two hours and engaged in a dialogue over many subjects; after this they met at least once per month for about two years. Abu Talib now feels that Sadat was putting him under examination during this period, and that this constituted part of Sadat's search for persons who could elaborate Sadat's thinking and sell Sadat's new programs to the people and the elite. This is one of the reasons Abu Talib was picked to participate in the televised political debates during 1974.

Early in 1975, the year during which Abu Talib was named president of Cairo University, Sadat had asked Abu Talib to write a book providing a political-philosophical basis for a new regime. The product was *Our Socialist Democracy,* a book whose subtitle is "The Ideology of the May Revolution, 1971."[134] In essence, the new book restated the ideas found in Abu Talib's *Arab Society* book, that is, it reflected Abu Talib's belief in socialism (but of a Western European—especially Scandinavian—variety), political democracy, and Islamic values. There is an explicit rejection of both communist and capitalist systems as "incapable of achieving happiness for mankind"[135] and basically incompatible with Arab civilizational values.

In Abu Talib's thinking, the means for achieving the proper balance between capitalism's wanton individualism and communism's shameful disregard for individual rights is to be found in the Arab civilization's values, primary among which is "faith." In his words, "through faith in God Almighty, man absorbs religious teachings which, above all, are social morals targeting individual's perfection physically, psychologically and socially, developing in him feelings of dignity and strength because faith fills him with a sense of eternity, a feeling of affiliation to the group and rids him of pessimism and seclusion."[136] Elsewhere, Abu Talib asserts that "religion is the most important means for achieving social peace."[137] While both Islam and Christianity have a role to play in Islamic society according to Abu Talib, he makes repeated reference to the special role assigned to Islam by Article 2 of the 1971 Constitution as a major source of legislation. "Thus, according to constitutional stipulation, the legislator is committed, in enacting new legislation after 1971, to go back to Islamic Sharia and shun from any regulation that appears contradictory to a given Islamic principle or origin."[138] (N.B. Indeed, in 1975, the Constitutional Court decreed that according to the 1971 constitutional amendment regarding *shari'a* law, all laws contravening the *shari'a* even those already in the books, were void.[139])

In *Our Socialist Democracy,* religious justification is provided for a socialist orientation, a socialism that leaves much room for the right to private property, but guarantees the state's right to override individual rights whenever a serious conflict of interests arises.[140] "[T]he public sector in

Egypt undertakes both important ventures which fall out of the ability of individuals and vital projects for the masses so that the State may ensure selling its products or rendering its services at prices which the masses can afford to pay regardless of the cost price. All this in addition to the strategic projects or those which threaten the State's sovereignty."[141] State economic planning, the maintenance of the public sector, and other forms of state economic intervention are essential to realize greater social harmony by creating greater equality of opportunity (not absolute equality) and a narrowing of income differences.[142] Social classes and class disparities exist in any society, but not in an antagonistic relationship to one another; and it is the state's duty to create conditions that will eliminate class conflict and create social solidarity.

For Abu Talib, the resulting system would be a democratic socialist one. That democratic socialism would be safeguarded by the sovereignty of law, as specified in the 1971 Constitution, which establishes a state of institutions, with a separation and balance of power among the major branches of government, such that no ruler or social group or class will be able to impose its will on the people. "The principle of democratic rule based on the alliance of the people's forces distinguishes our democratic socialism from scientific socialism (Communism), where power is centered in the hands of the proletariat."[143] "Achieving political equilibrium in society requires that no particular category grasps power exclusively and that no certain groups should be excluded from participating in the government. Consequently, sovereignty of all people as the sole source of power should be regarded as unquestionable. This is what is usually taken as: 'The rule of people by people for people,' a modern version of Al-Shoura principle, presenting the basis for government system of Arab civilization*[sic]*."[144]

Rule by the people is to be guaranteed by making the parliamentary body (People's Assembly) the ultimate repository of power, and by guaranteeing fair and open elections within a multiparty environment in which diverse political parties contest parliamentary elections at regularly scheduled intervals. However, Abu Talib noted that, as in keeping with Law 40 of 1977, the regime found it necessary to impose certain conditions aimed at "protecting the democratic experience against rifts and chaos by avoiding an unnecessary multitude of parties that may fragment national unity," as well as to block parties whose values contradict those of the July 1952 and May 1971 revolutions.[145] As Abu Talib put it in our interview, "Sadat's phrase was that he wanted to change everything in Egypt, and that 'the errors of democracy in one generation is not equal to the errors of totalitarianism in one year.' He wanted to open up democratically, but do it gradually."[146] So these [restrictive] conditions were seen as temporary and "ha[d] their equivalent in some states of deeply-rooted democracy which underwent radical changes" like Italy and Germany after the fall of fascism.[147] In essence, Abu Talib's vision was of a gradual transition to multi-party democracy, with a strong role for state activity and ownership in economic matters, and underpinned by a strong commitment to religious values.

When asked to compare himself with other regime thinkers, Abu Talib pegged Rif'at al-Mahgub as an Arab socialist of a leftist tendency—very near to the communists, but not a communist. Abu Talib stated that he is a socialist, but very near to Muslim thinking, like Kemal Abu al-Magd, but slightly less conservative than 'Abd al-'Aziz Kamel when it came to religious issues.[148] His thinking reflects an appreciation for Scandinavian-style social democracy, mixed with the powerful role played by the putatively value-based Christian Democratic parties of Western Europe. It is a mix, however untidy, that undoubtedly comes about as close as anything I could find that matched Sadat's political philosophical outlook at this juncture, which is why I have discussed it at such length. Sadat stated that Abu Talib's book would be the basis for the new politics in Egypt, and he opened a national dialogue about its values.[149]

By late 1978, Abu Talib would get his chance to have a more direct hand in introducing his ideas, as he was made speaker of the People's Assembly, replacing Sayyid Mar'ei. Winter portrays both Abu Talib, as well as another government official, Gamal al-'Uteifi, as cynical spokespersons for the implementation of *shari'a*. He asserts that Abu Talib, as People's Assembly speaker, "successfully thwarted all parliamentary initiatives to pass a resolution for the immediate implementation of the '*shari'a*' by arguing that 'taqnin al-shari'a' (codification of Islamic law) must precede 'tatbiq al-shari'a' (implementation of Islamic law), and that socio-economic conditions in Egypt (widespread poverty) made 'tatbiq' untimely."[150] Winter's assertion begs the question of how sincere Abu Talib, Sadat, 'Uteifi, and others were regarding the *shari'a*'s implementation. Were they cynical, or were they victims of the conundrums of a liberal/Muslim mind? Perhaps the correct conclusion is that these men, especially Sadat and Abu Talib, were torn by such issues and possessed no quick answers or logically compelling solutions to such difficult questions and issues. If so, they differed little from many of their counterparts at home and abroad.

Regardless, it is hard to endorse Winter's cynical viewpoint. As one can clearly see from this cursory examination of Abu Talib's principles, which he firmly embraces, there was much music to Islamists' ears imbedded in the steadfast references to Article 2 of the constitution, which made Islam "a major"—and in 1980 "the principal"—source of legislation. The con-

stitutional door was thus flung wide open to Islamists or others who did
not share the hybrid secular-Muslim sociocultural dispositions or orientations, whether more gradualist, "laid-back" or confused, of the likes of
Sadat or Abu Talib. For the latter, religious faith could yield principal values and means for building a more harmonious society and world. For
many Islamists (and some non-Muslims alike), faith was a sword brandished
to create a more exclusionary polity in which the dominance of their religion alone was guaranteed. And given some Islamists' interpretations of
faith, strife was certain to follow.

Sadat's shift toward a new set of values to underpin his regime had
important consequences on the domestic front. As will be demonstrated
below, this shift produced a rupture within Sadat's government, the media,
and elsewhere. In particular, as Arab nationalists and regime Leftists began
to take umbrage with Sadat's new orientation, they resigned or were
dumped by Sadat.

The Foreign Policy Cleavage Over Dependence on the United States

Another major split in Egypt resulted from Sadat's faith in the U.S. government to resolve the conflict with Israel. Most Arab nations' leaders,
including most Egyptians, were convinced that the pro-Israeli prejudices of
American policymakers left them incapable of delivering a just solution.
Accordingly, Sadat's reliance on the Americans was thought to be foolhardy
at best; and of course, this was a view that was strongly endorsed and reinforced by Soviet bloc representatives who still held great influence in many
Arab capitals. Thus, the further Sadat proceeded down the path toward peace
with Israel without key Arab leaders' approval, the deeper the contradiction
grew between Egyptian nationalist versus Arab nationalist forces in Egypt.[151]

The growth in this contradiction went hand-in-hand with Egypt's separation from the Soviet Union. That policy sprang from Sadat's genuine,
visceral dislike of the Soviets and his ardent desire, expressed to Kissinger,
to dissociate Egypt from the Soviet Union as quickly as possible.[152] The
reversal in relations with the Soviets created yet another rift, however, as
Egyptians inside the regime and beyond debated the wisdom of abandoning their affiliation with the Soviets and the world socialist camp in favor
of warmer relations with the United States and other capitalist nations.

By spring 1975, Sadat's foreign policy critics were crowing. More than
one year of step-by-step diplomacy by Kissinger had ground to an unsuc-
cessful halt. Kissinger had found it impossible to move the Israelis off their
position of suing for peace with Egypt by retaining control of the Sinai's
strategic Mitla and Gidi passes, or to shake their demand to retain control

of Syria's Golan Heights.[153] Ambassador Eilts recalls that "Kissinger's failure represented at the time a mini-crisis in Sadat's policy of relying upon
the U.S. He [Sadat] was bitterly disappointed and so was Kissinger, who
blamed it on the Israelis. It led to the U.S. administration's reassessment
[March 24] of its Middle East policy, which, while eventually meaningless,
did allow Sadat to get through a difficult period."[154]

Sadat's 1975 Cabinet Shift

Doubts about the new foreign policy orientation and *infitah* accentuated
internal regime divisions, and drove a wedge in Sadat's cabinet. The cabinet in place at the beginning of 1975 was a hodge-podge of individuals
distinguished by a combination of policymaking experience and strong
ideological convictions that ran the gamut from Marxism to Muslim
Brotherhood sympathies. Men like Isma'il Sabri 'Abdullah and Yehiya al-
Gamal were among the most prominent Marxists and Arab nationalists not
just in Egypt, but in the Arab world. Prime Minister 'Abd al-'Aziz Higazi
had considerable, high-profile experience dating back to the Nasser
regime. Now, each of these actors, from their own political-economic or
ideological perspectives, began to have serious reservations about Sadat's
new policies. Their one great common fear—one shared by some "statist"
technocrats as well—was that Sadat might allow the United States to lead
Egypt down the path of a separate peace with Israel, a development that
might irreparably destroy Arab solidarity. The leftists also shared a fondness
for the ASU, which Sadat was seeking to dismantle.

Sadat knew where he was heading, and he couldn't countenance the
presence of individuals whom he knew would not support his policies and
might embarrass him. So, in April 1975, he called for a change in government personnel to remove those most likely to prove obstructionist. Yehiya
al-Gamal had sensed an impending change. He told Higazi that their days
were numbered. Al-Gamal would resign because his pan-Arab stand would
not permit him to remain; Higazi would be ousted because he was too pro-
public sector; Isma'il Sabri 'Abdullah would be dumped because he was too
pro-planning and pro-public sector, and so on. "Kissinger and the U.S. role
had much to do with this. The Saudis may have had a role, too, but if so,
it's not well known," said al-Gamal.[155]

Although his assertion about a U.S. role is dubious, especially insofar as
any direct role is concerned, all of al-Gamal's predicted changes came to
pass. Higazi was replaced by Mamduh Salem as prime minister. Tahsin
Bashir goes so far as to claim that Salem had had a hand plotting demon-

strations against Higazi's government while Higazi was prime minister. According to Bashir, Sadat had phoned Higazi following the demonstrations to tell him "this policy is not clicking. You have to make changes. At the same time, Sadat had me [Bashir] write a paper saying we need radical changes: real *infitah,* real businesses!"[156]

Vice President Hussein al-Shaf'ei was also dumped in April. Sadat and Shaf'ei had never gotten along well with one another; his departure left Sadat as the only remaining high official with roots in the July 1952 revolution. Shaf'ei was replaced, as noted earlier, by the younger, politically inexperienced Air Force commander, Husni Mubarak.

Problems relating to *infitah* clearly offered one rationale for the cabinet shuffle. But Sadat was also preparing the way for foreign policy shifts of special importance. These came on September 4, 1975, when the Egyptians signed a second Sinai Disengagement Agreement, an agreement including a provision that there would be no recourse to force to resolve differences with Israel. Sinai II brought a storm of protest and condemnation from the capitals of the radical Arabs; namely, Syria, Iraq, Algeria, and Libya, not to mention the Palestinians. It was here that Sadat's grandiose visions and bold motions began to distance him from his more circumspect Arab cousins and compatriots. Ahmed Beha al-Din recalls that sometime around the signing of Sinai II, Sadat opined: "Hafez al-Assad is haggling with Kissinger; Assad's acting like a Syrian grocer, bargaining over the cost of a piece of cheese. I'm making a disengagement plan with the United States, not with Israel. This is a political issue, not a military geostrategic issue."[157]

The negative reaction and breach in Arab ranks was matched by a split on Egypt's domestic front, where elites of different ideological backgrounds shared "radical" Arabs' concerns. Many of these elites had equally serious reservations about Sadat's *infitah.* Lutfi al-Kholi asserted that, "All left and democratic forces cut completely with Sadat in 1975 [after the second disengagement agreement] due to his anti-democratic politics, *infitah,* and step-by-step diplomacy. We told him this would lead to a separate peace; we're now 100 percent certain he was on the CIA payroll, as later proven by the *Washington Post* and *International Herald Tribune* articles."[158] (These are the same articles discussed elsewhere.)

Minister of Cabinet Affairs Yehiya al-Gamal saw Sinai II as a watershed. "In early 1975, all members of Sadat's cabinet except two were former ASU Vanguard members, including the prime minister and vice-prime minister. After 1975, there was a new type of people; they were technicians who say yes. Sadat wanted his own men, not people who had made their mark under Nasser like Gamal, Sidqi, and Higazi. There was greater recruitment from those close to the Muslim Brothers."[159] Isma'il Sabri

'Abdullah echoed this sentiment: "Higazi was dumped, and Salem came in. I sensed a radical change because 'Uthman Ahmed 'Uthman and Hamed Mahmud were hovering around Sadat."[160] Both 'Uthman and Mahmud held Islamist sympathies; Higazi acquired such sympathies at a later date.

The appointment of Salem as prime minister, given his lifelong career in the police, signaled Sadat's willingness to steel his regime against the increasing political turbulence. In appointing 'Uthman as minister of housing and reconstruction, Sadat revealed his confidence in 'Uthman's ability to address one of Egypt's most pressing problems, but he also placed the fox in charge of a lucrative hen house.[161] But as with the appointment of Muhammad Hamed Mahmud as minister of state for local government and popular organizations, 'Uthman's appointment also indicated a rightward shift. Mahmud replaced one Fuad Muhi al-Din, who at this time was still seen as committed to socialism. Finally, Kemal Abu al-Magd shifted posts to become minister of information. Both 'Uthman and Abu al-Magd's presence gave the cabinet a stronger Islamist flavor.

Closer examination of the new cabinet's personnel indicates that al-Gamal, Sabri 'Abdullah, and Bashir slightly overstate the case for a radical cabinet change. Many of Salem's new ministerial recruits were still committed socialists and public sector defenders. For example, Sabri 'Abdullah's replacement as planning minister, Ibrahim Hilmi 'Abd al-Rahman, had extensive knowledge of economic planning in socialist India, and was a major figure behind the National Planning Institute's creation in 1960, as well as the first five-year plan of 1965. He was perhaps closer to Nasserite Rightists like Zakariyya Muhi al-Din than the Centrists, but he was still a socialist and public sector advocate.[162] His successor in the March 1976 cabinet, Muhammad Mahmud al-Imam, was also an avowed socialist and public sector defender. Al-Imam recalled how an influential professor, "Zaki Shaf'ei [one of the first deans of Cairo University Economics Faculty] had said that no economist working in lesser developed countries can avoid being a socialist. As an econometrician and a planner, I [al-Imam] became a socialist."[163]

Zaki Shaf'ei was himself the minister for economy and economic cooperation in Sadat's April 1975 cabinet, and retained that post in the 1976 cabinet. 'Abd al-Latif Bultia, whom some described as a "Moscow man," retained control of the Manpower (Labor) and Training Ministry during the mid-1970s. Bultia may have been more "chameleon" than committed socialist; Posusney has noted how he deftly abandoned his patron, 'Ali Sabri, to side with Sadat in May 1971.[164] Still, Bultia was a staunch defender of the public sector and many socialist principles.

Only with the formation of the November 1976 and October 1977 cabinets was there a clearer shift toward technocratic ministers less attached to socialism. In November 1976, 'Abd al-Mun'im al-Qaisuni was brought in as deputy prime minister for financial and economic affairs, with his Rightist technocratic friends, Hamed 'Abd al-Latif al-Sayeh and Muhammad Hamed Muhmud placed as minister of the economy and economic cooperation and minister of finance, respectively. Imam and Bultia retained the planning and manpower ministries until October 1977. Then Qaisuni added control of Planning to his other posts; and Sa'd Muhammad Ahmed, whom Sadat had found a cooperative ETUF president, replaced Bultia. In other words, it wasn't until October 1977 that all key economic posts in the government were occupied by pro-private sector individuals, and even they believed in the need to retain a strong public sector.

Thus, just as Nasser had attempted to build socialism without the most committed socialists at the helm, Sadat preached economic liberalization but was slow to place staunchly pro-capitalist elements in charge. The result was confusion and frustration on both ends. Muhammad Mahmud al-Imam noted, "I couldn't stay long because there was no real belief in planning, especially long-range planning. There was only belief in planning as a means of obtaining assistance."[165] Yet there Imam had remained, a committed socialist presiding over the Ministry of Planning for 11 months more than two and one-half years after the onset of *infitah*.

With these caveats in mind, the April 1975 cabinet still represented the beginning of a significant, qualitative shift. Even if some of the new ministers were pro-socialist, they were men of lesser stature and therefore weaker defenders of the public sector status quo than their predecessors. The cabinet changes helped pave the way for reform of the public sector. For example, the July 28, 1975 passage of Law 111 abolished the General Organization for Industrialization, which had overseen state industrial activity. The new law made public sector companies more autonomous, enabling their managers to make joint ventures arrangements with foreign firms, as well as "hire and fire" with greater ease.

The April 1975 cabinet shift was a watershed. The personnel changes, along with Sadat's new economic and foreign policies, cost Sadat important support from representatives of ideological currents——leftists and Arab nationalists—who had been assisting the regime.

Sadat's Postwar Foreign Policy Shift

During 1974 and the first half of 1975, several events destabilized the regional and international environment. First, in Israel, postwar elections held on December 31, 1973 brought a weakening of Prime Minister Golda Meir's Knesset majority and a strengthening of the hawkish Likkud party.

Israeli voters showed that Egyptians were not the only ones impressed by the October War canal crossing. Political fallout from the war compelled Meir to resign in March 1974, and Moshe Dayan lost his post as defense minister. They were replaced by Yitzhak Rabin and Shimon Peres, respectively.

Second, although the Arab oil embargo was lifted in March 1974, oil prices remained at their new, high rates. Again, the world economy was heavily affected by the massive shift in resources to oil-producing nations, and governments around the world went groping for answers to the attendant fiscal crisis.

Third, in the United States, the Watergate scandal came to a head in the summer of 1974, forcing Nixon's resignation in August. Nixon was replaced by President Gerald Ford, who had been a loyal supporter of Israel as a Congressman, but had little foreign policy experience. Ford retained the services of Kissinger as secretary of state.

Fourth, on October 28, 1974, at an Arab summit meeting in Rabat, the participants unanimously voted to recognize the Palestine Liberation Organization (PLO) as the sole legitimate representative of the Palestinian people. Given Israel's adamant rejection of the PLO, the vote brought further complications to any effort to resolve the conflict. In addition, the Syrians could see that the Israelis were trying to take Egypt out of the Arab fold, and began speaking out against such a likelihood.

Fifth, on March 25, 1975, Saudi Arabia's King Feisal was assassinated by a deranged relative. Feisal had long been supportive of Sadat and Western interests in general; he had told Kissinger that "he trusted me to proceed as I judged best even though he would have preferred another approach."[166] Now questions were posed as to the sentiments of his successor, King Khalid, who assumed the leadership of a country that in the two preceding years had metamorphosed into a financial superpower.

Not surprisingly, these conditions seriously hampered American efforts to promote peace in the Middle East. Indeed, as noted earlier, for 14 months following his Sinai I success, Kissinger's step-by-step diplomacy foundered, bringing the Ford administration to the aforementioned suspension of negotiations and "reassessment" of U.S. policy in the region. Kissinger could not convince the Israelis that it was in their interest to withdraw beyond the Sinai's strategic passes short of a promise of non-belligerency by the Egyptians, which Sadat was unwilling to offer. In a March 28 National Security Council (NSC) meeting, Ford expressed his frustration over the Israelis' lack of flexibility, and added, "I have never been so disappointed as to see people I respect unable to see that we are trying to do something for their interest as well as for our own. But in the final analysis our commitment is to the United States."[167]

At the same NSC meeting, the outlook was gloomy. CIA director William Colby spoke of the increased chance of war, noting that:

> the armies of Egypt, Syria and Israel are all in a state of alert and there is a substantial chance of hostilities breaking out either deliberately or by accident at any time in the next few weeks. If it does not happen quickly, then there will be negotiations at Geneva and if there is no progress there by early summer there are high odds that Egypt and Syria will launch a coordinated attack and even higher odds that Israel will attack first. Israel probably sees war as inevitable and may decide to hit now. Comparatively, they are well off. They can probably beat Egypt and Syria both in 7-10 days.[168]

Kissinger, too, predicted renewed warfare within one year or less in the absence of diplomatic progress. He also expressed fears that the Soviets would not permit the Arabs to suffer yet another humiliating defeat. "We have an interest in the survival of Israel but we also have broader interests with the Western Europeans and Japan and the Arabs. If there is another war we run the risk of antagonizing the Arabs definitively and of pushing them into the arms of the Soviets. We will also run the risk of a direct confrontation with the Soviets."[169]

Vice President Rockefeller commented, "Think what another war would mean for us. The OPEC countries would stick together in an oil embargo, particularly since the Latin Americans are already unhappy with us. This could cause paralysis of the East Coast and the United States."[170]

Top American officials' assessments remained bleak at the May 15, 1975 NSC meeting.[171] Kissinger now felt the Egyptians and Israelis were so dug into their publicly-expressed conditions that negotiating a second interim agreement would be extremely difficult: "Israel would demand non-belligerency and this is impossible for Egypt except in the context of total or almost total withdrawal."[172] He also thought Prince Fahd, now calling the shots in Saudi Arabia for King Khalid, was less likely to support a separate Egyptian negotiation.[173]

The Americans had little hope that a Geneva conference, co-sponsored by the Soviet Union, would advance the peace process, so they prayed that flexibility on the part of principal decision-makers would allow them to carry on their step-by-step diplomacy. Against the backdrop of the aforementioned regional and international conditions, Sadat provided Kissinger and the Americans that flexibility. Sadat met Ford in Sadat's favorite foreign country, Austria, on June 1-2, and Sadat displayed interest in a second interim agreement. When the Israelis finally concluded that it was in their interest to follow up on American diplomatic efforts in late June, Sadat proved willing to soften his own position to facilitate that process.[174] Most importantly, he granted the Israelis non-belligerency in exchange for retrieval of the strategic passes and the Sinai oil fields. These compromises, and others worked out by Kissinger during the summer of 1975, led to the September 4, 1975 signing of the Sinai II disengagement agreement in Geneva. One can only imagine what chaos the world might have witnessed if this agreement had not been struck.

Sinai II, with its heavy reliance upon American diplomats, helped drive a stake in Egyptian-Soviet relations. In a February 1976 speech before the Soviet Union Communist Party's General Congress, Brezhnev spoke of the Indian government's efforts to maintain sound relations with the Soviet Union, but when he spoke of Egypt, he spoke only of the Egyptian people and not the Egyptian government. No one missed the slight. On March 14, 1976, Egypt's People's Assembly voted at Sadat's behest to abrogate the 1971 friendship treaty and withdraw naval port facilities granted to the Soviets. This marked Egypt's formal departure from its position of international socialist, anti-Western imperialist solidarity being preached just four years earlier by Sadat himself. And as Hafez Isma'il said, "This was the beginning of an open clash."[175]

In October 1975, Sadat made the first official visit by an Egyptian president to the United States. His request for economic and military aid begot a favorable response from the U.S. administration, but did not bear significant fruit until after Sadat's March 1976 abrogation of the friendship treaty with the Soviet Union.[176] Resumed in 1975, U.S. economic assistance totaled $371.9 million, of which $110.7 was in PL 480 food aid.[177] But 1976 brought an impressive build-up of the U.S. Agency for International Development (AID) mission in Egypt, and U.S. economic assistance reached $986.6 million, of which just $191.7 million was for PL 480 aid.[178]

The major transformations of 1975 and early 1976 presaged Sadat's more serious attempt, discussed below, at political liberalization in 1976. In contrast to Yehiya al-Gamal's ruminations, the Americans appear to have steered clear of Sadat's domestic political reforms. The U.S. Ambassador to Egypt, Hermann Eilts, swears that at no time did he or anyone else tell Sadat or others that they had to democratize Egyptian politics; this included communications during the Carter years.[179] Abu Talib avers that there was "no influence from either the U.S. or the Gulf in the 1974–1975 changes. Sadat simply kept stating that "to open the door economically without democracy would bring nothing;" and that "democracy without *infitah* would be like a barking of dogs. The two must go together, hand-in-hand."[180] And so Sadat had convinced himself, at least, that Westerners would react most favorably if he took measures to democratize Egypt.

In sum, 1975 was an important turning point in Egyptian history. Sadat was trying to build a new Egypt, one with a more liberal political-economy and more peaceful relations with Israel. To promote these changes, he boosted supportive voices in the media, changed his cabinet, and sought greater help from major Western bloc countries, especially the United States. He also showed willingness to weather storms of protest and violent reactions by radical Islamists, Marxists, Nasserites, and Arab nationalists at home and abroad. Just five years earlier, he had bowed before Nasser's statue; now there was no mistaking the difference between Nasser's and Sadat's paths. Whether or not he could sustain his liberalization in the face of such domestic and foreign opposition remained to be seen.

Sadat's "Controlled" Liberalization

"I wish I had a button. I push it, and the Egyptian people wake up; I push it again, and they go to sleep." Nasser[181]

Nasser had maintained a closed, tightly controlled society. By comparison, Sadat was less desirous of micromanaging the nation's affairs, and although he retained his own authoritarian habits, he consciously sought to liberalize the political economy. Still, somehow, he and his close advisers believed they could control the pace of this liberalization, and that they would liberalize gradually. But in following this course of action, they exposed their countrymen to the previously discussed panoply of societal rifts, or "contradictions."

It is fascinating to examine Sadat's efforts to steer Egypt down this new path. To do so, it is essential to study not only how he sought to manage that transition, but how his political rivals responded to Egypt's new political, economic, and sociocultural realities: How did they create or react to new intra-state or state-society tensions? How did they seek to mobilize old and new constituencies? And what countermeasures did they face from the Sadat regime? To pursue this line of inquiry, I shall begin by examining the turn of events in the press, which served as one of the major arenas of political struggle in the post-October War period.

Controlled Liberalization of the Press

The freedom of the press that Sadat accorded did not mean freedom to criticize him. He was very unusual on this. He was so proud of the liberalization measures that he undertook, including greater freedom of the press, but seemed to assume that those who took advantage of such new freedom would use them to criticize government, but not him. At times, despite his cleverness, he could be a bit naïve. The thought seems never to have entered his head that people would criticize him." Ambassador Hermann Eilts[182]

Expanding the Search for Regime Philosophers

If Sadat's economic objective was to diversify Egypt's development options by attracting Arab petrodollars and Western capital and technology, he needed to find individuals able and willing to promote such ideas on the domestic front. Just as Sadat felt it important to enlist Abu Talib's assistance to draft a new regime political philosophy, he also found it desirable to alter the print media's ideological mix to reinforce fellow Rightists' power and influence. Just as Nasser had recruited independent Marxists and communists to promote socialism in the early 1960s, Sadat now introduced Rightists to herald changes that were leading Egypt away from what most viewed as the Nasserite mold.

For starters, Sadat needed voices to respond to the increasingly hostile statements by Syrians and other radical Arabs, including Egyptians living abroad. Harsh criticism began with those who accused Egypt of having damaged the overall 1973 war effort by failing to push on for a more significant victory in the early days of the war;[183] and it became more shrill with Sadat's signing of Sinai I and especially Sinai II. Thus, Sadat needed writers to project glorious images of the 1973 war's outcome in the Egyptian media and defend his postwar foreign policies.

One significant outgrowth of Egyptian–Arab discord was the development of an "Egypt first" attitude among Egyptian officials, a line pushed with considerable vigor in the media by Rightists and initially many national Leftists as well.[184] This "Egypt first" attitude developed further, and at the expense of the Arab unity ideal, as Sadat embraced the U.S.–chaperoned negotiations with Israel that led to Sinai I on January 18, 1974. That agreement caused considerable friction at home as it had abroad, most noticeably producing the removal of Heikal from his *al-Ahram* fiefdom on February 1, 1974. Heikal had been among those questioning why Egypt had not pressed its military advantage in the 1973 war. Now Heikal felt Sadat was taking Egypt too far out on the American limb.[185] Just one day prior to his removal, Heikal had written yet another article casting doubt on American motives in the Middle East, as well as Kissinger's ability to promote lasting peace.[186]

An Injection of Rightist Journalists

In anticipation of difficulties, Sadat gave the print media a strong injection of Rightist blood. In early January 1974, after continued urging by his journalist friend Musa Sabri, Sadat saw to the release of Mustafa Amin from prison. As noted earlier, Amin had been sentenced under Nasser for pro-American espionage. At the same time, Mustafa's twin, 'Ali, returned to Egypt after nine years of self-imposed exile. When Heikal was relieved of his duties at *al-Ahram,* 'Ali Amin was named editor while 'Abd al-Qader Hatem was appointed president of the board of directors. One will recall that Hatem was never much of a socialist, and had fallen out of Nasser's good graces by the late 1960s, much to Heikal's content. By February 27, Mustafa Amin was reinstated as editor of *al-Akhbar,* and the new government, announced on April 26, 1975, had as its Minister of Information Ahmed Kemal Abu al-Magd (the former MB member and YO leader).

Mustafa Bahgat Badawi, a former Free Officer known for his religiosity, had been made editor of *al-Gumhurriyya,* the third major, state-owned paper, on May 22, 1971. He also retained the post of *al-Gumhurriyya's* chairman of the board, which he had acquired in 1965. He was replaced by 'Abd al-Mun'im al-Sawi as chairman on March 13, 1975, with Muhsin Muhammad named editor on the same day. Both men were safely in Sadat's camp. One distinguished political observer described Muhsin Muhammad as "a young Musa Sabri; a professional journalist who considers journalism to be like shoemaking."[187] The observer took this metaphor from a comment made by Musa Sabri himself. It seems that one day he had crossed paths with Sabri, who was momentarily quite angry at Sadat for something he had done. When Sabri's column appeared the next day and was completely positive toward Sadat, the observer phoned him to ask what was up. Sabri answered, "I'm a shoemaker. On writing, I am a shoemaker"; that is, Sadat would order the article's size and shape, and Sabri would produce it.[188]

Sadat tried to combat any rancor caused by Heikal's removal with a February 9, 1974 announcement of an end to press censorship. Although Hatem followed up with a February 10 warning to journalists that they would still be held responsible for what they wrote, the end-to-censorship announcement had an easily recognizable impact on the print media's content. Many journalists shed the caution and inhibition that marked their earlier writing. Rightist journalists like Musa Sabri, Anis Mansur, Salah Gaudet, Sa'id Sunbul, Amina al-Sa'id, Galal al-Din Hamamsi, Ibrahim Salih, and 'Ali Hamdi al-Gamal, with the Amin brothers leading the pack, were among the journalists most aggressively exploiting this press liberalization to mount a campaign against the Nasser regime's police-state characteristics, socialism, or the way socialism had been applied.[189] Several of the new press leaders, like Galal al-Din Hamamsi, 'Ali Hamdi al-Gamal and Amina al-Sa'id hailed from prominent families, and they were highly critical of Nasser's socialism.[190] Salah Gaudet, editor of *al-Musawwar,* said of

Nasser's regime, "No one should deny its achievements . . . but neither should they forget its torture and oppression. It had created centres of power whose evil acts spread everywhere and culminated in the 1967 war."[191] Ahmed Hammadi asserted that the Nasser regime's property sequestrations were in part the cause of the 1967 defeat, because they left us "torn apart and living like strangers in our homeland."[192] At the same time Sa'd Fakhri 'Abd al-Nur wrote in *al-Ahram* on March 9 that the seizure of property, which affected 15,000 people, was "a barbarian act belonging to the Middle Ages and a weapon of material and moral terrorism."[193] Following quickly on the heels of the announced end to press censorship was the March 24, 1974 announcement of a lifting of film censorship. Movies like *The Sparrow* and *The Night Visitors* ensued, both of which were hugely popular cinematic repudiations of Nasser-era regime excesses.[194] A formal lifting of censorship on the foreign press came in the fall of 1974,[195] but had Egypt's media been freed just to attack Nasser?

That Heikal's removal coincided with the beginning of this liberalization period raises some obvious questions as to just how liberal Sadat's experiment truly was. Prominent leftist voices were clearly silenced. For example, Hussein 'Abd al-Razzeq was transferred to *Akhbar al-Yom* in March 1975, but given no permission to write,[196] and there were occasional seizures of domestic and foreign newspapers due to threatening articles. Yet, even in the estimation of self-described anti-Sadat journalists, the period from 1974 to 1976 was one of relatively open debate and freedom of expression within the confines of a basically state-owned press.[197]

Sadat allegedly communicated strong, personal objections to Amin for his writing in lurid detail of the torture practiced in "Nasser's prisons"; he was, reportedly, put off by the de-Nasserization crusade in the press because he had been, after all, a Nasser regime member.[198] But no matter how genuine Sadat's objections, he did not stop Amin or others from attacking Nasser's record, and his own Rightist orientation was initially abetted by Rightists' and liberals' books and articles.

Islamist writers were also beneficiaries of the print media's liberalization. Articles by Islamic authorities appeared with greater frequency in newspapers and magazines—particularly articles that assisted the regime through their criticism of the socialist practices of the past and attacks on Marxists and Nasserites.[199] In some respects, these articles were priming the pump for the reemergence of bona fide Islamists, including Muslim Brothers, in the media. But by general consensus among print media types, there were few prominent Islamist journalists in the Egyptian press in the 1970s.

On balance, Sadat engaged in a selective liberalization of the press. So long as articles to his disliking did not affect his interests directly, he remained tolerant of a more liberal exchange of views, especially on a theoretical plane. But once certain journalists began to test the limits of their freedom and criticize specific government policies, or expose regime corruption, they discovered Sadat and his watchdogs to be as quick on the censorship trigger as their predecessors, albeit now from a different, more Rightist, ideological viewpoint. Some journalists also earned regime opprobrium by penning vicious, inaccurate articles, or because they were seen as motivated by personal vendettas. Kemal Abu al-Magd labeled some journalists as "rotten people," given to misrepresentation of other political actors; for example, as with Ibrahim al-Wardani's attacks on Mustafa Bahgat Badawi and labeling him a Leftist.[200] Abu al-Magd also noted that he carefully reviewed the file on Mustafa Amin's espionage case and came away convinced that the charge had been sound. When both Abu al-Magd and Sadat initially refused to grant Amin a pardon, the Amins had orchestrated a press attack on Abu al-Magd.[201]

As Mustafa Amin also intoned, however, "Freedom of the press, to Sadat, did not mean freedom to criticize him."[202] And Sadat was not alone among those protected by the regime. Indications of Sadat and other regime officials' sensitivity to criticism appeared in both 1975 and 1976. In March 1975, prior to the signing of Sinai II, the directorships of the major daily newspapers were altered to put pro-peace writers in place.[203] Again, Muhsin Muhammad was appointed editor of *al-Gumhurriyya,* while Ihsan 'Abd al-Quddus and a Sadat-reformed 'Ali Hamdi al-Gamal were appointed chairman of the board and editor in chief of *al-Ahram* respectively. Other changes in the staffs of some publishing houses occurred, as did more frequent seizures of various publications, usually those written by Leftist and Marxist critics of the disengagement agreement.[204]

A New Supreme Press Council; and Additional Adjustments

In May 1975, a new Supreme Press Council was formed, headed by the ASU first secretary. The council's creation represented one small move to restore regime control over the press establishment to a level more closely approximating that enjoyed by the Nasser regime. Its creation also showed that the regime was growing increasingly skittish about its media liberalization policy. The removal of Information Minister Kemal Abu al-Magd in August and Heikal's house arrest in November 1975 were further indications of regime uncertainties.[205]

Even more wide-sweeping were changes undertaken in press directorships in March 1976; these were prompted by a well-oiled press campaign against corruption in high government positions, with "fat cats" Ashraf

Marwan and 'Uthman Ahmed 'Uthman two of the most prominent targets.[206] Some journalists had even accused Sadat of having violated the constitution.[207] Sadat was increasingly angered by what he viewed as the press's growing "negativism" and was ill at ease in the "liberalized" press environment that he had created. Even more alarmed were those whom Mustafa Amin referred to as the "thieves of the city" (of Cairo) who were now openly accused of high level corruption or "fat cat" profiteering under the regime's new economic policies.[208] The well-known journalist, Galal al-Din al-Hamamsi, for example, returned to the press to pen many scathing anti-corruption pieces during 1974-75. Hamamsi, arrested for his role in printing the famous "black book" exposing Wafdist corruption in the pre-1952 era, had met Sadat in jail in the 1940s and became a very close friend. However, this friendship did not override Hamamsi's independent-mindedness and courageous spirit, and he launched a vigorous, few-holds-barred attack on Sadat regime corruption. According to Amin, the "fat cats" then brought much pressure to bear on Sadat to muzzle the press rather than allow critics to undermine the new course charted by the regime.[209] At *Akhbar al-Yom,* Sadat changed the administrative structure, removing al-Hamamsi from his editorship. He then brought in Musa Sabri as editor in chief, enabling Sabri to censor or distort embarrassing anti-corruption pieces by Hamamsi and others.[210]

These pressures, combined with Sadat's own desire to push ahead with economic liberalization and his pursuit of peace through U.S. diplomacy, apparently convinced Sadat of the need to draw the reins of the press even more tightly. Sadat's decision was self-motivated; Ambassador Eilts wrote that "we *never* asked Sadat to rein in the press."[211] These were changes he had already been contemplating, attested Kemal Abu al-Magd, who as minister of information had personally witnessed Sadat's careful interviewing of all the prospective editors in chief.[212] In March 1976, Yusuf al-Seba'i replaced Ihsan 'Abd al-Quddus as chairman of the board at *al-Ahram,* Musa Sabri replaced 'Ali Amin as chairman of the board of the al-Akhbar publishing house, Amina al-Sa'id took the place of Fikri Abaza as chairman of the board of Dar al-Hilal publishing house, and Anis Mansur, editor of *Akher Sa'a,* became board chairman of the Dar al-Ma'arif publishing house, as well as editor of the new *October* magazine. (When Sadat appointed Musa Sabri to head *al-Akhbar,* Anis Mansur refused to work under him, so he asked to go to *al-Ahram.* A short time later, Sadat made Mansur chairman of Dar al-Ma'arif.) Mamduh Rida, former editor of *al-Gumhurriyya,* replaced Muhammad Subeih as chairman of the board of al-Ta'awun publishing house. 'Abd al-Hamid 'Abd al-Ghani, a Rightist, took Mustafa Amin's place as editor in chief of *Akhbar al-Yom,* while 'Ali Hamdi al-Gamal remained editor of *al-Ahram* and was appointed deputy chairman of the board of that newspaper. Both of the Amin brothers retained jobs as staff writers in the al-Akhbar establishment, although 'Ali Amin died in April 1976.[213]

Within this congeries, the two most prominent journalists, Sadat's two main writers, were Musa Sabri and Anis Mansur. Sabri's close relationship with Sadat has already been detailed. As for Mansur, he too came out of the Amins' stable of writers. A highly prolific, well-read polyglot and professor of literature at Cairo University, Mansur had been infuriated by the 1961 press nationalizations. His scathing, sarcastic criticism of that event in a 1961 article earned him Nasser's opprobrium, causing him to lose his journalistic and professorial jobs for a two-year period. Mansur met Sadat in an elevator at Akhbar al-Yom in early 1970, and Sadat had recruited him to write a literary page. With the intellect and inclination to serve Sadat well, Sadat propelled Mansur's career upward by appointing him to crucial press posts and, in essence, making him one of the leading regime voices by naming him editor in chief of the new *October* magazine. From 1976 until Sadat's death, Mansur was Sadat's most important journalist. His contact with Sadat was tight; they met two to three times per week for lengthy, walking discussions, and spoke many times per day.[214] Mansur became one of Sadat's major speechwriters; he also read books and summarized them and wrote briefs on political figures at Sadat's behest.[215]

At first sight, the aforementioned changes appear rather confusing, with Rightist elements being brought in to replace, by and large, fellow Rightists. In part, this massive transformation of the press directorship must be seen in terms of a clientelistic logic—that is, individuals installed as the new press directorate were to be seen, and to perceive themselves, as beholden to Sadat for their lofty appointments. As many Egyptians explained it, people like Anis Mansur, Muhsin Muhammad, and Ibrahim Nafi'a came from families of more modest means and were less well-known by the public. Accordingly, having acquired positions of prestige, they were more predisposed to unflinchingly serve regime interests so as not to jeopardize those positions. One cannot fail to notice the analogy with Yehiya al-Gamal's characterization of early- versus late-1975 cabinet members.

In contrast, those who were removed from their positions, although ideologically close to Sadat, were almost all individuals of such prestige and stature that they could dare to voice greater criticism of the regime. Also, many of these individuals now believed the time for opening up the political system had arrived and openly called for greater liberalization. They no longer fit the Nasserite regime-determined Rightist label.[216] Others were lifelong liberal democrats. Both groups had joined hands; they disapproved of many of Sadat's major policy orientations, Sadat's continued control of the press, and/or the pace of his reforms, and they embarrassed Sadat by constantly reminding him of how far he was falling short of his own promises of greater democracy and freedom of enterprise.

Given the dangerously unstable, jumbled political–economic situation of the mid-1970s, this was a state of affairs Sadat was no longer willing to abide. With "his own" Rightists in command of the press, he could expect in-house censorship that would spare him the embarrassments that derived from his earlier press liberalization. Ideologically diverse writers maintained their posts in the print media, but still had to watch what they wrote about the regime, its policies, and, especially, Sadat.

Finally, to offset whatever loss of support Sadat incurred by these changes, he curried favor from an altogether different constituency. In mid-June 1976, Muslim Brothers 'Umar Tilmesani, Salih al-'Ishmawi, and others were granted permission to resume publication of the weekly *al-Da'wa* magazine. Not long thereafter, other Brotherhood publications appeared, such as *al-I'tisam* and *al-Mukhtar al-Islami*. These publications all played their own role in denigrating Nasser's regime and heralding Sadat's liberalization, but they also served as new instruments trumpeting the return of the Islamists and propagating their beliefs. It is very safe to assume that 'Uthman Ahmed 'Uthman, who had had a close relationship with Hassan al-'Ishmawi, was very supportive of this development.

The Lawyers' Syndicate

Significantly liberated from the tight ASU control that had marked elections in the late 1960s, and with Barad'ei as syndicate chief, rival political currents were able to reassert themselves in the early 1970s. When ASU membership for syndicate members became voluntary in May 1975, the syndicate council postponed its elections from June until November to give non-ASU types a chance to compete. Wafdists continued to prosper under liberalization. They helped Barad'ei become reelected naqib in 1975, again defeating Khawaga, despite Khawaga's support from the regime. In general, council representation was consistently more diverse on the bar council than on the relatively polarized Journalists' Syndicate. Although here, as elsewhere, the regime succeeded in gaining a significant foothold, with the number of Sadatists increasing from zero in 1971 to four in 1975.

Table 4: Lawyers' Syndicate Council Elections*

Year of Election	1971	1975	1979
Partisan Identity			
Indep. Right	1	1	1
Wafdist	7	7	7
Right–Sadatist		4	4
Center–Nasser	1	1	
Leftist	1	1	1
Nat'l Ind. Left			
Chameleons	5	4	2
Professional synd.	3		
Coptic	1	1	1
Islamist (MB)	1	1	4
None			
Unknown			
TOTAL	20	20	20

Law 61 (1969) changed the syndicate's elections schedule to one election every four years instead of one every two years.

Dismantling the ASU

> Sadat was anxious to have the open door policy work, and in his mind the political infitah *was* directly related to and a necessary adjunct of getting the open door policy to "take off." Sayyid Mar'ei[217]

Sadat's immediate post-war popularity emboldened him to proceed with an incremental liberalization of politics alongside his economic opening. The April 1974 October Paper described the ASU as a "house of contradictions," suggesting that something had to be done to put the political system in order.[218] In an interview with 'Ali Amin, Sadat specifically stated that Egypt was not yet ready for a multiparty system, but that the ASU's decentralization was necessary and under review.[219] In August, an official "Paper on the Development of the Arab Socialist Union" was published in which several changes in the ASU were proposed.[220] It called for dropping ASU membership as a prerequisite for election to other organizations (e.g., syndicate councils), but recommended that the ASU remain the sole political organization. The paper also discussed the notion that special *minabir* might be set up inside the ASU to represent rival interests, echoing an idea presented by *al-Katib's* editor in 1972.[221]

Debate over the ASU's Future

A special discussion group was formed in the People's Assembly to consider the ASU's fate in early September. Some voices called for a return to a multiparty system, repeating arguments found in the press.[222] But on September 9, 1974, Speaker of the Assembly Hafez Badawi closed debate, declaring that a return to a multiparty system was impractical before termination of the state of war with Israel. Leaving the door cracked open, he added that should a multiparty system be allowed, there should be no encroachment on the ASU-inspired rule that guaranteed 50 percent of the assembly's seats to workers and peasants.[223]

As might be expected, clear indications that regime officials were publicly countenancing important modifications in the ASU's structure stimulated enormous debate over what political organization(s) should replace it. Due to press liberalization, representatives of nearly every ideological grouping—including long-silenced voices—joined this debate.[224] Only the perspectives of newly emerging radical Islamists and extreme leftists were not publicly aired. While regime officials smugly stuck to the line that they did not envision any wholesale dismantling of the ASU, they monitored public reaction to the debate to ascertain the breadth of consensus for the ASU's preservation.

The debate itself raged on for one full year, preceding the holding of new ASU elections from base units up to the CC level in the months of June and July 1975. Despite the onset of talk about establishing platforms in the ASU, the elections were lackluster. According to one report,[225] which focused on al-Gharbiyya governorate, no prominent political or social issues were raised during the elections. Rather, most friction derived from the new ruling that allowed People's Assembly members to participate in district and local level ASU conferences. Because these conferences represented the most important recruiting grounds for ASU candidates, efforts by parliamentarians to assure victory for their preferred candidates, including attempts to place the supervision of ASU elections in their hands rather than in those of the ASU governorates' secretaries, met with heavy resistance from ASU types. Interestingly, the latter received regime backing "in a way which showed that they didn't want ASU elections influenced by any other power."[226] Sadat, with Mar'ei and Khalil's help, had already significantly altered the ASU's leadership composition.

The Minabir Concept

On July 25, the first ASU National Congress following the war was convened. That Congress conveniently put an end to Sadat's public muttering about not seeking a second presidential term by nominating him to retain the presidency, and Sadat was duly re-elected in October 1976. But the Congress also initiated debate over how the ASU could be transformed into a more vital institution. What emerged from that debate was a majority rejection of both a multiparty and a single-party system, and an endorsement of the idea of allowing some kind of platforms to be set up in the ASU.[227]

Additional formal debate over the *minabir* issue took place in August and September in the People's Assembly, alongside the informal debate in the press. There was a surfeit of talk, but little action, as everyone remained uncertain as to what form—functionalist? ideological?—the platforms or forums were to take.[228] Also, there was some trepidation in taking the first step toward establishing a *minbar* for fear Sadat might disapprove. It was, therefore, not altogether surprising that the first man to take the plunge was Mahmud Abu Wafia, Sadat's brother-in-law. Sadat's daughter, Noha, described Abu Wafia as having "no political power aspirations"; "Father just said to him, 'Do me a favor : . . ' and he complied."[229]

On October 22, 1975, Abu Wafia announced the formation of his Social Democratic *minbar,* which he said derived from the July 23 "revolution."[230] He declared socialism to be his platform's ideological starting point, "a socialism that believes in God and His books and prophets, so as to put between it and Marxism certain boundaries."[231] The program called for: (1) support of the public sector; (2) an enhanced private sector role; (3) protection of the socialist gains against deviation either to the right or the left; (4) greater freedom of the press; and (5) a foreign policy vaguely defined as support for the policies of President Sadat.[232]

The Transition to "Limited Pluralism"

Once Abu Wafia had blazed the trail, it quickly became a well-beaten path. By January 24, 1976, just three months after Abu Wafia's declaration, the founding of some 43 *minabir* had been announced, with the ASU Secretariat having received formal applications from all but three.[233]

Conditions for the platforms' formation had been lain out in an ad hoc manner in a series of statements delivered by the ASU first secretary, Rif'at al-Mahgub. Mahgub, a professor at Cairo University's Faculty of Economics and Political Science, was a prominent Rightist theoretician with a strong Arab socialist bent during the Nasser era. On October 24, 1975, he announced that the only condition for creating a *minbar* was a commitment to the "coalition of the working forces" principle.[234] Four days later, he had established that the platforms would not be formed by the ASU, but that all of them must be committed to one philosophy and one ideology.[235]

By October 31, Mahgub had made his position even more specific, having declared that "it is not our intention that *minabir* appear within the Arab Socialist Union which espouse an individualistic philosophy and capitalism, relying on class oppression, or that a communist *minbar*, embracing Marxism and class struggle, be established."[236] Then, on November 3, Mahgub reportedly stated that the *minabir* were designed to give an organizational form to minority opposition views in the ASU; and that the majority current, which he did not specify, would remain without a *minbar*.[237] This theme was repeated on November 17 with news of Mahgub's assertion that the *minabir* would put an end to the era of individual opinions and allow for groups to emerge.[238]

Mahgub's pronouncements reflected concern that the *minabir* experiment was getting out of hand. Portugal had recently offered the spectacle of political instability produced by the sudden appearance of dozens of new political parties. Egyptian government observers complained that the platforms' proliferation derived from competing personalities, not from real political differences; and that most *minabir* lacked meaningful programs.[239] The criticism was valid as far as many of the proposed platforms were concerned, but certainly not true of them all. In fact, the most intriguing factor revealed by these platforms' emergence was the diversity of ideological viewpoints, especially when one keeps in mind that many of their founders were regime members: ASU CC and Secretariat members, People's Assembly deputies, etc. The platforms' creation confirmed the existence of diverse regime factions based in ideological and issue-oriented differences, not mere patron-client configurations. A leading Nasserite Leftist (Kemal Rif'at), Marxist (Khalid Muhi al-Din), and Rightist (Dr. Hilmi Murad) each formed *minabir*, as did others from those currents. Perhaps even more striking was the appearance of some eight to ten *minabir* (at least one fourth of the total number) giving greatest emphasis to religious ideals and principles. For example, there were two Science and Faith platforms, the Free Muslims, the Islamic Work platform, as well as one *minbar* which simply called itself the *minbar* of Allah. The whole liberalization experiment was also known to be rekindling the political hopes of pre-1952 party activists; that is, former members of the Wafd, Watani, Neo-Watani and Liberal Constitutionalist parties, as well as the Muslim Brotherhood.

So avid a response to the newfound freedom of assembly and organization went far beyond what Sadat originally had in mind; for Sadat, it raised concern that old, powerful, socially-divisive ideological forces were being unleashed. The need to diminish these fears acquired a sense of urgency because many platforms' leaders were busily and noisily proceeding with membership recruitment and other organizational activities, as if they had already received (or did not require) official sanction,[240] or believed that in constructing their platforms they could establish irreversible *faits accomplis.* Consequently, on December 21 Sadat called for the establishment of a special committee to review the platforms' applications. Mahgub and Sayyid Mar'ei, the new speaker of the Assembly, were entrusted with forming the committee, which they completed by January 28, 1976. The committee was composed of 130 members: 50 members from both the ASU-CC and the People's Assembly, one half of whom were "workers" or "peasants," 32 representatives from the syndicates, 20 members from the Supreme Press Council and 28 professionals and political experts.[241] The group—the Committee on the Future of Political Work in Egypt—began a series of open hearings to debate the *minabir* issue on February 2, with Sayyid Mar'ei presiding.

One day earlier, in Vienna, Mahgub had announced that *minabir* might be transformed into political parties. Therefore, the committee undertook its work against the backdrop of very liberal statements by top regime officials, as well as a most invigorating, heated debate in the Egyptian press in which nearly all of Egypt's leading (albeit predominantly secular) intellectuals participated.[242]

According to Mar'ei's assessment of these hearings, published on March 7, four major trends surfaced during the debate: (1) those who wanted to preserve the ASU but allow for permanent platforms to be set up inside it, represented the majority view, commanding 70 votes; (2) those who supported the ASU, but preferred the concept of "movable" or ad hoc issue-oriented platforms, garnered 33 votes; (3) seven individuals favored terminating the ASU and permitting the formation of full-fledged political parties; and (4) two individuals felt that the platforms should be allowed to form both inside the ASU and outside, with the door left open to their transformation into political parties if that conformed to the popular will.[243] Thus, there was considerable diversity despite the "in-house" selection of the committee's members.

The Officially Approved Minabir

Each group was instructed to draft official reports in defense of their positions and submit them to the committee chairman. On the evening of March 16, these positions were subjected to a formal vote with an outcome nearly identical to that mentioned above.[244] In conformity with the "fixed" platforms position, the majority agreed to a formula allowing creation of Right, Center and Left platforms within the ASU, which is what Sadat had hoped for all along.[245] Formal conditions were set for the platforms' formation; namely, that they accept the principles of the July 23 and May 15 "revolutions," that their founders include 20 ASU CC or People's Assembly members, and that one-tenth of the combined CC-People's Assembly membership approve the platform.[246] The ASU "coalition" concept was thus safeguarded, as was the 50 percent rule on "worker-peasant" representation. Here, as with the economic liberalization measures, the regime feared a Nasserite backlash and preferred gradual change.[247] It was now legal, however, for non–ASU members to join the platforms.[248]

The three *minabir* were established before the end of March. From the ASU Left platform, the Nationalist Progressive Unionist Grouping (NPUG) would emerge, headed by Free Officer core conspirator Khalid Muhi al-Din. The ASU Center platform metamorphosed into the Egyptian Arab Socialist Organization (EASO), led by Prime Minister Mamduh Salem, with Abu Wafia as secretary general. From the ASU Right platform emerged the Liberal Socialists Organization (hereafter referred to as the Liberals), presided by Mustafa Kamel Murad, also a former Free Officer.

Both the EASO and Liberal platforms grew out of the Rightist current of the Nasser era. Hoping to stake out what it perceived as the high middle ground, the EASO had Sadat's distinct backing, and immediately gained the support of government ministers, most state personnel, and legions of sycophants. The regime also made a concerted effort to draft the support of major trade union leaders, and experienced considerable success.[249] Because the EASO was, in essence, Sadat's party, and Sadat's political orientations and policy preferences have been carefully articulated, there is no need to dwell on the EASO members' orientations and preferences at this juncture; but it is beneficial to describe the Liberals and NPUG in greater detail.

The Liberals

The Liberals' leader, Mustafa Kamel Murad, was not only a former Free Officer, he had also been Anwar Sadat's close friend during their army days. Again, Murad was a former suitor of Jehan Ra'uf (Sadat), and Sadat had lived in a house owned by Murad's father. Murad had been a Nasser regime faithful, mostly working in the direction of a major public sector company. Both prior to and on the night of the May 1971 "revolution," he had provided valuable assistance to Sadat.

Murad objected to his platform being pegged to the right of the ground held by the EASO.[250] Indeed, initially, there were few substantive differences in the Liberals' and EASO's programs. Many Liberal Socialist Politburo members traced their political roots to the July revolution,[251] but Murad would demonstrate a stronger liberal penchant.

Murad's pro-liberalization orientation was a product of his Nasser regime experience. Murad told me: "I was a moderate socialist man. But after the socialist experiment, I thought it was too utopian. Socialism in practice becomes hell. I hated that system more than you can imagine. You can attract young boys with the pretty theory, but it can't be put into practice."[252]

Still, the anti-socialist, pro-liberalization rhetoric of Murad and many Liberals often had its limits; and this accorded well with Sadat's desire for a controlled liberalization. These limits were clearly demarcated in an interview with Muhammad Murad al-Subtacy, the man who became the party's number two official by 1978. Like Murad, al-Subtacy had belonged to all of Nasser's regime organizations, and in keeping with those organizations' precepts, he retained the belief that "absolute freedom regarding political party formation would bring chaos."[253] He characterized the Sadat multi-party system as "an experiment on the road to democracy."[254] In keeping with the 1971 Constitution, al-Subtacy said that religion should be "left out of politics," and parties based in religion and communist parties should not be allowed.[255] Similarly, freedom of the press should be circumscribed; he asserted that "the government should give *the existing parties* the right to express their views" and that there should be "no restrictions on the press *within the framework*."[256] [emphasis added] Al-Subtacy also expressed support for *shari'a* law as a basic source of legislation.[257] Regarding foreign policy orientations, al-Subtacy professed that the United States has popularity in the Arab world, not the Soviet Union, and noted that Israel caused most of the problems in the area, "forcing us to spend on the military, not the economy."[258]

The Liberals' Politburo did contain members with more pronounced, liberal democratic leanings; they were drawn to the organization out of their support for *infitah,* which Murad had helped champion in parliamentary debate. Clearly, Liberals represented the "blandos" of Nasser's authoritarian order; that is, many were regime actors whose experiences within an authoritarian system had led them to become most favorable toward a liberal democratic opening, and in general more predisposed to greater free enterprise and pro-Western relations than any other regime types. (Indeed, one such member quizzed me, *sotto voce,* asking if this author had any "special contacts" with the U.S. embassy in Cairo—contacts that might result in a flow of funds to the party coffers. If so, he would set up an appointment with me at a coffee house where we could get down to more serious business.)

The National Progressive Unionist Grouping (NPUG — Tagamu'a)

To clarify the ideological space occupied by the NPUG and its membership recruitment, it is essential to provide a brief sketch of the array of leftist political organizations in Egypt in the mid-1970s. To begin, on the far left, several communist organizations had reconstituted themselves or emerged in 1975: the ECP, the January 8 Communist Party of Egypt, the Egyptian Communist Workers Party (ECWP), and the Revolutionary Current. In brief, ECP types had worked with and felt disillusioned by the Nasser regime. The other three parties comprised individuals who rejected the communist party's 1965 dissolution and cooperation with Nasser. January 8 and the Revolutionary Current were created by old-guard communists, while the ECWP was formed by younger, extreme leftists with roots in the Writers of Tomorrow group.[259] These organizations remained underground, banned by provisions in the 1971 Constitution. In addition, there were many independent Marxists, such as Lutfi al-Kholi and Fuad Mursi.

As for the Nasserites, two basic currents emerged over time: First, the old guard types, like Leftist Kemal Rif'at, and Centrists Muhammad Fa'iq, Farid 'Abd al-Karim, and others, many of whom were still in prison; second, a younger generation of students and YO types. The first group "thought in terms of the value of the Nasser experience; the second saw Nasser as presenting a complete ideology—a third way between capitalism and Marxism."[260]

The NPUG drew from the Marxist, Nasserite Left, and Nasserite Center camps; put differently, it gathered support from independent Marxists, ECP types, old-guard Nasserites, and Nasserite youth. Many members had trained and worked in the old ASU Executive Bureaus, socialist institutes, and the YO.[261] The NPUG also recruited "enlightened Islamic" or Islamic socialist elements, like Muhammad Khalifallah. Finally, but importantly, it won the support of a significant fraction of the trade union leadership, as well as thousands of rank-and-file members.[262]

Khalid Muhi al-Din, himself an independent Marxist, headed the NPUG. He was backed in its creation by People's Assembly members Abu Seif Yusuf and Kabari 'Abdullah, and ASU Central Committee members Muhammad 'Abd al-Sami'a and 'Ali Talkham, among others.

Sadat picked a fight with Khalid Muhi al-Din over the NPUG's recruitment of Nasserites, 1960s Leftists, and Centrists.[263] Muhi al-Din had contested Abu Wafia's call for Nasserites to join the Center platform, claiming that their natural ideological affiliation was with the left. Sadat pretended that no such Nasserite current existed distinct from his own position, persisting in his refusal to acknowledge that he had betrayed any of Nasser's basic principles (e.g., Arab unity, socialism, anti-imperialism).

Sadat's argumentation was extremely coy. He was well aware of a distinct group that perceived itself as Nasserite and that many of its members were at ideological loggerheads with Marxists of Khalid Muhi al-Din, Lutfi al-Kholi, and Fuad Mursi's ilk. In fact, Nasserites attending the NPUG's first meetings tried to impose their control, proposing that Kemal Rif'at assume the platform's leadership.[264] Also caught up in this fray were the Arab Nationalists, led by Yehiya al-Gamal. They were at a loss as to whether or not to join the NPUG, perceiving themselves as "left of the EASO-Center, but right of the NPUG-Left."[265]

This confusion was consciously designed by Sadat, who calculated that if these potentially antagonistic factions were crammed into one organization, they would be preoccupied by debilitating internal debates.[266] Moreover, by helping the Marxist Muhi al-Din keep control of the NPUG, Sadat hoped to discourage hardcore, anti-Marxist (anti-communist) Nasserites from joining it in large numbers. In this regard, Sadat experienced some success, but most saw through Sadat's machinations and set aside their differences to come together in the grouping. As Hussein 'Abd al-Razzaq claimed, "We foiled Sadat's logic. He wanted a platform for communists, but controlled by the regime. We opened the *minbar* to all leftists and intentionally kept the communist representatives to just three of the 22 members in the general secretariat (Isma'il Sabri 'Abdullah, Rif'at al-Sa'id, and Lutfi al-Kholi). Sadat was very angry when he saw the left *minbar* included other leftists, not just the communists."[267]

The delicate nature of the NPUG's successful balancing act was highlighted by the fact that no one faction within the NPUG would endorse the NPUG program on its own.[268] Again, many erstwhile Youth Organization cadres were attracted to the NPUG. The *minbar* also garnered support and dual membership from Marxists (like Nabil al-Hilali of the ECP) who belonged to the newly reformed—1975—clandestine communist parties, although other Marxists refused to join out of the belief that any form of association with Sadat's regime would discredit them.[269] It is also interesting to note that all of the communist members of the NPUG would go on to call for genuine liberal democracy,[270] a position not endorsed by many Nasserites.

In many respects, Sadat had merely poured the regime factions of the 1960s into a new structural format in which former Rightists, especially those in the EASO platform, now had the upper hand. The leaders of the old, Nasser-era Centrist faction—Sabri, Gum'a, Sharaf, and others—remained in prison, while their ideological followers and non-Marxist Leftists were forced into an uneasy coalition in what was still perceived by many as a Marxist-led NPUG. Should NPUG activities become troublesome, regime authorities could brand the whole lot as communists or atheists and expect much of the general public to turn a blind eye to their repression. Sadat would employ this strategy repeatedly.

Beyond the "Limits": The Blossoming of Illegal Parties and Groups

Although the views of former Wafdists, Muslim Brothers and communists were now on display in the press, they remained formally banned from the political playing field. In retaining this authoritarian feature, the regime increased the likelihood that excluded political activists would have recourse to extra-legal means to advance their cause. This point has already been demonstrated regarding the reformation of the communist parties in 1975. Some of these parties were directly involved in mobilizing the workers' demonstrations of 1975. Elsewhere, the Fanniyya 'Askariyya incident represented another example of extra-systemic, regime-challenging behavior.[271] Again, the latter incident set a precedent for the use of violence by Islamist extremists under Sadat; and several of its members survived to establish other organizations. Although Sadat's major preoccupation was with the threat from the political left, Islamist extremism would prove much more problematic over the long run.

Roots of Egypt's Islamic Extremists

The Role of Sayyid Qutb

Egypt's Islamist extremists did not appear out of the blue. Muhammad al-Mismari, a lawyer and powerful figure in the Muslim Brotherhood, characterized the Fanniyya 'Askariyya types as one link in a chain of radical descendants of the Muslim Brotherhood.[272] For al-Mismari, the initial, radical link in the chain came with the followers of Sayyid Qutb.[273]

Qutb was a MB heavyweight whose travails and subjection to torture in prison during the Nasser years led him to a rejection of Egypt's society and political regime as *jahili* (ignorant of God) and even *kafir* (apostate). When tied to specific Koranic verses, Qutb's judgment was interpreted by some Muslims as giving license to kill the "kafirs." Qutb's views were presented in his radical treatise, *Signposts on the Road,* in 1964. For this, as well as his alleged complicity in anti-government plotting in the mid-1960s, Qutb was tried, then executed on August 29, 1966; but Qutb's ideas lived on.

Mainstream Muslim Brothers, most all of the MB's old guard and their followers, refrained from describing the society or political system as *kafir,* preferring to label it as "non-Islamic" and restricting themselves to efforts to Islamize Egypt by constitutional means. In doing so, they were adhering to a policy established by former MB Supreme Guide, Hassan al-Hudeibi, that MB members and all Muslims should be "preachers, not judges."

But in Nasser's prisons, Qutb had made a great number of converts to his way of thinking. Or perhaps more accurately, Nasser's prisons made many converts to Qutb's way of thinking. Muhammad al-Mismari says Qutb's influence was already apparent in the late 1950s by the number of Qutb's followers or "Qutbiyyun" (government authorities gave them the name Qutbiyyun, so the name was viewed with disfavor by its members).[274] Then in the mid-1960s, following the appearance of *Signposts,* there was rapid adoption of its basic tenets by many of the younger generation of Muslim Brothers imprisoned in the government's major crackdown of August 1965. Rival interpretations of Qutb's book caused young Islamist radicals to split into two groups: (1) the *Gama'at al-'Uzla al-Shu'uriyya* (Spiritual Detachment Group), which saw the society as kafir but chose to conceal those views while adopting an incremental approach to gain predominance in society; (2) the *Gama'at al-Muslimin* (Society of Muslims), which not only saw the society as kafir but preached physical withdrawal from mainstream society to build a new Islamic society.[275] The latter group was referred to by authorities and the press as *Gama'at al-Takfir wa-l-Higra* (Denunciation and Holy Flight group). Takfir w-al-Higra would give birth to another splinter, one of Egypt's most violent and long-lived Islamic extremist groups, al-Jihad (Holy War).

The Society of Muslims; and Shukri Mustafa's Role
The Society of Muslims was originally led by a young al-Azhar graduate, Sheikh 'Ali 'Abduh Isma'il, but Isma'il became persuaded by Hudeibi's moderate stand in 1969, renounced the group's goals, and the group fell apart.[276] Another member, Shukri Ahmed Mustafa, took it upon himself to build the group anew.

The personal history of Shukri Mustafa represents a poignant example of the trajectory of Islamist radicalization. Born in 1942 in a small town near the southern city of Assiut, Mustafa attended Assiut University to study agriculture, but became involved in politics and was imprisoned between 1965 and 1971 for membership in the banned Muslim Brotherhood. He was released on October 16, 1971 in Sadat's general amnesty, and almost immediately returned to his religio-political ways. He was only in his late twenties, but hardened by his prison experiences. The group he helped set up—the Society of Muslims—was one that rejected Egyptian society. Mustafa sought to build his group and reshape society through a three phase process: 1) a spreading of the word to obtain recruits; 2) *hijra*—a "holy flight" or withdrawal from society to build the new community and train its members in Islamic-prescribed warfare; and 3) a return to conquer "apostate" society by the use of violence.[277] Most of Mustafa'a recruits were, as with the Fanniyya 'Askariyya group, middle- and lower-middle-class youth and college graduates from rural backgrounds. By 1973, Mustafa had already moved into phase two of his three-phase plan, quietly building his new Islamic society on the outskirts of a southern provincial city called al-Minya.

The New Domestic Political Arena

All told, Sadat had opened a political Pandora's box by giving the citizenry a taste of greater political freedom and movement. But during the mid-1970s, back in the mainstream of politics, liberalization of the press and the formation of distinct political organizations with identifiable, ideological orientations created a new, broader environment in which peaceful political discourse was the norm. Firmer in the knowledge that the existing system was at best a transitional one, and faced with the stressful political-economic conditions of the mid-1970s, citizens felt both encouraged and compelled to voice opposition to regime policies, and were now afforded legal political and media resources to discuss and criticize regime policies. Regime officials could have recourse to forcibly silence those elements, but only at the cost of seriously undermining the anti-police state, liberal ideals on which Sadat was trying to base his regime's legitimacy.

The 1976 People's Assembly Elections

Just how much the political environment had changed was made evident by the People's Assembly elections, held in two rounds on October 28 and November 4, 1976. For the 352 contested seats, the EASO-Center fielded 527 candidates; the surfeit reflected its unwillingness to alienate individuals who desired to run on the EASO ticket.[278] The Liberals and NPUG fielded 171 and 65 candidates respectively, the deficit indicating that they had not developed strong popular bases and were unable to field candidates in many constituencies, especially in rural areas.

Also noteworthy was the regime's decision to permit independent candidates to stand for the elections. Of the 1,660 candidates in total, 897 were independents. Many independents presented themselves as "above ideological machinations," but a good number held Wafdist sympathies, while a few had moderate Islamist leanings. Thus, many independents represented strong—yet still illegal—political currents.

The People's Assembly elections were marked by incidents of violence,[279] but in general were hailed as fair and open by Egyptian standards. As one American diplomat commented, they were no worse than many elections held in earlier times in the United States.[280] The turnout was small; most political observers saw this as a reflection of a learned cynicism toward elections. The government-backed EASO captured 280 seats, roughly 80 percent of the vote, while the Liberals and NPUG won only 12 and two seats respectively.[281] Independent candidates, however, garnered 48 seats, approximately 14 percent of the vote.[282]

These results partially demonstrated the political potential of currents that remained without official government recognition: the liberal democratic and Islamist currents. Yassin Sirag al-Din[283] estimated that roughly ten of the elected independents were pro-Wafdist. One of the Wafdist victors, Sheikh Salah Abu Isma'il, also had strong links to the Muslim Brothers. In Alexandria, several thousand GI members campaigned vigorously for the independent lawyer, 'Adil 'Eid, portraying 'Eid as someone who would promote application of the rules of Islam.[284] 'Eid won, and he was joined by several other new People's Assembly members who agreed on the importance of the Brothers' return to politics.[285] Finally, successful independent candidates also included prominent individuals from Nasser's days, like core-group Free Officer Kemal al-Din Hussein and former minister, Hilmi Murad. Both had had the courage to pick ideologically-charged fights with Nasser and had exited Nasser's regime. Their presence in the Assembly was likely to provide a certain measure of frank debate.

Post-War Changes in University Political Struggle: 1973-1977

When you have some poor kid from the countryside trying to live in the dorm on L.E. 5 per month, you can give him another L.E. 5 per month and tell him he's fighting for Islam. But then the groups grew into huge organizations, far exceeding the government's original intentions. Rich Muslim Brothers and the Gulf states helped finance them.[286] Kemal al-Ibrashi

During the 1973-1974 academic year, the struggle on university campuses remained in a state of flux. Marxists and Nasserites maintained control in a number of university divisions, but almost overnight became outnumbered by Islamist elements in others, such as Cairo University's prestigious medical and engineering colleges.[287] Islamists' gains in those colleges were of special significance in that, due to Egyptian university admissions policy, high school students receiving the highest scores on the general secondary (entrance) examination were channeled directly into those colleges. In other words, Islamists, most all of whom at this time derived from the "reformist" current backed by the Muslim Brothers, were experiencing success among Egypt's best and brightest students. But Islamist students experienced even more widespread support in the new provincial universities cropping up about Egypt.[288]

Because of the war, no student elections were held during the 1973-74 school year, so there was no meaningful test of rival political currents' strengths. Nevertheless, most observers agree that the October victory damaged the Marxist-Nasserite position, while it boosted the political fortune of Islamist groups.[289] The victory deprived Marxists and Nasserites of what had been their principal issue for attacking the Sadat regime—its failure to go to war. Furthermore, widespread perceptions of victory and the general sense of euphoria following the war made it difficult for those same elements to speak out against Sadat's drift toward the United States.

Meanwhile, Islamist groupings benefited handsomely from the religious symbolism attached to the October victory by Sadat and the general public. In this environment, the path was cleared for more open cooperation between the regime and pro-regime Islamist students. This resulted in the ASU setting up a general camp for religious and social affairs instruction in the summer of 1974, attended by members of all the *gama'iyyat al-diniyya* (religious clubs) of Cairo University.[290] Again, the grouping of these clubs consolidated the formation of *al-Gama'aat al-Islamiyya* (the Islamic Groupings (GI).[291] In short, having failed to co-opt the GSI group, the regime successfully abetted the formation of another religious organization. Importantly, although Muslim Brothers repeatedly denied it, at this time the GI was virtually an MB extension or "front organization." Its leading figures, all from Cairo University, included 'Essam al-'Aryan and Hilmi al-Gazzar, both Faculty of Medicine students, and Abu al-'Ala Madi, from the Faculty of Engineering.[292] Al-Gazzar emerged as president of the GI's National Assembly.[293] As noted earlier, the GI would move on to provide political backing to individuals, like 'Adil 'Eid, whose views were not consonant with Sadat's. Nevertheless, there would be no real conflict between the GI and the government until 1977.

The reappearance of pre-1952 rightists and some liberal democrats in the press was paralleled by the reemergence of like-minded students on university campuses. However, importantly, because all political organizations, even legal platforms, were barred from recruitment on university campuses, secular organizations were disadvantaged compared to religiously-inspired organizations. The latter could enter the campuses under the guise of spiritual work. Of course, ideas respect no boundaries, so by the 1974-1975 academic year, the universities' ideological terrain was occupied by the representatives of four currents: Islamists, still dominated at this point by the GSI, but soon to be surpassed by the GI; Marxists, still "hidden" behind the same front organizations; Centrist and Leftist Nas-serites; and a smaller, amorphous set of liberal democrats.[294]

Relations between these groups were characterized by shifting coali-tions. For example, some GSI would side with the Marxists against *infitah,* back Rightists and liberal democrats against Nasserites' support of the original ASU concept, or single-handedly attack the regime for changes in the personal status law or the relative absence of Islamist writers in the government-controlled media.[295] Yet, the bottom line was that all of these currents and related groupings ultimately retained adversarial relationships. Even the Marxist-Nasserite tandem was tenuous, as Marxists scrambled to dissociate themselves from Nasserites in the wake of the de-Nasserization press campaign.

In this chaotic situation, Marxists mounted a protracted drive to reverse the growth of religious, Rightist and liberal democratic forces. They helped to fuel and show solidarity for workers' discontent from December 1974 to March 1975, voiced opposition to the first Sinai disengagement agreements of January 1974, and criticized the development of closer ties with the United States.[296] However, the presence of rival groups, such as those GSI who effectively mixed calls for workers' rights and a questioning of closer ties with the U.S. with attacks on Marxist influence in the press,[297] demonstrated that the Marxists were not without competition.

The student elections of the 1974–1975 academic year provided addi-tional confirmation of this reversal of fortune. With assistance from regime officials at the university, who blocked the candidacy of some Marxist stu-dents,[298] Islamist students made their most impressive showing. From this year forward, the Islamist groups, especially the GI, won an ever-increasing number of student union elections. At first, the GI did so with regime sup-port, (in 1975–1976 and 1976–1977).[299] But after its alienation from the regime in 1977 (discussed below), the GI won without that support, and even in the face of regime opposition, (from 1977–1978 onward).[300] From 1977 to 1981, the GI were the dominant force on all university campuses; and in the 1978–1979 student union elections, they won by a landslide.[301]

Prior to 1976–1977, the Islamists' electoral successes did not mean that leftist students had been delivered a knockout punch. Nasserite Leftist stu-dents and Marxists carved out a niche of student supporters both by mounting a vigorous campaign against Sinai II and any agreement grant-ing any form of recognition to Israel, and by slightly de-legitimizing their GI opponents via sound accusations that the regime had helped rig some university student union elections.[302] A new leftist group, the Club for Nasserite Thought, was established at Cairo University's Faculty of Engi-neering. Although this club was shut down by the official student union in

January 1976, in May the official union rescinded its decision, and the club reappeared as the Club for Progressive Socialist Thought.[303] The club's success helped revive broader interest in the leftist movement, and gave rise to the creation of many popular student newspapers and wall-posters. In November 1976, though outvoted by other student representatives, the leftists staged an anti-Sadat march to the National Assembly in which some 300 students participated.[304]

Growth of the Islamists' Strength

Although leftist students remained active, especially on university campuses in Cairo, they were being rapidly outpaced by the Islamist movement. How does one explain the growth in strength of the Islamist groups, especially the GI, on university campuses during the postwar period?

To begin, it is essential to qualify the Islamists' electoral victories. Whether or not either the Islamists, or the leftists before them, represented a majority student viewpoint during their respective periods of dominance, is unknown, but seems unlikely. Most students did not involve themselves in politics. What they did constitute, one after the other, was the dominant force among student political activists; namely, that force most capable of dominating student assembly debates, whether through bully tactics or not, and of skillfully mobilizing a critical minority of student support to win student union elections.

Student elections were almost always a two-ballot affair. For candidates to win election on the first ballot required that a majority of the students vote. This rarely happened due to student apathy and alienation, so a second ballot was taken after two days in which only a 25 percent turnout was required. On the second ballot, the Islamists, taking a page from leftist students, became more adept at mobilizing voters by offering free rides to campuses and other incentives. In this fashion, groups that represented the sentiments of perhaps one quarter of the student body could totally dominate student elections.[305]

This said, many students were heavily imbued with religious values, just like the bulk of Egypt's populace. In this environment, Islam and Islamist political ideals were far easier "sells" than Marxism. Sa'd al-Din Ibrahim put is best:

> In Egypt particularly people are said to be quite religious. There is a positive sociocultural sanction to being religious. Even the most avowed liberal or leftist secularist regimes in the area find it necessary and expedient to invoke Islam when they try to institute any major new policy. The point is that for any militant movement, nearly half its task of recruiting members is already done by socialization and cultural sanctions since childhood. The other half

of their task is merely to politicize their consciousness and to discipline their recruits organizationally . . . As we have seen, the typical recruit is usually of recent rural background, a newcomer to a huge impersonal city . . . In such cases the militant Islamic groups with their emphasis on brotherhood, mutual sharing, and spiritual support become the functional equivalent of the extended family to the youngster who has left his family behind. In other words, the Islamic group fulfills a de-alienating function for its members in ways that are not matched by other rival political movements."[306]

The high religiosity of many students and the sociocultural environment in general made it extremely difficult for anyone to oppose Islamists on campus once the regime allowed them to get the ball rolling because opponents would appear to be preaching blasphemy or could readily be accused of doing so. Islamists also had the advantage of claiming that they were assembling for religious, not political purposes, making it more difficult for regime authorities to block their organizational activities than those of alternative political organizations. On-campus prayer rooms doubled as gathering places and recruitment sites; Islamist activists merely had to show up to perform their prayer obligations each day and keep an eye out for religiously devout students to identify prospective recruits. In this fashion, the Islamist groups' growth accelerated, especially that of the more moderate, MB-backed GI, with sub-groups in diverse university divisions selecting their own *amir* (literally, prince) to guide their activities and coordinate with other groups. The GSI, some members tainted by organic links to the regime, was rapidly eclipsed.

The rapid expansion of universities in provincial areas, as well as the increased attendance of urban universities by provincial students, all produced a huge increase in the number of students feeling "uprooted" and disoriented. On top of this, the overwhelming socioeconomic contradictions, moral dilemmas, and psychological pressures generated by *infitah* were felt acutely by an equally great number of students, on whose shoulders rested many families' hopes for upward social mobility. Because many university students came from humble backgrounds, they found it difficult to cover the cost of books and other course materials, or afford clothing on a par with more affluent students. Islamist student organizations, funded internally as well as via clandestine contributions from conservative Muslims in neighboring countries, offered free books and materials, and subsidized Islamic-style clothing to interested students. Young female students wearing Islamic dress were provided transportation to and from university, sparing them the hassles and indignities associated with public transportation.

Beyond this, while some graduates found employment with new, higher-paying companies, the majority were fated to accept low-paying jobs in the ridiculously overcrowded and decreasingly prestigious bureaucracy or public sector. So for the majority of students, whose material future looked bleak, solace could be found in reinforcing the value of their spiritual identity.

In the opinion of many disgruntled students, and despite the fact that some Islamists were enriching themselves, the perceived return to capitalism under the name of *infitah* was judged a failure. Little mattered that the experiment had only just begun. And if capitalism was a failure, and socialism had led to the catastrophic defeat of 1967, then "following God's path" seemed the only viable, untested alternative. The October War victory had given them a view of what might be accomplished if they "got right with God," and they now sought to extend that lesson from the battlefield to the domestic political arena.

Egypt's burgeoning university student body now contained many individuals who were among the first members of their family to achieve literacy. Again, it is hard to miss possible parallels here with the extremely rapid development of Christian ecclesiastical base communities (CEBs) in Latin America. Newly literate Latinos rejoiced in their ability to read and study the Bible. In a country like Brazil, where multitudes of newly literate people faced economic hardship and the often-humiliating impact of the forces of globalization in an authoritarian political environment, the number of CEBs grew from zero to 80,000 during the 1970s and early 1980s, "reinventing the church" in the process.[307] Egyptian youth faced many of the same challenges as their Brazilian counterparts, but Egypt, of course, is a predominantly Muslim country. Therefore, a more direct, hands-on discovery of the Muslim faith, combined with the joy and solace this brought many, perhaps also helps explain the rapid growth of Islamist groupings during this period.

Finally, the thrust of the media's de-Nasserization campaign redounded to the advantage of Islamist groupings. Because the campaign, which Islamists themselves helped to feed, focused on condemnation of the police-state excesses of the Nasser era, the victims of torture and abuse became celebrated as martyrs. Although many communists suffered greatly under Nasser, no group had been more consistently subjected to such repression than the Brothers, and graphic depictions of the fate they had suffered now made their way into print.[308]

In ever-increasing numbers, students turned to Islam to find solace from the pressures of the day, dramatically augmenting the recruitment base of Islamist associations. This advance went unchecked by the government. As noted by Dr. Yehiya al-Kabil, dean of Cairo University's prestigious School for Engineering from 1977 until 1981, "from 1975 until even the early 1980s, there was some let-go for the Islamist Groupings at the universities. No one predicted that it would turn out the way it did."[309]

Untried and untested, no one really knew exactly what form an Islamist alternative would take in terms of political-economic structures and institutions. But once the regime had responded to pressures, in part of the students' making, to permit Islamists the right to publish magazines and other materials, Islamist student activists were provided a steady diet of instruction in the teachings of Hassan al-Banna, Sayyid Qutb, and other Egyptian and foreign Islamic thinkers advocating establishment of an Islamically-based society. The role played in this regard by the glossy, monthly publication *al-Da'wa* (*The Call*) was particularly noteworthy. *Al-Da'wa* resumed publication in January 1976 after more than two decades of silence. Its staff cleverly provided a steady diet of articles by al-Banna and Qutb, as if resurrecting these figures from their graves to speak to an entire new generation of Muslims.[310] Importantly, the magazine also included a special "Youth and University News" section that kept young people informed as to recent developments, including information on the Islamist Groupings' activities. At the same time, students began creating their own publications. For example, at Cairo University's Law School, the GI obtained permission in late 1976 to publish their own journal, called *al-'Adala* (*Justice*).[311]

Elsewhere, once they had consolidated their strength on campuses, circa 1976-1977, *gama'aat* activists began to assert themselves and went so far as to impose their groups' values and mores on fellow students. Thus, there began to unfold a campaign to "Islamize" behavior on campus, including the raising of such issues as guaranteeing the serving of *hilal* (Islamically correct) food in university cafeterias, separated seating for men and women in classrooms, gender-designated use of staircases, interruption—often by force—of "secular" sociocultural activities like dances, introduction of common prayer areas and mass prayers, ordering students and professors to pray, and insistence on recruitment of Islamist speakers for university assemblies.

The January 1977 "Food Riots"

> In January 1977, Sadat practically lost power. He was president by default, because there was no organized force to take over. No government, no power, existed on January 18 and 19. Isma'il Sabri 'Abdullah

The April 1974 Military Technical Academy incident was the first serious incident to grow out of the contradictions engendered by Sadat's new foreign and domestic policies. As previously discussed, a rash of incidents ensued between 1974 and 1976, with various Islamist groupings or leftist-inspired workers and students as the protagonists. Collectively, these political disturbances were indicative of profound social malaise, of a society becoming unhinged. In retrospect, some of the incidents also served as "dress rehearsals" for a disturbance of far greater magnitude. Nevertheless, government officials were not alone in failing to be fully impressed by these incidents, as most observers were psychologically unprepared for the scale of the popular explosion that occurred on January 18-19, 1977.

Between 1973 and 1976, Egypt's total foreign debt had almost tripled and government subsidies had increased over more than thirteen-fold.[312] In consequence, Egyptian officials came under increasing pressure by foreign aid donors, and particularly the International Monetary Fund (IMF), to cut government spending. However, government spokespersons repeatedly denied reports that any significant reduction of subsidies would be undertaken in response to that pressure.[313] In the People's Assembly, just one day before the riots, there was word that there would be no increase in prices.[314] But in a crass contradiction of those statements, on the morning of January 18—one of those rare, dark and dreary days in Cairo—the daily newspapers announced that subsidies would be reduced on some 30 commodities, including many basic items.[315]

The economy czar, 'Abd al-Mun'im al-Qaisuni, is most often cited as having made the decision to lift the subsidies, but Qaisuni was just one member of a team of economists including Hamed al-Sayeh, Salah Hamed, 'Ali Nigm, and 'Abd al-Razzaq 'Abd al-Magid that formulated the measure. According to 'Ali Nigm, the Egyptian government was in arrears on sizable loan payments to its major creditors, the Gulf Organization for the Development of Egypt (GODE) countries were not being as helpful as anticipated, and therefore an IMF standby agreement was deemed essential. To obtain an agreement, the Egyptian government would have to put its financial house in order. The IMF offered very general advice on how the Egyptians might proceed; but the Egyptian team determined how to cut the deficit, and selected the commodities to be subjected to price hikes. The team then presented their recommendations to the cabinet, and all ministers in attendance, including Prime Minister Salem, gave their approval.[316]

To most elites, the price hikes did not appear exorbitant. For example, there was no change to the cost of bread, a two *piaster* hike on the cost of a pack of cigarettes, and a five *piaster* increase for a bottle of *butagas* (the principal means used for cooking and heating). However, these small increases represented a truly burdensome change to the country's legions of poor. This author was living in Egypt at the time of the riots. I can recall being aboard a bus awaiting departure to Zamalek from downtown Cairo when a *galabiyya*-clad man and what appeared to be his grandson boarded the bus. The old man asked how much the bus cost and when he was informed that the ride was 5 piasters, as opposed to a more "normal" fare of 2-3 piasters, he shook his head, muttered that it was too much, and got off. To all kinds of people, "pennies" made a huge difference, and so the sense of popular outrage over the price hikes was readily comprehensible. It was all the more easily understood in light of the government's botched communications. Indeed, many government officials would later lay the lion's share of blame for the riots on the doorstep of the minister of public information for his woeful failure to psychologically prepare the public.

The government's announcement triggered rioting, burning, and looting from Alexandria to Aswan. Sadat, who was at a meeting in Aswan, felt compelled to call upon the army to restore order. Major boulevards and city squares were rife with the stench of tear gas and the sound of guns firing buckshot and bullets. The riots were the worst disturbances that Cairo had witnessed since Black Saturday in January 1952, when the Egyptian masses vented their wrath against British imperialist control and set fire to many major hotels, department stores, and buildings. By the time the January 1977 rioting ended, the government had rescinded its austerity measures. At least 79 persons had been killed by security forces and another 800 wounded.[317]

There is evidence of premeditated leftist provocation of these events, and leftist workers and students led the anti-regime demonstrations.[318] Leftist political-economic analysts had been expecting the credit crunch to force government adoption of austerity measures, and believed this would present a moment laden with revolutionary potential; but leftist parties' leaders failed to anticipate the actual depth of popular outrage. As General Secretary of the NPUG Rif'at al-Sa'id put it, Tagamu'a [NPUG] and the Egyptian Communist Labor Party had a role in January 1977, and leftist workers and students were the principal leaders of street demonstrations, "but there were demonstrations everywhere; I didn't know what to do."[319] Indeed, most Marxist student activists note that they "regrettably" were caught by surprise by these events; other veteran Marxists reiterated this view.[320]

However surprised, there were visibly successful efforts by workers and students to occupy major city intersections and squares, or attack commuter rail stations to disrupt the flow of workers to job sites, thereby putting more people in the streets. Leaflets were distributed castigating the government's economic policies, although the message sometimes fell on deaf ears. One friend of mine reported observing a worker who was handed such a tract; the worker gave it a cursory glance, turned to his colleague and said, disdainfully, "*da kalam shuyu'i*" ("That's communist talk"), and threw down the paper.[321] Still, on balance, the leftist role must be viewed as significant and impressive, and their anti-regime behavior had great popular resonance.

That many bars and cabarets along the Pyramids Avenue were ransacked produced speculation that Islamists had exploited the breakdown of order to perpetrate these acts, but this speculation was largely unfounded. Those who broke into the cabarets were more concerned with carting off bottles of whiskey and other spirits than giving them a "fundamental" smashing.[322]

Yet another source of rioters came from those who benefited handsomely from the whole system of subsidies; namely, the private traders, wholesalers, and their assistants who spirited subsidized goods into the black market. Fuad Sultan says this "mafia" of middlemen and *shallalin* made sure that only about 30 percent of subsidized goods reached the intended consumers. This mafia was directly threatened by the price increases, and "they could move the mobs in demonstrations" to restore the status quo.[323]

In general, however, most of the rioting was spontaneous, a profound expression of pent-up popular frustration, not premeditated acts by political organizations. While students and workers clashed with security forces, much destruction was caused by juveniles who found great sport in throwing rocks through downtown windows.[324] Interior Minister al-Nabawi Isma'il pejoratively summed up the events by asserting that "the communists helped instigate the riots, then the rabble joined in to take advantage, to break and steal things."[325]

The army's intervention, combined with a late afternoon government curfew, effectively terminated the riots. Rif'at al-Sa'id noted, "When the tanks came into the streets, we decided to withdraw. You can't fight with tanks; also, we didn't want the army to be strengthened by these events. January 1977 proved there are limits to what you can do if the army is with the regime."[326]

Sadat's Reaction to the January Riots

Sadat's response was double-edged. On the one hand, he tried to pass off the events as an *intifadat al-haramiyya* (a thieves' uprising). On the other hand, he both saw a broad leftist hand in these events and needed a scapegoat, so Marxists and Nasserites shared the brunt of his wrath. He blamed the riots on communists posing as Nasserites and remnants of the pro-Moscow Centrist faction. Incensed by demonstrators' chants targeting his wife, "Jehan labsa fi akhir moda w-ihna nayyimin 'ashra fi-l-uda" ("Jehan's dressing in the latest fashions and we're sleeping ten to a room"), or again asking "ya battal al-'ubur, feen al-futur?" ("Oh hero of the crossing, where is our breakfast?"), Sadat publicly declared that:

". . . there was no longer any difference between the communists and those who claim to be the heirs of Gamal 'Abd al-Nasser. There are no more Nasserites . . . Nasser was finished after the defeat of June 1967. After that date, Nasser relinquished his power to Sha'rawi Gum'a and Sami Sharaf who, with 'Ali Sabri, gave the Soviet Union a free hand in Egypt."[327]

Such pronouncements, delivered on national television, were accompanied by announcement of a decree banning all political activity outside the three political organizations and making all strikes, demonstrations, and sit-ins punishable by life imprisonment with hard labor.[328] Sadat placed no blame on Islamists, despite rumors of their involvement in the riots. Radically-inclined Islamists undoubtedly participated in some fashion, while more moderate Islamists were less involved; but Sadat completely absolved them, perhaps adopting Nasser's early 1950s strategy of dividing and conquering the opposition. For his part, MB leader 'Umar al-Tilmesani backed Sadat and also blamed the communists for the January 17-18 riots.[329]

All told, at least 2,000 arrests were made during and after the January riots. Those arrested as alleged organizers included 108 ECP members, 44 Egyptian Communist Workers Party members, 44 from the Revolutionary Current, 6 from the "8 January" organization, and most importantly, 146 members of the NPUG.[330] (Rif'at al-Sa'id estimated that 1,000 individuals were arrested in January, and another 2,000 were arrested between 1977 and 1982, with many transferred to jobs in the provinces.[331]) NPUG leader Khalid Muhi al-Din was abroad when the riots happened, and therefore was left untouched, but other NPUG notables like Rif'at al-Sa'id and Hussein 'Abd al-Razzaq were apprehended. All were later released for lack of evidence, but some, like 'Abd al-Razzaq, spent months in prison.[332] Sa'id, blamed by Sadat for the riots and arrested in the night of January 21-22, was put in the Citadel prison. His luck proved good in that the attorney general, Mustafa Tahir, was a secondary school friend and a former HADETU (pre-1952 Marxist party) member. "Tahir helped clear me, as did a word from Mustafa Khalil, with whom I had communications during the events. Khalil was very fair with me."[333]

Participation in the January riots proved to be leftist students' last hurrah. The regime's extensive arrests decapitated the leftist student movement, leaving it in considerable disarray. Within months of the riots, Sadat restored the university guards to campuses, and undertook other measures to stifle campus political activity. On February 11, a referendum was ratified giving government the right to impose a penalty of life imprisonment, even capital punishment, for involvement in subversive activities.[334]

Meantime, the People's Assembly voted to remove former Vice President Kemal al-Din Hussein from his parliamentary seat. During parliamentary debate, Hussein had launched a scathing attack on the regime for its bloody handling of the riots. Political liberalization was on the ropes, or so it seemed.

Conclusion

Although *infitah* was slow to attract foreign direct investment and boost Egyptian manufacturing in general, the rapid growth of revenues from petroleum exports, tourism, the Suez Canal, and Egyptian workers' foreign remittances greatly altered the country's socioeconomic picture. These changes created great optimism among many citizens, especially *infitah's* beneficiaries, as well as pessimism and anger among pro-public sector citizens and a great many national capitalists. In contrast to the years of austere socialism, Egypt now seemed awash in money. However, this money was very unevenly distributed, and most of it either went toward increased consumption or was kept abroad; not enough was channeled into productive investment in Egypt. Both the inflationary pressure induced by private sector activity, as well as real and anticipated competition brought on by the flood of imported goods and increased prospects of FDI, caused considerable anxiety among public sector workers, bureaucrats, and domestic manufacturers.

As a complement to economic liberalization, and a nod to Egypt's new superpower patron, Sadat undertook a "controlled liberalization" of Egypt's political system. Political liberalization, from his perspective, had the additional salutary effects of destroying the Arab Socialist Union, and channeling restive political forces into the legal political arena. They also represented steps in Sadat's deliberately slow-paced, gradual move toward democracy. However, political liberalization failed to absorb the political, social, economic, cultural, and religious interests and sensitivities stirred up by Sadat's new domestic and foreign policies. Diverse political activists— Islamists, Marxists, Nasserites, and liberal democrats—vehemently opposed various aspects of those policies, and all were gaining force in different civil societal arenas. Meanwhile, although most Egyptians remained without party affiliations, they were increasingly "polarized" into pro- and anti-Sadat opinion groups.

Regime elites failed to appreciate the depth of public anger caused by infitah–induced socioeconomic transformations. In most regards, opposition elites also failed to appreciate just how active this opposition volcano was. After January 18-19, 1977, this was no longer the case. Suddenly, Sadat's confidence was deeply shaken, and the entire *infitah* strategy seemed seriously compromised by these events. Sadat's opponents were like sharks smelling blood.

5

Sadat's High–Risk Bid for Peace and Prosperity

The January Riots' Impact on Sadat

"Sadat was completely depressed about what had happened. He never imagined the people would rise up against him. I was very close to him. He was 100 percent changed by this experience. His domestic policy was completely different. He became aggressive; he decided not to give people too much freedom. He made referenda to keep power in his hands, and through these laws he silenced his opponents; then we didn't have any democracy in Sadat's period. His condition kept deteriorating until his death." General Gamassi[1]

The January riots had a profound impact on Sadat.[2] To many firsthand observers of these events, Sadat's post-riot public fulminating against communists sounded like a lame search for a scapegoat; yet even behind closed doors among insiders, Sadat was blaming "communists" for the riots. For example, Sadat said to Kemal Hassan 'Ali, "What are these communists doing? What do they want? *Da nizam hash.* (That [communism] is a fragile system.) It will collapse after ten years."[3]

Sadat's prophecy was off by a few years, but prophetic or not, his narrow, post-riot focus on the left was significant, both in and of itself, and also because it may have delayed his realization that an even greater threat was developing in Islamist circles. In addition, it is noteworthy that beyond his complaints about the communists, Sadat saw the riots as a conspiracy against him *personally,* not the product of popular dissatisfaction with his economic policies.[4] He was all the more disturbed because the demonstrators had attacked not only him, by name, but also his wife. (Many Egyptian elites commented that "perhaps you, as a Westerner, can not adequately appreciate the depth of outrage that such an insult would cause most Middle Eastern men."[5])

Sadat's reaction to this event marked the beginning of a retreat to more of a "bunker mentality." After the riots, Sadat literally spent less time physically in the "hostile environs" of Cairo, retreating to the relative serenity of various rest houses.[6] This physical withdrawal was associated with an important attitudinal change. Sadat increasingly saw himself both as victimized by various nefarious political forces, and as alone possessing the clarity of vision to bail the country out of its difficult political-economic circumstances.

Post-Riot Assessment of Egypt's Development Strategy

The riots underscored *infitah*'s failure to produce the economic miracle that Sadat had promised and which the media had turned into a powerful image. The January crisis called for a critical evaluation of the political-economic situation to reveal the major stumbling blocks, followed by bold decisions aimed at removing them. Sadat's "fundamental orientations" would weigh heavily in this decision-making process. His long-term objective was a democratic polity with a mixed economy, and he had already taken Egypt several steps in that direction. In his mind, however, it was still much too early to introduce full-fledged democracy to Egypt. He saw maintaining a powerful, rightist authoritarian state as essential during this stage of political-economic development. Alongside Sadat's transitional authoritarian predilections, the strength of various pro-statist forces— elites, mid-level employees, and workers alike—combined with Egypt's political-economic conditions to eliminate consideration of any radical leap of faith toward political democracy and unfettered capitalism.

In most regime elites' eyes, a more profound liberalization of the political economy was blocked internally by inability to "tighten the belt" to generate sufficient savings for investment. Egypt's population growth rate was running above 2.5 percent; it represented, in the opinion of World Bank President Robert McNamara, Egypt's "main obstacle to economic development" in that population growth alone would absorb 75 percent of all expected investment.[7] As much as 50 percent of the national budget was being set aside for military expenditures, but the continued state of war, need to rebuild the military with Western weapons, and regime dependence upon the military as key base of support eliminated discussion of defense cutbacks. At the same time, total public sector production for 1977 was expected to value L.E. 3,897 million, or 40 percent of GNP, but the net return to the state would be L.E. 134 million,[8] that is, it would produce no significant income for investment.

Consumption could have been cut because there was considerable waste. Animals were being fed bread and pastries because subsidies made these items cheaper than feed, and one ton of *baladi* bread cost the same as one ton of feed corn. However, regime leaders, and here Sadat proved no different than Nasser, lacked the political will, and perhaps strength, to coerce or convince the public to accept such measures. Yet another lesson Egypt's leaders derived from the January riots was that political liberalization could not be conducted concurrently with an economic austerity program. Something had to give.

External Shortcomings

Sadat's key economic advisers saw two major "external" factors as responsible for much of Egypt's continuing economic difficulties: a shortage of foreign aid, and a failure to attract adequate foreign direct investment. Both shortcomings went to the heart of *infitah* in its original, grand design.

The Shortage of Foreign Aid

Proponents of *infitah* had hoped for significant Arab and MDC development assistance. So far as the Arabs were concerned, Egyptians saw Arab assistance as falling far short of their capabilities.[9] As Said Aly has shown, Arab oil revenues, which had been a mere $2.169 billion in 1965, rose to $51.5 billion in 1970, then skyrocketed to over $204 billion by 1980.[10] With these figures as well as the enormity of Egypt's sacrifices to pan-Arab causes in mind, the $7-$10 billion in aid provided by Egypt's Arab cousins looked like peanuts. 'Abd al-Razzaq 'Abd al-Magid, who became Egypt's economic czar in May 1980, noted that:

> between 1974-1977, Sadat was a very disappointed man. He saw the Arabs as delaying a political settlement with Israel, but worse, he felt he was cheated of funds from the 1973 war. The Arabs had gotten huge oil revenues after Egyptian soldiers paid the price. He was very anti-Arab because of this. When 1977 came, he put all his anger on the Arabs. He didn't fire Qaisuni [who was managing the economy]. He said, "They have to understand that instability in Egypt or an end to myself will mean an end to their regimes." The Arabs gave money after January 1977, but Sadat's trip to Jerusalem [in November 1977] was because of anger over the lack of funds and Arab timidity regarding negotiations. He decided he had to go it alone. But it [January 1977] was the point of departure in his thinking toward the Arabs—Sadat was saying: "They don't help enough . . . They can't be trusted . . . King Feisal wouldn't have allowed this neglect to happen" and so forth.[11]

As Sadat's discussion with 'Abd al-Magid made clear, it was hoped that the riots would now impress upon Arab and other foreign donors the gravity of Egypt's economic situation, yielding greater assistance. Some cynics even argued that the riots had been intentionally triggered by the regime for just this purpose.

Significant Arab financial assistance did materialize in the months following the riots. By May, the GODE, whose members included most of the Gulf's oil-rich states, promised to deliver $1.5 billion in aid to Egypt in 1977 alone.[12] In the same month, the first meeting of a World Bank Consultative Group was held in Paris, attended by nearly all of the major Western powers, Iran, major Arab aid donors, and representatives of 10 financial institutions. This group's sole purpose was to discuss financial and economic assistance to Egypt, and aid and supplier credits from these countries increased dramatically in the aftermath of this meeting. U.S. economic aid had already been increased after Sinai II, but it was eventually boosted to roughly $1 billion per annum in funds and PL 480 wheat.[13] Important assistance came on line from Japan and several Western European nations as well.

Making Egypt Attractive to Foreign Direct Investors

Increased development assistance from Arab states, the United States, Iran, Japan, and Western Europe was of great help, but a second essential ingredient of *infitah* was the attraction of massive foreign direct investment. Egyptian planners expected that MNC's would bring capital and new technologies, generate employment, and establish competitive industries on Egyptian soil. Alarmingly, there had been no substantial investment by any major foreign manufacturer.

By comparison with the 1967-1973 period, when MDC foreign investment hit rock bottom, FDI increased after 1974. (See Appendix B.) Oil companies were the major foreign investors throughout the 1970s. While the bulk of what Law 43 foreign investment had occurred was in banking, tourist projects, and investment and consulting services, major investing had not occurred in manufacturing.[14] Foreign investment by Law 43 companies represented just 2.6 percent of gross fixed investment in 1977. Moreover, although dozens of foreign banks had established branches in Egypt, their managers had been and "remained reluctant to invest in long-term projects due to uncertainty about the future of the Egyptian economy."[15] Sizeable foreign exchange earnings belonging to Egyptians were transferred abroad by these banks.[16]

What was inhibiting a more active MNC role in Egypt? Of course, there were the countless complaints of bureaucratic "red tape" and excessive gouging on commissions by Egyptian officials.[17] For some MNC directors, there were all too many bureaucratic hoops to jump through to do business in Egypt, although at times Sadat personally helped grease the wheels of this process.[18] Some MNC directors were bothered by the Arab "blacklist" against companies doing business with Israel. But still others felt, as Fuad Sultan noted, that the whole legal framework discouraged MNC investment.[19] Existing legislation required foreign investment projects to be self-sufficient in foreign exchange and keep their accounts in banks registered with the Central Bank of Egypt. Also, foreign companies could not obtain full hard currency value for their Egyptian earnings and smoothly repatriate their profits and capital because the government fixed such transactions at the official exchange rate of 39.96 piasters per U.S. dollar,[20] well under its market value. Labor laws and international trade regulations were seen as onerous, and existing infrastructure as weak. In comparison with terms offered in Latin America and the Far East, the Egyptian investment environment was less seductive. Now, in the wake of the riots, MNC "risk analysts" had new domestic concerns to consider alongside the longstanding ones caused by Egypt's continued state of war with Israel.

New Economic Policies and Legislation

What was to be done? In February 1977, a workshop held to consider revisions to Law 43 brought together over one hundred key businesspersons, government officials, and legal advisers.[21] Foreign parties also entered this process. In April 1977, the American ambassador, Hermann Eilts, and Egyptian planners reached an understanding that met some potential investors' concerns and targeted many bureaucratic obstacles to foreign investment.[22] Such discussions led, ultimately, to the June 1977 issuance of Law 32, which modified Law 43, removing many foreign investors' concerns by liberalizing capital transfers and foreign exchange transactions.[23]

In essence, the strategy for addressing Egypt's economic problems was to beseech greater foreign aid, and create a more positive environment to attract FDI. Not everyone, however, saw eye-to-eye with this strategy, and doubters included the minister of planning, Muhammad Mahmud al-Imam. Al-Imam had approved the stabilization plan that brought on the riots, although he says that he had done so against his own belief. For al-Imam,[24] Egypt was facing a structural problem that could not be overcome by monetary tinkering via currency devaluations and subsidy reforms as called for by the IMF. What was needed was a fundamental attitudinal change designed to improve worker productivity and a more export-oriented approach. But instead, Imam said, "Egypt just kept the subsidies to bribe the people, and maintained the public sector while dismantling it."[25] "Sadat's problem was he had no clear economic strategy. He just begged for money; and this offered no solution to the structural problem. He didn't say, 'Egyptians, sit down and build your own country!'"[26] Imam had helped oversee the drafting of a 1976-1980 five-year plan, but it was never truly implemented.

Given the public sector's obvious difficulties, one might think that greater attention should have been paid to promoting the large, yet shackled, small- and medium-enterprise private capitalists. In fact, Law 32 did bring some change in government attitudes and regulations concerning the private sector, as Egyptian investors using foreign exchange acquired the same privileges previously extended to foreign investors.[27] But as shall be discussed shortly, no significant modifications of existing laws were made to invigorate the great number of existing small and private enterprises operating with local capital. In other words, under *infitah,* state policies continued to discriminate against and inhibit many national capitalists, especially those in manufacturing. Agriculturists growing fruits and vegetables had seen their situation improve, but government pricing and regulatory policies remained in effect, constituting a net tax on agriculture. Meanwhile, "fat cat" importers and government subcontractors, many of whom operated beyond legal boundaries, proliferated, as did the number of state officials taking kickbacks from foreign and local capitalists.[28] But the attention of government planners was elsewhere; they kept their fingers crossed, hoping in particular for a flood of MNC investors.

The Response of Domestic and Foreign Capitalists

Domestic Capitalists' Mixed Review

Although Law 32 appeared to represent an important breakthrough, serious blockages remained. Egyptian private investors' projects still were not guaranteed against nationalizations, and they had to be approved by the General Authority for Arab and Foreign Investment. Moreover, the new privileges applied only to Egyptian capitalists utilizing foreign exchange for their new investments. Many owners of existing firms were left in the cold. Berger conducted interviews with many Egyptian small and medium enterprise owners and managers in January and June of 1977, and January of 1978.[29] Most of her interviewees were discouraged by numerous factors, including continuation of the 95 percent rate of taxation on profits above L.E. 10,000, burdensome social insurance laws, and exasperatingly numerous bureaucratic constraints and interventions.[30] By May 1978, the threshold at which one started paying taxes at the 95% rate was raised to L.E. 100,000, a considerable increase. But Fuad Sultan complained to authorities that, "Private investment must expect a net return of 15-20 percent if one expects it to go into the productive economy. The 95 percent tax rate is crippling."[31] And a report by Nathan Associates noted that well into 1979 "the rate of taxation imposed on dividends on stocks and interest on bonds, loans and bank deposits" was "so high as to constitute a clear disincentive to all forms of saving and investment."[32] In brief, government policy weighed heavily against many Egyptian private sector manufacturers. It remained very difficult for them to enrich themselves by legal means, so incentives to expand production remained low.

As previously noted, Egyptian capitalists who used local currency were not placed on the same playing field with private sector investors using foreign capital until the period from 1980 to 1981.[33] And these modifications were not made palpable until the passage of Law 159 of November 1981, one month after Sadat's death. Only then were the 1961 socialist provisions setting ceilings for salaries and annual profits finally dropped, although other measures affecting profit-sharing and worker-employee representation on management boards were retained.[34] Thus, throughout the entire Sadat presidency, national capitalists in the manufacturing sector operated in what they perceived as a hostile environment. This bias against local private sector manufacturers was extremely important given the size of that sector regarding overall employment—over 50 percent—and recognized potential for growth. This sector was a major engine of growth in many "Asian Tigers;" Egypt's remained relatively stultified.

This said, the new economic environment still provided a boost to private sector activity writ large. There is no gainsaying the fact that many consumer-oriented capitalists—compradors and government sub-contractors—continued to thrive under *infitah*. And national capital was not totally excluded from the list of those making gains. All told, between 1974 and 1977, private sector investment had risen from 9 percent to 16 percent of gross fixed investment.[35] Overall private sector activity was expanding at a rapid pace.

Continued Foreign Reluctance

As for foreign investors, the 1979 Nathan Associates report indicated initial sluggishness following the introduction of Law 32, and highlighted the continued absence of heavy investment by foreign manufacturers.[36] The study reported that "Foreign investors are still troubled by the difficulties of doing business in Egypt and, in particular, by the lack of infrastructure and the uncertain availability of foreign exchange and raw materials."[37] An increase in investment was occurring, but at a pace much slower than anticipated and desired. In 1977, foreign investment accounted for ten percent of gross fixed investment, but most of this was by oil companies; less than three percent of the total was accounted for by Law 43 companies.[38] In short, Isma'il Sabri 'Abdullah's prediction—that "foreign capital will not come"—appeared disturbingly accurate.

Perceptions of the Absence of Peace as an Obstacle to FDI

While numerous economic obstacles to foreign and national private investors existed, others saw the "real" reason for the weak MNC response to Egypt's open door as lying elsewhere: MNC's would not enter Egypt so long as Egypt remained in a state of war. If Sadat's headache in the early years had been the situation of "No peace, no war," his predicament now was one of "No peace, no heavy FDI." For many, if not all, MNC board directors, the risks were simply too great. How many foreign interests were prepared to invest large sums of money in Egypt if there was a high probability of it all being blown up? Not many. And for those who were, they still faced the conundrum posed by Egyptian adherence to the Arab "blacklist." Investment in other developing markets was far more attractive.

On January 21, 1977, with the dust barely settled from the riots, the *Egyptian Gazette* had editorialized that Egypt's "most economically beneficial" option was to "opt out of the war with Israel altogether."[39] That move alone would start the money and investments flowing in from the West. This idea, which ten years earlier could not have been printed, constituted a certain clairvoyance with regard to Sadat's ruminations. For Sadat, such thinking was not new. Raphael Israeli notes that Sadat first publicly linked the vision of economic development in Egypt with the necessity for peace in an address to a U.S. Congressional delegation in August 1975.[40] "He [Sadat] made it plain that he saw no point in rebuilding his country as long as the threat of war might jeopardize the entire effort of reconstruction; therefore, he longed for peace."[41] Sadat was not wont to share this view with his fellow Egyptians, however, and it would take over two years before such thinking, eventually galvanized by the slow MNC response to post-riot economic legislation, produced concrete action. In early November 1977, just weeks before Sadat's historic trip to Jerusalem, Ford Motor Company, Coca-Cola, Colgate-Palmolive, Motorola, and Xerox were all reportedly poised to enter Egypt; but all were also on the Arab "blacklist,"[42] and Egypt's own Boycott Office was opposing these deals.[43] Given *infitah's* design, Sadat could not ignore such concerns. In the meantime, with no economic miracle visibly in the making and other sociocultural tensions coming into play, the domestic political cauldron began to simmer.

Intra- and Extra-Regime Dissent

Regime Tensions and Defections

Government ministers' heads did not roll after the riots; a government shuffle occurred in February 1977, but virtually all principal actors, including economic ones, retained their posts. Qaisuni kept his key role of guiding the economy for over a year and a half. But the fallout from the January riots was significant and took its toll among other regime insiders, including individuals who had worked very closely with Sadat.

Ahmed Beha al-Din, who had returned to Sadat's good graces, was asked by Sadat to write a speech following the food riots. For this purpose, he met with Sadat for three consecutive days at the president's Barrages rest house north of Cairo, with their private discussions lasting until midnight. Sadat wanted the speech to reflect his view that the riots were caused by a bunch of thieves and leftist rabble-rousers, not by widespread public discontent. Beha al-Din felt differently. He tried to convince Sadat that he was in "too big a rush to spend the money that came after the war, to give people immediate prosperity. I was bothered by the number of profiteers and corruption. I thought we should be tightening our belts and saving for two or three years, but Sadat disagreed."[44] At the end of marathon talks, Beha al-Din looked at Sadat and said, "I am of a completely different view."[45] Beha al-Din would maintain his special relationship with Sadat until December 1977, but from January onward he felt increasingly uncomfortable about his commitment to the regime.[46]

Another, more clear-cut, riot-induced government dropout was 'Aisha Ratib. Ratib says she opposed the price hikes, but was in Saudi Arabia at the time of the cabinet discussion and denied the opportunity to voice her opposition. In post-riot cabinet discussions, Ratib countered Sadat's notion that it was an *"intifadit al-haramiyya"*; "I said, "No, it was a popular uprising."[47] "I quit the cabinet because of the January riots," said Ratib, "it [when I resigned] was the only time Sadat got angry with me; he made me sit at home for one month."[48] When Sadat's February 1977 plebiscite garnered a 99 percent vote in support of Sadat's regime, Sadat called Ratib out of the blue and told her, "You see, it wasn't a popular revolt." Ratib asked, "Do you believe this [the referendum's results]?" Ratib added, "He didn't answer me."[49]

The riots also brought some friction to relations between Sadat and Sayyid Mar'ei. Sadat became angered when he learned that Mar'ei had held a closed door meeting with parliamentarians, including opposition figures, following the riots. When Mar'ei informed Sadat that, given the country's difficult circumstances, he was only hoping to ensure cooler heads would prevail during parliamentary question time, Sadat rebuked his effort. He told Mar'ei that the MPs should be left to criticize the government at will, with the government left to carry the burden of its responsibilities.[50]

Opposition Optimism

Beyond the silent departures and distancing of regime confidants, there were more threatening developments. The broad political opposition saw that the regime was shaken badly; they smelled weakness and believed it was time to press their luck. During the first half of 1977, there were several interesting developments: students chanting religious slogans demonstrated in February; rumors about a revival of the liberal democratic Wafd Party were confirmed by a noisy reunion of Wafdists in May; and continued pressure by Marxists led Sadat to pronounce in June that there was no room for atheists in top government posts, the media, or in official cultural organizations.[51]

Political "Carrots" and "Sticks"

Sadat responded to his predicament by what amounted to a "carrot and stick" approach. As for the "stick," in addition to the repressive powers acquired through the February 1977 referendum and specific, anti-opposition measures already noted, Sadat took important steps to enhance the regime's ability to deal with powerful internal challenges. The events of January 1977 proved that the police force was too small; the need to call in the army was both embarrassing and threatening to regime stability in and of itself. So, a quantitative and qualitative strengthening of the Ministry of Interior was deemed essential. Al-Nabawi Isma'il, a no-nonsense career police officer and friend of 'Uthman Ahmed 'Uthman, was promoted to vice minister of the interior in February 1977, and named Minister of Interior in October. Under his guidance between 1977-1981, the interior ministry's capabilities were improved to enable the police to "face all situations." The police force's size more than doubled, police personnel engaged in more extensive training, and police equipment was greatly modernized.[52]

Indeed, the police force was strengthened to the point where it could effectively deter a threat by the armed forces. According to security personnel, in the pre-1967 period under Nasser, the power-ranking of the security forces put General Intelligence first, Military Intelligence second, and the State Security Services (Mabahith) third. Because of the 1967 war, Military Intelligence briefly supplanted the GIA as the strongest agency. Under Sadat, following the 1973 war, the Mabahith had been strengthened to the point where it became the most powerful agency. At the same time, the Central Security Forces (Amn al-Markazi) expanded in size by leaps and bounds. When Egypt received armored vehicles from the Soviets in 1975, Sadat saw that they went to the CSF units, not the army. This move angered army officers.[53] The Amn al-Markazi developed, in effect, into a second army. Because both the Mabahith and Amn al-Markazi were under the direct command of the minister of interior, the holder of that post became even stronger than under Nasser, when his power had been deemed considerable. After al-Nabawi Isma'il was appointed minister, he positioned armored vehicles in new camps ringing the major cities. This was widely perceived in elite military and security circles as Sadat's desire to present a counterbalance to the possibility of a military coup.

As for the "carrot," Sadat pushed on with a controlled political liberalization. He oversaw Mustafa Khalil's selection as general secretary of the ASU. Khalil admitted that his main task as general secretary was to do away with that organization and introduce a multiparty system.[54] "Sadat took the multiparty decision on his own. I called for a one-year trial of the *minabir* system—I wanted parties to come *after* our experiment and *not* be based on the *minabir* because they were of our, the government's, creation, not the people's. Sadat said, 'No, the elections took place on the basis of the *minabir*, so the parties should come out of these *minabir*.' He was anxious to have the open door policy work, and in his mind the political infitah was directly related to and a necessary adjunct of getting the open door policy to 'take off.'"[55]

Of course, there were to be limits to party formation; the "carrot" was cooked to Sadat's taste. In June 1977, the Political Parties Law 40 was legislated. The law established several criteria that blocked the free formation of political parties, criteria that had been stiffened in light of the January riots.[56] It was illegal, for example, to establish any party on the basis of social class, religion, or geographic region. In addition, the law established a seven member Supreme Committee for Political Parties. Chaired by Khalil, the committee also included the Ministers of Justice and the Interior, as well as one Minister of State; therefore, regime elites were guaranteed majority control.

Sadat was not introducing a truly liberal democratic system; democratization, like economic liberalization, would occur at a gradual pace. But it was obvious that the "parties criteria" would not, for example, prevent Wafdists from re-forming their own party. Thus, Egypt was making a transition to a limited-pluralist authoritarian system.[57] Much of Sadat's motivation came from wishing to please the West; and one should recall that President Carter, with his new emphasis on human rights, had arrived in power in January 1977. As Mustafa Khalil put it, "a multiparty system would be closer to the Western systems."[58] That is, political liberalization was seen as a move that would please Western allies. There was no pressure from the U.S. or other parties to liberalize politically; it was "just understood that this would help."[59] Thus, on June 29, 1977, the single-political organizational format initiated by Nasser in January 1953 was laid to rest, as the ASU was declared officially defunct.

Khalil had spent years occupying influential posts under Nasser and Sadat. Interestingly, when I asked this polished political veteran about his personal political philosophical ideals, he said, "I can adopt the political system that would be most beneficial to my country at a given time in accordance with existing realities and under certain conditions."[60] I smiled; and he smiled sagely and broadly in return.

As the ASU went into eclipse, there were preliminary indications of Sadat's political philosophical ruminations as well. In July 1977, there were reports of new "theocratic laws" being prepared by the Ministry of Justice: making apostasy a capital offense, prohibition of alcohol, amputation for theft, and so on.[61] From all appearances, the regime was now introducing an Islamization program of its own.

Reactions to Regime Change

Moderate Opposition

There was no strong opposition from the labor federations to the ASU's death; only a few, greatly weakened Nasserite voices expressed dissatisfaction. Posusney has shown how Sadat used incentives to attract and co-opt important labor elites to join the EASO party, alongside intimidation of more obstreperous labor elements.[62] Sa'd Muhammad Ahmed was made minister for labor after the January riots, a move some saw as a reward for keeping many workers out of the disturbances, and also as actually strengthening the syndicate's ability to protect the public sector.[63] Many communists, socialists, some old regime party leaders, and religious elements were upset by the new parties law because of its exclusionary parameters, but their opposition was diminished by regime tolerance of their extensive informal political activities. Leftists were also pleased that Sadat had kept the rule safeguarding 50 percent representation for workers and peasants. Sadat did so because he feared a negative reaction by these sociopolitical forces, the rule was in the constitution, and some saw it as premature to change the rule during his presidency.[64]

More Troublesome Opposition

Despite Sadat's "carrots" and "sticks," more frequent challenges to the regime were being issued by diverse illegal, clandestine political organizations. In July 1977, former Minister of Waqfs and al-Azhar Affairs, Sheikh Muhammad Hussein al-Dahabi, was abducted by the largely unknown Society of Muslims (Takfir wa-l-Higra) group. He was ransomed for the release of Takfir members, who had been apprehended while undergoing military-type training. When the government refused to make a swap, Dahabi was killed. Egypt was by no means accustomed to such violence at this time, and news of Dahabi's death shocked the nation. The ensuing manhunt brought the arrest of 620 of Takfir's estimated 2,000 to 3,000 group members, with 54 put on trial for the assassination on August 2.[65] Its leader, Shukri Ahmed Mustafa was arrested on July 8, tried, condemned to death, and executed along with four colleagues in March 1978. In August 1977, arrests of roughly 200 members of two other radical Islamic organizations, *Jund Allah* (the Army of God) and *al-Jihad* (Holy War) were reported.[66] Interior ministry officials remained vigilant against leftists as well. In September, 34 members of the underground ECP and Egyptian Communist Workers Party were apprehended for alleged subversive activity.[67]

The growth of various Islamist forces in Egypt, combined with lurid accounts of Muslim-Christian bloodletting in the Lebanese civil war, caused strains in Muslim-Coptic relations in many geographical areas and institutional settings. In January 1977 there were numerous clashes in Assiut and Samalout,[68] and tension grew on university campuses.

Islamists' fortunes were further strengthened during this period by the behavior of the Sheikh al-Azhar, the most prominent religious "official" in Egypt. Sheikh 'Abd al-Halim Mahmud had scored major points with Sadat by backing his accusations against communists as responsible for the January 1977 riots. He had also served the regime admirably by convincing the Saudis and others to come to Egypt's financial aid.[69] To Sadat's chagrin, however, the sheikh also pushed very hard for the implementation of *shari'a* law and greater autonomy for al-Azhar, while remaining staunchly opposed to any calls for reform of the personal status law. Until his death in 1978, he remained a thorn in Sadat's side.

Sadat's problems with Pope Shenouda III continued, also. In August 1977, the government presented a draft bill to the People's Assembly to make apostasy punishable by death. At the same time, as previously noted, there were reports of calls for the implementation of *shari'a* law emanating from high government circles. In protest, Shenouda began a fast, and called upon all Copts to fast for five days. Also, whether prompted by Shenouda or not, Egyptian Copts residing in the United States staged an embarrassing protest coinciding with Foreign Minister Fahmi's meeting with President Carter; and there were howls of protest from Copts in

Canada and Australia. During the first week of September, Sadat threatened Shenouda with cancellation of his papal appointment if he didn't "put an end to this nonsense."[70] This brouhaha led to a September meeting between Sadat, Shenouda, and 50 Coptic Holy Synod members in which Sadat voiced his anger over the protest fasting.[71] Shenouda finally relented, and on September 15 issued a message to reassure the world Coptic community and urge calm. The government, for its part, withdrew the draft bill relating to apostasy.

Sadat's Calculations: A Bid for Regional Peace

Due to all these new domestic political concerns, Sadat appears to have concluded that removing the external impediments to his political-economic development strategy entailed fewer political costs than would eliminating the internal constraints. Just like Nasser, who had perceived cutting consumption in 1965, or "making the present generation sacrifice for future generations," as too difficult a task, Sadat now deemed greater austerity as incompatible with political liberalization. Reneging on political liberalization measures also might prove unpopular with both his Saudi and American benefactors, because the Saudis were pleased by the reemergence of Islamist elements in Egypt, while the Carter administration preferred liberalization in keeping with its emphasis on human rights. On balance, heavier dependence on MDC foreign aid and investment appeared more feasible than trying to squeeze the Egyptian public. The major difference was that the foreign option's feasibility meant making peace with the lifelong enemy and therefore contained potentially high political costs of its own on both the domestic and foreign fronts.

Sadat's Trip to Jerusalem

> From day one, Sadat's policy was a policy for peace. Sadat, by nature, was an impatient man. He didn't want to wait fifteen years for peace like al-Assad. It was Sadat's deep feeling that the October 1973 war should be the last war."
> Ambassador 'Abd al-Ra'uf al-Reidi[72]

Important shifts had occurred on the international political scene in the first half of 1977. In the United States, President Carter's became president in January. This brought the departure of Kissinger, but Kissinger's step-by-step diplomacy had basically exhausted itself anyway. The new secretary of state, Cyrus Vance, arrived in Cairo in February, urging a resumption of the Geneva conference format and a comprehensive settlement of the Arab-Israeli conflict. Sadat doubted the ability to make progress toward peace with the Soviets and Syrians brought back into the picture. But if Sadat privately opposed a comprehensive approach to peace in Geneva, then he would have to conjure up an alternative.

An alternate route presented itself through a second important shift in the regional political constellation—Menachim Begin's emergence as Israeli prime minister following May 1977 elections, and Moshe Dayan's appointment as foreign minister. One will remember that Sadat and Dayan had already engaged in an exploratory diplomatic dance in the early 1970s; now Dayan's appointment rekindled Sadat's optimism for another try. Sadat's hopes were also enlivened by the Romanian president, Nikolai Ceaucescu. As early as May 1977, Ceaucescu had proposed to Sadat that he meet Begin because peace with Begin might be possible. Indyk has shown how Sadat began sending out "feelers" in June by using language about going "to the ends of the earth" to avoid another war.[73] This overture elicited a friendly response, as Israeli intelligence informed Sadat, via Morocco, of an alleged Libyan-inspired coup attempt against Sadat; the news provoked brief fighting, initiated by Egypt, along the Egyptian-Libyan border. The intelligence report also produced extensive discussions between Sadat and Moroccan King Hassan II regarding the preconditions for a Sadat meeting with Begin.

In August, while Begin was visiting Romania, Sadat quietly sent Sayyid Mar'ei to hear Begin's views.[74] This set the stage for Egyptian envoy Hassan al-Tuhami's secret, direct meeting with Moshe Dayan in Morocco on September 16, followed by Sadat's visit to Romania in October, during which Ceaucescu confirmed Begin's readiness to advance the peace process. Sadat called Foreign Minister Isma'il Fahmi from Romania to discuss his idea of going to Israel. Fahmi, incredulous, told other foreign policy aides, "Can you imagine? The man's got a hashish idea and it appears he's taking is seriously?"[75] This development caused Egyptian foreign ministry officials to hurriedly put together an alternative scheme involving the U.N. Security Council to divert their own president, but this scheme came to no avail. Thus, by the time Sadat received a private note from Carter saying that hopes for a Geneva conference had hit rock bottom, and urging Sadat to make a "bold and imaginative" move by publicly endorsing Carter's proposal for a Geneva conference, Sadat was already well down the road to taking a "bold and imaginative" move of his own inspiration.

On November 9, 1977, in a speech before the People's Assembly, Sadat announced that he was ready to go anywhere, including the Israeli Knesset, to see that peace came to the Middle East.[76] According to Mustafa Khalil, Sadat's speech, though it still caught most Egyptian insiders off guard, did not come out of the blue. "When Begin came to power, Sadat met Ceaucescu and Ceaucescu told Sadat that Begin will negotiate peace. Sadat had the impression that peace [here] meant the return of the Sinai. This was all discussed at a National Security Council meeting [of which Khalil was a member] prior to Sadat's "I'll go to Jerusalem" statement. I supported Sadat's thinking; Isma'il Fahmi said he didn't take Sadat seriously. That's why he resigned."[77]

What exactly was Sadat's thinking? Still according to Khalil, "Sadat thought that there was no other alternative to peace, because the 1973 war proved that the United States was ready to defend Israel to the hilt. Therefore, 'if I [Sadat] have to make peace with Israel, I have to talk to them directly.'"[78] Once again, détente's impact was pronounced in that it was putting Middle East issues on the back burner; so in order to promote a solution, Sadat had the idea of pushing for peace by going to the Knesset. For Khalil, "the economic motivation for Camp David was not there. After all, the Arabs offered him an option. He knew the Arab world would boycott Egypt; he didn't have any offer from the U.S. side or others at the time, so it was a genuine effort by him to make peace."[79]

Within less than two weeks of Sadat's People's Assembly statement—on November 20 to be precise—Sadat was to be found, to the total amazement and dismay of many of his closest foreign policy advisers and cabinet ministers, speaking before another parliamentary body: the Israeli Knesset. This historic breakthrough was arranged via the mediation of Ambassadors Hermann Eilts in Cairo and Samuel Lewis in Tel Aviv, the skillful prodding of two U.S. Congressional delegations that rushed to see Sadat following his "I'll go anywhere" comment, and encouragement from American media stars like Walter Cronkite and Barbara Walters.[80] Though Sadat's Knesset speech was frank and contained no note of abandoning the Arabs' "realistic" objectives, the sheer weight of Sadat's presence and the implicit recognition of Israel's right to exist shattered the longstanding psychological barrier, turning a new page in the region's history.

Foreign Reactions to Sadat's Trip and the Camp David Peace Process

Response in the Arab World

So far as foreign audiences were concerned, Sadat's peace initiative touched raw nerves and hopeful hearts alike; few remained indifferent. During 1976, the Saudis had used their influence to bring a reconciliation between Egypt and Syria over Sinai II. The Jerusalem trip obliterated this reconciliation, with Syria joining Algeria, Iraq, the People's Democratic Republic of Yemen (PDRY), Libya, and the PLO in condemning Sadat. Diplomatic relations between these parties and Egypt were frozen. Morocco, Sudan, Somalia, and Oman initially supported Sadat's move, while Jordan, Saudi Arabia, and other Gulf Arab nations adopted a more cautious, wait-and-see attitude.

When the Camp David peace talks were initiated in September 1978, the Steadfastness Front formed by the radical Arab states was joined by Tunisia, Jordan, and eventually Morocco. Sadat had had numerous run-ins with Jordan's King Hussein over the years—he even developed somewhat of a penchant for public references to the diminutive king as "the dwarf"—but he felt hurt and betrayed by the reactions of Morocco's Hassan II and Tunisia's President Bourguiba.[81] After all, Hassan II had quietly helped set up and host the secret talks between Hassan al-Tuhami and Moshe Dayan, and Bourguiba had been the first Arab leader to call for direct negotiations with Israel. Noha Sadat remembers her father feeling particularly betrayed by King Hassan II—"King Hassan sold me!" he said.[82] However, Sadat himself was much to blame on this point. Even advisers approving his peace effort, as well as key American policymakers, believed much of this negative response owed to Sadat's failure to display enough patience in explaining to fellow Arab leaders the nature of the steps he was taking.[83]

Arab leaders assembled to denounce Sadat's overture. Eventually, they tried to buy Sadat back into the Arab fold, offering billions of dollars in economic assistance if Sadat would ditch his peace initiative. But their efforts were to no avail. Sadat signed the Camp David Peace Accords in September 1978. Sadat would always point to rejection of their offer as a sign he made his trip for peace, not for Egypt's economy. Perhaps this was so, and Sadat's position is backed by the aforementioned testimonies of Mustafa Khalil and Ambassador al-Reidi. But for the cynics it never sounded completely convincing. Sadat himself could not have failed to calculate that the Americans, West Europeans, and others would feel indebted to him for his initiative and that peace with Israel would bring its own rewards.

By November 1978, all Arab states with the exception of Oman and the Sudan adhered to the Baghdad summit resolution to suspend economic aid to Egypt and boycott Egypt economically if a separate peace treaty with Israel was signed. For all intents and purposes, these measures were implemented from the beginning of 1979, several months prior to the actual signing of the Camp David peace treaty in March 1979. A second Baghdad Arab summit, organized by Saddam Hussein in late March 1979, brought the breaking off of diplomatic relations between the Arab states and Egypt, as well as the decision to transfer Arab League headquarters from Cairo to Tunis and expel Egypt from that body. In May 1979, the Islamic Conference met in Fez, Morocco and its members also voted to expel Egypt and reject the Camp David treaty. Sadat responded by trying to establish a League of Islamic and Arab Peoples, but little came of this effort.

The Soviet Response
Soviet officials also reacted negatively to Sadat's peace bid, although relations with the Soviets had already hit a low point. Ambassador Eilts recalled, "They were furious at being excluded from the peace process from January 1974 onward."[84] With Egypt allowing the United States to negotiate their disengagement agreements with Israel, the Soviets had refused to resupply Egyptian armed forces with essential spare parts or to reschedule payments on Egypt's multi-billion ruble debt.[85] This friction had prompted Sadat's unilateral abrogation of the 1971 Egyptian-Soviet friendship treaty in March 1976, and in August 1976 Egypt halted its massive cotton exports to the Soviet bloc. Just three weeks before his trip to Jerusalem, Sadat unilaterally declared a ten year moratorium on repayment of Egypt's debt to the Soviet Union in retaliation for continued arms shipment deferrals and other economic sanctions.[86] Soviet disapproval of the Camp David process just added one more grievance to an already lengthy list, and allowed the Soviets to earn political capital in the region by its display of solidarity with anti-Camp David forces. For Egypt, the strain brought additional risks and consequences because the Soviet Union was still the largest importer of Egyptian goods.

Western Governments' Strongly Favorable Reaction
Western governments' reactions were diametrically opposite those of the Soviets. Sadat was transformed overnight into an heroic figure by his Jerusalem trip, and his engagement in the Camp David peace talks boosted his admiration in the West to previously unimaginable heights. In a word, Sadat became the darling of the Western, especially American, media. In November 1977, U.S. Democratic House Leader James Wright stated that Egypt could write its own aid requests if Sadat's Jerusalem trip produced favorable results. Wright's statement proved inflated. Sadat would receive an increase in American assistance after Camp David, although he would never reap U.S. aid on a scale that he had hoped for and requested.[87] Employing Marshall Plan metaphors, Sadat eventually asked for a "Carter Plan" that would yield $21 billion over five years;[88] Egypt ended up receiving roughly half that amount. Still, Egypt rapidly found itself on the

receiving end of $2.2 billion in annual American assistance. Roughly half that amount went to economic development and support projects overseen by the U.S. Agency for International Development (AID) mission in Egypt, the largest of its kind in the world. Simultaneously, military aid and military transfers, which had begun very cautiously as early as 1975, grew quantitatively and qualitatively after the Camp David process began. American military assistance reached a plateau of $750 million to $1 billion per year by the end of the decade. With $2.2 billion in annual assistance, Egypt became and has remained to this day the second largest recipient of U.S. aid after Israel.

Overall, MDC financial and economic development assistance flowed into Egypt in quantities that offset the withdrawal of Arab aid.[89] France and other nations also engaged in arms sales and transfers. Moreover, the development of Egypt's petroleum resources by Western companies, the dramatic increase in Western tourists, and revenues from the reactivated Suez Canal boosted foreign exchange earnings at this crucial moment, while remittances from Egyptians working abroad jumped to $1.8 billion the preceding year.[90] Finally, foreign investment responded very favorably, jumping to 14 percent of gross fixed investment by 1979, compared to 10 percent in 1977. (See Appendix B.) Once again, oil companies led the way; they accounted for ten percent of gross fixed investment, and Law 43 companies for just four percent.[91] Still, on balance, these were positive signs for Egyptian planners. In two years, total foreign investment went from L.E. 204 to L.E. 497 million, and foreign investment in Law 43 companies rose from L.E. 49 to L.E. 126 million.[92]

Domestic Reactions to the Peace Process

The domestic reaction to Sadat's peace initiative was mixed. On the basis of extensive conversations with "people-in-the-street," it is safest to conclude that most Egyptians initially supported the peace initiative. Meanwhile, nearly all important opposition leaders and some regime elites vehemently opposed it.

General Reaction of the Citizenry

The army truly comes from the people and the Egyptians are not a martial people. There is a deep yearning for peace in Egypt. Egyptians are loathe to continue to pay the highest price in the frustrating battle for the fulfillment of the national aspirations of the Palestinians. But, along with this, is a truly morbid and fatalistic obsession with concepts of "honor" and "dignity."
Donald Bergus, November 1970[93]

The reasons for broad public support for peace with Israel, as well as the reservations accompanying it, deserve careful consideration. First, the state of war represented a psychological burden that nearly all citizens had long wished to erase. For the nation's youth, it meant the constant, real possibility of going to war against a militarily superior adversary. For citizens in general, it meant the everyday anxiety brought by the sound of high-speed aircraft flying overhead, the ubiquitous presence of army personnel, and the perennial drain on the nation's budget. Following the October "victory," Egyptians were free of their "morbid obsessions" with "honor and dignity." They were ready for an honorable solution that would restore their peace of mind and allow them to concentrate their efforts on the country's enormous socioeconomic needs.

Second, the regime actively played upon the citizens' hopes and anxieties. The government-controlled Egyptian media presented the peace initiative as heralding a new era of affluence.[94] In speeches and media interviews, Sadat repeatedly told his countrymen that peace would bring a reduction in military expenditures, as well as Carter's imitation of a Marshall Plan for Egypt. After a peace treaty was signed, Egyptians would find themselves on easy street. In a country where most people toiled to eke out a meager existence, this was powerful imagery.

Third, Egyptians' feelings of Arab solidarity had been seriously eroded. As noted earlier, most Egyptians have no primordial self-identification as Arabs; to Egyptians, Arabs are people from the Gulf: Saudis, Kuwaitis, and so on. Most of Egypt's citizens retain a primary Egyptian identity, anchored in such factors as its 7,000-year civilizational track record (which long predates the occurrence of the Arab/Islamic stamp on Egyptian life), the Egyptian dialect, a sense of cultural supremacy in the Arab world, and Egypt's distinct, contemporary history. For some Egyptians, a sense of belonging to the Arab world was very strong, especially among those who wholeheartedly embraced the Arab nationalist dream, but for most people it remained a secondary identity. In the late 1970s, "Egypt first" sentiments were reinforced by most Egyptians' belief that they had by no means been adequately compensated by their Arab cousins for the horrendously heavy price they had paid in defense of the Arab cause in their wars against Israel.[95] The Sadat regime would play heavily upon these sentiments as it charted its independent foreign policy path and encountered a severe Arab backlash.

Popular "Egypt-first" sentiments were also strengthened by Egyptians' envy of the good fortune that had befallen their relatively uneducated, unsophisticated, Gulf Arab and Libyan neighbors, about whom most Egyptians, in private, referred condescendingly. Older Egyptians were quick to recount stories of a not-so-distant past in which "the Arabs" who came to Egypt did so with hands outstretched, supplicating alms. Seeing themselves, through their own—perhaps inflated imagery—as having assisted their Arab cousins during their time of hardship, Egyptians now felt it incumbent upon the Arabs to return the kindness. Instead, what Egyptians were more likely to witness or hear were the stories of Arab men's misbehavior in and about Cairo. Such behavior, so much of which was not just immoral, but even sacrilegious in most Egyptians' eyes, stirred considerable animosity toward the highly visible, white-robe-and-*kefiyya*-clad visitors.

Elsewhere, the repeated attribution of violent incidents in Egypt to Qaddafi's mischief-making also exacerbated antagonistic attitudes toward foreigners like Qaddafi, who preached that Sadat was a traitor. During 1976-1977, Libyans were held responsible for terrorist bombings of the central administrative building in downtown Cairo and the Cairo-Alexandria train, as well as other acts. Animosity growing out of such events helped precipitate the aforementioned skirmish along the Egyptian-Libyan border in July 1977, further intensifying Egyptian nationalist sentiment. Similarly, there was a common perception, whatever its veracity, that Palestinians residing in Egypt had prospered while Egyptians suffered in the name of the Palestinian cause. Therefore, criticism from Arafat and other Palestinian leaders tended to fall on deaf ears among most Egyptian citizens. With these considerations in mind, the majority of the Egyptian populace supported Sadat's peacemaking, as evidenced by the enthusiastic, largely spontaneous mass reception he was afforded upon his return from Jerusalem.

Over the two year period following the Jerusalem trip, radical Palestinians and their Arab supporters directed other attacks against Egypt and Egyptians; e.g., Palestinians' assassination of the popular journalist, Yusuf al-Siba'i; and the skyjacking of an EgyptAir flight to Larnaca, Cyprus by Palestinians, which resulted in an embarrassingly botched and bloody rescue effort by Egyptian commandos. Such incidents only caused most Egyptians (opposition political activists and many intellectuals notwithstanding) to show even more support for Sadat. Thus, when Sadat signed the Camp David Peace Treaty in March 1979, he received a massive, tumultuous hero's welcome upon his return to Cairo. Of course, the government had a hand in mobilizing this demonstration of support, for as Yehiya al-Gamal wryly noted, "only Umm Kalthum [the renowned singer of classical Arab music] ever received entirely spontaneous mass demonstrations in Egypt."[96] But by Egyptian political standards, the measure of support for Sadat's peace treaty was truly impressive.

The Mostly Negative Reactions of Legal Opposition Elements

The broad political elite's reaction to Sadat's peace efforts was marked by varying degrees of opposition and minimal consent. All Marxist and Nasserite Leftists observed a strict rejection of the peace negotiations with Israel, motivated by a perceived affront to the principles of Arab unity and solidarity with the PLO. The Muslim Brothers also proved vociferous critics, an opposition deriving from a steadfast refusal to surrender any Islamic land, especially the prospect of ceding Jerusalem (the third holiest city of Islam), to infidels.[97] The Brothers' sentiments were echoed, in spades, by the university-based Islamist Groupings, while more radical Islamists saw Sadat's "treachery" as fulfillment of their worst predictions.

Most New Wafdists opposed the trip because it violated their pan-Arab sympathies. Yassin Sirag al-Din, brother of the party's president and a party big-wig, thought Sadat was completely crazy.[98] Other New Wafdists adopted a wait-and-see posture.

Mustafa Kamel Murad's small Liberal Socialist party was alone among opposition organizations in supporting the trip; Murad had even accompanied Sadat to Jerusalem. Murad had been called at 2:00 A.M. and told by Mamduh Salem, "You're going today with Sadat to Israel." Murad accepted. "I walked as if in a dream-like state in Jerusalem," said Murad.[99]

Opposition Within the Regime

The opposition's broad rejection of Sadat's initiative was hardly surprising considering the decidedly mixed views within his own diplomatic corps and government. As noted, Foreign Minister Isma'il Fahmi resigned, as did Minister of State for Foreign Affairs Muhammad Riyad and some Egyptian ambassadors. One need only read Boutros Boutros-Ghali's memoirs to appreciate the depth of shock, consternation, and disapproval that reigned among Egypt's insiders, including the foreign policymaking elite.[100] Even confidants like Sayyid Mar'ei were cool to Sadat's peace initiative. Such reactions added to Sadat's sense of political isolation.

Sadat's New Frame of Mind, New Sources of Tension

Sadat's mindset was modified by the varying responses to his peace initiative. There is no doubt but what Sadat was affected by his adulation in the West, which included acclamation like his selection for the Nobel peace prize in December 1978. Dr. Mustafa Mahmud, a well-known Marxist-turned-moderate Islamist television personality, thought Sadat's peace initiative was "brilliant." But Mahmud also believes that this stardom went to Sadat's head to the point where Sadat believed that only his view was correct; an attitude set in of 'I'm the best leader—no one has the right to oppose me.'[101] As Rutherford notes, many elites, including those close to Sadat like Sufi Abu Talib, admit that Sadat "became convinced that he was the lone visionary destined to lead Egypt and the Middle East to greatness."[102]

On the domestic front, major difficulties for Sadat grew out of his inability to tolerate opposition criticism, and a major, old-time nemesis was reappearing on the horizon. The *minabir* had been granted legal political party status in November 1976. By February 4, 1978, Wafdists had met the Political Parties Law 40 requirements to gain formal recognition on February 4, 1978. The so-called New Wafd was headed by none other than Fuad Sirag al-Din, the pre-1952 Wafdist prime minister, and drew instant support from many of Egypt's most famous, landed families: Abaza, Lamlum, Badrawi, 'Allam, al-Fiqqi, and so on.

From Sirag al-Din's vantage point, "Sadat had approved the party's reemergence because he thought it would be weak; because most of its members had died. He was wrong. At a May 1978 meeting, we had a huge turnout. The New Wafd was less powerful among workers, but we were very strong in the countryside."[103] Within three months of the party's formation, nearly one million people had reportedly joined.[104] And of course, New Wafdists were highly critical of Sadat's foreign and economic policies. Meanwhile, rumors flew that old Watani Party members were meeting to reconstruct that party.[105] In short, by early 1978 all significant, pre-1952 political forces had returned to the domestic political scene except the king, and they all lined up squarely against Sadat.

Sadat had good cause for concern about these opponents, especially after he signed the September 1978 Camp David peace accords, because there were efforts to form a national opposition coalition. Acting as independents, individuals like Seif al-Islam Hassan al-Banna, Lutfi al-Kholi, Muhammad Ahmed Khallafallah, and many NPUG types issued a declaration, published in the NPUG's publication *al-Taqqaddum,* to encourage this effort. By early 1979, this evolved into the formation of a "Group of 100," an informal, broad-based coalition speaking out against Camp David and calling for democracy.[106]

Sadat did not bear up well under opposition attacks against the vagaries of *infitah,* government corruption, constraints on political liberalization, and peace negotiations with Israel. In March 1978, Sheikh 'Ashur, a moderate Islamist member of parliament who helped sponsor the New Wafd's formation, was expelled by the government's majority for having insulted Sadat. Of far greater importance, in May Sadat called a referendum on a National Unity law to deny political rights to those who had been tried and convicted for political corruption. The move was clearly designed to strike at New Wafdist leaders Fuad Sirag al-Din, Ibrahim Farag, Hamed Zaki, and 'Abd al-Fattah Hassan, although it also opened the door to a far-reaching attack on leftists. When the referendum passed, it prompted an assembly of roughly 600 New Wafdists at which they adopted a protest decision to freeze party activities on June 2. "Sadat was going to issue a law to dissolve the party," said Sirag al-Din, "so we froze our activities to prevent this."[107] Subsequently, government officials argued that the New Wafdists had dissolved their party, so that its members would have to reapply to the Political Parties Committee for new legal status; but New Wafdists successfully pleaded in court that they had merely frozen party activities.

Even some of Sadat's longest-standing confidants and fellow regime leaders could not stomach the reversals and opposition crackdowns started in 1978. Said Sayyid Mar'ei,

> This was the beginning of our serious differences with Sadat. As I said, I first opposed quick moves to a multiparty system. I didn't join the Misr [EASP] party or any other one out of my conviction that the multiparty experiment was too early and not based on grass roots involvement. But once we *had* a multiparty system, "let it be" was the way I was thinking, and of course I was telling Sadat as much. I felt the debate within the Wafd with people was better than what we were doing with the Misr party's contact with people. I told Sadat we should play the political game more intelligently—expose the Wafd's past, debate the Wafd openly, show it had supported Faruq.[108]

But Sadat did not endorse Mar'ei's viewpoint, and the deterioration of relations with individuals like Mar'ei was indicative of Sadat's increasing isolation within his own regime. Prime Minister Mamduh Salem was yet another victim of this turn in events. He was blamed by Sadat for not doing enough to make the EASP the kind of vibrant party the New Wafd threatened to be, and resigned as party president in September. By October 1978, Sadat had dumped Salem. Salem went from being prime minister to driving about Cairo all by himself with a forlorn look on his face.

Sadat's New National Democratic Party (NDP)

> Why create a new party? It occurred to me when we started negotiations with the Israelis. I suggested to Sadat that we are going into a difficult time, needed a new party's support, and the chairman of the party must be you. Mustafa Khalil[109]

To draw attention away from his problems with the opposition, and turn a new page in regime politics as well, Sadat announced on July 9, 1978 that he was forming a new party based on the July 23 and May 15 revolutions. Sadat had expressed a desire to form a new party in July 1977. Mar'ei noted that the idea to establish a new party was born at the time of the January 1977 riots, because Mamduh Salem and the EASP were associated in people's minds with the riots.[110] Numerous meetings were held during summer 1978 to lay the party's foundations and discuss its principles. Key participants included Sadat's political philosopher, Sufi Abu Talib, along with Mansur Hassan, 'Abd al-Hamid Radwan, Mahir Muhammad 'Ali, Muhammad al-'Uqaili, and Fikri Makram 'Ebeid. New party elites represented a combination of *infitah* millionaires and rural elites. In a mid-August speech before NDP founding committee members, Sadat attacked opposition parties for wanting to take Egypt back to pre-1952 politics.[111] And in a clear effort to derive support for the new party from rural elements, and steal some thunder from the New Wafd, he asserted that land ownership should be raised to 200 feddans.[112]

The founding committee's efforts culminated in formal approval of the National Democratic Party (NDP) on October 2, 1978. The signing of the Camp David peace accords in September had reinvigorated thinking as to the need for a party.[113] Sadat took the party's presidency, despite discouragement from Mar'ei, Sufi Abu Talib, and others who felt that this was a mistake because Sadat would be blamed or criticized for the party's shortcomings.[114] "If the Misr party wasn't efficient, let me try to run one efficiently," Sadat told Mar'ei. To which the latter responded, "One man, especially a president, can't run a party efficiently." "There was no anger between us, just disagreement. He was perhaps influenced by the logic that Nasser should have created a party while he was alive."[115]

Fikri Makram 'Ebeid, from a prominent, Coptic landowning family, was named as the party's general secretary. Beyond successful private capitalists, the party's other 140 founding members included a mishmash of university professors, 'ulama, and presidents of labor federations and professional syndicates.[116]

Sadat had seen the EASP as too weak, a shortcoming he attributed to Mamduh Salem's failure to follow his advice and build the party from village-level formations. The new party was to seek help from old families and leadership personalities to build party cells on the Muslim Brotherhood model.[117] This would give the party a quality of being "rooted" in the society, unlike the EASP.

Inspiration for the new party derived from a genuine change in Sadat's thinking over the 1977-1978 period, reflecting a real desire to move beyond the strong pro-public sector and statist authoritarian attitudes of many regime elites.[118] But the peace initiative as well as domestic political developments obviously reinforced Sadat's desire for new thinking and new faces. This shift included further Islamization. Sufi Abu Talib notes that during November and December 1978 he formed a committee to codify *shari'a* law that included representatives from al-Azhar. He says Sadat asked explicitly for this work because "Sadat now believed that any Arab Muslim leader who didn't codify the shari'a couldn't succeed. He asked me to move quickly on this project."[119] The NDP's basic goals were: "(1) the building of a modern state founded upon science and faith, (2) the affirmation of spiritual values, (3) the reconciliation of individual and collective interests, (4) the affirmation of national unity and social peace, (5) striving for Arab unity, and (6) the *shari'a* is the principal source of law."[120] Sufi Abu Talib's handwriting was clear.

There was disagreement among regime elites as to the NDP's relationship to the EASP. Sadat did not want the NDP to simply replace the EASP. Well prior to his departure, Mamduh Salem had sent a memo to Sadat asking whether the EASP should stay or go; Mansur Hassan convinced Sadat that it should stay and serve as a loyal opposition party.[121] Some EASP members were convinced that the EASP should remain and began organizing meetings to this end. But while the NDP was still in formation, 'Ebeid publicly invited EASP members to join.[122] Al-Nabawi Isma'il went so far as to crash a meeting of EASP People's Assembly deputies in Fuad Muhi al-Din's office to tell them to join the NDP, saying "don't worry about the party's principles."[123] By August 1978, 200 People's Assembly members had already asked to join the NDP; the figure climbed to 275 by mid-month.[124]

With the NDP's broad leadership in place, in October 1978 Sadat dropped Mamduh Salem from the prime ministership and replaced him with the quintessential technocrat, Mustafa Khalil. Khalil also filled the foreign minister post, left empty when Muhammad Ibrahim Kamel split with Sadat during negotiation of the Camp David Accords. Regime change in October affected other key figures as well. Sayyid Mar'ei stepped down as speaker of the assembly, with Sufi Abu Talib taking his place. Mansur Hassan was brought into the cabinet as minister of information, while Field Marshal Gamassi was eased out of the defense ministry and replaced by Kemal Hassan 'Ali. In addition to their association with Sadat's new NDP orientation, many of these shifts also related to his desire to put in place individuals who would stand more firmly behind him as he moved toward the March 1979 signing of the Camp David peace treaty with Israel.

Sadat would experience the same travails as Nasser in trying to build his own tighter-knit party. Neither he nor other party leaders could prevent opportunistic elites and masses from joining the party for fear of angering and alienating them. EASP members, sycophants, and all, abandoned that party en masse to join the NDP; the EASP, like Prime Minister Salem, headed to political oblivion.[125]

Sadat spoke with resolve about making the NDP a coherent, vibrant organization.[126] By August 1979, he was disgruntled enough with the party's composition to tell regime insiders that he wanted base-to-top elections to lift it out of its quagmire. He entrusted Mansur Hassan with the task of remaking the NDP by recruiting new faces, getting university professors (e.g., Dr. Abu Talib) to embellish its program and attract the *shabab* (youth). In September 1979, Hassan beseeched each provincial governor to nominate five persons known for their integrity and genuine nationalism, without stipulating that they be party members. However, intra-elite sensitivities emerged; NDP parliamentary deputies protested these developments, believing that the new elements would be used to undercut their own positions, and the governors' recruitment process was quashed.[127]

Later, Mansur Hassan would make one final bid to rejuvenate the party, calling upon parliamentary figures to nominate new youthful cadres. In response, some 1100 new cadres were recruited across 11 provinces, but this endeavor ultimately fell victim to Abu Wafia's warnings to Sadat, beginning in May 1981, that former VO members, including people who allegedly planned to kill Sadat in May 1971, were exploiting the recruitment process to infiltrate the regime party. Sadat told Hassan to "be careful" so many times that Hassan decided to suspend his effort.[128] In the end, Sadat never did succeed in creating a full-fledged party—one rooted in a solid societal base—to provide backing for his major policies.

Building a Less-than-Loyal Opposition

As the EASP was folding its tent, the issue of a loyal opposition party presented itself. Several members of the long defunct Young Egypt/Egyptian Socialist Party, headed by Ibrahim Shukri, had been waiting for the moment to revive that pre-revolutionary party. Shukri had been a devout follower of Young Egypt party founder, Ahmed Hussein. Under Hussein, the Young Egyptians had been known for their xenophobic Egyptian nationalism, high Islamic religiosity, and imitation of European fascist youth groups. In the early 1950s, Hussein felt Nasser had stolen his party's ideals, and was imprisoned in Nasser's March 1954 crackdown on opposition political parties.[129]

Shukri himself had a checkered political track record under Nasser. He did not participate in the Liberation Rally or National Union, but he did join the ASU in 1963 after being urged to do so by Nasser regime Rightist, Nur al-Din Tarraf, and was appointed ASU General Secretary for the Delta region. As with many Rightist elements, Shukri had been very supportive of Egyptianization measures. He had also backed the regime's strong anti-imperialist stand, land reform, construction of the Aswan Dam, and the creation of state economic planning and a public sector. But as with some Nasser-era Rightists, he came to see Nasser's regime as too closed to permit free and frank exchanges of ideas and questioning of decisions, having gone too far with many post-1961 nationalizations, and being altogether too disrespectful of legal parameters, especially in the way the Defeudalization Committee mistreated middle class farmers for political reasons.[130] Such thinking brought a clash with Centrists, especially Sabri; when Sabri became ASU general secretary in 1965, Shukri's political activity was frozen.

When Sadat reorganized the ASU after May 1971, Shukri renewed his ASU and regime involvement, becoming ASU secretary of professional syndicates, then Governor of the New Valley (1974-1976), then minister of agriculture. He joined the Center *minbar* upon its formation, and won election to the People's Assembly in 1976, but he never saw eye-to-eye with Mamduh Salem. Shukri says "I had much more history [experience] than Salem, much deeper historical roots than Salem and others, and this may have made them ill at ease and somewhat wary of me."[131]

From Shukri's perspective,[132] when Sadat decided to set up the NDP, it provided him with the long-awaited moment to form his own party. He knew Sadat would have a difficult time denying him the opportunity, both because he was a well-known nationalist figure, wounded in an anti-British struggle in 1935, and because he had cooperated closely with Sadat's regime.

Shukri's dream dovetailed with Sadat's desire to create a loyal opposition party. Shukri was happy to ride on Sadat's coattails, for he needed 20 People's Assembly members to set up his party. In the end he got 28 deputies to back him, five to six were sympathizers of the old Egyptian Socialist Party, another five to six were independents, and the rest were brought along by Sadat's brother-in-law, Mahmud Abu Wafia, at Sadat's behest. Abu Wafia was also Shukri's friend. Abu Wafia had hoped for an NDP position, but Sadat had seen otherwise, inveighing upon him to do this favor, with Shukri and others the happy beneficiaries.

On December 12, 1978, the Socialist Labor Party (SLP) gained legal recognition. Shukri was pleased to allow Sadat to introduce the party, "because this would have a better popular impact."[133] While opposition elements attacked Shukri, questioning his acquiescence to major regime policies and claiming his undertaking was nothing more than an effort to assist Sadat in a difficult moment, Shukri was content to ride out the criticism, seeing it as a small price to pay for obtaining admission into the legal political arena and restoring the Young Egypt party tradition. The SLP quickly became dominated by those who openly professed Young Egypt/Egyptian Socialist roots.[134] They embraced a populist socialism that left much room to attract national capitalists, while holding an intensely nationalistic attention to Egyptian, pan-Arab, and pan-Islamic foreign policy issues.

The party was first seen as an answer to Sadat's hopes for a loyal opposition, a function it initially fulfilled according to his expectations.[135] In its infancy, SLP elites voiced approval of Sadat's peace initiative. Yet once the party was more firmly established and a brief honeymoon had elapsed, Shukri found numerous ways to address "my biggest problem; i.e., how to distance myself from the NDP."[136] Issues like Egyptian arms shipments to Morocco for use in the Western Sahara conflict, the deposed shah of Iran's January 16, 1979 visit, and the offer to the U.S. to act as a guarantor of Suez Canal traffic, were all opposed by the SLP. And the party's acquisition of a print media arm, a newspaper called *al-Sha'b*, equipped it with a potent weapon for denouncing regime policies. Over time, the pages of *al-Sha'b* were also opened up to Islamist and other regime opponents.

Sadat's Clashes with Domestic Opponents

Taming a Not-So-Unruly National Assembly

Sadat's moves in the political party arena may have been made in anticipation of his signing a peace treaty with Israel, in the hope that he would at least reduce the number of legal opposition critics of such a move. That he profoundly disliked the sign of any disapproval of such a treaty was demonstrated by his post-treaty presidential dissolution of the People's Assembly. The assembly's dissolution provided Sadat the opportunity to arrange, via electoral engineering, the elimination of the 17 members—out of its 352 elected members!—who vehemently opposed the treaty.[137]

When elections were held in June 1979, NDP candidates won 320 seats, the SLP won 29 seats, the Liberal Socialists 3, and the NPUG none.[138] Only two members who had opposed the peace treaty retained their seats and their victories were allegedly assured only as a result of their ability to employ superior force at the polling places given the distance of their constituencies from the capital.[139] Former core Free Officer Kemal al-Din Hussein, an opponent of Camp David, alleged that 30,000 soldiers were sent to vote against him in his constituency of Benha.[140] Despite this alleged electoral fraud, he survived the first round of balloting and went into a runoff election. In the runoff, claimed Hussein, regime authorities "kicked out my representatives, put in fake ballots, and did everything imaginable to make me lose, but I still won despite the rigging to ensure a pro-Camp David People's Assembly."[141] By general consensus, the 1979 elections involved far more widespread vote-rigging and fraud than the 1976 elections, all for the sake of removing a handful of critics of the peace treaty from the assembly and guaranteeing next to no opposition in the new one.[142] Even regime loyalist Sufi Abu Talib confessed there were irregularities, although he preferred to characterize the elections as "controlled" rather than falsified, a pre-election control that "helped some pro-peace candidates and put obstacles before others."[143]

Curbing Opposition by the Journalists

Regime Relations with the Journalists' Syndicate

Great opposition to Sadat's peace efforts was played out in the press. That criticism reflected the extent to which Sadat had become the victim of contradictions of his own creation. A look at the Journalists' Syndicate council elections (see Table 3) helps point out the strength of Marxist and Nasserite Leftist forces in the press corps, and therefore the potential for opposition to Sadat's foreign and domestic policies.

During Sadat's presidency, the regime did manage to increase its influence in the syndicate. While some journalists were in general agreement with Sadat and his policies all along, the authorities also improved, over time, in utilizing regime resources to influence the outcome of syndicate elections and other syndicate activities.

Although the elections were relatively free from government influence in the early 1970s, in later elections the names of council candidates had to be approved by the Socialist Prosecutor and some regime critics experienced difficulties or were blocked from candidacy.[144] This may account in part for why more Sadatists were elected in those years. Nonetheless, Nasserite and Marxist journalists maintained a strong grip on the Journalists' Syndicate throughout the 1970s, despite repeated regime efforts to weaken their control.

The important position of *naqib* was often won by opposition-backed individuals (1971, 1975, 1977). 'Ali Hamdi al-Gamal won election in 1971 and 1975 with support from Marxists and Nasserites, who were voting against Sadat's preferred candidate;[145] Kamel Zuheiri, a leftist, won in 1977. Even when the *naqib* elected was Sadat's preferred candidate (Yusuf al-

Seba'i in 1973, Salah Galal in 1980), this was not to be misconstrued as reflecting the superiority of Sadatist forces in the syndicate. Many journalists stated that it was common practice to elect a *naqib* who could work well with regime officials and thereby safeguard or advance the syndicate's material interests. With a president like Sadat, who was a prodigious provider of patronage, this practice seemed highly pragmatic. For example, in May 1981, with Sadat's man Salah Galal as *naqib,* the Ministry of Information delivered a check to the syndicate worth L.E. 120,000.[146] Thus, chairpersons were typically individuals with sufficient ideological flexibility to cooperate with the regime, but Nasserites and Marxists combined maintained a majority of seats throughout the entire Sadat period.

One additional observation should be made. The low or declining number of professionals and "chameleons" (those whose ideological orientations changed more than two times), especially when comparisons are made with the Nasser era,[147] reflected the greater ideological clarity and assertiveness resulting from Sadat's liberalization.

The Regime's Press Relations

As noted earlier, opposition forces mounted an increasingly strong press attack against Sadat's policies. At the time of the January 1977 riots, the regime's momentary loss of control was seized upon by many journalists to castigate regime policies.

Once again, Sadat was unwilling to brook such dissent; and as in other arenas, the January riots provided the basis for a regime clampdown on press opponents. Some 14 journalists, mainly Marxists and Nasserites, were arrested at the time of the riots and accused of incitement.[148] The February issue of the leftist journal *al-Tali'a* was seized shortly after hitting the newsstands. Its editor, Lutfi al-Kholi, resigned under pressure, and within months all Leftists had been canned and the journal itself reoriented toward science and technology. Thus, one of the Marxists' major print media organs was silenced in what remained an ostensibly socialist country.

Elsewhere, the creation of legitimate opposition platforms in the ASU had brought pressures by those groupings for their own press organs. Because the authorities wished to give the Egyptian Arab Socialists a mouthpiece, they couldn't do so without granting other parties the same privilege. Therefore, a party press gradually emerged, beginning with the EASP's June 28, 1977 publication of its *Misr* paper, edited by 'Abd al-Mun'im al-Sawi. The Liberals' newspaper, *al-Ahrar,* first appeared in late 1977; although the first issue of the NPUG's paper, *al-Ahali,* did not hit the stands until early 1978. The first issue of the SLP's paper, *al-Sha'b,* reached newsstands in May 1979. Again, the Muslim Brothers had obtained the right to publish magazines carrying political commentary in 1976, the principal publications being *al-Da'wa* and *al-I'tisam*.

All party newspapers were weeklies, subsidized by the government. The government also retained control over the supply of newsprint, so all editors operated under the threat of the government's ability to cut off essential financial and material resources. Confiscation, however, remained the major weapon deployed by the regime, as seen above and below.

Syndicate and Press Reactions to Sadat's Peace Initiative

Only one of the press syndicate's 13 members backed Sadat's trip to Jerusalem. That one person, 'Abduh Mubashir, was seen as a *mukhabarat* (intelligence) agent appointed to *al-Ahram* as a war correspondent. The syndicate council refrained from issuing a public declaration against the Jerusalem trip and, later on, Camp David, "so as to reduce the clash with the *sulta* [power; i.e., the authorities]."[149] Much later, the council did issue a report against the Israeli ambassador's presence in Egypt, and called upon journalists not to travel to Israel.

Sadat's Jerusalem trip was backed in *al-Ahrar,* but criticized in *al-Da'wa.*[150] However, the strongest opposition came from *al-Ahali,* as well as from Egyptian journalists publishing articles in the Arab press. This opposition contributed directly to the regime's decision in May 1978 to submit the National Unity Law to a public referendum. Once "approved" by the public, the regime used that law as a powerful weapon against Egyptian journalists penning articles—whether appearing at home or abroad—that were deemed "defamatory to Egypt and a threat to the security of the home front."[151] Several dozen journalists, including the likes of Heikal, and Marxists Muhammed Sid Ahmed and Ahmed Hamrush, were called in for questioning by the Arab Socialist prosecutor for writing allegedly subversive articles. Many journalists were blocked from writing and from leaving Egypt, and a general ban was placed on "communist, atheist and monarchist journalists."[152]

Meanwhile, *al-Ahali's* attack on the regime's foreign policy vis-à-vis Israel, along with its call for public opposition to the National Unity Law, resulted in repeated confiscation of the paper in 1978. As the first Camp David talks were being held in September, neither *al-Ahrar* nor *al-Ahali* reached newsstands, although the temporary suppression of *al-Ahrar's* publication had more to do with its articles on regime corruption.[153] In response to their attacks on the government, government-owned publishing houses had suddenly required these newspapers' managers to pay double the usual amount before printing.[154] After the October 17 issue of *al-Ahali* was confiscated, an issue devoted almost entirely to an attack on the Camp David talks, the newspaper's publication was suspended indefinitely. Mustafa Amin was secretly blocked from writing by Sadat between August 15 and September 25, 1978 for his rebuke of parliamentarians who opportunistically flocked to join Sadat's new party.[155]

The clampdown on the press demonstrated just how intolerant Sadat had become, the obvious irony being that he himself had made a greater measure of press criticism possible in the first place. Sadat started adding journalists to newspapers' staffs to change the press from within, as he had done before. Between 1977 and 1980, some 45 new journalists were added to the *Rose al-Yusuf* staff; roughly 1,000 new journalists were added to all press establishments. Sadat was hoping to create a new, post-October war generation of supportive young writers; instead, many of the new journalists turned against him.[156]

When the Camp David agreement was finally signed in March 1979, Sadat benefited from *al-Ahali's* continued absence, but the April issues of both *al-Da'wa* and *al-I'tisam* were seized because of anti-Camp David invective. This appeared to have had a partial and temporary "calming effect" on *al-Da'wa's* editorial staff. The May issue was much milder and even reproached the Arabs for their punitive actions against the Egyptian government.[157]

Following the SLP's founding, a new party newspaper, *al-Sha'b,* began publication on May 1, 1979. Again, given Sadat's role in setting up the party, the party's leaders kept their regime criticism limited in the paper's infancy. *Al-Sha'b's* editor, Hamed Zeidan, was a strong supporter of the July 23 revolution and a former editor of a workers' syndicate paper; he had Sadat's total confidence.[158] As the party became more firmly established, however, its leaders' ideological orientations (Arab unity, solidarity with the Palestinians, populist socialism, greater democracy, nonalignment) placed them at odds with the Sadat regime as well. Also, more specifically, once Hilmi Murad began contributing to the paper, problems began because Zeidan found it impossible to control Murad.[159] Murad was a former government minister who had been dumped by Nasser in the late 1960s for criticizing the regime's inability to deliver on its March 30 reform program. Ten years later, this indefatigably critical spirit was producing articles accusing Mustafa Khalil of taking money in the Siemens telephone deal, and attacking Jehan Sadat, putting him at loggerheads with the Sadat regime.

Following the 1979 elections, Sadat cut off relations with the SLP altogether.[160] Abu Wafia, party vice president, threatened to resign from the party if Murad didn't stop writing. Shukri didn't desire either outcome, so he stopped publication of the paper; but Abu Wafia soon let him off the hook by resigning. Shukri learned of his resignation by reading about it in *Akhbar al-Yom.*[161]

Paradoxically, despite *al-Sha'b's* writers' clashes with the regime, regime officials were capable of displaying evenhandedness on many occasions. For instance, Ibrahim Shukri avers that Khalil himself arranged for government funds on the order of L.E. 4,000–5,000 per month to help *al-Sha'b* surmount its debts.[162]

Al-Sha'b was to contribute significantly to efforts to form an opposition coalition during the 1980-1981 period. The SLP's leaders occupied an interesting middle ground between Islamists, Arab nationalists and advocates of political liberalization, and provided space to these voices in their party newspaper. This enhanced *al-Sha'b's* effectiveness in acting as a rallying point for opposition elements. SLP leaders and *al-Sha'b's* editors alike knew that opposition to Israel and the Camp David peace treaty was the one common denominator among nearly all opposition elements, and they hit hard upon this theme. On many occasions, they engaged in catchy displays that played upon anti-Israeli sentiments. For example, in February 1980, when the Israeli flag was to be raised publicly for the first time on Egyptian soil, the paper's editors called for one million Palestinian flags to be raised in response, and backed that effort by printing the Palestinian flag on the back page of *al-Sha'b.* At the same time, in this author's opinion, its editors had no qualms in presenting sensationalist, hyperbolic, yellow journalism in its effort to attract buyers and party supporters.

The dilemma of a desirably more liberal, yet intolerably critical press would plague Sadat until his assassination. Over time, opposition criticism weakened Sadat and his regime, while putting wind in the sails of his diverse, ideological adversaries. In a direct sense, the opposition press heated up the political atmosphere, and set the stage for Sadat's assassination. By the late 1970s, Marxists, Nasserites, and Muslim Brothers all possessed the means, either in opposition weeklies or glossy magazines, to inform and incite their constituencies. While New Wafdists did not yet have their own newspaper, they could make their voices heard through general media coverage, as well as special opportunities provided to them by the opposition press.[163] This variegated, ideological assault, a cacophony to which many Egyptians were unaccustomed and some found difficulty comprehending, elevated political tension to great heights.

Ami Ayalon has written that:

> In February 1974, President Sadat proclaimed the abolition of censorship. Important steps toward the reorganization of the press were taken in April 1979, July 1980, and August 1981: The press was declared an autonomous

'Fourth Estate' (alongside the legislative, executive, and judiciary), a new press law was enacted, and a Supreme Press Council was formed to supervise journalistic articles in the country. Despite serious shortcomings, these changes did open opportunities to Egyptian journalism that had nearly been forgotten during the previous two decades."[164]

There is no gainsaying the advances registered toward press liberalization under Sadat, but Ayalon has misinterpreted matters. Most of the changes that occurred between 1979 and 1981, namely, the new press law and Supreme Press Council, were designed to maintain or reinvigorate regime control, not loosen it. As Bianchi notes, one half of the new council's members were appointed by the new Maglis al-Shura (Consultative Council, or Senate), half of whose members were picked by President Sadat.[165] The other half of the press council's members were drawn mainly from editors and managers of state-owned media concerns,[166] many of whom, as previously demonstrated, were also picked by the president. As Bianchi correctly concludes, "These arrangements placed control of the press more firmly than ever in the hands of nonjournalists and diminished the syndicate's already marginal authority to the vanishing point."[167]

Still, Sadat's problems persisted. By March 1981, Sadat was so perturbed with the press that he held a closed door meeting with the major newspapers' editors and board chairpersons to warn that if his candidates did not win the syndicate elections, heads would roll. So editors, heeding Sadat's instructions, gave support to regime candidates, and provided financial rewards, voyages abroad, raises, threats of transfers, free meals, and employed all manner of "carrots" and "sticks" to influence the syndicate vote. This time, however, journalists spurned the patronage, elected Lutfi al-Kholi *naqib*, and returned an opposition majority to the Press Syndicate council.[168]

One saving grace for Sadat was the presence of four staunch supporters among the council's members: Muhammad 'Abd al-Gawad, 'Abduh Mubashir, Salah Galal, and Ibrahim Sa'da. (The latter, who would go on to assume great media prominence, was a former intelligence worker under Salah Nasr.) These four individuals were able to maintain a policy of silence vis-à-vis many of Sadat's more contentious undertakings, including his mass arrests of opposition elements in 1981. Moreover, although the Press Syndicate held seminars with speakers who were critical of regime policies, it never held regular conferences or seminars to fuel and steel the opposition in the manner of the Bar Syndicate.

The Lawyers' Syndicate-Opposition Melting Pot

The Lawyers' Syndicate had experienced rapid growth during Sadat's presidency. From 1971 to 1979, membership grew from 9,816 to 13,812, and the budget rose from L.E. 12,000 to L.E. 87,000.[169] Having remained relatively quiet during the first half of the 1970s, the Lawyers' Syndicate became a veritable hotbed of political activity in the latter years of the decade. As Sadat opened up the political system, syndicate *naqib* Mustafa al-Barad'ei cranked up the association's public efforts to promote greater liberalization and full-fledged democratization.[170]

When al-Barad'ei died in office in November 1977, regime leaders struck a deal with former *naqib* Ahmed al-Khawaga whereby he presented himself as the NDP's candidate in a special by-election in 1978. Khawaga was reelected *naqib* in the regularly scheduled elections of 1979. To this day, many feel that al-Khawaga won the post in those years by virtue of the regime's support,[171] and that subsequently he either betrayed the regime's confidence in him or remained the regime's double agent in the syndicate in the desperate summer days of 1981. More will be said on these points shortly.

Critical to political action in the late Sadat era was the Lawyers' Syndicate's development into a true cauldron of political opposition. In many regards, the Bar Syndicate came to occupy a position of political importance exceeding that of individual opposition groupings and parties. To begin, as one lawyer noted, the "lawyers were above [many of] the political parties, mobilizing or activating them from the syndicate."[172] But even more significant was that the diversity in the Lawyers' Syndicate, coupled with the liberalism of its dominant Wafdist current, made that syndicate a natural meeting ground for opposition forces. Lawyers were present in the leadership ranks of most major political groupings (New Wafdists, MB, other Islamists, SLP, NPUG), and they used the syndicate as a forum for opposition activity once it regained substantial autonomy after the ASU's demise.

No grouping or current took more advantage of this than did the Wafdists. It was in the relative sanctity of Lawyers' Syndicate headquarters, in fact, that Wafdists had tested the waters for a formal return to political organization and activity. In 1976, celebrations were held in the syndicate to mark the anniversaries of the deaths of former Wafdist leaders Sa'd Zaghloul and Mustafa al-Nahhas; and additional Wafdist rumblings were heard early in the summer of 1977. Wafdists combined with Muslim Brothers and old Watani Party sympathizers (the Watani and New Watani party were small, pre-1952, right-wing nationalist parties) to hold other huge, commemorative rallies. A rally in memory of Muslim Brother 'Abd al-Qader 'Awda, hanged by regime authorities in 1954, was attended by 5,000 people.[173]

At the time of the January 1977 riots, the syndicate called for a return to multiparty politics, denouncing existing parties as void of content.[174] This position matched what had been Barad'ei's longstanding, publicly expressed, negative view of the *minabir* experiment as falling far short of genuine multiparty politics.[175] Importantly, MB lawyers backed these calls for democratization, although doubts remained as to their long-term regime-type preference. By thus demonstrating the renewed vitality of these pre-revolutionary organizations, their shared opposition to major regime foreign and domestic policies, and common desire for democratization, the lawyers sorely tested regime officials' commitment to political liberalization. In fact, regime officials sought ways to block Lawyers' Syndicate activities rather than incur repeated public embarrassments. In many instances, they had recourse to brute force to accomplish this goal.[176]

Although many lawyers were upset by the shift in foreign policy of the immediate postwar period, Sadat's trip to Jerusalem was the critical event that set opposition wheels in motion in the syndicate. Opposition was not limited to the issue of peace with Israel, as evidenced by strong stands against the Pyramids' Oasis deal,[177] the restrictive 1978 press code, the rumored sale of Nile water to Israel, and military basing rights for the United States, and many other issues. The syndicate also publicly opposed the regime's efforts to rein in the increasingly independent-behaving judiciary and make the Supreme Constitutional Court subordinate to the presidency.[178] Still, the initial thrust of joint opposition activity and its major axis derived from the issue of peace with Israel.

Yehiya al-Gamal, Sadat's former minister and a prominent, Arab nationalist lawyer, "was shocked by Sadat's trip. It was a total surprise. I sent him a telegram pleading him not to go to Jerusalem; I said, 'You will cut the Arab world into pieces and make the Israelis more conceited.'"[179] Al-Gamal's view was shared by many lawyers.

A Hotly Contested Election for Naqib, Ahmed al-Khawaga's Role
When Mustafa al-Barad'ei died, a special election was held in 1978 to fill his post as *naqib*. The election pitted Ahmed al-Khawaga, the government's candidate, against 'Abd al-'Aziz al-Shurbagi. Shurbagi[180] was a venerable lawyer, a one-time friend of Nasser's who had held the post of *naqib* during the Nasser years, but had parted with Nasser in the 1960s due to neglect of abuses of human rights and civil liberties, as well as the depth of Nasser's socialist policies. Shurbagi was also a founding member of the New Wafd Party. While Shurbagi was a likely candidate as one of the select few with

widespread popularity in the syndicate, his candidacy also assumed an anti-Camp David character; this garnered him support from Nasserites, leftists, many New Wafdists, and others. Because Shurbagi's victory would have acquired a symbolism most unflattering to the regime, regime officials doubled their efforts to ensure his defeat.

The election results were too close to pick a winner after one ballot, so a second ballot was held. Khawaga drew heavy support from public sector lawyers, whose admission to the syndicate he had helped engineer back in 1968. Rumor had it that regime officials secretly asked Pope Shenouda to intervene on their behalf and instruct the disproportionately influential Copts in the syndicate to vote for Khawaga as well. According to this rumor, which Shenouda denied,[181] his intervention provided the decisive margin of victory for Khawaga. Khawaga then proceeded to keep the syndicate quiet throughout 1978-1979, "just as he had promised the regime."[182]

Khawaga was a repeat winner in December 1979. Shurbagi was ill, Barad'ei dead, and 'Ali Mansur had been offered an appointment to the Political Council of the National Democratic Party, perhaps to draw him away from the syndicate's election; so Khawaga ran virtually without opposition. NDP and public sector lawyers were urged to back Khawaga, and promised government largesse if he won. Khawaga's easy victory allowed him to work effectively to ensure the success of other NDP candidates as well. For these reasons, regime officials felt confident at the end of 1979 that syndicate-based opposition would decline.

This perception was gravely flawed. By all estimations, Khawaga was a quick study, capable of reading briefs just one hour prior to a major court case, then arguing brilliantly before the court. But he was also, says Yehiya al-Gamal, a "very flexible political figure; a man who kept one eye on power, and the other eye on the masses. He could speak with great enthusiasm with many 'different' people."[183] So while Khawaga may have played watchdog for the regime, he also allowed opposition elements great room for maneuver. Besides clearly cooperating with the regime on many occasions and being considered a member of the NDP,[184] Khawaga was also a founding member of the New Wafd, as well as a founding member of the NPUG.[185] In many respects, he was the quintessential political chameleon.

Syndicate as Opposition Rallying Point

In the early months of 1980, political activists in the syndicate turned their headquarters into a veritable bastion of opposition activity and rallied people from all sectors of society to their frequent, critical discussions of regime policies. Those discussions revolved around two basic issues: opposition to the peace treaty, and opposition to all anti-liberal democratic measures and actions initiated by the regime. As regarded the first issue, an important development occurred in the summer of 1980 when some 200 Egyptian lawyers, representing a variety of currents, attended the Rabat Conference of Arab Lawyers. Although most were public-sector lawyers who backed the government, a smaller group of delegates denounced their own government's signing of the peace treaty. Many prominent lawyers, including Yehiya al-Gamal, were questioned by the Socialist Prosecutor after their return to Egypt, and five (Muhammad Fahim Amin, Muhammad al-Azhari, 'Abd al-'Aziz Muhammad, Ahmed Nasir, and 'Abd al-'Aziz Maghribi) were placed on trial in September for treasonous behavior.

Khawaga had adopted a somewhat ambiguous formal position at the conference, calling upon conferees to stop short of censuring Egypt. Nonetheless, he was denounced as a traitor by the regime upon his return home, and Bianchi concludes that this brought his break with Sadat.[186] Though it appeared that Khawaga had become one of Sadat's major opponents, he remained *naqib,* and others believe that he continued to inform Sadat of what was going on in the syndicate. Noted 'Abd al-'Aziz Gabr, a well-known lawyer, "This is why Khawaga and Muhammad al-'Ilwani were about the only ones not arrested in that crowd [of Egyptian lawyers speaking against Camp David in Rabat]."[187]

The Lawyers' Syndicate's Political Seminars
Khawaga did abet regime opponents by turning syndicate discussions into regularly scheduled, weekly seminars in October 1980. The seminars were of two types: the New Wafdists' Muhammad Fahim Amin organized "secular" seminars every first and third weeks of the month on "hot" contemporary issues, while the MB's Muhammad al-Mismari took responsibility for organizing "religious" seminars during the second and fourth weeks. Thus, liberals were by no means alone in using the syndicate to project anti-regime barbs, although most of the "Islamic conferences" were tamer, and focused on the economy, presenting strong, pro-free enterprise views.[188]

Despite regime hostility, Bar members' denunciations of the peace treaty continued in syndicate seminars. At the first of the secular seminars,[189] where the rumored sale of Nile water to Israel was the topic of discussion, 700 lawyers of mixed ideological affiliations took an oath to condemn Sadat to life-long enmity if such a sale were made. On February 26, 1981, upon the occasion of the Israeli embassy's opening in Egypt, lawyers of diverse ideological persuasions held a large rally at which the Israeli flag was burned and the Palestinian flag hoisted. Some lawyers called for the downfall of Sadat "the traitor" and an end to the Egyptian-Zionist coalition. Equally intense meetings were held to denounce the regime's peace with Israel as the unfolding of events in the effervescent Middle East afforded new opportunities and causes to do so (e.g., Israel's unilateral annexation of Jerusalem, the Israeli bombing of Beirut and the Iraqi nuclear reactor, the granting of military facilities to the United States).

Many of the secular seminars were devoted to advocating more democracy. Opposition lawyers had done their best to expose the coercive aspects of the regime's Law of Shame (1980) before it was legislated—the law would empower the government to transfer state employees from one occupation to another—and to oppose continuation of other legislation that sanctioned police-state actions and authoritarian control mechanisms, like Law 32 (1964).

Amin and Mismari's seminars continued until Sadat ordered the syndicate dissolved in late July 1981 (discussed below). The seminars consistently attracted a minimum of 200–300 lawyers, but attendance often approached 1,000.[190]

The seminar discussions dovetailed with efforts to gain or retain the right to establish political parties engaged in by New Wafdists, Muslim Brothers, *Islamiyyin* (Islamists—as the slightly younger generation preferred to call itself), Marxists, and lawyers of other political persuasions.

The Growth and Radicalization of Islamist Forces

During the mid-1970s, Islamists had become the dominant political force on university campuses throughout Egypt. As noted earlier, many of Egypt's "best and brightest" had joined the broad Islamist movement. Much of this occurred with the regime's silent blessing. 1977 represented a watershed in regime-Islamist relations, especially as a result of Sadat's peace overture. Nearly all Islamists were enervated and energized by that development. The Islamists received another inspirational boost from the Iranian revolution, which built up momentum throughout 1978 and culminated in chasing the shah from the Peacock throne in January 1979. As noted, the overthrow of the shah, one of America's principal regional allies and the object of Sadat's admiration, bred optimism for a similar performance among many of Sadat's opponents. The Iranians' establishment of an Islamist regime, in turn, was as heartening to many Islamists in Egypt as to Islamists around the globe. Even if Egypt's Sunni Islamists disapproved of the Iranian regime's Shi'ite doctrine, they admired the revolutionary model.

Islamist Advances at Egypt's Universities

On university campuses, the Islamic Groupings were deeply affected by these developments. Sadat's peace initiative, more than any other issue, caused GI members to part with the regime. The GI were split by Sadat's trip to Jerusalem. Though all voiced disapproval, more militant members came to the fore, seizing direction of the GI and remaking it in a more radical image, while more moderate elements slipped more snugly into the MB fold. In response, the government withdrew its support for the GI, and began working against them by withholding subsidies for the largely GI-controlled student unions.[191] In the summer of 1978, the Interior Ministry prevented the GI from holding summer camps at Cairo University and Alexandria University, although Islamist camps were held at Minufiyya, al-Minya and Assiut universities.[192]

Student union elections in 1978-1979 were overwhelmingly won by GI candidates, and they used their control to issue numerous declarations, such as: condemnation of the new personal status law of 1979,[193] rejection of newly imposed regulations constraining the university student unions and Islamic groups,[194] opposition to peace with Israel,[195] praise for the new Iranian constitution,[196] condemnation of violence by Islamist extremists,[197] assertion of Islam as the only path for Egypt to follow,[198] and calls for full application of *shari'a* law.[199] By 1978, GI leaders had started calling mass prayers in huge public squares, attended by thousands. The revived Islamist summer camp at Cairo University in the summer of 1979 reportedly attracted 10,000 attendees[200]; an October 1979 mass prayer in 'Abdin Square called by the GI to celebrate the feast ending Ramadan drew 70,000 participants.[201] MB Supreme Guide 'Umar al-Tilmesani or other MB dignitaries were often invited to speak, revealing the close MB-GI ties.

Islamist Gains in the Broader Egyptian Society

Islamization was underway among Muslim men and women throughout the country. Everyday conversations focused increasingly on correct Islamic behavior; for example, whether or not it was proper to wear gold, or a recounting of what had appeared on Sheikh Sha'rawi or Dr. Mustafa Mahmud's Islamically-oriented television programs. Religious consciousness, which always seemed high in Egypt, was now running in overdrive. Kiosks were crammed with small paperback books by Sheikh Sha'rawi and others, all placed alongside the revitalized Islamic magazines and new, Islamically-oriented newspapers. Mosques filled up as they hadn't in years, and a whole new set of charismatic preachers delivered Friday sermons to capacity crowds. The more successful ones, like the blind Sheikh Muhammad Kishk, were totally unabashed in their railings against Sadat, the lifestyles of his wife and children, the woeful state of the economy, and the perfidious peace with Israel.[202] Kishk and others also showered much of their invective upon the Copts, instigating numerous acts of violence against Copts between

1979 and 1981.[203] Kishk's sermons were recorded, as were those of other preachers, and cassettes were produced that circulated in Egypt and abroad.

Equally ominous from Sadat's perspective, prominent Islamist spokesmen attacked Sadat in thinly-veiled language, or called for a change of regimes. Sadat had succeeded in eliciting *fatwas* from the Sheikh al-Azhar and Minister of Religious Endowments supporting the Camp David accords.[204] But numerous, well-known men of the cloth such as Sheikhs Mahallawi, Yusuf al-Badri, Hafez Salama, Adam Salih and 'Abdallah al-Samawi, opposed Sadat's policy and acquired large followings.

Again, many individuals in this current had wealthy foreign and domestic Islamist benefactors. Although this author remains unaware of its documentation, foreign funding of the Islamist movement in Egypt—by foreign governments and individuals alike—is widely seen as a given. As regards foreign government involvement, one need only recall the activities of Kemal Adham in Egypt in the early 1970s, not to mention separate, and at times more hostile, clandestine efforts by Libya's Colonel Qaddafi to promote his own Islamic political philosophy. Meantime, foreigners like 'Usama Bin Ladin owned residences in Cairo. In light of Bin Ladin's track record, it would be astonishing if he did not abet Islamists in Egypt during the Sadat era. Gaffney recounts that he dismissed rumors in al-Minya that money smuggled into Egypt from Saudi Arabia and Libya was used to offer stipends of L.E. 3-7 per month to students and others to grow beards; then he met a young rural school teacher who, on the basis of personal experience, confirmed the rumors.[205]

At the same time, as Lesch has shown, many Egyptian Islamists and Islamist sympathizers fared well as entrepreneurs, financiers, and commercial agents during the 1970s.[206] In addition, all the free professions were replete with successful, even wealthy, Islamists. A detailed history of Egypt's Islamist bourgeoisie and Islamist middle-class has yet to be written, but no one can deny that it existed, and its presence had a heavy impact on Egyptian society and Egypt's political-economy.

In March 1980, the Iranian shah and his family finally took up Sadat's longstanding offer of asylum in Egypt. For Islamists in particular, it was as if the devil himself had arrived in town; and Sadat bore the brunt of Islamist preachers' attacks for allowing the shah's presence. In April 1980, a prominent MB lawyer, Mustafa Mashhur, appealed to youth to make the building of an Islamic state their principal aim.[207] His words resonated.

Radicalization of the GI, Emergence of Jihad and the IG
A sufficiently rich and historically deep tradition of radical Islamist thought facilitated the construction of a radical Islamist force. In the strug-

gle for Egyptians' hearts and minds, radical Islamists easily presented their own potent political philosophy. Beyond the inspiration provided by Sayyid Qutb, many young Islamists now focused on readings by jurists. Ibn Taymiyya was a favorite, as were Ibn Kathir, Abu al-A'la al-Mawdudi, Abu al-Hassan 'Ali Nadvi, and Malik al-Nabbi.[208] To paraphrase Hassan Hanafi,[209] 90 percent of the books read by *gama'aat* types were written by jurists, not philosophers, mystics or theologians, because questions of authority were of utmost importance to them. For example, "What is the legality of the present regime? Who has sovereignty? And if one answered sovereignty to Nasser, or to Michel 'Aflaq [Ba'th party founder], or to God? Then, isn't the answer clear? Popular sovereignty didn't gain the respect of those in the *gama'aat* at all. *Al-hakimiyya li-Allah* (Sovereignty is to God), and the Koran is the only valid source of legislation." So many *gama'aat* members clearly saw Egypt, as well as the Arab and Islamic worlds in general, as threatened by a decadent, anti-Islamic "West" that sought to impose its cultural hegemony. Accordingly, they also read the jurists because, as Hanafi explained it, "A jurist always defines himself vis-à-vis 'others'—he defends the fort against threats to one's identity."[210]

What was particularly alarming in this was that the writings of Ibn Taymiyya and company sanctioned the labeling of rulers who did not apply Islamic law as apostates. And on the basis of such a judgment, one could provide justification for removing offending rulers from office, if necessary through the use of force. Apostates could be sentenced to death.

In August 1977, Interior Ministry personnel discovered a new Jihad organization in Alexandria. It had been set up earlier that year by two Fanniyya 'Askariyya group members, Salim al-Rahhal and Hassan al-Halawi, who had averted arrest in 1974. When these two were apprehended, the group's leadership passed to a 24-year-old Cairo University graduate, Kemal al-Sa'id Habib.[211] One of the group's members during 1978 was an electrical engineer in his mid-twenties named 'Abd al-Salam Farag. Farag left the Alexandria group when he moved to Cairo to take a job at Cairo University, and in 1979 he began setting up his own Jihad organization.

Farag described his group as an extension of Jihad, and confirmed its links to Salih Sirriyya's group.[212] A self-styled *faqih* (Islamic jurisprudent), Farag encouraged his followers to read the works of Ibn Taimiyya and Mawdudi, both of whom advocated violence against those not ruling in accordance with God's law. Farag incorporated these ideas in his own manual, entitled *al-Farida al-Gha'iba* (*The Missing Obligation;* namely, jihad) in which he called for establishment of an Islamic state and the return of the caliphate. For recruitment purposes, he printed up some 500 copies of his treatise for selective circulation.[213]

What remained of the Alexandria Jihad group fused with Farag's Cairo-based Jihad in 1979, and the united groups experienced increasingly good fortune in coordinating efforts with more radical GI and Islamic Group types, and/or converting them into Jihadists. In part, the GI's radicalization was perhaps facilitated when some of its more moderate leaders left the GI to join the MB in 1978,[214] but the heady events of the late 1970s, including images emanating from Iran, sufficed to bring about an important radicalization of many GI members.

In keeping with the membership profiles of the Fanniyya 'Askariyya and Takfir wa-l-Higra groups, this radicalization was more pronounced at provincial universities. There, both offended by and farther removed from the financial blandishments used by the Muslim Brothers to keep younger GI types in tow in Cairo and Alexandria, GI leaders—especially in the South—began circa 1979 to adopt a distinct line, drifting much closer to the more strident, aggressively anti-regime, violence-prone position advocated by the new Jihad organization.[215]

Radicalization of southern GI in al-Minya is brilliantly depicted by Gaffney. First, he notes that on the night of February 10, 1979, just one week after the Ayatollah Khomeini's triumphant return to Iran, GI members broke into al-Minya's city hall and "claimed to be holding it as a step toward their declaration of Egypt as an Islamic Republic."[216] Second, Gaffney writes that on March 6, 1979,

> a meeting was held in the auditorium at the College of Arts of the University of Minya which included representatives from Islamic societies from other universities throughout Egypt. It proclaimed itself to be the First General Congress of Islamic societies and it not only passed resolutions rejecting the Camp David Accords and explicitly insist[ed] that there must be no separation between religion and politics (thus contradicting Sadat's much repeated slogan, "no politics in religion and no religion in politics"), but it pronounced on certain matters of pending disciplinary proceedings involving members of the Islamic Society at Minya who had severely beaten approximately a dozen students in early January 1979. . . . This First General Congress posted its resolutions defiantly on the bulletin board of the College of Arts, where it hung for a few days and then was removed. About a month later, the Disciplinary Board concluded that the student members of the Islamic Society were guilty of this unprovoked attack. Some were suspended and others were dismissed from the university.[217]

Third, Gaffney's comparison of developments at the provincial campus of al-Minya and Egypt's more cosmopolitan universities is also instructive. He notes that,

During 1977-1979, in other universities this same pattern of convergence of the formal structures of student representation and activist Islamic Societies was also occurring, but at Minya, the combination of bullying tactics and the general novelty of the institution allowed the Islamic society to proceed with almost no organized opposition. It was not simply a matter of militants winning the elections in which they presented themselves as the only hope in a society where every other ideological platform was viewed as historically discredited or as currently failing, *but it was also a case of radicalizing representatives who initially seemed more moderate* [Emphasis mine].[218]

Without knowing it, it would appear Gaffney was bearing witness to the emergence of *al-Gama'at al-Islamiyya* (the Islamic Group, IG), and signs of IG-Jihad rapprochement.

Clashes with Christian students, violent acts against Coptic citizens, and brutish interventions to break up campus parties and impede "anti-Islamic" behavior were undertaken with far greater frequency. By mid-1980, almost all southern GI leaders now felt it a mistake to work within the system to promote change[219]; they had broken ranks with the more moderate, MB-aligned, GI types and had become IG or Jihad members. Many were busily assessing the prospects for a violent confrontation with the state.

Sadat's Reaction to the Islamists' Growth

As a self-perceived, genuinely devout Muslim and a promoter of a certain degree of Islamization, Sadat remained unalarmed by the Islamists' success much longer than one might think. It was he, after all, who had let the Islamist genie out of Egypt's political bottle. He had done so not only because he was encouraged by major Arab benefactors, and it had served his domestic political needs, but also because he himself found much that was laudatory in the values held by moderate Islamists, including many Muslim Brothers. His views were shared by many close friends and advisers, like 'Uthman Ahmed 'Uthman and Sufi Abu Talib.

Musa Sabri's writing is instructive as regarding Sadat' thinking during this period because he was especially close to Sadat.[220] As Sabri says, Sadat's analysis of the Islamic groups produced a three-fold categorization: (1) a large group comprised of youths who were true believers in Islamic principles, were disturbed and annoyed by signs of corruption, and saw their religion as a refuge and escape from that which was bad in their society; (2) a much smaller group of youths who had come to embrace extremism and terrorism, and the need to change society by blood and the sword; and (3) a tiny group of communists—infiltrators of sorts—who sought to push the

Islamic groups to play with fire to wreak havoc in the country. According to Sabri, Sadat thought he could win over the "innocent youth" of the first, largest component, and therefore he focused his efforts on devising means to attract these youth to "the correct meaning of Islam."[221] Sadat felt his security forces could handle any threat posed by the smaller groups.

One might surmise that after the shah's demise—especially given Sadat's fondness for the shah and contact with him—Sadat's attitude toward Islamists in general might have been negatively affected. This happened, but again, not as quickly as one might surmise. Evidence of this can be found in Boutros Boutros-Ghali's account of the following insightful exchange he had with Musa Sabri as the two men stood observing the shah's post-revolution arrival in Egypt on January 16, 1979:

> I [Boutros-Ghali] asked Musa Sabri, "Is there a risk that the Iranian revolution can spread to Egypt?" Sabri, one of the few journalists who dared to criticize the Ikhwan (Muslim Brotherhood) . . . replied, "The Iranian revolution is a sickness that cannot spread to Egypt. This country is Sunni while Iran is Shia; the two countries are geographically and religiously separated by Saudi Arabia, the stronghold of Wahhabism, a third force in Islam." Then he added thoughtfully, "The successive governments of Egypt have contributed in no small way to building up the Ikhwan as a political force. . . . President Sadat is on the point of making the same mistake in tolerating not only their reappearance but their activism."
>
> I interrupted . . . and asked, "You see him so often and can talk freely with him. Why don't you talk to him about this very real danger?"
>
> "Yes, this is a subject that I regularly mention to him. Jehan al-Sadat agrees with me and she insists that this danger must be averted. Sadat answers. . . . that we overestimate their importance and that he would not hesitate to intervene with force should this become necessary."
>
> I asked, "Do you think, now that the shah's regime has fallen, the 'Raiss' [President] will act?"
>
> "I don't think so, . . . half of the people present imagine that the shah will return victorious, and the other half think that the Ikhwan can never take over Egypt. Sadat himself still thinks that the real danger comes from communism."[222]

Thus, even for a certain period after the shah's fall, and in contrast to what one might surmise, Sadat perceived no grave threat from the Islamist movement. Rather, he saw "communists" and Nasserites as more threatening, and for the record, the late 1970s and early 1980s were replete with reports of government security forces "smashing" small, clandestine groups like the "Organization of the ECP—8 January" and the Committee for the

Defense of the Nation and Democracy.[223] Simultaneously, Sadat oversaw measures to thwart radical Islamists, but he made no serious effort to stem the broad Islamist tide. He kept his focus primarily on how to maintain a good relationship with the "largest component" of Islamists, and even raised moderate Islamists' hopes. He had even greater media light shined on his attention to Islamic holidays and regular appearances at mosques, his regime's support for Sufist orders, and his opening of the print and broadcast media to new Islamic publications and programming. And following the Iranian revolution, instead of clipping all Islamists' wings, he chose to go further to assuage Islamist sentiment.

For example, Sadat initiated contacts with Dr. Zakariyya al-Birri, a professor of Islamic law, to discuss changes that would meet Islamist youths' needs and demands.[224] Sadat felt these meetings so constructive as to turn them into regular weekly meetings, held every Monday, beginning circa November 1979 and continuing until Sadat's turbulent trip to Washington, D.C. in August 1981.[225]

In the end, regime stalwarts were correct in believing that any successful Islamization of the polity would have to be sanctioned by Sadat, and be decreed from on high. Unless, of course, there was a revolution. Why? Because as push came to shove, "clubs were still trump," and the state maintained the ability and willingness to use its "clubs" to keep radical Islamists in check. As many Islamist groups entered into what gave the appearances of an exponential growth spurt, regime leaders tried to apply the brakes. Still, regime efforts to block the Islamists' summer camps in 1978 and 1979 were halfhearted. In 1979, some student unions were banned, depriving GI of important organizational and material resources.[226] Yet, despite the numerous obstacles faced by Islamist students competing for student union seats in January 1980, they still performed well.[227]

An Opposition National Front?

Cooperative efforts in the Lawyers' Syndicate spilled over into the broader political arena. During 1979 and the first half of 1980, some political activists sought formation of an opposition national coalition, if not a national front.[228] This activity was inspired, at least in part, by the momentous developments in Iran. That revolutionary effort was achieved by an impressive combination of Islamists, Marxists, and liberals, and supported by broad sectors of the Iranian public. The Iranian revolutionary model had many admirers in Egypt, many for its content, but even greater numbers for its form.

In Egypt, against a backdrop of threats and invective from Arab nations and the new Iranian regime, the collapse of negotiations with Israel was highlighting Sadat's inability to show progress toward a broader peace and compounded his difficulties by late 1979 and early 1980. For Sadat, such strains were perhaps most problematic due to the way they affected his fellow citizens' thoughts about what, exactly, peace with Israel had wrought. Once again, opposition to the treaty was serving as the primary unifying force among regime challengers.

In Egypt, principal figures seeking to build a national front in opposition to Sadat's regime included Free Officers 'Abd al-Latif al-Boghdadi and Kemal al-Din Hussein, Heikal, 'Abd al-Salam al-Zayyat, Mahmud al-Qadi, Sheikh Salah Abu Isma'il (Wafdi with MB links), Sabri Mubaddah, Muhammad Nassar (independent), and some NPUG types.[229] On February 26, the day relations with Israel were normalized, an opposition petition was published; it was signed by dozens of well-known political figures, including numerous, high-ranking post-1952 elites. Next, on May 12, 1980, a five-point statement was issued by Boghdadi, Hussein, Khalafallah, Nassar, 'Aziz Sidqi, Ahmed Seif al-Islam Hassan al-Banna, Murad Ghalib, Muhammad Riyad, Muhammad 'Asfur, Fathi Radwan, Lutfi al-Kholi, Isma'il Sabri 'Abdullah, Fuad Mursi, 'Abd al-Salam al-Zayyat, Zaki Hashem, Muhammad 'Atia Khamis (president of the Shabab Muhammad), and 'Abdullah Salim (president of the Association for Promoting the Culture of the Koran, which had 2,000 branches all over Egypt), as well as syndicate representatives, Wafdists, and SLP members.[230]

Ultimately, efforts to form a pro-democracy, anti–Camp David coalition would fail for numerous reasons. From the Brothers' perspective,[231] there were too many July 23 types present for some people's liking. From a New Wafdist and Leftist vantage point,[232] the Iranian revolution's Thermidor, Khomeini's repression of liberals, as well as leftist revolutionary forces, soured attitudes toward building a broad revolutionary coalition in Egypt. Though national front efforts would fail, they first provided signs that members of diverse ideological leanings were attempting coalition formation in opposition to Sadat's regime. Such actions piqued Sadat's anxiety; he had no desire to suffer the same fate as the shah.

The May 1980 Government: Cookies, Islamic Crescents, and Clubs

By May 1980, the autonomous growth in power of the Islamist groups, radicalization of many GI elements, and signs of opposition national opposition activity elicited a strong response from Sadat. In the new May 15, 1980 cabinet announced by Sadat, Sadat himself assumed the post of prime minister. The only other time he had done this was prior to the 1973 October War. This time, the battle was at home.

To safeguard his position at home, Sadat found it imperative to provide signs of tangible economic progress to his citizenry. To enable his economic and foreign policies to ripen, he needed to buy time, and he proceeded, quite literally, to attempt just that. The original budget drafted for 1980, presented in late 1979 and revised in February 1980, called for imposition of a new sales tax, price increases for public sector companies, higher rates for electricity, and reductions in subsidies for numerous items, including butagas, medicine, wheat, and flour.[233] "Following considerable social tension in early 1980, some of these measures were dropped as a new government announced a major change in the direction of policy in May 1980."[234]

With the new May 1980 cabinet, Sadat introduced his new economic czar, 'Abd al-Razzaq 'Abd al-Magid, who was instructed by Sadat to keep the economy "rosy." For 'Abd al-Magid, the good news was the enormous improvement in Egypt's balance of payments position due to unexpectedly high oil revenues. While these revenues presented a window of opportunity to alleviate Egypt's foreign debt, or introduce reforms from a position of relative economic strength, Sadat found it politically expedient to loosen the belt. Accordingly, the minimum wage was increased by 25 percent, import duties were reduced for a wide range of commodities, including consumer durables, the government recommitted itself to hiring all graduates, starting salaries were raised for graduates taking public sector jobs, and exemptions from certain taxes were offered public sector employees.[235]

Sadat's new cabinet also included his behind-the-scenes Islamist adviser, Zakariyya al-Birri. Al-Birri was appointed minister of religious endowments. According to Musa Sabri, both Sadat and al-Birri discussions produced agreement over the need to implement *shari'a* law, and that there should be no problem in modifying the civil code to bring it into conformity with the *shari'a*.[236] They also concurred on the need to create youth associations, first for Muslims, then for Christians, to propagate "correct" visions of these faiths.[237] Al-Birri also proposed establishing human rights committees in each town, village, and city district; their members would be chosen from among individuals known for their nationalism and moral rectitude, and their goal would be to eliminate acts of oppression by tyrannical *umdas* and police officials at the local level.[238]

Sabri's assertions accord with those made by Sufi Abu Talib, who was among the principal legal minds charged with the task of revising the civil code.[239] (Abu Talib would complete this work in the early 1980s, but under Mubarak his endeavor came to naught.) For Abu Talib,[240] the Iranian revolution had led Sadat to the conclusion that it was impossible to imagine a democratized Islamic nation in which Islamic law did not feature prominently. Taken collectively, these assertions suggest that Sadat, long characterized as the ultimate pro-Westerner, and long vilified as such by his Islamist opponents at home and abroad, was promoting an interesting Islamization of the Egyptian polity.

As Dekmejian notes, "Sadat's response to the growing opposition to his economic and foreign policies was to intensify his pursuit of Islamic legitimacy. The regime introduced a series of bills on Islamic penalties for usury, apostasy, theft, adultery, and drinking, most of which were withdrawn after protests by both Copts and liberal Muslims. [But in his] May 1980 speech before the People's Assembly, Sadat proposed a constitutional amendment to make *shariah* law *the* main source of legislation."[241] There was even an independent motion put before the People's Assembly to declare Sadat as the fifth rightly guided caliph; although Sadat himself was embarrassed by it and vehemently objected to it.[242] Article 1 of the May 1980 Law of Shame, passed by referendum on May 22, stipulated that "the prosecution of the basic values of society is the duty of each citizen"; and Article 3 criminalized "[a]dvocating any of the doctrines which imply a negation of divine teachings or which do not conform to the tenets thereof."[243]

In many respects, in the struggle for Sadat's mind on the issue of Islamization versus secularization, the advice of his moderate Islamist friend, 'Uthman Ahmed 'Uthman, was winning out over that of Sadat's more secular-minded wife, Jehan. As Beha al-Din observed, "Perhaps her influence on him [Sadat] might have remained greater, until 'Uthman Ahmed 'Uthman won away a big share of her influence on him, as the president came to spend even more time in his diverse rest houses with 'Uthman than he spent with her in his house. And the reputation of her influence shrank alongside the growth of 'Uthman Ahmed 'Uthman's influence, a matter that led her, despite their family relationship, to despise him to a great extent."[244]

From all appearances, 'Uthman Ahmed 'Uthman and others encouraged Sadat to go farther down an Islamic path during this period. They encouraged Sadat to approach university Islamists through his longstanding contacts with the MB's old guard. Several meetings were held, but they bore no fruit.[245] The attempt to find common ground with Muslim Brothers and more moderate Islamist elements had come too late. The more radicalized GI factions were off and frenziedly running on their own fateful course.

But the May 22 referendum brought much more than signs of Islamization. It lifted the constitutional provision limiting a president to two terms, opening up the possibility of Sadat becoming president for life. It also created a new Maglis al-Shura (Consultative Council), a senate-like body whose membership was heavily controlled by the presidency and would operate to enhance executive control. And last but not least, there were other potent, repressive instruments contained in the Law of Shame, for it also criminalized "advocating opposition to, hatred of, or contempt for the state's political, economic or social systems," or "broadcasting or publishing false or misleading news or information which could inflame public opinion."[246] All told, these changes clearly indicated Sadat's decision to steel himself against his opponents to weather the domestic and foreign political storms.

Regime Clampdown

The Law of Shame may have helped to keep the general public quiescent. But as already seen, it did little to dissuade active regime opponents from pursuing their mobilizational efforts, and therefore the regime went on the offensive. By mid-1980, all Islamist student activities were forbidden, and several "princes" and Islamist student leaders had been incarcerated for promoting sectarian strife.[247] Tilmesani and others were banned from speaking to student and youth assemblies[248]; and all attempts to form Islamist camps on university campuses in the summer of 1980 were thwarted.[249] Yet in a true display of grit, gumption, and regime defiance, Islamist youth still managed to mobilize mass prayer gatherings, score well in certain colleges' student elections,[250] and hold successful conferences during the 1980-81 academic year.[251] Thus, Islamist revolutionary spirits continued to run high, despite regime repression. All things considered, compared to Nasser, Sadat's bark always remained worse than his bite.

Continued Islamization in 1980-1981

At the turn of the decade, continued Islamization was readily observed in numerous ways. More and more men were sporting beards in imitation of the Prophet Muhammad, and more women were adopting the *hijab,* that is, Islamically-prescribed dress. To cite just one example, this author arrived in Egypt in the fall of 1980 for formal registration at the Faculty of Economics and Political Science at Cairo University. In the main clerical office, there were roughly ten employees, all but one were women. When I first entered the office, there was only one woman who was *muhaggaba* (in conformity with the Islamic dress code) but on each of the occasions I had cause to reenter the office in the ensuing months, there were one or two more women who had become *muhaggaba.* By the time of my final visit there at the end of academic year, all but one of the women had "covered herself." I asked the one woman why she hadn't followed suit, and she gave me a rather ambiguous "in sha' Allah" ("if Allah wills it") response. I felt as if I was bearing witness to a "domino theory" of Islamist expansion at Egypt's principal university.

During the same time frame, the language and actions of moderate Islamists grew bolder. In September 1980, Muhammad 'Abd al-Quddus, son of the famed journalist Ihsan 'Abd al-Quddus, wrote an article referring to the bad fate suffered by pharaohs and authoritarian rulers like Hafez al-Assad, Saddam Hussein, Mu'ammar al-Qaddafi, the shah, and Nasser.[252] Two months later, MB leader Tilmesani wrote in *al-Da'wa* that "the Koran, the Prophet, Jihad and death for the sake of God is the first of our concerns."[253] And in 1981, the GI-MB tandem sponsored mass prayers in 'Abdin Square and Alexandria's university stadium that attracted 250,000 individuals each.[254]

Radical Islamists' Advances

In 1980, a *shura* (consultative) council was formed whose membership reflected close coordination between Jihad, radical GI, and IG elements. This same council selected the 43-year-old blind sheikh, 'Umar 'Abd al-Rahman, as their religious leader. 'Abd al-Rahman, a formally trained religious scholar who was teaching at al-Azhar University's Assiut branch at the time, was seen as possessing the religious credentials permitting him to issue a *fatwa*. Many of his religious injunctions countenanced the use of violence by radical Islamists.

Jihad adopted a relatively open, mass recruitment system. However, as Dekmejian notes, unlike the Society of Muslims, Jihad also recruited from the military, security services, and other government personnel.[255] Its structure was cell-like; and as it grew in size it acquired a healthy list of regional leaders, called princes, who had significant decision-making autonomy. By 1981, the group had grown to include some 200-300 members,[256] most of whom resided in Cairo, especially in the poor district of Bulaq al-Dakrur, or the southern cities of Assiut and al-Minya. Its most important princes included 'Abd al-Salam Farag (Cairo and Giza), Fuad al-Dawalibi and 'Essam Darbala★ (Minya), 'Asim 'Abd al-Magid 'Asa,★ 'Usama Ibrahim Hafiz and Nagih Ibrahim★ (Assiut), Hamdi 'Abd al-Rahman 'Abd al-'Azim (Sohag), Tal'at Fuad Qasim and Muhammad al-Sharif (Nag'a Hamadi and Qena).[257] This list constitutes a miniature *Who's Who?* of Islamic extremists whose deeds were a pox on the Egyptian regime well beyond Sadat's demise.[258] The asterisk designates those who were also GI and/or IG princes.

An additional, noteworthy recruit in 1980 was 'Abbud 'Abd al-Latif al-Zumur. Al-Zumur was a 33-year-old lieutenant colonel in Military Intelligence. He had been greatly inspired by the Iranian revolution. After about one year of religious reading, he had met with Farag in August 1980, was given Farag's treatise to digest, and began concocting his own revolutionary plans for Jihad.[259] His skills as an intelligence officer made him an invaluable asset. He quickly became the group's master strategist, and by January and February 1981, he and Farag initiated the planning that culminated in Sadat's assassination.[260]

Al-Zumur served as a principal link between Farag's primarily northern group, and the *sa'idi* (south of Cairo) group. Later testimonies revealed that the *sa'idi* group members were acutely concerned that Coptic Christians were stockpiling weapons and gearing up for a Lebanese-style conflict, with the objective of making Assiut the capital of a breakaway Coptic state.[261] Al-Zumur met often with Fuad al-Dawalibi, a 28-year-old, Minya-based prince, to teach military strategy. Their meetings revealed that their capabilities were limited to making only one concentrated strike on a significant government target, which they determined to be the security headquarters in Assiut.[262]

Sadat at Bay

There was a Lebanonization of Egypt at the elite level and an Iranization of Egypt at the mass level. Kemal Ibrashi[263]

By May 1981, Sadat had reached yet another level of frustration. He felt he could no longer tolerate the threat posed by the Lawyers' Syndicate's activities, in particular because they held the potential for promoting a broad-based, anti-regime coalition. Short of reopening Nasser era-type internment camps, almost everything possible was being done to block many opposition groups' activities, but a frontal assault on the legal parties would be very damaging to the Sadat regime's image at home and abroad. Taking on the Lawyer's Syndicate, by comparison, represented a safer target to demonstrate the regime's anger, and a means to send a strong message to all opponents.

To this end, Sadat met with a group of public sector lawyers in Alexandria in May 1981. In this meeting, which was nationally televised, Sadat lashed out at the "small group of dissidents" who were controlling the Lawyers' Syndicate. The implication was that the syndicate should purge itself of those elements just as some other syndicates had "cleansed" their ranks.[264] On June 26, Sadat's suggestion was acted upon when, according to the official version,[265] a large number of lawyers smashed their way into the syndicate headquarters in Cairo, declared a withdrawal of confidence from the existing council, and demanded its dissolution. Sadat responded promptly to this plea, calling upon the People's Assembly to investigate the matter. On July 26 the elected council was dissolved, and a provisional council headed by a regime insider, Gamal al-'Uteifi, was put in its place.

The "dissident" lawyers' pro-regime action was far from spontaneous. According to many sources,[266] many promises were made to public sector lawyers. These included a new requirement that all joint ventures employ legal advisers, as well as the NDP's pledge to grant each lawyer L.E. 300 at marriage and L.E. 400 to open a new office. In exchange, the "Alexandria" lawyers and other regime supporters had launched their June 26 assault on syndicate headquarters, their ranks reinforced by Mabahith agents. These agents, trying to pass as lawyers, had blown their cover by mistakenly attacking the Journalists' Syndicate headquarters, located directly adjacent to the lawyers' headquarters. Others had shouted for an end to the Council of Administration, which didn't exist in the Lawyers' Syndicate.[267] Nevertheless, Sadat had been provided the pretext to quash the opposition in the syndicate and he used his preponderant control of the media to drown out the opposition's outcry.

The confrontation with the lawyers was just the first in a series of events that turned the summer of 1981 into a scalding hot one for Egypt's president. Utterly shattering to his image at home were three other major events, two of them regional, the third domestic.

Israel's Military Strikes in Iraq and Lebanon

Two consecutive bombing raids were conducted by the Israeli Air Force against Arab foes, one in early June on an Iraqi nuclear reactor whose construction was nearing completion, the second in mid-July in which hundreds of civilians in Beirut were killed or wounded. Both Israeli bombings came within 48 hours of face-to-face meetings between Sadat and Israeli Prime Minister Menachim Begin. Sadat had no prior knowledge of either raid and was infuriated by both events. Ashraf Ghorbal says Sadat felt he had been "stabbed in the back by Begin."[268] Noha Sadat was with her father at their summer house in Ma'mura, on Egypt's Mediterranean coast, when he got the news of the nuclear reactor bombing. She says he called the Israeli ambassador and "shouted at him so loudly you could have heard him all the way back in Cairo."[269] Jehan Sadat says her husband was "extremely angered and upset" by the bombings; she had never seen him any angrier.[270] Still, the Egyptian government's public response was muted, and thus created an altogether different image to the broader public.

To most observers, the timing of both events made Sadat appear either complicit in the bombings, or the ultimate *humar* (literally, donkey; fool).

Animosity toward the regime rose precipitously. The opposition press screamed bloody murder, and SLP members and other parliamentarians stormed out of the People's Assembly after shouting objections to the regime's "ostrich policy" response to the bombings.

The regime's unwillingness to respond with any punitive action against Israel was understood by all elite actors, foreign and domestic alike. Sadat was temporarily handcuffed. Because the Camp David accords scheduled the return of all Egypt's occupied territory for April 1982, Sadat was determined to do nothing to jeopardize the tangible gains to be realized by that date. Israeli decision-makers understood Sadat's predicament perfectly well. But if this schedule enabled the Israeli government to go beyond testing Sadat's commitment to peace and exploit his predicament to attack other Arab nations, it also mobilized his domestic opposition. With regard to Egypt's policy toward Israel, there was little disagreement among regime opponents about what ought to be done. In short, this issue, replete with its intensely nationalistic, anti-Zionist, anti-American, anti-Western imperialist, and religious dimensions, provided a potential basis for the formation of a revolutionary coalition. Combined with the common desire to terminate Sadat's limited pluralist authoritarian regime, this issue placed Sadat in a genuinely precarious position.

Again, it took no stretch of the imagination to find a model for such a revolutionary coalition, for one had just been placed on successful display in Iran. Interestingly, Mustafa Khalil said that, "Sadat didn't draw parallels between Iran and Egypt. The mullahs were much more powerful there; the shah had angered all the clergy, whereas here the clergy support the regime."[271] Perhaps, in general, Sadat had not made such comparisons; and Khalil's assessment certainly matches that of Musa Sabri cited earlier. But on this matter, one is well-advised to recall Camelia Sadat's words about her father's admonition, "Don't show you are weak." There is much reason to believe that in the specific historical moment in which Sadat found himself in 1980–1981, the lessons of the Iranian revolution pressed upon him more sharply. After his fall, the shah himself repeatedly warned Sadat not to trust the Americans. He told Sadat, "When I was dancing with Mrs. Carter in Teheran, I found out later that the head of the CIA was preparing for Khomeini's return. Don't trust them, my dear friend Anwar; they have no ethics."[272]

Of course, for Sadat's opponents, there was one new, major psychological barrier to coordination of efforts by the disparate ideological forces. Again, ironically, this derived from observations of the Iranian revolutionary coalition's dissolution. The Iranian regime's crushing of non-Islamist groupings raised serious doubts among secular opposition types in Egypt

over the wisdom of such an alliance. Given a choice between more of
Sadat's rule or life in an Islamist society, most non-Islamists much preferred
the "tyrant" at hand.[273]

For this crucial reason, a coordination of efforts by opposition forces did
not advance very far in Egypt. Individual opposition groupings became less
inhibited in attacking the regime. Their activities were splashed across the
front pages of opposition newspapers,[274] and thereby contributed to a rapid
growth in political ferment. But of crucial importance was the opposition's
continued inability to form any broad-based revolutionary coalition, despite
interesting attempts by individuals like Hilmi Murad and Fathi Radwan to
link up with Islamist youth groups and Arab rejectionist states.[275]

Needless to say, Sadat couldn't appreciate his opposition's difficulties. For
Sadat, the mere appearance of efforts to form such a coalition now sufficed
to heighten his sense of danger. Regime security officials encouraged him
to nip in the bud any hint of revolutionary activity. Indeed, some individuals, al-Nabawi Isma'il among them, were seen as self-servingly heightening
Sadat's concerns. Mansur Hassan, Sadat's former minister of Information,
opined that: "You gain power in the system from the president. To show
him that you are loyal, you have to find enemies. It is in my interest to create enemies for you to make you realize you need me and I am with you.
I believe Sadat's enemies were mainly artificially created and enlarged by
others who wanted to keep their positions."[276] The sagacity of Hassan's
comment is quickly undermined by Sadat's ultimate fate; but it must be
pointed out that he was not alone among insiders in making this evaluation. To the extent that Sadat's paranoia produced the massive September
1981 arrests, which in turn precipitated his own assassination, Hassan's
words are well worthy of consideration.

Fitna ta'ifiyya (Sectarian Strife), the Zawia al-Hamra Explosion
In the Middle East, the word *fitna* carries the weight of references to a
plague, or to some deadly virus lying dormant in its victim's body, then
suddenly choosing the dreaded moment to strike. In Egypt, for centuries
on end, the Islamic crescent and the Christian cross have appeared alongside one another, in general peacefully filling the skyline between heaven
and earth; but the relationship always carried the potential for discord dis-
integrating into the worst forms of violence.

Relations between Sadat and the Coptic Christian community had
deteriorated badly from 1978 onward. In March 1978, there were clashes
between Muslims and Copts in Assiut and al-Minya; many churches were
burned and some priests were attacked.[277] The Abu Zabaal church in Cairo
was burned, also, and this was followed by a protest march by 90 priests.[278]

During the same month, the Supreme Court decided that according to *shari'a*, "which is valid for all," Copts too could marry four women. The decision was later repealed, but the challenge to the Coptic personal status law was clearly understood.[279]

These events led Pope Shenouda to a frank discussion of matters with Sufi Abu Talib. With the apparent drift toward *tatbiq al-shari'a* (implementation of *shari'a*) through the effort to amend Article 2 of the constitution, Shenouda expressed concern about Copts' equality. Despite some measure of political liberalization under Sadat, no Copt was elected to parliament in either the 1976 or 1979 elections. This kept the Copts' parliamentary record intact; although they were granted representation by presidential decree, they won no seats in the 1960s and 1970s in national legislative elections. In addition, the pope had taken a dim view of Sadat's peace with Israel. Indeed, he banned Coptic Christians from making pilgrimages to Jerusalem;[280] yet another stance that did little to endear him to Sadat.

During November and December 1979, Sufi Abu Talib was following through on Sadat's instructions to form a committee for the codification of Islamic law.[281] Sadat had issued two caveats to Abu Talib relating to this work: (1) that conditions were still not right in Egypt to permit implementation of the *hudud*, the "punishments" meted out for specific crimes according to Islamic prescription; and (2) not to touch anything regarding the Christians. Abu Talib says he contacted Shenouda to provide these reassurances, and to discuss *taqnin al-shari'a* (codification of shari'a law), not *tatbiq al-shari'a*," but Shenouda's response ultimately proved aggressive and hostile.[282] In the early months of 1980, Shenouda sent Sadat a letter asserting that Christians were eight million strong, that is, roughly 20 percent of the population. (Shenouda apparently repeated the claim to President Carter in a private meeting.)[283] Official government's figures put the Copts' demographic weight at only five to seven percent of the total. In the same letter, Shendoua asked Sadat to name two vice presidents, one Muslim and one Christian, as well as guarantee a number of state posts (especially police and judiciary jobs) to Christians proportionate to their demographic weight. Shenouda believed there should be twenty, not ten, People's Assembly seats set aside for Christians, and more Christians appointed to the Foreign Ministry and public sector managerial positions.[284] Sadat was greatly offended by Shenouda's letter.[285]

These developments came against the backdrop of other events that disturbed Coptic-Muslim relations. The civil war in Lebanon, heavily laden with the most heinous forms of Christian-Muslim conflict, continued to create anxiety over duplication in Egypt. Rumors became widespread in the late 1970s and early 1980s that Coptic Christians were purchasing and stockpiling weapons, preparing for the eventuality of armed confrontation with Muslims. In early 1980, there were many attacks on Coptic churches,[286] and heightened Coptic-Muslim tension on university campuses. At al-Azhar University, Islamist groups staged a huge rally on January 18 at which they heaped much invective upon the Copts.[287] In addition, there were reports of girls being abducted for the purpose of "forced conversions to Islam."[288] On March 21, the niece of a priest who was the pope's secretary was allegedly abducted and raped by a radical Islamist.[289] While members of the community were searching frantically for her, the Holy Synod met on March 26. In response to the degeneration of the Copts' standing, and for Sadat's refusal to endorse Shenouda's political advice, the Synod decided to spurn the government's traditional offer of Easter-time congratulations. When Egyptian television crews showed up at the Coptic Vatican to broadcast the services as usual, they were sent away. In essence, the Easter celebration was canceled. The pope and his bishops prayed in the seclusion of a monastery, and there was news that Shenouda was again fasting.

Sadat was again greatly angered by Shenouda's actions. During Sadat's People's Assembly speech of May 14, 1980, a fiery two-hour speech delivered on national television just eight days before passage of the Law of Shame, Sadat attacked Shenouda and the Coptic church's hierarchy. He accused Shenouda of fomenting religious strife, of plotting for seven years to split Egypt and establish a Coptic capital in Assiut. Said Sadat, "I'm a Muslim leader of an Islamic state," and to reiterate, he proposed amending the Constitution to make Islam the principal source of legislation.

In the speech's wake, Coptic-Muslim relations became a tinderbox; or as Musa Sabri put it, the situation became so dangerous that there was a risk of bloodletting in the streets. Only the intervention of Coptic People's Assembly deputies and Mansur Hassan helped calm Shenouda and Sadat's spirits.[290]

Meanwhile, others persisted in fanning the flames. At the Islamic Conference held on August 4, 1980 at Cairo University, Hilmi al-Gazzar, prince of Cairo University's GI, blamed Christians for sectarian strife through their demands for more ministerial jobs and more churches. "They already have their rights," said al-Gazzar.[291] Prominent Copts were not without their own sharp appraisals. Milad Hanna, NPUG member and a pillar in the Coptic community, characterized Sadat's behavior as "fascistic; Sadat, consciously or subconsciously, liked Hitler's concept of minority opposition, so he accused Copts of being Egyptian Jews. He could easily build up Islamic nationalism to absorb the genuine Islamic movement by exaggerating the anti-Coptic mood. Subjectively, Pope Shenouda fell into the trap."[292]

Coptic-Muslim tension persisted throughout the first half of 1981, then in June, in a poor, northeastern district of Cairo called Zawia al-Hamra, a violent confrontation occurred. A group of Islamist militants began setting up a tiny mosque on a plot of land owned by a Copt and already proposed as the site of a church. The Coptic owner, along with several relatives, machine-gunned several of the Islamists as they were performing their Friday prayers, and there were additional, inflammatory rumors of Christians burning a mosque. The news caused Muslims to seek reprisals, eliciting an eruption of violence. By the time the army and police put an end to the fighting—it took three days to restore calm—35 were dead, 50 wounded, and 165 had been arrested.[293] A French arms dealer who saw armored vehicles used to quell the clashes said they looked like they had been involved in full-scale warfare;[294] and there were particularly gruesome reports of combatants carving religious symbols into their victim's bodies.[295]

Islamist publications interpreted these events as wanton, Coptic aggression against the Muslim community, further aggravating tensions between the two religious communities.[296] Curiously, Sadat saw the incident as related to Papa Shenouda's efforts to embarrass him prior to his visit to Washington, D.C.[297] And there were rumors that the interior ministry had intentionally responded slowly to first reports of the disturbances to give time for the enraged Muslims to teach the Copts a lesson.[298] Despite the placing of guards in front of the city's churches, the rest of the summer was marked by violent reprisals against Coptic sanctuaries.

In early August 1981, Sadat traveled to Washington, D.C. for his first meeting with the new president, Ronald Reagan. During this visit, Sadat was angered by the presence of Coptic demonstrators, some of whom hurled eggs along with their invectives against him. Sadat had allegedly received intelligence reports to the effect that demonstrations would occur in Washington, and that these were orchestrated by Shenouda.[299] To Sadat, Shenouda had not been persuaded by his Coptic emissaries to realize that because the Islamists were targeting the government, Shenouda should cut Sadat some slack to deal with them as opposed to presenting even more challenges; Sadat saw Shenouda as playing both cards—talking conciliation, but still plotting against him.[300] After the Washington trip, Sadat refused to meet Shenouda.

Strains in Relations with the Reagan Administration

By the time of the Washington trip, as Ghorbal noted, Sadat believed the U.S. had helped oust his friend the shah from power, if only by permitting the U.S.—as was true in some Western European countries—to serve as a base for embarrassing anti-shah demonstrations and anti-shah media campaigns.[301] Now Sadat may have read the same type of message into the opposition demonstration that occurred during his visit to Washington. To Ahmed Beha al-Din, it was not surprising that Sadat cracked down on the political parties after his visit with Reagan. "Sadat was very upset after the visit: he had hoped Carter would win; but here was Reagan telling him, 'you got the Sinai back, that's all.'"[302] Ambassador al-Reidi also noted that the change in Washington had a big impact on Sadat: "He didn't find in Reagan the same kind of man he found in Carter."[303]

Reagan's presence affected Sadat's thinking in other ways. Reagan told Sadat he couldn't base U.S. foreign policy on human rights performances—in keeping with the new Kirkpatrick Doctrine, versus Carter-era thinking—so Sadat felt he had nothing to worry about by a democratic renege and opposition crackdown.[304]

Ghorbal declined comment on some of these points. But Ghorbal did say that Sadat was disappointed by Carter's loss due to the deep relationship he had built up with Carter, and Sadat's feeling that Carter still had Part II of Camp David to complete. Now Sadat would have to start anew with Reagan.[305] Sadat had been president just over ten years; Reagan represented the fourth American president with whom he had to negotiate.

For his part, Hermann Eilts, who was no longer serving as ambassador to Egypt, saw Sadat during his Washington visit and could sense his discontent. "He [Sadat] was an unhappy man because a) the Reagan administration had not invited him for eight months; b) contrary to his hopes, he had gotten no commitment from Reagan that the U.S. would remain on as a "full partner" in the peace process; and c) he clearly feared that the various anti-Sadat groups would stage demonstrations that Begin would seize upon to delay the final Israeli withdrawal from Sinai."[306]

Maneuverings of the Legal Opposition

All opposition forces blasted the regime for its handling of the Zawia al-Hamra flare-up. While secular opposition attacked the regime and the Interior Ministry in their newspapers, mosque pulpits were filled by speakers, including opposition party leaders, addressing their criticism of the regime to increasingly large congregations. With Friday sermons being delivered by well-known opposition figures from both secular parties and Islamist groups, and *al-Sha'b* carrying pictures of rallies attended by representatives of all opposition forces,[307] regime officials grew fearful that a revolutionary coalition was actually in the making.

In the end, no opposition "national coalition" emerged. New Wafd leader Fuad Sirag al-Din preferred to "lie low";[308] and NPUG president Khalid Muhi al-Din took a similar posture.[309] Liberal democrats and leftists alike were crucial components of Iran's revolutionary coalition. Having witnessed that coalition's post-revolution collapse, most of Egypt's secular political elite were loathe to see that phenomenon repeat itself in Egypt.

While there was no coalition in Egypt, *al-Sha'b* served as an impressionistic symbol of a national front, running pictures showing popular opposition rallies attended by representatives of diverse opposition parties.[310] Sadat, who had hosted the shah following his exile from Iran, was not about to allow an Iranian scenario to repeat itself in Egypt.

The Mass Arrests of September: Setting the Stage for Assassination

Near his end he became tired; a father feeling the ingratitude of his children. He felt he'd done so much for Egypt, yet the people were ungrateful. He felt embittered. Anis Mansur[311]

My father's reaction to the political parties' exploitation of this period's events was that their behavior was *"'aib"* (shameful). The nation's security was at stake. People [in the opposition] became like hyenas snatching at a corpse. Noha Sadat[312]

Pope Shenouda passed me, this book's author, a Bible and said read this: John 16:2. I read the verse, 'They will put you out of the synagogues; yes, the time is coming that whoever kills you will think that he offers God service.' Then, looking me in the eyes, the Pope said, 'It happens in every generation.'[313]

On September 2, Sadat took the unanticipated, draconian measure of arresting 1,536 individuals, including almost all key opposition figures. Leading figures, including party presidents, from the NPUG, SLP, New Wafd, Muslim Brothers, GI, IG, Jihad, and communist parties, as well as suspected activists in numerous smaller Islamist groups, prominent Nasserites, important lawyers and journalists of the independent opposition, prominent Islamist preachers, Pope Shenouda III, and several Coptic bishops all were apprehended by state security forces, and most were packed off to prison. Pope Shenouda was cloistered under "monastery arrest" in Wadi al-Natrun. Publication of all major opposition press organs, such as *al-Sha'b, al-Da'wa, al-I'tisam,* and three other religious magazines, was stopped. All mosques were placed under the direct supervision of the Ministry of Religious Endowments with sermons required to receive prior government approval. Popular private mosques set up by Islamist groupings were banned.

Why did Sadat crack down in this fashion? Said Hamdi Fuad, "The shah had spoken to Sadat about a U.S. conspiracy against him. This frightened Sadat. He took the decisions in September 1981 because he thought he was in a shah syndrome."[314] But importantly, as Ambassador al-Reidi noted, "Sadat was nervous. He needed to make it past April 1982. This is why he put the opposition in prison in September 1981—so they couldn't botch his peace drive."[315] Mustafa Kamel Murad concurred: "Sadat was very afraid the Israelis wouldn't leave Sinai. I told him, 'They'll leave because you paid the price to the U.S.' He said, 'You're too optimistic.'"[316]

According to all insiders,[317] Sadat's plan was to release all the detainees after Israel returned the Sinai in April 1982. He told members of his entourage that big changes would come after April. Restrictions against parties and more conservative economic policies were only temporary until April, then everything would change.

Sadat's economy czar, 'Abd al-Razzaq 'Abd al-Magid, had told his boss that Egypt needed "surgery regarding prices, interest rates, subsidies, wages, etcetera, not just aspirin. I have already printed food coupons; I know all the names of the poor people; I have their addresses." Sadat's response was fever pitch: "Just shut up! Keep quiet! Pray for the help of God for things to hold together until we get Sinai back then you can make surgical changes to the economy the next day!"[318] As 'Abd al-Magid added, "Sadat didn't trust Begin. He was almost fanatical about April 26."[319]

So, no excuse was to be offered the Israelis to allow them to change their minds or delay the April evacuation.[320] Noha Sadat recalled, "Every time I mentioned April 26, 1982, my father responded, 'if only Allah will allow me to live to see the day.' He said it repeatedly; it sounded very strange at the time."[321]

The Sadat who appeared on television to justify his draconian measures, which his own vice president and interior minister opposed,[322] appeared to most observers a desperate man. His speech was full of invective that insulted Muslim leaders and incensed *gama'aat* members; but he railed against the alleged excesses of all those whom he had incarcerated and gave every impression of having lost his self-control. I asked a secular-minded Egyptian friend what she had thought of the speech, and she responded, *"Ittagannin."* ("He went crazy.") She stopped, as if to measure her words, then stated with even greater conviction, *"Ittagannin!"*

Terminal Opposition Responses

Following the Iranian Revolutionary Path?

The arrests of September were followed by many disturbances, particularly on Fridays when the faithful were afforded the opportunity to congregate in large numbers at the mosques. Despite the presence of formidable security forces, these settings were exploited to instigate anti-regime demonstrations, again in keeping with the Iranian pattern, albeit still on a much smaller scale. The opposition, after all, had been decapitated; and it would have taken some time for non-elite regime opponents to respond to Sadat's preemptive strike. But Egypt's broad masses proved disinclined to demonstrate any outpouring of mass support for those targeted by Sadat's arrests. Perhaps they were cowed by the state security forces, but they were undoubtedly also stymied by the lack of unity within their ranks. Whether the Friday mosque-gathering phenomenon might have matured into a movement with full revolutionary potential in the absence of nearly the entire opposition leadership cannot be known, but it seems unlikely. Secular regime opponents in Egypt, not to mention Copts, were keen observers of the Iranian Thermidor; most did not like what they had seen.

By contrast, a small number of radical Islamists chose a proactive course. Most southern IG leaders and Jihadists had avoided arrest in September. Galvanized by those mass arrests, the southern IG princes met with 'Abd al-Salam Farag. They agreed to form an 11-member shura council, and talked 'Umar 'Abd al-Rahman into accepting the position of council *amir* (prince). The council members then set before themselves the task of settling scores with Sadat, and perhaps precipitating a revolution, through one brazen initial act—the assassination of the president—and 'Abd al-Rahman "legitimized" the undertaking by issuing his infamous *fatwa*.

The Plot

The specific plan to kill Sadat came from a young military officer, who was informed by his commanding officer that his unit would be participating in the October 6 parade attended by Sadat. First Lieutenant Khalid al-Islambuli of Artillery Battalion 333, whose brother, Muhammad, had been arrested in September, presented the idea to 'Abd al-Salam Farag. Al-Islambuli, 24 years old, held great respect for major Islamic figures like 'Umar al-Tilemsani, Sheikh Hafez Salama, and Sheikh Kishk,[323] but had also been sensitized by Islamist preachers in the southern city of Nag'a Hamadi about one and a half years prior to the assassination. He had then become a disciple of Muhammad 'Abd al-Salam Farag, who preached in a small private mosque near al-Islambuli's house, although in his trial Farag would deny any relationship.[324]

Farag, now 27, had taken to lecturing on the Tatars on several occasions some three to four months before Sadat's assassination.[325] Again, Ibn Taymiyya, writing at a time when the Tatars controlled Islamic lands, had issued a *fatwa* justifying killing Tatars for ruling Muslims without regard for God's law. Because of Sadat's references to the *ziyy al-islami* as a "tent," his criticism of keeping women at home as backward, and his failure to implement *shari'a* law, Farag denounced Sadat's rule as worse than that of the

Tatars.[326] He claimed that those who didn't respond to the call for jihad were *munafiqun* (hypocrites), and that *munafiqun* were the lowest form of *kuffar* (pl. of *kafir*, a non-believer).[327]

Members of Farag's group and likeminded organizations had been greatly agitated by the Zawia al-Hamra incident. Sheikh 'Umar 'Abd al-Rahman, regarded by many as the spiritual leader of all violence-prone Islamists, was so incensed that he issued a *fatwa* condoning the killing of Christians who funded church activities directed against Muslims' interests,[328] such as Christians' alleged acquisition of weapons. This gave rise to the targeting of Christian shop owners, often those who owned gold shops, to rob them and use the proceeds to fund their own organizations and purchase their own weapons. Money from such proceeds was spent to purchase the grenades and ammunition used in Sadat's assassination from arms smugglers.[329] To assassinate Sadat, al-Islambuli assembled a squad, all men in their twenties. They included Hussein 'Abbas 'Ali, a champion army sharpshooter.

Al-Islambuli's squad was not alone. The assassination was to set the stage for a Bastille-like storming of police headquarters in Assiut directed by a southern IG and Jihadist prince, Karam Zuhdi. Zuhdi's desire to go ahead with this revolutionary thrust won out over a more sober appraisal of its chances of success introduced by 'Abbud al-Zumur at a fateful September 26 meeting.[330] The Assiut attack and attempt to incite widespread guerrilla warfare or revolution would come immediately after al-Islambuli's assassination squad had struck down Sadat. If a revolution succeeded, they would establish an Islamic regime, with an *imam* as leader, surrounded by *ahl al-hall wa-l-'aqd* (literally, the people who loose and bind; i.e., a coterie of religious and technical personnel) as advisers.

The Assassination

On October 6, 1981, al-Islambuli's team took its place in the military parade held to celebrate the October 1973 war victory. As an officer, Islambuli had been able to give a leave to the three soldiers originally signed to the unit and replace them with his assassins.

Al-Nabawi Isma'il had warned Sadat of a possible assassination attempt the night before the parade. He didn't warn Sadat against attending the parade, but he did say that he was fearful and anxious.[331] Isma'il's anxiety was based on internal security's knowledge that something was afoot; they also knew al-Zumur was involved. In fact, just eight days prior to his assassination, Sadat was referring to al-Zumur, without using his name, in a public speech in which he warned that security forces were onto him.[332] Indeed,

'Abbud al-Zumur had narrowly escaped arrest when returning home from the September 26 meeting; and on October 3, Isma'il had given Sadat a tape of extremists' threats to kill him.[333] But Sadat chose to attend the festivities, and as he sat watching the parade, resplendent in his military uniform, his assassins went into action. One put a gun to the head of a parade truck's driver, forcing him to stop the truck in which his accomplices were riding. For reasons we shall never know, Sadat rose from his seat. Hussein 'Abbas 'Ali, from the back of the truck, fired a deadly shot into Sadat's body. Khalid al-Islambuli ran forward, hoisting his Kalashnikov over the reviewing stand wall and angling it downward to fire off a round of bullets into Sadat's body for the coups de grace.[334] "I killed the pharaoh!," al-Islambuli later boasted at his trial, "I killed the pharaoh!"

Conclusion

Unfortunately for Sadat, *infitah* did not provide rapid relief to Egypt's tired and teeming masses. MDC investors were responding, but heavier foreign investment and other revenues had not produced the economic miracle Sadat had mistakenly promised. Wealth accumulated in the hands of "fat cat" importers, government contractors, and corrupt state officials, or was flaunted by Arab and foreign visitors. Considerable income trickled down to those who were employed by or provided services to these individuals, worked in the tourist sector, or received remittances from Egyptian relatives working abroad, such that the welfare of many people improved. But for many others, especially among the legions employed by the state, a sense of relative deprivation grew more acute. State employees (both bureaucrats and factory workers) were either forced into moonlighting or experienced status reversal, and alienation of these segments of the citizenry rendered the regime politically vulnerable. Too much of too many Egyptians' new profits was being squirreled away in foreign accounts.

Sadat failed to use whatever public support he might have won by his political and economic liberalization to stay the economic course. Both the EASP and NDP remained ineffectual as bases of support for his political-economic development strategy; and his efforts to develop a new regime formula based in a vague synthesis of Islamic values and liberal democracy failed to attract serious attention. If anything, these efforts introduced a new source of intra-regime conflict and promoted intra-regime polarization into "moderate Islamist" versus "secular" factions. This split reflected the ambiguity in Sadat's own mind, as well as disagreement within his own extended family (his wife and Sayyid Mar'ei versus 'Uthman Ahmed 'Uthman).

Lacking a popular mandate anchored in a clear political-economic formula, when push came to shove in January 1977, Sadat's regime was compelled to renege on austerity policies designed to reduce foreign debt and
free up more capital for productive investment. With the austerity policy
blocked, Sadat again placed his bet on foreign capital, seeing fit to eliminate what he perceived as the major obstacle to MDC investment in Egypt;
namely, the state of war with Israel. But the price of peace proved very
high. It caused discord and defections within his own regime, invigorated
opposition parties and groupings, and brought Egypt's ostracism in the
Arab and Islamic worlds. The rupture of relations with the Arabs pushed
Sadat deeper into the American camp, and although Western and Far Eastern nations offset the loss in Arab economic support, they could deliver
neither the economic miracle nor the foreign policy victory that was necessary to save Sadat from his foreign and domestic critics. Ironically, October 5, 1981 [one day before Sadat's assassination] was the zenith of the
influx of capital and investments; 58 major projects were approved on that
day.[335] Many positive changes were in the making, but most people could
not see them, and Sadat was denied the opportunity to see them through.
For that, he needed to survive until April 1982.

Successful economic liberalization requires time and political stability;
political liberalization can produce overnight change where permitted.
Sadat's hope of being able to regulate the pace of political liberalization
was quickly dashed. Instead, political liberalization cleared the way for the
return of major pre-revolutionary ideological forces—Muslim Brothers,
Wafdists, Young Egyptians, and Marxists—and created an environment in
which many new, radical or radicalized, Islamic groups emerged as well.
Rather than confront these forces, where possible, through democratic
debate, Sadat chose to renege on his democratic promises and govern by
referenda, whose outcomes were never in doubt, or simply have recourse
to force. Though the regime ultimately maintained firm control of the
instruments of coercion, employment of such means against regime challengers in the media, syndicates, university campuses, and the labor movement came at the expense of Sadat's liberalization-based legitimacy.

The introduction of parties and parliamentary elections might have
marked a positive renewal of civil society, but Sadat proved incapable of tol-
erating criticism, even from parties fostered by his own regime. By falling
back on his authoritarian ways, Sadat undermined his early legitimacy formula and provided his political opponents with a rallying cry—the call for
democratization—second only to their rejection of Camp David.

As Hamdi Fuad astutely observed,

One could easily tick off the yearly accomplishments that Sadat was so fond of racking up, but he hanged himself along the way, as each step earned him the enmity of a different group within Egyptian society. First he angered the Marxists, then the Arab nationalists, then the democrats, then the church and the mosque. He lost the church establishment simply because he couldn't tolerate Shenouda's call to Copts to not go to Israel. He alienated almost all the important sectors of Egyptian society and he became very isolated from reality at the end."[336]

By the time of his assassination, Egypt's economic picture showed signs of promise, but life for most people remained bleak. Sadat's political isolation was almost total. Indeed, he had returned Egypt to a situation comparable to that of the early 1950s, replete with powerful, rival, civilian political forces, all battering on the regime's door. And again, as was true in that earlier period, no one of these forces appeared capable of seizing power on its own, and each remained too wary of their rivals' long-term intentions to permit coordinated action. The growth in political instability reinforced the unlikelihood of *infitah* succeeding, as well. A new Egyptian bourgeoisie was emerging, but it, too, was divided into Islamist, liberal democratic, and pro-regime camps. There was no hope of it playing its "classic" role as handmaiden of liberal democracy.

In passing judgment on Sadat's regime, it would be easy to conclude on this note. To do so, however, would be to ignore the broader historical context—to ignore what the French call the *conjoncture*. To do so would also ignore Sadat's essence.

Sadat was a visionary, an iconoclast, a maverick, and a gambler. These qualities enabled Sadat to envision a region at peace, a region that made room for both Israel and a Palestinian state. But Sadat's visionary quality, though pie-in-the-sky thinking to some, was not devoid of a base in reality. Sadat realized that Israel's nuclear capability served as one potent guarantor of its long-term existence; unflinching support from the United States served as another. If Israel were there to stay, then to deny its right to exist and maintain a state of war would only prolong Egypt's socioeconomic development difficulties. Peace seemed the only logical response; only peace could bring prosperity.

Sadat the iconoclast, maverick, and gambler was willing to buck the powerful wave of domestic and regional opposition to this vision. But as is true of even successful gamblers, Sadat experienced alternating periods of boom and bust. Long before assuming the presidency, time and again he had risked his life in the name of lofty national objectives, and either reaped the rewards or suffered the dire consequences. During his presidency, he repeatedly rolled the dice, again risking either his physical and/or political life. He did so when he took on his Centrist foes in 1971, went to war in 1973, flew to Jerusalem in 1977, and made peace in 1979. At the time of his assassination, he was involved in yet another enormous—one cannot even fairly say biggest—gamble.

From Sadat's vantage point, he knew that if he survived until the complete return of the Sinai, he would have once again won. Not only would he have fully restored Egypt's national sovereignty, he would also have been free to harden his foreign policy stance against Israel if deemed necessary, use his tremendous influence to advance other Arabs' causes in the court of world public opinion, release most opposition elements from prison, and turn to a more vigorous pursuit of his socioeconomic development priorities. With Sadat present, the Middle East peace process might have been accelerated by more than a decade, and Egypt's economic position vastly improved. Alas, Sadat's gamble failed.

Much was said at the time, and one still hears recalled, how relatively few Egyptians turned out for Sadat's funeral compared to that of his predecessor. Well beyond the fact that many citizens might have feared violence at the time of Sadat's funeral, one must acknowledge that a great number of citizens stayed home because they had come to dislike, even detest, their president. To this day, I remember vividly how one young student at The American University in Cairo, a moderate Islamist, recounted not long after the event how he had sat watching the parade on television with friends, and had stood up, pretending as though he had a machine gun in his hands. He said, "I just wish that someone would . . ." and just as he was feigning spraying Sadat with bullets, the television went blank—his wish was coming true. Another young Egyptian, after commenting to an American friend on how bad the assassination was for the country, smiled wryly and added, "wa lakin takhtit bitt al-kalb, mish kida?" ("But it was damn good planning, don't you think?)"[337]

Years after the events, there were still many individuals who retained a critical or caustic view. When I interviewed SLP leader Ibrahim Shukri in July 1986, for instance, and noted that Sadat would likely have changed many policies after April 1982, he answered, "Yes, I'm sure he would have; but if you ask me what would have been better—if he had lived or not—my answer is that, as a person who believes in Allah, the best thing is that which happened."[338] In short, past and present detractors of Sadat abound.

But Sadat was greatly loved and admired as well, both in Egypt and abroad. And so I also recall the young taxi driver who, with pride and great emotion in his voice, quoted verbatim the words that Sadat delivered in his famous speech to the Knesset. And the man who lauded Sadat for his vision, then proclaimed that Sadat's biggest problem was, "He was one thousand years ahead of his time." But perhaps the greatest tribute that one can pay to this man has come from all those voices, so shrilly or even calmly opposed to his regime and policies at the time of his assassination, who later acknowledged his courage and wisdom.[339]

When Anwar Sadat died, he was just 62. But during his lifetime, itself cut short by assassins' bullets, he participated in numerous revolutionary struggles, and fought or was otherwise involved in no less than five wars. Indeed, he lived his entire life in a country that was either at war or in a state of domestic political upheaval, and one of his brothers was killed in the war over which Sadat himself presided. Sadat felt that he and his fellow citizens had seen enough death and destruction, so he devoted most of his presidency to the pursuit of peace. No one can deny that Sadat tried his best to give peace a chance.

Notes

Chapter 1

1. Kirk J. Beattie, Egypt During the Nasser Years (Boulder, CO: Westview Press, 1994), 66-102.
2. See Seymour Martin Lipset, "Some Social Requisites of Democracy: Economic Development and Political Legitimacy," American Political Science Review, vol. 53, no. 1, March 1959, 69-105. Lipset's article was seminal. What is interesting is that the Egyptian government's behavior and that of U.S. foreign policymakers, both years before and long after the article, reflected endorsement of its basic argument; i.e., that liberal democracy cannot exist in a nation lacking a large middle class, high rate of literacy, and sociocultural norms conducive to the widespread acceptance of democratic principles.
3. Beattie, 102.
4. Patrick O'Brien, The Revolution in Egypt's Economic System: From Private Enterprise to Socialism, 1952-1966 (London: Oxford University Press, 1966).
5. Heba Handoussa, "The Impact of Foreign Aid on Egypt's Economic. Development: 1952-1986," Conference on AID Capital Flows and Development, Talloires, France, September 13-17, 1987: 10-14, Unpublished.
6. Ibid.
7. Ibid.
8. Ibid., 17-19.
9. Interview with Hassan 'Abbas Zaki.
10. Beattie, passim.
11. 'Amer's wife and other family members never accepted the official version. "Insiders" that I interviewed offered diverse viewpoints on this issue. Sadat's behavior led Ahmed Gami'a to believe 'Amer's death was not a suicide. See Ahmed Gami'a, A'raftu al-Sadat (Cairo: Modern Egyptian Press, 1998), 88.
12. Based on extensive interviews with elites of varying ideological convictions.
13. Beattie, 171-175. Also see Afaf al-Kosheri Mahfouz, Socialisme et pouvoir en Egypte (Paris: Librairie Generale de Droit et de Jurisprudence, 1972), 131-169.
14. Joel Migdal, Strong Societies and Weak States (Princeton: Princeton University Press, 1988).
15. Unless otherwise indicated, data in this section is taken from Beattie, 237-8.

16. Robert Mabro, The Egyptian Economy, 1952-1972 (Oxford: Clarendon Press, 1974), 167. Writes Mabro, "…the annual percentage increase of GDP fell steadily from 8.7 percent in 1963/1964 to −1% in 1967/68. This was followed by a short recovery in 1968/1969 and 1969/1970." Mabro, 168.

17. John Waterbury, Egypt: Burdens of the Past, Options for the Future (Bloomington, IN: American Universities Field Staff, 1978), 146-150.

18. Ibid., 113-124.

19. Ibid., 16.

20. Ibid., 204.

21. Anwar Sadat, In Search of Identity (Glasgow: Fontana/Collins, 1977).

22. Raphael Israeli, Man of Defiance: A Political Biography of Anwar Sadat (Totowa, NJ: Barnes & Noble Books, 1985), 16; Joseph Finklestone, Anwar Sadat: Visionary Who Dared (London: Frank Cass, 1996), 25; Sadat, 21, 78, 101.

23. See Beattie. Also see Joel Gordon, Nasser's Blessed Movement (Oxford: Oxford University Press, 1992).

24. Muhammad Hassanein Heikal, Autumn of Fury (New York: Random House, 1983), 12-13, 18-20.

25. Ibid., 21-24.

26. Anwar Sadat later shortened his last name.

27. Sadat, 5-6; Israeli, 15.

28. Interview with Mansur Hassan.

29. Sadat, 6-10.

30. Heikal, 10-15; Israeli, 11-12; interview with Camelia Sadat.

31. Finklestone, 7.

32. Sadat, 6-16; Beattie, 157-8.

33. Sadat, 12.

34. Ibid., 59.

35. Finklestone, 15.

36. Ibid., 4-5.

37. Israeli, 18.

38. Sadat, 12-13.

39. Interview with Muhsin 'Abd al-Khaliq. He says at least 70 to 80 percent were from middle- and upper-class families.

40. Sadat, 14-15.

41. Beattie, 158.

42. Heikal's account of what occurred on this point is more accurate than Sadat's, in which Sadat inflates his own role. Heikal, 14-15; Sadat, 17-24. Interviews with various Free Officers.

43. Finklestone, 17; interview with Khalid Muhi al-Din.

44. Heikal, 16; Sadat, 22-6.

45. Interview with Boghdadi; and Wagih Abaza.

46. Mahmud Fawzi, Hukkam Misr: al-Sadat (Cairo: Markaz al-Raya li-l-Nashr w-al-I'lam Ahmed Fikri, 1997), 35. Fawzi interview with Muhsin 'Abd al-Khaliq.

47. Sadat, 53; Musa Sabri, Watha'iq 15 Mayo (Cairo: n.d.), 176-88.

48. Sadat, 54.

49. Ibid., 57-8.

50. Heikal, 20.

51. Sadat, 68-93; Israeli, 22-25; interview with Carmelia Sadat.

52. Heikal, 21-24.
53. Sadat, 97.
54. Ibid., 97-98.
55. Ibid., 98.
56. Heikal, 25.
57. Sadat, 99.
58. In my book on Nasser, I put the year at 1942, but this is patently incorrect, as Faruq had not yet met Rashad. Beattie, 44.
59. Sadat, 98.
60. Heikal, 19-20.
61. Sadat, 46.
62. Ibid., 57.
63. Mohamed Ibrahim Kamel, The Camp David Accords (London: Routledge & Kegan Paul, 1986), 2.
64. Interview with 'Abd al-Khaliq; see Rashad Kamel, Al-Mar'a al-Latti Hazzat 'Irsh Misr (Cairo: Markaz al-Raya li-l-Nashr wa-l-I'lam, 1994), 24-38.
65. Kamel, 206.
66. Ibid., 206-207.
67. Interview with Jehan Sadat conducted by Nayrouz Tatanaki, January 1999.
68. Kamel, 206-207. Heikal says Sadat's involvement in these attempts is recorded in the files relating to Iron Guard activities found in the royal archives after the revolution. Heikal, 21.
69. Sadat, 92. Daughter Camelia was conceived during one leave.
70. Heikal, 21.
71. Sadat, 99.
72. Ibid., 99-103.
73. Heikal, 26.
74. Interview with Muhsin 'Abd al-Khaliq.
75. Heikal, 27; Beattie, 51 (based on extensive interviews with former Free Officers).
76. Heikal, 27; also see Kamel, 181-190.
77. Sadat, 103-104.
79. Supportive voices include Khalid Muhi al-Din, Hassan Ibrahim, 'Abd al-Latif al-Boghdadi, Muhsin 'Abd al-Khaliq, and others. Based on personal interviews and numerous readings.
79. Interview with Muhsin 'Abd al-Khaliq.
80. Interview with 'Abd al-Khaliq; also see his statement in Kamel, 257-63.
81. Beattie, 67.
82. Sadat, 117.
83. Heikal, 29-30.
84. Interview with Wagih Abaza, June 15, 1991.
85. Sadat, 74. Sadat speaks of not being fond of socializing, and says that he declined an offer to dance from Peal Bailey because he never learned how to dance. He could have been thinking of Western-style dancing as opposed to "Eastern" dance.
86. Interviews with Sadat's peers. Sadat did not drink alcohol, but hashish use was quite socially acceptable in many circles, and less frowned upon than alcohol consumption.
87. J.D. Mayer and P. Salovey, "The Intelligence of Emotional Intelligence," Intelligence, 17(1993), 433-442; D. Goleman, Emotional Intelligence (New York: Bantam, 1995); A.R. Damasio, Descartes' Error: Emotion, Reason and the Human Brain (New

York: Grosset/Putnam, 1994); R.K. Cooper and A. Sawaf, Executive EQ (New York: The Berkley Publishing Group, 1996). Several prestigious graduate schools of management have recently started using examinations based on EQ-testing as opposed to relying on the standard GMAT exam.

88. Beattie, 70.
89. See Mahmud Fawzi, 74.
90. Israeli, 19.
91. Heikal, 30.
92. Gordon, 133-149.
93. Sadat, 136.
94. Heikal, 30-1.
95. Israeli, 20.
96. The Protocols of the Elders of Zion. A document fabricated in Tsarist Russia purporting to contain a Jewish conspiracy for world domination.
97. Interviews with Kemal al-Din Hussein and Hussein al-Shaf'ei.
98. Sadat, 146-7.
99. Interview with Michael Sterner. Interestingly, Freedom of Information Act (FOIA) records show that both U.S. State Department officials and their Egyptian counterparts had reservations about Sadat. "Both Department officers familiar with Sadat and UAR Embassy (protect) question wisdom his holding press conference..." Department of State telegram, January 14, 1966; FOIA file number 198803126.
100. Ibid.
101. Interview with Jehan Sadat.
102. Sterner draft memorandum, March 16, 1966, FOIA file number 198803126.
103. Interview with Michael Sterner.
104. Sadat, 162-63.
105. Ibid., 163-71.
106. Interviews with Dia al-Din Dawud, 'Ali Sabri, and other Centrists.
107. Ahmed Gami'a, 83-5.
108. Beattie, 162-75.
109. Heikal, 33.
110. See Beattie, 159-62.
111. Beattie, 161.
112. Sadat, 175.
113. Interview with Jehan Sadat.
114. Sadat, 177-178.
115. Interview with Wagih Abaza.
116. Heikal, 33; interview with Jehan Sadat.
117. Musa Sabri, 197.
118. Interviews with Jehan Sadat and Noha Sadat.
119. Heikal, 35, says Jehan Sadat spent L.E. 650,000 on redecoration of the villa after Nasser's death.
120. Interview with Zakariyya Muhi al-Din.
121. Letter from Hermann Eilts to Kirk Beattie, August 22, 1986.
122. Interview with Sharaf.
123. Interview with Zakariyya Muhi al-Din.
124. Interview with Hoda 'Abd al-Nasser.
125. Beattie, 68, from interview with Hamdi Fuad.
126. Interview with Michael Sterner.

127. Interview with Jehan Sadat.
128. Sadat, 148.
129. Ibid., 163-71.
130. Ibid., 154.
131. Interview with Boghdadi.
132. Jon Alterman ed., 4-5.
133. Camelia Sadat's response during question and answer session of Washington Institute for Near East Policy conference on Sadat twenty years after his trip to Jerusalem, November 1997.
134. Interview with Sayyid Mar'ei.
135. Interview with Michael Sterner.

Chapter 2

1. Ahmed Gami'a, 165.
2. Interview with Ahmed Beha al-Din.
3. Fuad Mattar, *Aina Asbaha 'Abd al-Nasser fi Gumhurriyyat al-Sadat?* (Beirut: Dar al-Nahar li-l-Nashr, 1972), 78.
4. Gamal al-Ghitani, *Mustafa Amin Yatathakkir* (Cairo: Maktabat Madbuli, 1983), 112-113. Amin recalls Nasser's prediction that Sadat was his most likely successor, because Sadat's readiness to comply with Nasser's directives and self-effacing behavior made him a more likely survivor of regime infighting.
5. Interview with Mahmud Amin al-'Alim.
6. Interview with Hussein Kamel Beha al-Din.
7. Interview with Mahmud Amin al-'Alim.
8. Interviews with Sami Sharaf and Hafez Isma'il; also see Sharaf in 'Abdullah Imam, 400.
9. Interview with Hussein al-Shaf'ei.
10. *Arab Report and Record,* October 1-15, 1970, reporting an *AP* wire of October 13. Dubcek led the 1968 "Prague Spring" liberalization in Czechoslovakia.
11. Interview with 'Abdullah Imam.
12. Interviews with Kemal al-Din Hussein and Salah Dessouki.
13. Interview with Kemal al-Din Hussein.
14. Interviews with 'Abd al-Muhsin Abu al-Nur, Muhammad Fawzi, Dia al-Din Dawud, and others.
15. Interviews with Dia al-Din Dawud, Muhammad Fa'iq, and Sha'rawi Gum'a.
16. Mahmud Fawzi, *Hukkam Misr: al-Sadat* (Cairo: Markaz al-Raya li-l-Nashr w-al-I'lam Ahmed Fikri, 1996), 87-8. This Giza group included Farid 'Abd al-Karim, Ahmed al-Khawaga, and Sa'd Zayyid, the governor of Cairo.
17. Nearly everyone has recounted this story.
18. Interviews with Boghdadi, Z. Muhi al-Din, Salah Dessouki, Kemal al-Din Hussein, all the prominent Centrists and Leftists.
19. Ibid.
20. Interviews with Dia al-Din Dawud, 'Abd al-Muhsin Abu al-Nur.
21. Interviews with Dia al-Din Dawud, Sha'rawi Gum'a, Ali Sabri.
22. Interviews with Dia al-Din Dawud, Muhammad Fa'iq, Sha'rawi Gum'a.
23. Interview with Hamdi Fuad.
24. Interview with Muhsin 'Abd al-Khaliq.
25. Interview with Samir Hilmi.
26. Mattar, 72. Sadiq's promotion coincided with the dumping of the communist

Mahmud Amin al-'Alim at *Akhbar al-Yom,* and the appointment of Hassan al-Tuhami, a Rightist, to replace the Sabri's Centrist protégé, 'Abd al-Magid Farid, as general secretary for the presidency. See Mattar, 71.

27. Interviews with numerous Egyptian officers.

28. "It was a considerable presence: four thousand to five thousand advisors with the Egyptian forces; ten thousand to fifteen thousand other personnel, some manning the fifty SAM-2 and SAM-3 missile sites; two hundred pilots with ground crew for the MiG-21J and Sukhoi-11 fighters; and heavy Soviet contingents at four Egyptian ports and by now virtually in control of seven airfields. Effectively, the Soviet Union could veto any of Sadat's military plans. This caused enough trouble for Sadat with his own officers. Many were pro-western; others were simply fed up with what they saw as Soviet arrogance toward them." Insight Team of the *London Sunday Times, The Yom Kippur War* (Garden City, NY: Doubleday & Company, Inc., 56.

29. Interviews with Egyptian officers.

30. See also Muhammad Hassanein Heikal, *The Road to Ramadan,* 162-171, 179-182. Interviews with numerous Egyptian officials.

31. Kemal Hassan 'Ali, *Mishawir al-'Umr* (Cairo: Dar al-Shuruq, 1994), 252-253.

32. Interview with 'Adil Shuhdi; Shuhdi, a 1956 War College graduate and Rangers division Infantry officer, was among those cashiered and restored.

33. Beattie, 216-217, based on interviews with numerous Leftists.

34. Leonard Binder, *In a Moment of Enthusiasm: Political Power and the Second Stratum in Egypt* (Chicago: University of Chicago Press, 1978).

35. Hamied Ansari, *Egypt: The Stalled Society* (Albany, NY: State University of New York Press, 1986).

36. John Waterbury, *The Egypt of Nasser and Sadat* (Princeton, NJ: Princeton University Press, 1983).

37. Yahya M. Sadowski, *Political Vegetables?* (Washington, D.C.: The Brookings Institution, 1991).

38. Interview with Dia al-Din Dawud.

39. See the excellent study on Mar'ei by Robert Springborg, *Family, Power, and Politics in Egypt* (Philadelphia, PA: University of Pennsylvania Press, 1982).

40. Gen. Muhammad Fawzi, *Istratigiyyat al-Musaliha* (Heliopolis, Egypt: Dar al-Mustaqbil al-'Arabi, 1986), vol. II, 174.

41. Interviews with Dia al-Din Dawud, Muhammad Fawzi.

42. Interview with Dia al-Din Dawud.

43. Numerous interviews, including Jehan Sadat, Michael Sterner.

44. Interviews with Sami Sharaf, Lutfi al-Kholi, and others.

45. Jim Hoagland, "Hussein Payments Only a Part; CIA's Operations in Mideast Held Wide-Ranging, Effective," *Washington Post,* February 22, 1977.

46. Ibid.

47. FOIA file 198803126.

48. General Records of the U.S. Department of State (GR-State), Subject Numeric Files 1970-1973, Political-UAR and Egypt, National Archives (NARA) II, College Park, Maryland.

49. Interviews with Hermann Eilts, Michael Sterner, and Richard Parker.

50. Interview with Sami Sharaf.

51. General Records of the U.S. State Department, op. cit. Specific examples are provided elsewhere in this text.

52. Mustafa Amin's contacts with the United States went too far for Nasser's liking. The Americans seem to have picked up on Amin's idea that a cancellation of wheat ship-ments would put the squeeze on Nasser's regime. Amin was convicted of treason and spent many years in prison, where he was repeatedly tortured.

53. On Hassan al-Tuhami and his CIA contacts, see Miles Copeland, *The Game of Nations: The Amorality of Power Politics* (New York: Simon and Schuster, 1969).

54. Muhammad 'Abd al-Salam al-Zayyat, *Al-Qina'a wa-l-Haqiqa* (Cairo: Sharikat al-Amal li-l-Taba'a wa-l-Nashr, 1989), 98-102.

55. Ibid., 175.

56. Anwar Sadat, *In Search of Identity* (Glasgow: Fontana/ Collins, 1977), 276.

57. Ibid., 277.

58. Cable from US Interest Section Cairo (Bergus) to Secretary of State, September 28, 1970. GR-State, Political-UAR 1970-1973, Egypt, NARA II. RG 59, Entry 1613; Box 2640.

59. Mahmud Fawzi, 151. Fawzi interview with 'Abd al-Mun'im Amin. A former State Department official confirmed to me that Amin did play a role during this period, although I could not pinpoint the timing of his activities.

60. Ibid.

61. U.S. Interest Section Cairo (Bergus) to Secretary of State, October 3, 1970, GR-State, Political-UAR 1970-1973, Egypt, NARA II. RG59, Entry 1613, Box 2641.

62. U.S. Department of State telegram to U.S. Interests Section Cairo, December 15, 1970. GR-State, Political-UAR, Egypt, 1970-1973. NARA II. RG 59, Entry 1613, Box2642.

63. U.S. Interest Section Cairo (Bergus) to Secretary of State, November 9, 1970, GR-State, Political-UAR, Egypt, 1970-1973. NARA II. RG 59, Entry 1613, Box 2642.

64. Muhammad Fawzi, vol. II, 176-177.

65. U.S. Interests Section Cairo (Bergus) to Secretary of State, December 24, 1970, GR-State, Political-UAR, Egypt, 1970-1973, NARA II. RG 59, Entry 1613, Box 2642.

66. Sadat, 278.

67. Ibid., 278.

68. Kemal Hassan 'Ali, 284-5.

69. U.S. Interests Section Cairo (Bergus) to Secretary of State, January 4, 1971, GR-State, Political-UAR, Egypt, 1970-1973, NARA II. RG 59, Entry 1613, Box 2642.

70. Department of State telegram, January 19, 1971, drafted by M. Sterner and W.B. Smith II, GR-State, Political-UAR, Egypt, 1970-1973, NARA II. RG 59, Entry 1613, Box 2642.

71. Interview with Dawud. See Muhammad Fa'iq in Mahmud Fawzi regarding Sadat's secret contacts with Joseph Sisco.

72. Interview with Muhammad Fawzi.

73. General Fawzi, vol. II, 177-8. Interview with Yehiya al-Gamal.

74. Interview with Michael Sterner.

75. Sharaf in Imam, 403.

76. Interviews with Dawud, Fa'iq, Gum'a.

77. Interview with 'Ali Sabri.

79. Heikal, *al-Ahram,* March 19, 1971.

79. Heikal, *al-Ahram,* March 5, 1971.

80. Heikal, *al-Ahram,* March 12, 1971.

81. *Newsweek,* January 12, 1971.

82. 'Abd al-Hadi Nassef, *al-Gumhurriyya,* March 18, 1971.
83. *Al-Hawadith,* March 26, 1971.
84. Fawzi, vol. II, 183.
85. Ibid., 188.
86. Interviews with Kemal Hassan 'Ali and Muhammad 'Abd al-Ghani al-Gamassi.
87. See Hassan 'Ali, 478; interview with Gamassi.
88. Hassan 'Ali, 288.
89. Lt. Gen. Saad el Shazly, *The Crossing of Suez* (San Francisco, CA: American Mideast Research, 1980), 18. Shazly spells out the major weaknesses at the time-—the air force was too weak to provide adequate ground support or serve as a retaliatory deterrent; the SAM missile sites were not completed, so air defense was weak; absence of good bridging equipment; etcetera.
90. Mattar, 124.
91. Interview with Gum'a.
92. Eilts letter to Beattie, August 22, 1986.
93. Corroborated by Michael Sterner in a phone interview with him.
94. Sharaf in Imam, 404; also, interview with Michael Sterner.
95. Mahmud Fawzi, 53-54. Fawzi interview with Magdi Hassanein.
96. Interview with Dia al-Din Dawud.
97. Ibid.; and interview with Mahmud Amin al-'Alim.
98. Robert D. Kaplan, *The Arabists* (New York: The Free Press, 1995), 166-167.
99. Mahmud Fawzi, 50. Fawzi interview with Muhammad Fa'iq.
100. Telephone interview with Michael Sterner.
101. U.S. Interests Section Cairo (Bergus) to Secretary of State, April 22, 1971, GR-State, Politics-UAR-US, NARA II. RG 59, Entry 1613, Box 2642.
102. Sharaf in Imam, 405.
103. Muhammad Fawzi, vol. II, 216.
104. Beattie, 215-17.
105. Imam, 179-92.
106. Interview with Hafez Isma'il.
107. Mattar, 61; Muhammad Fa'iq in Mahmud Fawzi, 50.
108. Interviews with Sami Sharaf, 'Abd al-Muhsin Abu al-Nur, Sha'rawi Gum'a.
109. Sharaf in Imam, 417. Sharaf said "with regard to the false notion of shillaliyya, there was no "shilla"; no personal connections; rather, just connections via [policy] orientations."
110. I first heard of this in an interview with Mahmud Amin al-'Alim. Sharaf later admitted this was true, albeit overblown by Heikal in an effort to discredit Sharaf and others.
111. Interview with Mahmud Amin al-'Alim.
112. See Musa Sabri, 268.
113. Muhammad Fawzi, 203.
114. Ibid., 203-210.
115. Ibid., 205.
116. U.S Interests Section Cairo (Bergus) to RUEHCR/Secretary of State, May 9, 1971, GR-State, Political-UAR, Egypt, NARA II. RG 59, Entry 1613, Box 2642. See also Muhammad Fawzi, vol. II, 198, 206. These conditions included agreement on a permanent ceasefire, reopening the canal to all ships, no Egyptian forces on the East bank of the canal, continued presence of Israeli personnel in civilian clothing along the East bank, return of Egyptian civilians to Suez Canal cities, and other demands.

117. Muhammad Fawzi, 206.

118. U.S. Interests Section Cairo (Sisco) to Secretary of State, For Secretary of State, May 9, 1971, GR-State, Political-UAR, Egypt, NARA II. RG 59, Entry 1613, Box 2642.

119. Musa Sabri, 268.

120. Interview with Gum'a. Of course, in my interviews with Sharaf, Sabri, Fa'iq, Abu al-Nur, Dia Dawud, Muhammad Fawzi, Farid 'Abd al-Karim, and others, all averred there was no coup conspiracy.

121. Jehan Sadat, *A Woman of Egypt* (New York: Simon and Schuster, 1987), 263.

122. Interview with Mustafa Kamel Murad.

123. See also Gami'a, 177–80.

124. Interview with Farid 'Abd al-Karim.

125. Sharaf in Imam, 419.

126. Interview with Samir Hilmi. General Hilmi, former chief of the Planning Department in Military Intelligence, told me that "General Fawzi and Sami Sharaf were tracked by Military Intelligence at Sadiq's request for several months before the May events, so Sadat's version is fiction. The whole thing was plotted well in advance." Hamied Ansari, *Egypt: The Stalled Society* (Albany: State University of New York Press, 1986), 161–2. Ansari is quoting Sadiq; see footnote 21, p. 282.

127. Muhammad Fawzi, 204–10.

128. Interview with Muhammad Fawzi.

129. Muhammad Fawzi, 204–210.

130. Ibid.

131. Interview with Mahmud Amin al-'Alim.

132. Musa Sabri, 292.

133. Ibid., 270.

134. Sharaf in Imam, 412–413, 436. Interview with Sharaf.

135. Ibid., 423.

136. Muhammad Fawzi, 219.

137. Interview with Mustafa Kamel Murad.

138. Muhammad Fawzi, 219–20.

139. Interview with Muhammad Fawzi.

140. Interview with Dia al-Din Dawud. Repeated by many others.

141. The exact timing of these events is difficult to reconstruct. Gum'a told me that he phoned Fawzi at 9:00 P.M., telling him to come to the house. Interview with Gum'a. Elsewhere, Fa'iq maintains that he gave the letter of resignations to Marwan at 8:00 P.M., fully expecting that Sadat would receive them before the announcement was broadcast at 11:00 P.M. See Mahmud Fawzi, 48.

142. Interview with 'Abd al-Muhsin Abu al-Nur.

143. Interview with Sha'rawi Gum'a.

144. Interview with Muhammad Fa'iq.

145. Dawud, 87.

146. Interview with Jehan Sadat. When I asked Mrs. Sadat if it were possible that the Centrists' moves were misconstrued, her response was, "No, it was a real plot. They were against his policy—they adored Nasser and they wanted the president to follow his steps exactly as Nasser had presented them. But each president must have his own way, for example, Mubarak does what he feels is most suitable given Egypt's circumstances; he didn't follow my husband's path perfectly. Anwar Sadat loved Nasser so much; but circumstances change, so policies must change."

147. Murad says he was dining with 'Ali Shafiq in Ma'mura and Shafiq asked him if he had heard the 11:00 news, which he hadn't. Murad exclaimed: "This is a coup." He sped back to Cairo, retrieved his revolver at home, and went to Sadat's house, where he found "about 30 people sitting around, looking gloomy, like at a funeral."
148. See also Ansari, 163-4.
149. Interview with Mustafa Kamel Murad.
150. Interview with Ahmed Darwish.
151. Interview with Mustafa Kamel Murad.
152. Interviews with Farid 'Abd al-Karim and Dia al-Din Dawud; see also Ansari, 64 quoting 'Abd al-Karim in an interview with *al-Ahali,* May 11, 1983.
153. Interview with Mustafa Kamel Murad.
154. Dia al-Din Dawud, *Sannawat 'Abd al-Nasser, Ayyam al-Sadat* (Cairo: Dar al-Khiyyal, 1998), 229-231. Dawud claims anyone who looks at the signatures on the official register can see that many were written in the same handwriting with the same pen.
155. Interview with Dia al-Din Dawud.
156. Interviews with 'Abdullah Imam, Sha'rawi Gum'a.
157. Interview with 'Abd al-Salam al-Zayyat.
158. Ibid.
159. Interview with Sharaf and others.
160. Interview with Mahmud Amin al-'Alim.
161. Interview with 'Ali Sabri.
162. Interview with Hussein 'Abd al-Razzaq.
163. Dawud, 85-86.
164. Interview with Yehiya al-Gamal.
165. Interview with Lutfi al-Kholi.
166. Interview with Rif'at al-Sa'id.
167. Interview with Isma'il Sabri 'Abdullah.
168. Ibid.
169. Marsha Pripstein Posusney, *Labor and the State in Egypt* (New York, Columbia University Press, 1997), 94-95.
170. Ibid., 95.
171. Interview with 'Abd al-Salam al-Zayyat.
172. Muhammad Fawzi, 224.
173. Interview with Mustafa Kamel Murad.
174. Sadat speech, June 2, 1971.
175. *Al-Ahram,* February 18, 1972.
176. Abdel Magid Farid, *Nasser: The Final Years* (Reading, NY: Ithaca Press, 1994), 72-90.
177. To wit, the idea was first put in print by Ahmed 'Abbas Salih, "'An al-Dimuqratiyya wa-l-Ittihad al-Ishtiraki," *al-Katib,* June, 1971, 2-10.
178. Interview with Lutfi al-Kholi.
179. Muhammad 'Abd al-Salam al-Zayyat, *Al-Qina'a wa-l-Haqiqa* (Cairo: Sharikat al-Amal li-l-Taba'a wa-l-Nashr, 1989), 157-163.
180. Ibid., 175-8.
181. Interview with Sami Sharaf, who went over the lists with me, identifying many individuals with Centrist identities and sympathies.
182. *Al-Ahram,* July 18, 20, 21, 1971.
183. Interviews with Dia al-Din Dawud, Lutfi al-Kholi.
184. Interview with Lutfi al-Kholi and others.
185. Interview with Muhammad 'Abd al-Salam al-Zayyat.

186. Interviews with numerous elites, especially Sami Sharaf.
187. Ansari, 167.
188. *Al-Ahram,* July 27, 1971.
189. *Al-Ahram,* February, 18, 1972.
190. Interview with Muhammad 'Abd al-Salam al-Zayyat.
191. Interview with Sayyid Mar'ei.
192. Ibid.
193. Ibid.
194. Interview with Lutfi al-Kholi.
195. *Arab Report and Record,* August 16-31, 1971.
196. Ibid.
197. Sharaf in Imam, 402.
198. Gami'a, 189.
199. Ibid., 189.
200. *Arab Report and Record,* September 1-15, 1971.
201. Interview with Mustafa Khalil.
202. See the discussion in Bruce K. Rutherford, *The Struggle for Constitutionalism in Egypt: Understanding the Obstacles to Democratic Transition in the Arab World,* Ph.D. thesis, Yale University, 1999, 215-20.
203. Zayyat, 234-40.
204. See Rutherford, 220-51. His description of the give-and-take by the representatives of various currents during the drafting of the constitution is particularly enlightening and provides corroborating evidence for the hegemonic struggle depicted in this book.
205. For a solid overview of Law 32, see Denis J. Sullivan and Sana Abed-Kotob, *Islam in Contemporary Egypt* (Boulder, CO: Lynne Rienner, 1999), 25-6.
206. Sadat speech on shift to "state of institutions."
207. Sadat speech on the introduction of the idea of the state being based on "science and faith." See *al-Ahram,* September 20, 1971.
208. Reference to Article 2 of new Egyptian Constitution.
209. The irony here is that Sadat was complicit in ousting the judges at Nasser's behest. See Ahmed Hamrush, *Qissat Thawrit 23 Yuliu: Kharif 'Abd al-Nasser* (Beirut: Arab Organization for Studies and Publishing, 1979), vol. V, 313. Rutherford is undoubtedly correct in pointing out that the Centrists desired this "massacre" far more than did Sadat. Rutherford, 259-60, 266, 272, 283-5.
210. Interview with Ahmed al-Khawaga.
211. Interviews with Wafdist lawyers, especially Muhammad Fahim Amin and Ahmed Nasir.
212. Interviews with MB and Islamiyyin lawyers, particularly MB member Muhammad al-Mismari and his Islamiyyin colleagues in the same office.
213. Interview with Nasserite journalist 'Abd al-'Aziz 'Abdullah.
214. Ansari, passim; Binder, passim. Both discuss at length the success of rural middle-class elements in the parliamentary elections under Nasser.
215. *Arab Report and Record,* November 1-15, 1971.
216. Sharaf's connection to the KGB was alleged in a book by John Barron, *KGB* (New York: Reader's Digest Press, 1974).
217. Interview with Hafez Isma'il. See Sadat, 225.
218. Interview with Hafez Isma'il.
219. Interview with Wagih Abaza.
220. Interview with Muhammad 'Abd al-Salam al-Zayyat; also see Zayyat, 195, 248-54.

221. Interview with Kemal Abu al-Magd.

222. Zayyat, 195, 248-54.

223. Viewed on a PBS documentary on Richard Nixon aired in Boston in April 2000.

224. Secret memo from Secretary Rogers to President Nixon, November 17, 1970, GR-State, Political-UAR, Egypt, 1970-1973, NARA II. RG 59, Entry 1613, Box 2642. These included improvement of cultural exchanges, like reactivating the Fulbright program; aid to the Catholic Relief Services Food Program; consideration of debt rescheduling; Ex-Im Financing for the UAR; and the possibility of Rogers visiting Cairo.

225. Interview with Ashraf Ghorbal. For the record, Ghorbal told me that, to the best of his knowledge, Sadat did not have a transmitter enabling direct contacts with the Americans or others. Hermann Eilts, interview, also found this unlikely.

226. Memo from NEA-Sisco to Undersecretary of State [sic], March 12, 1971, GR-State, Political-UAR, Egypt, 1970-1973, NARA II. RG 59, Entry 1613, Box 2642. "Ghorbal has never been a central figure in our ongoing discussions with the Egyptians on the Arab-Israeli settlement situation for several reasons. Both we and the Egyptians have found it more effective to do our business with the UAR through our Minister in Cairo, Donald Bergus, who has access to high Egyptian officials. Furthermore, the UAR leadership has not kept Ghorbal current on the more sensitive aspects of our Cairo talks. Specifically, we do not believe Ghorbal is aware of the exchanges which have taken place with us in Cairo on Sadat's proposal for a partial Israeli withdrawal and reopening of the Suez Canal." The memo goes on to recount how the Americans do keep Ghorbal generally abreast of developments.

227. Zayyat, 182.

228. Interview with Ahmed Beha al-Din.

229. Memo to Kissinger from Theodore Eliot, Jr., Executive Secretary, Department of State, March 25, 1971, GR-State, Political-UAR, Egypt, 1970-1973, NARA II. RG 59, Entry 1613, Box 2642. The memo reviews the background to Sadat's letter to Nixon.

230. U.S. Interests Cairo (Bergus) to RUEHC/Secretary of State, March 5, 1971, GR-State, Political-UAR, Egypt-U.S., 1970-1973, NARA II. RG 59, Entry 1613, Box 2642.

231. Ibid. Included along with this memo is Sadat's letter to Nixon in Arabic.

232. State Department memo on Nixon's response to Sadat, March 31, 1970, GR-State, Political-UAR, Egypt, 1970-1973, NARA II. RG 59, Entry 1613, Box 2251.

233. Interview with Michael Sterner.

234. Kaplan, 166-167.

235. Interview with Michael Sterner.

236. Interview with Hafez Isma'il.

237. U.S. Interests Cairo (Bergus) to Secretary of State, May 17, 1971, GR-State, Political-UAR, Egypt, 1970-1973, NARA II. RG 59, Entry 1613, Box 2642. Bergus also wrote, "Much of what Sadat said was going on is true. But would minister of interior planning a coup arrange only for the surrounding of the radio station without taking any other measures to ensure success? It seems unlikely. Rumors existed Sadat wanted to dump some people—Sharaf, Gomaa, but all of this seems very hastily done, not premeditated." "In sum, it appears as though Sadat had planned certain changes in the ASU and his cabinet for some weeks, and seized the opportunity to charge his opposition with conspiracy when it arose. He may not have intended to dismiss six ministers at once, but was forced to do so when they resigned together."

238. Interview with Michael Sterner.

239. From Sisco to Action U.S. Interest Cairo, June 17, 1971, GR-State, Political-UAR-US, 1970-1973, NARA II.

240. U.S. Interest Cairo (Bergus) to Secretary of State, July 6, 1971, GR-State, Political-UAR, Egypt, 1970-1973, NARA II.

241. U.S. Interest Cairo (Bergus) to Secretary of State, July 7, 1971, GR-State, Political-UAR, Egypt, 1970-1973, NARA II.

242. Interview with Ricky Romano.

243. Zayyat, 202-214.

244. Ibid., 258-60.

245. Interview with Hafez Isma'il.

246. Zayyat, 258-60.

247. Near East Affairs memo: S.S.Hanley/M.Sterner; A.L.Atheron, May 22, 1972, GR-State, Political-UAR, Egypt, 1970-1973, NARA II.

248. *Arab Report and Record,* December 16-31, 1971.

249. U.S. Interests Cairo (Bergus) to Secretary of State, December 30, 1971, GR-State, Political-UAE, Egypt, 1970-1973, NARA II. RG 59, Entry 1613, Box 2642.

Chapter 3

1. Ahmed Abdalla, *The Student Movement and National Politics in Egypt* (London: Al-Saqi Books, 1985); Haggai Erlich, *Students and University in 20ᵗʰ Century Egyptian Politics* (London: Frank Cass, 1989).

2. Erlich, 203.

3. Heba Handoussa, "The Impact of Foreign Aid on Egypt's Economic. Development: 1952-1986," Conference on AID Capital Flows and Development, Talloires, France, September 13-17, 1987: 10-14, Unpublished, 19.

4. Ibid.

5. Mahmud al-Maraghi, "Al-Mustahil fi Burnamig l-il-'Amal al-Watani," *Rose al-Yusuf,* no. 2251, August 2, 1971, 26-28.

6. Clement H. Moore, *Images of Development* (Cambridge, MA: The MIT Press, 1980), 126.

7. See Erlich, 203-204. He notes that in some faculties, the student-teacher ratio reached 666-1 in 1977.

8. Read Tewfiq al-Hakim and others' pronouncements on the mass anxiety caused by the authorities' incessant talk of the elusive battle in Ghali Shoukri, *Egypte: la contre-revolution* (Paris: Editions le Sycomore, 1979), 172-173.

9. *Arab Report and Record,* August 16-31, 1971.

10. 'Abd al-Sitar al-Tawila, "Al-Gami'a: Huna Sari'a al-Agyal," *Rose al-Yusuf,* no. 2211, October 26, 1970, 14-16.

11. *Rose al-Yusuf,* no. 2234, April 5, 1971, 41. No author or title.

12. Abdalla, 266, note 9.

13. 'Abd al-Sitar al-Tawila, "Ittihadat al-Talaba Tanzimat 'ala al-Waraqa," *Rose al-Yusuf,* no. 2216, November 30, 1970, 14-17.

14. "Harakat al-Shabab fi Misr w-al-'Alim," *Rose al-Yusuf,* no. 2278, February 7, 1972, 11-13.

15. Abdalla, 177, and note 8, 266.

16. Ibid., 176-177, notes 2-4, 266.

17. Muhammad 'Abd al-Salam al-Zayyat, *Al-Qina'a wa-l-Haqiqa* (Cairo: Sharikat al-Amal li-l-Taba'a wa-l-Nashr, 1989), 286-290.

18. The first use of the term in an article that I detected was by Kamel Zuheiri, "A'azam fi al-Nasirriyya," *Rose al-Yusuf,* No. 2210, October 19, 1970, 5.
19. Based on interviews with former student activists.
20. Shoukri, 134–139.
21. Ibid., 134.
22. Interviews with former student activists.
23. Wa'il 'Uthman, *Asrar al-Haraka al-Tulabiyya* (Cairo: al-Sharikat al-Misriyya li-l-Taba'a, 1976), 68; Abdalla, 177.
24. Abdalla, 180.
25. 'Uthman, 69–70.
26. 'Abdalla, 182.
27. Shoukri, 136.
28. Interview with 'Abbas al-Tunisi.
29. Shoukri, 136; Abdalla, 183–184.
30. Abdalla, 184–185.
31. 'Uthman, 68; interviews with former student activists.
32. 'Uthman, 55,68.
33. Zayyat, 292.
34. Michael Winter, "Islam in the State: Pragmatism and Growing Commitment," in *Egypt: From Monarchy to Republic,* Shimon Shamir, ed. (Boulder, CO: Westview Press, 1995), 44–58.
35. Interviews with former student activists and diverse elites. 'Uthman makes repeated mention of the *Mabahith's* presence on university campuses; 'Uthman, passim.
36. Kepel, *Muslim Extremism in Egypt: The Prophet and the Pharaoh,* translated by Jon Rothschild, (Berkeley, CA: University of California Press, 1985), 133.
37. Ahmed Gami'a, A'rift al-Sadat (Cairo: Modern Egyptian Press, 1998), 190.
38. Interviews with Kemal Abu al-Magd, Sufi Abu Talib, and al-Nabawi Isma'il; see Gami'a, 190-192. Al-Nabawi Isma'il blames Muhammad 'Uthman Isma'il for selling the idea to Sadat, absolving both his friend, 'Uthman Ahmed 'Uthman and Abu al-Magd of connivance in this matter. Both Sufi Abu Talib and Kemal Abu al-Magd maintain that 'Uthman was involved.
39. Zayyat, 292-293. Gami'a, 191, speaks of the GSI's use of knives and whips in clashes with the leftists.
40. Gamal Salim, "Asrar Hamma fi Mu'tamarat al-Ittihad al-Ishtiraki," *Rose al-Yusuf,* no. 2304, August 7, 1972, 10-13; and no author, "Al-Wahda al-Wataniyya Hiyya al-Latti Harrakat al-Muslimin li-Yadfa'u 3 Alaf Ginay li-Bina Kanisa," *Rose al-Yusuf,* no. 2304, August 7, 1972, 14.
41. Interview with Kemal Abu al-Magd.
42. Ibid.
43. *Al-Ahram,* May 25, 1971.
44. *Al-Ahram,* March 29, 1972.
45. Kirk J. Beattie, Egypt During the Nasser Years (Boulder, CO: Westview Press, 1994), 181.
46. Carré, "From Banna to Qutb and 'Qutbism': The Radicalization of Fundamentalist Thought Under Three Regimes," in Shimon Shamir, ed., 190.
47. 'Adil Hamuda, "Nahnu Mas'ulin Amama Allah wa-l-Mu'tamar al-Qawmi," *Rose al-Yusuf,* no. 2306, August 21, 1972, 11-14.
48. Interview with Kemal Abu al-Magd.
49. 'Uthman, 88-89, 113-114.

50. Ibid., 114.
51. Gami'a, 191.
52. 'Uthman, 89.
53. Ibid., 82-83.
54. See articles by David Hirst, *Daily Telegraph,* November 14, 15, and 21, 1972 as noted in *Arab Report and Record,* November 1-15, 1972.
55. Gami'a, 191.
56. Ibid.
57. Hala Mustafa, *Al-Islam al-Siyyasi fi Misr: Min Harakat al-Islah illa Gama'aat al-'Unf* (Cairo: Markiz al-Dirasat al-Siyyasiyya wa-l-Istratigiyya, 1992), 158-159.
58. Mustafa, 159. Mustafa relies heavily on note 82, p. 208, Salih al-Wardani, *Al-Harakat al-Islamiyya fi Misr, Ru'ya Waqi'a li-Marhalat al-Saba'inat al-Bidaya* (1986), 125-127.
59. Interview with Pope Shenouda III.
60. Nadia Ramsis Farah, *Religious Strife in Egypt* (New York: Gordon and Breach Science Publishers, 1986), 1.
61. See Daniel H. Levine, *Religion and Political Conflict in Latin America* (Chapel Hill, NC: University of North Carolina Press, 1986); and Jeffrey Klaiber, S.J., *The Church, Dictatorships, and Democracy in Latin America* (Maryknoll, NY: Orbis Books, 1998).
62. Farah, 48-51.
63. Interview with Pope Shenouda III.
64. Farah, 2.
65. Ibid.
66. U.S. Interests Cairo to Secretary of State, August 16, 1972, GR-State, Political-UAR, Egypt, 1970-1973, NARA II. RG 59, Entry 1613, Box 2249.
67. Interview with Lutfi al-Kholi.
68. Farah, 2.
69. Musa Sabri, 107; Heikal, 162-163.
70. Ibid.
71. Interview with Pope Shenouda III.
72. Ibid.
73. Musa Sabri, 112.
74. J.D. Pennington, "The Copts in Modern Egypt," *Middle Eastern Studies* 17, 1981, 168.
75. Interview with Jehan Sadat.
76. Interview with 'Aisha Ratib.
77. Ibid.
79. Ibid.
79. Ibid.
80. Nancy Y. Reynolds, "Discourses of Social Change: An Analysis of the 1985 Personal Status Law Debate in Egypt," B.A. thesis, Harvard University, 1989, 23.
81. Ibid.
82. Ibid., 23-24.
83. Interviews with numerous Islamists. See articles in *al-Da'wa* on the problem of increasing numbers of women in constrained physical space.
84. CAPMAS, *Statistical Yearbook, 1981* (Cairo: Central Agency for Public Mobilisation and Statistics, 1981), 172-174.
85. Saadedin Ibrahim, "An Anatomy of Egypt's Militant Groups," *International Journal of Middle East Studies,* 1981.
86. Ibid., 160-165.

87. Ibid.; and CAPMAS, *Statistical Yearbook, 1975* (Cairo: Central Agency for Public Mobilization and Statistics, 1975), 162, in Arabic.

88. See the books by Daniel H. Levine and Jeffrey Klaiber, S.J., op. cit.

89. Kepel, 105.

90. Ibid.

91. Carré, in Shamir, ed., 191.

92. See Denis J. Sullivan and Sana Abed-Kotob, *Islam in Contemporary Egypt* (Boulder, CO: Lynne Rienner, 1999), 59-65.

93. Kepel, 173, 175.

94. Ibid.

95. See the text of Sadat's speech in the People's Assembly, January 31, 1973. Sadat referred to them as "the adventurous Left." *Speeches and Interviews of President Mohamed Anwar el Sadat, January-December 1973* (Cairo: Ministry of Information,1975), 27-58.

96. Ibid.

97. Wa'il 'Uthman, 90.

98. Ibid.

99. Ibid., 92. *Arab Report and Record,* December 16-31, 1972.

100. Ahmed Abdalla, 204-211.

101. Abdalla says 35 participated; Abdalla, 273, note 98. 'Uthman says 60; 'Uthman, 96.

102. *Arab Report and Record,* December 16-31, 1972.

103. 'Uthman, 101-106, 117.

104. Ibid., 101-102.

105. Ibid., 102-105, 130.

106. Interviews with Sayyid Mar'ei and Kemal Ibrashi.

107. Interview with Sayyid Mar'ei.

108. Interview with Sufi Abu Talib.

109. Sullivan and Abed-Kotob, 73.

110. Interview with Fuad Hussein.

111. Winter, in Shamir, ed., 52.

112. Israeli, xiv. Sadat's founding of the regime's new paper, *al-Gumhurriyya,* is discussed in chapter one.

113. Musa Sabri, 529; interview with Rif'at al-Sa'id.

114. Based on interviews with numerous journalists.

115. Sabri, 530.

116. Abdalla, 181; and interviews with numerous journalists.

117. *Bayan* (official document) issued by the Journalists' Syndicate, January 25, 1972.

118. *Arab Report and Record,* December 16-31, 1972.

119. Interview with 'Abd al-'Aziz 'Abdullah.

120. Shoukri, 171-174.

121. Ibid., 174.

122. Ibid., 174-175.

123. Speech by Sadat, January 31, 1973, op. cit.

124. Posusney, 99-100.

125. Interviews with Ahmed Beha al-Din, Lutfi al-Kholi, and others.

126. Shoukri, 178.

127. Interview with Ahmed Beha al-Din.

128. Interviews with numerous journalists.

129. Sadat, 245.

130. Heikal, *The Road to Ramadan* 162-166, 168-171, 175; and interviews with Hafez Isma'il and Kemal Abu al-Magd.
131. Interview with Hafez Isma'il.
132. Interview with Erik Jensen.
133. Insight Team of the London Sunday Times, *The Yom Kippur War* (Garden City, New York: Doubleday & Company, Inc., 1974), 52-57.
134. Ibid., 54-55.
135. Interview with Hafez Isma'il; see also Sadat, 228.
136. Insight Team, 54.
137. Ibid., 55-56.
138. Isma'il Fahmy, *Negotiating for Peace in the Middle East* (London: Croom Helm, 1983); Fahmy and Hassan al-Tuhami were among the Soviets' most vocal critics at the seminar.
139. *Arab Report and Record,* May 1-15, 1972; interview with Salah Dessouki.
140. Raymond A. Hinnebusch, Jr., *Egyptian Politics Under Sadat* (Boulder, CO: Lynne Rienner Publishers, 1988), 52.
141. See Murad Ghalib in Mahmud Fawzi. Ghalib's view, probably correct, is that Sadiq's charge was grossly exaggerated.
142. *Arab Report and Record,* July 16-31, 1972, quotes articles from *France Soir,* July 24, 1972 and the *Financial Times,* July 20, 1972.
143. Interview with Hamdi Fuad.
144. Department of State Memo of Conversation, July 12, 1972, GR-State, Political-UAR, Egypt, 170-1973, NARA II. RG 59, Entry 1613, Box 2251.
145. Sadat interview by Alyaa El Solh, *al-Ahram,* March 28, 1974; *Speeches January-December 1974* (Cairo: Ministry of Information, 1976), 90; Sadat interview with Selim el Lozy, *al-Hawadith,* 29 April 1974; *Speeches . . . January-December 1974,* 244-246.
146. Insight Team, 56-57.
147. Mahmud Fawzi, 123. Fawzi interview with Ghalib.
148. Interview with Noha Sadat.
149. Interview with Sayyid Mar'ei.
150. Interview with Hafez Isma'il.
151. Interview with Gamassi.
152. Sadat continued to refer to the Soviet Union as Egypt's friend and ally. See his speech of May 1, 1973 in *Speeches January-December, 1973,* 152.
153. Interview with Hafez Isma'il.
154. Sadat, 237.
155. American Embassy in Moscow to Secretary of State, October 17, 1972, GR-State, Political-UAR, Egypt, 1970-1973, NARA II. RG 59, Entry 1613, Box 2249. The U.S. Interests Section in Cairo detected a resuscitation of Soviet economic assistance. U.S. Interests Cairo to Secretary of State, October 19, 1972, GR-State, Political-UAR, Egypt, 1970-1973, NARA II. GR #59, Entry #1613, Box #2251.
156. See Kemal Hassan 'Ali, *Mishawir al'Umr* (Cairo: Dar al-Shuruq, 1994).
157. Interview with Noha Sadat.
158. Interview with Hamdi Fuad.
159. Interview with Gamassi.
160. Kemal Hassan 'Ali, 52.
161. Interview with Gamassi.
162. Ibid.
163. Sadat, 238.

164. Kemal Hassan 'Ali, 283-284; Alvin Rubenstein, *Red Star on the Nile* (Princeton, NJ: Princeton University Press, 1977), 216.
165. U.S. Interests Cairo (Bergus) to Secretary of State, November 27, 1971, GR-State, Political-UAR, Egypt, 1970-1973, NARA II. RG 59, Entry 1613, Box 2642.
166. Sadat, 287.
167. U.S. Interests Cairo to Secretary of State, February 22, 1972, GR-State, Political-UAR, Egypt, 1970-1973, NARA II. RG 59, Entry 1613, Box 2251.
168. U.S. Interests Cairo (Sisco) to Secretary of State, February 20, 1973, Political-UAR, Egypt, 1970-1973, NARA II. RG 59, Entry 1613, Box 2249. Sisco was reviewing Egyptian – American relations from 1971 to 1973.
169. NEA/Egypt: SSHanley/MSterner; NEA: ALAtherton, May 22, 1972, GR-State, Political-UAR, Egypt, 1970-1973, NARA II.
170. Ibid.
171. Heikal quotes Kissinger in Heikal, *The Road°,* 186-187; Kissinger, on why Sadat asked for nothing in exchange for his 1972 expulsion of the Soviets.
172. Interview with Sayyid Mar'ei.
173. Sadat, 232-233.
174. Kissinger, 205. Note that Kissinger says "reactivated."
175. U.S. Interests Cairo to Secretary of State, July 25, 1972, GR-State, Political-UAR, Egypt, 1970-1973, NARA II. RG 59, Entry 1613, Box 2251.
176. Ibid.
177. Memo from Theodorre L. Eliot, Jr. to Kissinger, drafted by NEA: ALAtherton, Jr. on July 28, 1972, memo sent to Kissinger July 31, 1972, GR-State, Political-UAR, Egypt, 1970-1973, NARA II. RG 59, Entry 1613, Box 2251.
178. American Embassy Tel Aviv to Secretary of State, August 13, 1972, GR-State, Political-UAR, Egypt, 1970-1973, NARA II. RG 59, Entry 1613, Box 2249.
179. Sadat, 238; interview with Hafez Isma'il; Kissinger, 213-215.
180. U.S. Interests Cairo (Greene) to Secretary of State, April 6, 1973, GR-State, Political-UAR, Egypt, 1970-1973, NARA II.
181. U.S. Interests Cairo (Greene) to Secretary of State, May 2, 1973, GR-State, Political-UAR, Egypt, 1970-1973, NARA II. RG 59, Entry 1613, Box 2249.
182. Kissinger, 226-227.
183. Heikal, *Autumn of Fury,* 49-50 also says the notion that the Middle East situation needed to be "hotted up" before the U.S. could move toward a resolution of that conflict was subtly communicated to the Egyptians by Kissinger, and even David Rockefeller, during the February-October 1972 period.
184. Memo for Kissinger, July 25, 1973, GR-State, Political-UAR, Egypt, 1970-1973, NARA II. RG 59, Entry 1613, Box 2249.
185. Bureau of Intelligence and Research note, August 30, 1973, GR-State, Political-UAR, Egypt, 1970-1973, NARA II. RG 59, Entry 1613, Box 2250.
186. Ibid.
187. William B. Quandt, *Peace Process* (Washington, D.C.: The Brookings Institution, 1993), 146.
188. Interview with Hafez Isma'il.
189. Interview with 'Aisha Ratib.
190. Sadat, 241; Kemal Hassan 'Ali, 286.
191. Kemal Hassan 'Ali, 286.
192. Memo from Nixon to Sadat, April 25, 1973, GR-State, Political-Egypt, 1970-1973, NARA II. RG 59, Entry 1613, Box 2250.

193. Sadat, 232.
194. Sadat, interview in *Newsweek,* March 18, 1974 noted in *Speeches January-December, 1974,* 64-65, and Sadat speech of April 3, 1974 in ibid., 130-138.
195. Interview with Mustafa Khalil.
196. Insight Team, 62; citing Arnaud de Borchgrave interview with Sadat in *Newsweek* in late March 1972.
197. Ibid., 62.
198. Speech of August 26, 1974 in *Speeches January-December, 1974,* 502, and speech of August 28, 1974 in ibid., 512-513. In these speeches, Sadat noted that prior to the war, "economically, we had reached rock bottom."
199. Sadat, 245.

Chapter 4

1. Interview with Hafez Isma'il. See also Kemal Hassan 'Ali, 285.
2. Interview with Ashraf Ghorbal.
3. Interview with Hafez Isma'il.
4. The story was repeated far and wide in Egypt.
5. Speech by Sadat on 6 June 1974 in *Speeches January-December, 1974,* 368.
6. Profound economic and political instability was produced by the failure of Western governments to respond to the oil shocks of 1973 and 1979. This failure gave rise to "a significant shift in economic thinking in the advanced Western democracies from Keynesianism to what Alain Lipietz (1992, p. 30) has called 'liberal-productivism'. . . In order to stop the deterioration of their competitive position, Western societies had to reverse course. Instead of continued welfare state expansion and state intervention in the economy, governments had to 'withdraw from control of the economy, dismantle public ownership, cut public expenditure, revive private welfare, remove trade union privileges, and promote mobility of capital and labour'" (Aimer, 1988, p. 1). It was not until the rise of Thatcherism in Great Britain that the "neoliberal creed," as the radical departure from traditional economic thinking came to be know, became the dominant approach to solving the twin problems of the mid- and late-1970s—economic stagnation and inflation. By the early 1980s, not only center-right, but also left-wing parties like the French Socialists had adopted it to cure Western Europe's economies suffering from "Eurosclerosis."" Hans-Georg Betz, *Radical Right-Wing Populism in Western Europe* (New York: St. Martin's Press, 1994), 109.
7. Interview with Mustafa Khalil.
8. *Speeches January-December, 1974,* 368. Sadat was referring to a statement issued by the London Institute of Strategic Studies.
9. Interview with 'Abd al-'Aziz Higazi.
10. Interview with Fuad Sultan.
11. *The Economist,* November 10, 1974.
12. Interview with Mustafa Khalil.
13. *International Herald Tribune,* October 2, 1974.
14. *Arab Report and Record,* January 1-15, 1974.
15. *Arab Report and Record,* February 1-14, 1974.
16. Sadat asked to see members of the financial community in New York prior to his visit in 1966. I do not know if he met Rockefeller then, but what is certain is that Rockefeller played an interesting role as a go-between in the highly secret interim settlement discussions of the early 1970s. See FOIA file 198803126 regarding Sadat's

visit to the United States; also see David Rockefeller letter to Joseph Sisco, November 4, 1970, GR-State, Political-UAR, Egypt, 1970-1973, NARA II. RG 59, Entry 1613, Box 2640. There are other references to Rockefeller in these declassified State Department documents.

17. Waterbury, *The Egypt of Nasser and Sadat,* 130.

18. Ibid., 131-132.

19. Ibid.

20. Marsha Pripstein Posusney, *Labor and State in Egypt,* 173.

21. Interview with Mustafa Khalil.

22. Mikhail Gorbachev, *Perestroika* (New York: Harper & Row, 1987).

23. Interview with Hassan 'Abbas Zaki.

24. Interview with Isma'il Sabri 'Abdullah.

25. Interview with Fuad Sultan.

26. Interview with Isma'il Sabri 'Abdullah.

27. Ibid.

28. Interview with Ahmed Sultan.

29. Ibid.

30. Posusney, 173.

31. Suzanne Berger, "Problems and Prospects of Egyptian Small-Scale Industry," Massachusetts Institute of Technology, draft paper, August 1978, 2; and Waterbury, 162-164. The author thanks Ms. Berger for permitting citation of this paper.

32. Mourad M. Wahba, *The Role of the State in the Egyptian Economy, 1945-1981* (Reading, MA: Ithaca Press, 1994), p. 194. Wahba puts these ceilings at L.E. 5,000 for annual salaries, and L.E. 10,000 for profits. Ceilings were kept, but raised, in the late 1970s, see p. below; the 95 percent tax rate was retained, however.

33. Ibid., 194-195.

34. Ibid.; also see Suzanne Berger, *op. cit.*

35. Waterbury, 287.

36. Sadowski, 82; Waterbury, 287.

37. Waterbury, 285-286.

38. Interview with Sufi Abu Talib.

39. Interview with Jeswald Salacuse.

40. Posusney, 179.

41. Based on interviews with past and present Salon Vert employees.

42. Interview with Gamal Khouzzam. Khouzzam worked as an employee, then manager at Salon Vert from 1946 to 1968.

43. Samir Youssef, *System of Management of Public Sector Enterprises* (Cairo: Center for Middle East Management Studies, American University in Cairo, 1983), 26-27.

44. Interview with Hassan 'Abbas Zaki. Also confirmed by interviews with numerous others, including 'Abd al-Razzaq 'Abd al-Magid.

45. Interview with Fa'iqa 'Abd al-Rahman, Vice-Governor of the Egyptian Central Bank at the time of the interview.

46. Interview with 'Adil Gazarin.

47. Posusney, 173. See her excellent discussion of this issue, 173-180.

48. Monte Palmer, et al., *The Egyptian Bureaucracy* (Syracuse, NY: Syracuse University Press), 4,8; Waterbury, 243.

49. Waterbury, 243.

50. Sadowski, 261-262.

51. Posusney, 174–176.
52. Interview with Ahmed Beha al-Din.
53. Interview with Ashraf Ghorbal.
54. Interview with al-Gamassi.
55. Kissinger, *Years of Upheaval,* 636–646, 768–770.
56. Heikal, 67–69.
57. Presentation by Harold Saunders at Harvard University, March 23, 2000. I would like to thank Mr. Saunders for permitting me to use his remarks from that presentation.
58. Letter to author from Hermann Eilts, August 22, 1986.
59. Interview with Kemal Abu al-Magd.
60. Handoussa, 20.
61. For example, see Ibrahim 'Izzat, "Misr Dawlat Bitruliyya Kubra," *Rose al-Yusuf,* no. 2406, July 22, 1974, 3; or look at the cover of *Rose al-Yusuf,* No. 2387, 11 March 1974, which shows a drawing of Sadat inundated with money, that bears the label *infitah.* Sadat is standing before a poor woman, and in the background is a bus teeming with people, headed down a road toward a bright sun labeled socialism. The caption reads, "The will arrive in peace, if Allah wills it, but this (the money from *infitah*) is to relieve them a bit from the crowded buses, the long lines of the coops, etc."
62. Richard Adams, 15.
63. Ibid., 15. Adams gives figures of $128 million and $2,214 million.
64. World Bank Report 2738—EGT, "Arab Republic of Egypt: Recent Economic Developments and External Capital Requirements," November 12, 1979, 29.
65. *Arab Report and Record,* May 1-15, 1974.
66. Interview with 'Abd al-Razzaq 'Abd al-Magid.
67. Alan Mackie, "IMF approval gives weight to new economic package," *Middle East Economic Digest,* vol. 21, no. 2, January 14, 1977, 3.
68. *Middle East Economic Digest,* vol. 21, no. 9, March 4, 1978, 17.
69. Interview with Fuad Sultan.
70. Interview with Hassan Mar'ei.
71. Waterbury, 291–297.
72. Salah Hafez, "Laisa Waqt al-Muhakimat!," *Rose al-Yusuf,* no. 2482, January 5, 1976, 18-19. The article refers to a recent disclosure in the People's Assembly.
73. Interview with Isma'il 'Uthman.
74. Ibid.
75. 'Uthman Ahmed 'Uthman, *Safahat min Tugribati* (Cairo: al-Sharikat al-Misriyya li-l-Taba'a, 1976), 578; and Raymond Baker, *Sadat and After* (Cambridge, MA: Harvard University Press, 1990), 25.
76. Baker, 33.
77. His wealth was estimated at $1.5 billion in 1987 in "The Billionaires," *Fortune,* October 12, 1987, 125.
78. 'Abdullah Imam, *Jehan: Sayyiddat Misr al-Ula wa-l-Akhira* (Cairo: Mu'ass'assat Rose al-Yusuf, 1985, 114.
79. Waterbury, 259.
80. Salah Hafez, op. cit., 18-19.
81. See Sadowski, 123–129.
82. Interview with 'Abd al-Razzaq 'Abd al-Magid.
83. See 'Abdullah Imam, 142–156.

84. See 'Abdullah Imam; Sadowski, 122-123; for a strong defense of Jehan Sadat, read Ahmed Beha al-Din, *Muhawirati ma'a Sadat* (Cairo: Dar al-Hilal, 1987), 182-188.

85. Posusney, 175-176.

86. Interviews with numerous employers and employees.

87. Ragui Assaad and Simon Commander, "Egypt: The Labour Market Through Boom and Recession," World Bank, May 1990, 26, as cited in Posusney, 137. According to Waterbury, elite civil servants and public sector managers legally earned about L.E. 4,000 per annum (L.E. 333 per month), high ranking civil servants and managers earned L.E. 900-1,500 per annum (L.E. 75-125 per month), mid-level bureaucrats and white collar company workers earned L.E. 144-540 per annum (L.E. 12-45 per month), and beginning level civil servants earned L.E. 13.50-15 per month. Waterbury, 248-248, 362.

88. Sa'd al-Din Ibrahim, "Social Mobility and Income Distribution," in G. Abdel-Khaleq and R. Tignor, eds. *The Political Economy of Income Distribution in Egypt* (New York: Holmes & Meier, 1982).

89. Mahmud al-Maraghi, "Ganun al-As'ar wa Muwagihat al-Ghila" al-Qadim," *Rose al-Yusuf,* no. 2417, October 7, 1974, 11. There were many other articles in the same vein.

90. Assaad and Commander, 26, cited in Posusney, 137.

91. Posusney, 136-138, 181.

92. Nazih N.M. Ayubi, *Bureaucracy and Politics in Contemporary Egypt* (London: Ithaca Press, 1980), 8-9.

93. Adams, 15.

94. Ibid., 143.

95. Ibid., 15.

96. Ibid., 15, 197 footnote 12.

97. Ibid., 13-14.

98. Ibid., 14.

99. I experienced this on numerous occasions in Cairo during 1976-1977, as did many other friends and acquaintances.

100. Story recounted to me by Magda al-Sanga.

101. Central Agency for Popular Mobilization and Statistics (CAPMAS) *Statistical Yearbook, 1952-1982,* August 1983.

102. Ibid.

103. Interview with Fa'iqa al-Rifa'i.

104. See Waterbury, 170-178.

105. Interview with Yusuf Mansur.

106. Interview with 'Ali Nigm. He was with the National Bank of Egypt from 1955 until 1986, and was named governor of the Central Bank in 1985.

107. Waterbury, 291. Waterbury found that the holders of three to ten feddans were the real gainers of this era.

108. Posusney, 136.

109. *Arab Report and Record,* January 1-15, 1975.

110. Ibid.

111. Ibid.

112. Interview with Rif'at al-Sa'id.

113. *Arab Report and Record,* August 1-15, 1975; interview with Rif'at al-Sa'id.

114. Interview with Hussein 'Abd al-Razzaq.

115. Ibid.

116. Sayyid Qutb, who was hanged in the mid-1960s by the Nasser regime for his radical Islamic writings, had lived in the United States. His experience was largely negative, leading to a pronounced reinforcement of his Islamic value system.
117. The dark callous formed on the forehead as the result of extensive prayer and friction with the prayer rug.
118. I experienced this firsthand. In my interview with Shaf'ei, he preferred to focus on religious and mystical concerns. Shaf'ei noted that a Western correspondent had once shown impatience with his mystical responses to questions, so I sat there patiently listening to Shaf'ei speak, not understanding half of what he was saying. Interview with Hussein al-Shaf'ei.
119. 'Uthman Ahmed 'Uthman, 359.
120. Interview with Noha Sadat.
121. Imam, 115. The assassin's defense team showed a picture of daughter Jehan with Julio Iglesias that appeared on the cover of an Italian magazine just days before the assassination. They claimed this photo and other behavior proved her rejection of Eastern traditions.
122. In the face of much opposition to a more liberal personal status law, a bill finally appeared in 1968, but received no serious push from Nasser and got nowhere. See 'Abdullah Imam, "Wa Akhiran. . .Hatha Huwwa Qanun al-Ahwal al-Shakhsiyya al-Gadid," *Rose al-Yusuf,* no. 2069, February 5, 1968, 11-13; Su'ad Zuheir, "Tanfagir Mushkilat Qanun al-Ahwal al-Shakhsiyya," *Rose al-Yusuf,* no. 2390, April 1, 1974, 20-24; 'Aida al-Azab Musa, "Hatha Huwwa Ra'yi bila 'Asabiyya wa la Khawf," *Rose al-Yusuf,* no. 2392, April 15, 1974, 20-21.
123. Interview with 'Aisha Ratib.
124. Mustafa, 141.
125. Ibid., 140.
126. Kepel, 93.
127. Mustafa, passim. See also R. Hrair Dekmejian, *Islam in Revolution* (Syracuse, NY: Syracuse University Press, 1985), 90-96.
128. *Arab Report and Record,* June 1-15, 1975.
129. Gleaned from 1975-1976 issues of *Arab Report and Record.*
130. Mustafa Kamel Murad, "Makan al-Mu'arda fi-l-Ittihad al-Ishtiraki," *Rose al-Yusuf,* no. 2393, April 22, 1974, 5-6.
131. Interview with Mustafa Khalil.
132. Interview with Sufi Abu Talib.
133. Sufi Abu Talib, *Al-Mugtama'a al-'Arabi* (Cairo: publisher unknown, 1965).
134. Sufi Abu Talib, *Ishtirakiyyiatina al-Dimuqratiyya* (Cairo: publisher unknown, 1978).
135. Ibid., 17.
136. Ibid., 22.
137. Ibid., 26.
138. Ibid., 13-14.
139. Winter, in ed. Shamir, 51.
140. Abu Talib, *Our Socialist Democracy,* 24-33.
141. Ibid., 52.
142. Ibid., 72.
143. Ibid., 80.
144. Ibid., 80.
145. Ibid., 85.

146. Interview with Sufi Abu Talib.
147. Abu Talib, *Our Democratic Socialism,* 85.
148. Interview with Sufi Abu Talib.
149. Interviews with Sufi Abu Talib and Jehan Sadat. When I asked Mrs. Sadat about Abu Talib's credibility, she responded, "You can believe whatever Dr. Abu Talib told you."
150. Winter, in Shamir, ed., 52.
151. See Salah Hafez, "Azmat al-Ittifaqiyyat wa Azmat al-'Arab," *Rose al-Yusuf,* no. 2465, September 8, 1975, 3; 'Abd al-Rahman al-Sharqawi, "Badalan min al-Tamziq," *Rose al-Yusuf,* no. 2465, September 8, 1975, 4-6; 'Abd al-Sitar al-Tawila, "Misr Taht Rahmat al-'Askarriyya al-Amrikiyya!," *Rose al-Yusuf,* no. 2465, September 8, 1975, 7-9.
152. Kissinger, *Years of Upheaval,* 768.
153. Read Quandt's excellent discussion of this period. William B. Quandt, *Peace Process* (Washington, D.C.: The Brookings Institution, 1993), 227-246.
154. Eilts letter to the author. In a closed cabinet meeting, Kissinger informed his American cabinet colleagues that when the Israelis asked him if he thought they were being unreasonable, he responded, "not only were you unreasonable, you were disastrous." Cabinet Meeting Minutes, March 26, 1975, Box 4, James E. Connor Files, Gerald R. Ford Library, Ann Arbor, Michigan.
155. Interview with Yehiya al-Gamal.
156. Interview with Tahsin Bashir.
157. Interview with Ahmed Beha al-Din.
158. Interview with Lutfi al-Kholi. This is yet another reference to the Hoagland article cited elsewhere.
159. Interview with Yehiya al-Gamal.
160. Interview with Isma'il Sabri 'Abdullah.
161. I can remember a brief, hallway discussion with Boutros Boutros-Ghali in the early 1980s when he was a professor at Cairo University's Faculty of Economics and Political Science. He said, "If you want to understand what's going on, follow the money."
162. Interview with Ibrahim Hilmi 'Abd al-Rahman.
163. Interview with Muhammad Mahmud al-Imam.
164. Posusney, 83, 95, 101.
165. Interview with al-Imam.
166. National Security Council meeting, March 28, 1975, Box 1, National Security Adviser, National Security Meetings File, Gerald R. Ford Library, Ann Arbor, Michigan.
167. Ibid.
168. Ibid.
169. Ibid.
170. Ibid.
171. Minutes: National Security Council Meeting, May 15, 1975, Box 1, National Security Adviser, NSC Meetings File, Gerald R. Ford Library, Ann Arbor, Michigan.
172. Ibid.
173. Ibid.
174. See Quandt, 239-243.
175. Interview with Hafez Isma'il.
176. Congress approved the commercial sale of $50 million worth of transport planes to Egypt. "The pickings" were still slim.
177. William J. Burns, *Economic Aid and American Policy Toward Egypt, 1955-1981* (Albany, NY: State University of New York Press, 1985), 220.
178. Ibid.

179. Interview with Hermann Eilts.
180. Interview with Sufi Abu Talib.
181. Interview with Mustafa Amin.
182. Eilts letter to author.
183. Whether or not the Egyptians could have pressed their initial military advantage remains subject to debate. The view of the "radical" Arabs was endorsed by Egypt's chief of staff at the time of the war, Gen. Sa'd al-Din Shazli. Shazli's criticism caused Sadat's regime considerable embarrassment, and resulted in Shazli's self-imposed exile. See al-Shazly's book, op. cit.
184. Salah Hafez, "Sheikhukhat al-Thawra wa Dawa' al-Sadat," *Rose al-Yusuf,* no. 2409, August 12, 1974, 3-4.
185. Freedom of Information Act 199102323, file on Heikal. The file includes a communiqué from the American Embassy in Cairo to the State Department reporting on a discussion with Heikal. Heikal told his interlocutor that he disagreed with Sadat about Sinai I, but had maintained his friendship with Sadat. Sinai II, however, had caused him to vow not to associate or speak with Sadat because this meant that 'the balance of power has been shifted irrevocably in favor of Israel; Egypt can never recover.'
186. *Arab Report and Record,* February 1-14, 1974, 44.
187. Interview with Rif'at al-Sa'id.
188. Ibid.
189. *Al-Musawwar* magazine and *al-Akhbar* newspaper were leading sources of anti-Nasser articles. See *Arab Report and Record,* February 1-14, 1974, March 1-15, 1974, and May 1-15, 1974. The latter issue refers to the debate over the Nasser era between Lutfi al-Kholi and the exiled Wafdist journalist, Ahmed Abu al-Fath, in *al-Tali'a.*
190. Interview with Ibrahim Salih.
191. Salah Gaudet, *Al-Musawwar,* March 7, 1974, quoted in *Arab Report and Record,* March 1-15, 1974, 79.
192. Ahmed Hamadi, *Akhbar al-Yom,* quoted in *Arab Report and Record,* March 1-15, 1974, 79.
193. Sa'd Fakhri 'Abd al-Nur, *al-Ahram,* March 9, 1974.
194. See Waterbury, 338–9, on the de-Nasserization campaign.
195. *Le Monde,* October 16, 1974.
196. Interview with Hussein 'Abd al-Razzaq.
197. Interviews with numerous journalists of diverse ideological leanings.
198. Interview with Mustafa Amin.
199. In an interview with *Akher Sa'a* magazine, the well-known Sheikh 'Ashur was critical of socialism and asserted that Islam did not oppose individual wealth. Rebuttal by socialists produced rejoinders by other religious figures in support of both sides, and fueled a largely conservative religious versus leftist debate. Read: 'Abd al-Rahman al-Sharqawi, *Rose al-Yusuf,* no. 2461, August 11, 1975; 'Aryan Nasif, "Haram ya Sheikh 'Ashur!," *Rose al-Yusuf,* no. 2415, September 23, 1974, 16-17; or see the exchange between Khalid Muhi al-Din and Hussein Muhammad Hassan: Khalid Muhi al-Din, "Al-Markisiyya. . .al-Din. . .al-Ishtirakiyya," *Rose al-Yusuf,* no. 2435, February 10, 1975, 6-8; Hussein Muhammed Hassan, "Bal al-Fikr al-Islam. . .la Ghair," *Rose al-Yusuf,* no. 2438, March 3, 1975, 12-13; Khalid Muhi al-Din, "Ma'a al-Markisiyya wa-l-Din wa-l-Ishtirakiyya," *Rose al-Yusuf,* no. 2440-1, 28-30, March 1975.
200. Interview with Kemal Abu al-Magd.
201. Ibid.

202. Interview with Mustafa Amin.

203. *Arab Report and Record,* March 1-15, 1975.

204. 'Abd al-Mun'im al-Sawi was made head of al-Tahrir publishing house. On March 16, 1975, copies of *Rose al-Yusuf* were seized; copies of the first issue of the leftist *al-Hurriyya* were seized on April 8, 1975; see *Arab Report and Record,* March 16-31, and April 1-15, 1975.

205. *Arab Report and Record,* August 16-31 and November 1-15, 1975. Eilts says Abu al-Magd was removed because Sadat was annoyed by a TV interview Abu al-Magd had allowed. Letter from Eilts to author.

206. Articles abounded attacking Ashraf Marwan and 'Uthman Ahmed 'Uthman for corrupt business practices.

207. Interview with Mustafa Amin. The article in question was written by Nu'man Gum'a in *al-Akhbar.* Gum'a would later become a major figure in the New Wafd party.

208. Interview with Mustafa Amin.

209. Ibid.

210. Interview with Galal al-Hamamsi.

211. Letter from Eilts to author.

212. Interview with Kemal Abu al-Magd.

213. The author thanks Ibrahim Salih for his assistance in sorting out these changes.

214. Interview with Anis Mansur. Corroborated by other regime elites.

215. Ibid.

216. Interview with Mustafa Amin. One of the most vocal proponents of a liberal-democratic system was Ibrahim al-Ba'thi, "Al-Ahzab? Na'm wa Laakin...Matta?," *al-Musawwar,* no. 2584, April 19, 1974; al-Ba'thi, "Al-La'ibun bi-l-Nar...," *al-Musawwar,* no. 2585, April 26, 1974, 19; al-Ba'thi, "Matlub Infitah Sahafi 'Agil," *al-Musawwar,* no. 2586, May 3, 1974, 20; al-Ba'thi, "Al-Sura al-Manshuda li-l-Tanthim al-Siyyasi," *al-Musawwar,* no. 2594, June 28, 1974, 25.

217. Interview with Sayyid Mar'ei.

218. *Waraqat Uktubur* (Cairo: Ministry of Information, 1974).

219. 'Ali Amin, *al-Ahram,* April 12, 1974, reported in *Arab Report and Record,* April 1-15, 1974.

220. *Arab Report and Record,* August 1-15, 1974; and Mark Cooper, 179.

221. Ahmed 'Abbas Salih, "'An al-Dimuqratiyya wa-l-Ittihad al-Ishtiraki," *al-Katib,* June, 1971, 2-10.

222. *Arab Report and Record,* September 1-15, 1974.

223. *Al-Ahram,* September 9, 1974.

224. Read Gamal Salim, "Al-Ahzab la Tinsha' bi-Qirar!," *Rose al-Yusuf,* No. 2414, September 16, 1974, 7; Ahmed Hamrush, "Ishtirakiyyat 'Ali Amin," *Rose al-Yusuf,* no. 2414, September 16, 1974, 7.

225. Yusuf Sabri and Samir 'Izzat, "Intikhabat al-Ittihad al-Ishtiraki," *Rose al-Yusuf,* No. 2456, July 7, 1975, 4-7.

226. Ibid.

227. Mark Cooper, *The Transformation of Egypt* (Baltimore, MD: Johns Hopkins University Press, 1982), 181.

228. Ibid.

229. Interview with Noha Sadat.

230. *Al-Ahram,* October 22, 1975.

231. Interview with Abu Wafia by Sami Metawalli, "Hadith ma'a Abu Wafia," *al-Ahram,* 23 October 1975.

232. Ibid.
233. *Al-Ahram,* January 24, 1976.
234. *Al-Ahram,* October 24, 1975.
235. *Al-Ahram,* October 28, 1975.
236. *Al-Ahram,* October 31, 1975.
237. *Al-Ahram,* November 3, 1975.
238. *Al-Ahram,* November 17, 1975.
239. Read the articles in *al-Ahram* by 'Abd al-'Aziz al-Shurbagi, November 7, 1975; Muhammad 'Unbur, November 19, 1975; and Muhammad Hilmi Murad, November 20, 1975; inter alia.
240. *Al-Ahram,* November 1, 1975.
241. See *al-Ahram,* January 26-28, 1976.
242. From February 2 to March 8, 1976, the major newspapers carried articles by Nagib Mahfuz, Tewfiq al-Hakim, Louis 'Awad, Ihsan 'Abd al-Quddus, Lutfi al-Kholi, Boutros Boutros-Ghali, and many others.
243. *Al-Ahram,* March 7, 1976.
244. *Al-Ahram,* March 17, 1976.
245. Interview with Ahmed Beha al-Din.
246. *Al-Ahram,* March 19, 1976.
247. Interview with Sufi Abu Talib.
248. *Al-Ahram,* March 16 and 20, 1976.
249. Posusney, 108-111.
250. *Al-Ahram,* March 18, 1976.
251. Interviews with Mustafa Kamel Murad, Muhammad Murad al-Subtacy, and 'Abd al-Magid Shatir. Subtacy used the term Politburo in describing the party's board of directors.
252. Interview with Mustafa Kamel Murad.
253. Interview with Muhammad Murad al-Subtacy.
254. Ibid.
255. Ibid.
256. Ibid.
257. Ibid.
258. Ibid.
259. See Tareeq Isma'il and Rif'at al-Sa'id, *The Communist Movement in Egypt, 1920-1988* (Syracuse, NY: Syracuse University Press, 1988), 127-150.
260. Interview with Hussein 'Abd al-Razzaq.
261. Interview with Khalid Muhi al-Din.
262. Posusney, 109.
263. Reported in *al-Ahram,* March 28, 1976.
264. *Al-Ahram,* March 29, 1976.
265. *Al-Ahram,* March 25, 1976.
266. Interviews with Ahmed Beha al-Din, Rif'at al-Sa'id, Muhammad Sid Ahmed, and Milad Hanna.
267. Interview with Hussein 'Abd al-Razzaq.
268. Interview with Rif'at al-Sa'id.
269. Ibid.
270. Interview with Lutfi al-Kholi.
271. *Arab Report and Record,* April 16-30, 1974. This article points out that some claimed the Fanniyya 'Askariyya group was backed by Libya's Colonel Qaddafi.

272. Interview with Muhammad al-Mismari.

273. Sullivan and Abed-Kotob assert that the roots of Egypt's Islamic extremists date to the late 1960s influence of a Muslim Brother, Sheikh 'Ali 'Abdu Isma'il, who as a prisoner briefly held the position that both the ruler and the ruled in Egypt were guilty of apostasy. Denis J. Sullivan and Sana Abed-Kotob, *Islam in Contemporary Egypt* (Boulder, CO: Lynne Rienner, 1999), 75-77. 'Abdu Isma'il's influence was undoubtedly significant, but Sayyid Qutb's influence and renown both predated and far surpassed that of 'Abdu Isma'il. Mismari's version is more accurate. Qutb was, as Dekmejian calls him, "The Crucial Link." Dekmejian, 90-93. Also see Emmanuel Sivan, *Radical Islam* (New Haven: Yale University Press, 1985), 21-28 and passim.

274. Ibid.

275. Kepel, 74-75; interview with Muhammad al-Mismari.

276. Kepel, 75-76.

277. Mustafa, 148.

278. Mark Cooper, 205.

279. Ibid., 215-217.

280. Comment made to the author by Henry Precht.

281. *Arab Report and Record,* November 1-15, 1976.

282. Ibid.

283. Interview with Yassin Sirag al-Din.

284. *Al-Da'wa,* no. 7, December 1976, 13.

285. Ibid.

286. Interview with Kemal Ibrashi.

287. 'Uthman, 73-74.

288. See, for example, Patrick Gaffney, *Shaykh, Khutba and Masjid: The Role of the Local Islamic Preacher in Upper Egypt,* Ph.D. thesis, University of Chicago, 1882. Gaffney was at al-Minya University in the late 1970s and recorded many stories about the Islamist students' strength there.

289. Ibid., 134; interviews with former student activists.

290. 'Uthman, 130.

291. Ibid., 130-131.

292. Gami'a, 191.

293. Sullivan and Abed-Kotob, 73.

294. Wa'il 'Uthman, 148; and interviews with former student activists.

295. 'Uthman, 149.

296. Ibid., 148, 153.

297. Ibid., 155-157.

298. Interviews with former student activists.

299. See *al-Da'wa,* no. 9, February 1977, 52.

300. See *al-Da'wa,* no. 20, January 1978, 52, 55.

301. Abdalla, 226-227.

302. Erlich, 213-214.

303. Ibid.

304. Ibid., 215.

305. Interview with Yehiya Kabil. Kabil was dean of Cairo University's School of Engineering from 1977 to February 1981.

306. Sa'd al-Din Ibrahim, "Anatomy of Egypt's Militant Islamic Groups," *International Journal of Middle East Studies* 12, 1980, 448.

307. Scott Mainwaring, "Brazil: The Catholic Church and the Popular Movement in Nova Iguacu, 1974-1985," in Levine, op. cit., 126.

308. Such as Gabr Rizq, *Madabih al-Ikhwan fi Sugun Nasser* (Cairo: Dar al-I'tisam, 1977), and Gabr Rizq, *Madbahat al-Ikhwan fi Liman Tura* (Cairo: Dar al-I'tisam, 1979).

309. Interview with Yehiya Kabil.

310. See *al-Da'wa*, no. 5, October 1976, 46; *al-Da'wa*, no. 6, November 1976, 57; and *al-Da'wa*, no. 7, December 1976, 36.

311. *Al-Da'wa*, no. 7, December 1976, 39.

312. See Appendix B for total foreign debt. Subsidies had risen from L.E. 39.8 million in 1973 to L.E. 116.2 million in 1974, L.E. 433.4 million in 1975, and L.E. 622 million in 1976. See *Middle East Economic Digest*, vol. 21, no. 34, August 26, 1977, 18.

313. Prime Minister Mamduh Salem had made such an announcement in the weeks preceding the price increases.

314. Interview with 'Ali Nigm.

315. Price increases were as follows: rice, 16 percent; sugar, 3.3 percent; petroleum, 31 percent; cigarettes, 12 percent; butagas, 46 percent; cars, 33 percent; imported textiles, 50 percent; imported electrical household good, wool, and alcohol, 100 percent. From *Middle East Economic Digest*, vol. 21, no. 3, January 21, 1977.

316. Ibid.

317. *Arab Report and Record*, January 1-15, 1977.

318. I saw the student demonstrators in the Midan Tahrir and Bab al-Luq area. They were more intent on chanting anti-regime slogans than anything, but when they encountered the security forces using buckshot and tear gas to defend the Bab al-Luq metro station, rocks were thrown by the students and others at the security forces. On the leftists role in inciting the riots, see Erlich, 216-217. For a fuller discussion in Arabic, see Hussein 'Abd al-Razzaq, *Misr fi 18 wa 19 Yanayir* (Cairo: Matba'at Ikhwan Muraftili, 1985).

319. Interview with Rif'at al-Sa'id.

320. Interviews with numerous Marxists.

321. Interview with John McDougal.

322. Interviews with residents of the Pyramids Avenue district.

323. Interview with Fuad Sultan.

324. I witnessed this personally: watching children and teenagers throw stones at the windows of The American University of Cairo on the heels of the student demonstrators. Not that there weren't some older individuals who did the same.

325. Interview with al-Nabawi Isma'il.

326. Interview with Rif'at al-Sa'id.

327. Statement by Sadat on February 3, 1977, reported in *Arab Report and Record*, February 1-14, 1977.

328. Ibid.

329. 'Umar al-Tilmesani, "Laisat al-Gawla al-Akhira...," *al-Da'wa*, no. 11, April 1977, 2-3.

330. *Arab Report and Record*, January 1-15, 1977.

331. Interview with Rif'at al-Sa'id.

332. Interview with Hussein 'Abd al-Razzaq.

333. Interview with Rif'at al-Sa'id.

334. Erlich, 217.

Chapter 5

1. Interview with 'Abd al-Ghani Gamassi.
2. Based on interviews with numerous insiders, especially Sayyid Mar'ei, Hamdi Fuad, Kemal Hassan 'Ali, and Ahmed Beha al-Din.
3. Interview with Kemal Hassan 'Ali.
4. Interview with Ahmed Beha al-Din.
5. Interviews with numerous elites. Several of them employed the term "Oriental" men, rather than "Middle Eastern" men.
6. Interviews with Hamdi Fuad and others.
7. *Middle East Economic Digest,* vol. 22, no. 4, January 27, 1978, 17.
8. *Middle East Economic Digest,* vol. 21, no. 34, August 26, 1977, 18.
9. *Egyptian Gazette,* January 21, 1977 reported that only ten percent of total arms expenditures between 1967 and 1975 had been covered by Arab aid. See *Arab Report and Record,* January 1-15, 1976 and July 16-31, 1976. The latter report contains information on GODE and its plan to provide $2 billion in aid to Egypt, a sum Sadat found insufficient. The Saudis later countered the Egyptian authorities' criticism by claiming that they had provided $7 billion in aid between 1973 and 1978, but it must be noted that at least one-third of this arrived after the January 1977 riots. See "Cover Story," *The Middle East,* June 1979, 26-30.
10. Abdel Monem Said Aly, "Privatization in Egypt: The Regional Dimensions," in I. Harik and D. Sullivan, eds., *Privatization and Liberalization in the Middle East* (Bloomington, IN: Indiana University Press, 1992), 48.
11. Interview with 'Abd al-Razzaq 'Abd al-Magid.
12. *Arab Report and Record,* April 1-15, 1977, and May 1-15, 1977. The latter reports on the first meeting of the World Bank Consultative Group in Paris to discuss Egypt's economic and financial situation.
13. *Arab Report and Record,* 16-30 June, 1977. Also, letter from Ambassador Eilts to author.
14. Robert R. Nathan Associates, "A Study of the Feasibility of a Private Investment Encouragement Fund for the Egyptian Private Sector," submitted to U.S. Agency for International Development, Department of State, September 1979, 20. Also see Waterbury, *The Egypt of Nasser and Sadat,* 147, 155.
15. Nathan report, 28-29.
16. Waterbury, 149-150.
17. Alan Mackie, "Last Tango in Cairo?," *Middle East Economic Digest,* vol. 20, no. 31, July 1976.
18. Interviews with Sadat insiders.
19. Interview with Fuad Sultan.
20. Mourad M. Wahba, *The Role of the State in the Egyptian Economy, 1945-1981* (Reading, MA: Ithaca Press, 1994), 190; and Waterbury, 132-133.
21. Waterbury, 132.
22. Interviews with an aide to 'Abd al-Razzaq 'Abd al-Magid and Jeswald Salacuse.
23. For a slightly more detailed description, see Waterbury, 132-133.
24. Interview with Muhammad Mahmud al-Imam.
25. Ibid.
26. Ibid.
27. These included "exemptions from prevailing labor legislation, the right to dispose freely of foreign exchange earned by the project, free importation without license

of goods necessary to the production process, the right to export directly without permit, exemption from corporate profits tax for eight years, exemption from taxes on all foreign currency loans, etc." Waterbury, 170.

28. Waterbury, 171–188.

29. Suzanne Berger, "Problems and Prospects of Egyptian Small-Scale Industry," MIT, unpublished paper, August 1978.

30. Ibid. Other factors included the poor quality of local materials, the absence of space in workshops, inadequate banking services, and restrictions regarding incorporation.

31. *Middle East Economic Digest,* vol. 22, no. 22, June 2, 1978.

32. Robert R. Nathan Associates, 26.

33. Wahba, 194–195.

34. Ibid, 194–195.

35. World Bank Report 2738—EGT, "Arab Republic of Egypt: Recent Economic Developments and External Capital Requirements," November 12, 1979, 32; and World Bank Report 3253—EGT, "Egypt: Recent Economic Developments and External Capital Requirements," December 19, 1980, 37.

36. Nathan, 40.

37. Ibid.

38. World Bank Report 3253—EGT, 37.

39. *Egyptian Gazette,* January 21, 1977.

40. Raphael Israeli, 209.

41. Ibid, 209.

42. Alan Mackie, "Influx of funds increases confidence," *Middle East Economic Digest,* vol. 21, no. 44, November 4, 1977, 23.

43. Ibid., vol. 21, no. 45, November 11, 1977, 18.

44. Interview with Ahmed Beha al-Din.

45. Ibid.

46. Ibid.

47. Interview with 'Aisha Ratib.

48. Ibid.

49. Ibid.

50. Interview with Sayyid Mar'ei in Mahmud Fawzi, 144.

51. *Arab Report and Record,* February 1–15, 1977, May 16–31, 1977, and June 16–30, 1977.

52. Interview with al-Nabawi Isma'il.

53. Interviews with Fuad Hussein and al-Nabawi Isma'il.

54. Interview with Mustafa Khalil.

55. Interview with Sayyid Mar'ei.

56. Compare the bills discussed in *al-Ahram,* January 3, 1977 and June 2, 1977 as regards the criteria for party formation.

57. Juan Linz, "Totalitarian and Authoritarian Regimes," in Fred Greenstein and Nelson Polsby, eds., *Macropolitical Theory* (Reading, MA: Addison-Wesley Publishing Co., 1975), 174–411.

58. Interview with Mustafa Khalil.

59. Ibid.

60. Ibid.

61. *Middle East Economic Digest,* vol. 21, no. 29, July 22, 1977, 15.

62. Posusney, 110–113.

63. Interview with Ahmed Gam'a.

64. Interviews with Kemal Abu al-Magd and Sufi Abu Talib.
65. *Arab Report and Record,* July 1-15, 1977.
66. *Arab Report and Record,* August 16-31, 1977.
67. *Arab Report and Record,* September 16-30, 1977.
68. Farah, 2.
69. Baker, 165-166.
70. Musa Sabri, 107-111.
71. Interview with Pope Shenouda III.
72. Interview with Ambassador 'Abd al-Ra'uf al-Reidi.
73. Speech by Martin Indyk, Washington Institute for Near East Policy, November 1997.
74. Israeli, 226.
75. Interview with Isma'il Fahmi in Mahmud Fawzi, 161.
76. Sadat, *Khitab wa Ahadith al-Ra'is Muhammad Anwar al-Sadat* (Cairo: Ministry of Information, n.d.).
77. Interview with Mustafa Khalil.
79. Ibid.
79. Ibid.
80. Interview with Hermann Eilts.
81. Interview with Ashraf Ghorbal.
82. Interview with Noha Sadat.
83. Interview with Ashraf Ghorbal; discussion with Harold Saunders.
84. Letter from Eilts to author.
85. *Arab Report and Record,* April 16-30, 1975, July 16-31, 1975, and February 14-29, 1976.
86. *Middle East Economic Digest,* vol. 21, no. 43, October 28, 1977.
87. Letter from Eilts to author.
88. *Middle East Economic Digest, Arab Report,* January 1979.
89. Assem Abdul Mohsen, "Arab boycott far from fatal," *Middle East Economic Digest,* April 1979, 73-74; and Alan Mackie, "West could make up for loss of Arab economic support," *Middle East Economic Digest,* vol. 22, no. 46, November 1978, 7.
90. Alan Mackie, "Unforseen payments strength gives room for manoeuvre," *Middle East Economic Digest,* February 15, 1978. See also Hussam al-Qudsi, "The danger of fool's gold," *The Middle East,* March 1980.
91. World Bank Report 3253—EGT, 37.
92. Ibid.
93. U.S. Interests Cairo (Bergus) to Secretary of State, November 14, 1970, GR-State, Political-UAR, Egypt, 1970-1973, NARA II. RG 59, Entry 1613, Box 2640.
94. One need only review the covers of popular magazines like *Rose al-Yusuf* and *October* during this period for proof.
95. Again, see the *Egyptian Gazette,* January 21, 1977, reporting that only 10 percent of total arms expenditures between 1967-1975 had been covered by Arab aid. Even many with strong pan-Arab sentiments felt the Arabs were not doing enough.
96. Interview with Yehiya al-Gamal.
97. See *Arab Report and Record,* December 1-31, 1977.
98. Interview with Yassin Sirag al-Din.
99. Interview with Mustafa Kamel Murad.
100. Boutros Boutros-Ghali, *Egypt's Road to Jerusalem* (New York: Random House, 1997), 3-55.
101. Mahmud Fawzi, 102-103.

102. Rutherford, 315; based on his interviews with numerous Egyptian elites.
103. Interview with Fuad Sirag al-Din. Ansari, 202, quotes Sirag al-Din as estimating that 40,000-50,000 turned out in cold weather to listen to the former prime minister speak.
104. Ansari, 202. The figure is undoubtedly exaggerated.
105. Kuwait's *Al-Siyyasa,* June 23, 1978.
106. Interview with Hussein 'Abd al-Razzaq.
107. Interview with Fuad Sirag al-Din.
108. Interview with Sayyid Mar'ei.
109. Interview with Mustafa Khalil.
110. Interview with Sayyid Mar'ei.
111. *Al-Gumhurriyya,* August 15, 1978.
112. *Al-Gumhurriyya,* August 16, 1978.
113. Interview with Sufi Abu Talib.
114. Interviews with Sayyid Mar'ei and Sufi Abu Talib.
115. Interview with Sayyid Mar'ei.
116. *Al-Gumhurriyya,* August 14, 1978.
117. Musa Sabri, 628.
118. Interviews with Sufi Abu Talib and Mansur Hassan.
119. Interview with Sufi Abu Talib.
120. Waterbury, 370.
121. Musa Sabri, 631.
122. *Al-Gumhurriyya,* August 7, 1978.
123. Musa Sabri, 642-643.
124. *Al-Gumhurriyya,* August 13 and 16, 1978.
125. *Al-Ahram,* September 22, 1978.
126. Interview with Mansur Hassan.
127. Musa Sabri, 634-636.
128. Ibid., 635-636.
129. See Beattie, 27-29, 45-46, 75-76, 94-98.
130. Interview with Ibrahim Shukri.
131. Ibid.
132. Ibid.
133. Ibid.
134. Ibid.; and see *al-Ahram,* July 28, 1978.
135. Assem Abdul Mohsen, "Egypt's Tame Opposition," *The Middle East,* February 1980, 27-29.
136. Interview with Ibrahim Shukri.
137. Interview with Ahmed Nasir.
138. Stanley Reed, "Egyptian Assembly Elections: Sadat Does it Again," *Middle East Economic Digest, Arab Report,* no. 11, June 20, 1979, 4.
139. Interview with Ahmed Nasir.
140. Interview with Kemal al-Din Hussein.
141. Ibid.
142. Stanley Reed, op. cit.; Stanley Reed, "Egypt after the Elections: new government, old problems," *Middle East Economic Digest, Arab Report,* no. 12, July 4, 1979, 5-6.
143. Interview with Sufi Abu Talib.
144. Interviews with numerous journalists.
145. Musa Sabri, 529-531.

146. *Al-Ahram,* May 6, 1981, 16.

147. See Beattie, 186.

148. *Arab Report and Record,* January 16-31, 1977.

149. Interview with Sami Mansur.

150. *Arab Report and Record,* December 1-31, 1977.

151. Ibid., May 16-31, 1978; quote by the Socialist prosecutor.

152. Ibid.; interviews with journalists.

153. Interviews with leaders of the Liberal Socialist Party.

154. *Arab Report and Record,* vol. 17, September 1-15, 1978.

155. Interview with Mustafa Amin.

156. Interviews with 'Abdullah Imam, 'Aouni 'Izz al-Din, and other journalists.

157. See *al-Da'wa,* May 1979.

158. Musa Sabri, 528.

159. Ibid.

160. Interview with Ibrahim Shukri.

161. Ibid.

162. Ibid.

163. *Al-Musawwar* was quite supportive of the liberal current. See especially the articles written by Ibrahim al-Ba'thi from 1974 to 1976 such as in *al-Musawwar,* nos. 2584, 2585, 2593, 2594, 2715, and 2717.

164. Ami Ayalon, "Journalists and the Press: The Vicissitudes of Licensed Pluralism," in Shamir, ed., 267-279; quote is from 274.

165. Bianchi, 110.

166. Ibid.

167. Ibid., 110-111.

168. Interview with Sami Mansur.

169. Rutherford, 316.

170. Bianchi, 100-101.

171. Interview with pro-Sadat lawyer and NDP member, 'Abd al-'Aziz Gabr.

172. Interview with Muhammad Fahim Amin.

173. Ibid.

174. *Al-Ahram,* January 20, 1977.

175. Bianchi, 100.

176. Interviews with diverse opposition lawyers.

177. Muhammad Fahim Amin et. al., *Nadwat Niqabat al-Muhamin 'An Mashru'a Hadbat al-Ahram* (Cairo: Dar Wahdan li-l-Taba'a wa-l-Nashr, n.d.). This involved a plan formulated by a maverick foreign businessman to develop areas adjacent to the pyramids into a major tourist complex, complete with golf courses and so forth.

178. The syndicate was successful in several of these pursuits. See Rutherford, 320-324, on its protection of the Supreme Constitutional Court's autonomy.

179. Interview with Yehiya al-Gamal.

180. Interviews with Mahmud and Mamduh al-Shurbagi, the sons of 'Abd al-'Aziz al-Shurbagi. Both sons also became lawyers.

181. Interview with Pope Shenouda III. Shenouda denies it.

182. Interview with Muhammad Fahim Amin.

183. Interview with Yehiya al-Gamal.

184. Interview with 'Abd al-'Aziz Gabr.

185. Interview with Rif'at al-Sa'id.

186. Bianchi, 102.

187. Interview with 'Abd al-'Aziz Gabr.

188. Interviews with Muhammad al-Mismari, Muhammad Fahim Amin and other lawyers.

189. The secular seminars were organized by Muhammad Fahim Amin, while the religious seminars were organized by Muhammad al-Mismari. The seminars alternated use of the Lawyers' Syndicate meeting hall every other week, with each thus meeting twice per month.

190. Interviews with Muhammad Fahim Amin, Muhammad al-Mismari, and others.

191. Rudolph Peters, *Jihad in Classical and Modern Egypt* (Princeton, NJ: Markus Wiener Publishers, 1996), 153.

192. *Al-Da'wa,* no. 27, August 1978, 54.

193. *Al-Da'wa,* no. 25, June 1978, 47; *al-Da'wa,* no. 39, August 1979, 56-57.

194. *Al-Da'wa,* no. 39, August 1979, 56-57; *al-Da'wa,* no. 42, November 1979, 58-59.

195. *Al-Da'wa,* no. 38, July 1979, 54-55.

196. *Al-Da'wa,* no. 43, December 1979, 54-55.

197. *Al-Da'wa,* no. 37, June 1979.

198. *Al-Da'wa,* no. 37, June 1979.

199. *Al-Da'wa,* no. 41, October 1979, 56.

200. *Al-Da'wa,* no. 39, August 1979, 56-57.

201. *Al-Da'wa,* no. 41, October 1979, 54.

202. See Kepel, passim.

203. Mahmud A. Faksh, *The Future of Islam in the Middle East* (Westport, CT: Praeger, 1997), 49.

204. *Al-Ahram,* May 10, 1979.

205. Gaffney, 61.

206. Ann M. Lesch, "The Muslim Brotherhood in Egypt: Reform or Revolution?" in Matthew C. Moen and Lowell S. Gustafson, eds., *The Religious Challenge to the State* (Philadelphia, PA: Temple University Press, 1992), 201.

207. *Al-Da'wa,* no. 47, April 1980.

208. See Sivan, 23-28; Dekmejian, 90-93; and interview with Hassan Hanafi.

209. Interview with Hassan Hanafi.

210. Ibid.

211. Mustafa, 150.

212. Musa Sabri, 86; see also Sullivan and Abed-Kotob, 78-82; Dekmejian, 97-101;

213. Sabri, 97-98; Sivan, 103.

214. Sullivan and Abed-Kotob, 82.

215. Mustafa, 158-163; Gaffney, 57-80.

216. Gaffney, 72.

217. Ibid., 63-64.

218. Ibid., 64-65.

219. Hala Mustafa, 159-160.

220. Ibid., 127.

221. Ibid., 127.

222. Boutros Boutros-Ghali, 181-182.

223. 8 January organization began work in 1975 after the union of the Workers and Peasants Organization and the ECP organization. See *al-Ahram,* October 26, 1978.

224. Musa Sabri, 127.

225. Ibid., 127-129.

226. Peters, 153.

227. *Al-Da'wa,* no. 44, January 1980, 59.

228. Interviews with Fuad Sirag al-Din and Lutfi al-Kholi.

229. Interview with Muhammad al-Mismari.

230. Interview with Lutfi al-Kholi. Also see Waterbury, 372–373.

231. Interview with Muhammad al-Mismari.

232. Interview with Hussein 'Abd al-Razzaq.

233. World Bank Report 3253—EGT, 10.

234. Ibid.

235. Ibid., 11–12.

236. Sabri, 129.

237. Ibid., 127–129.

238. Ibid.

239. Interview with Sufi Abu Talib.

240. Ibid.

241. H. Hrair Dekmejian, *Islam in Revolution* (Syracuse, NY: Syracuse University Press, 1985), 87.

242. Ibid., 88.

243. Heikal, *Autumn of Fury,* 110.

244. Ahmed Beha al-Din, *Muhawirati…,* 188.

245. Musa Sabri, 130.

246. Heikal, 110.

247. *Al-Da'wa,* no. 50, July 1980.

248. *Al-Da'wa,* no. 48, May 1980.

249. *Al-Da'wa,* no. 51, August 1980, 61.

250. *Al-Da'wa,* no. 56, January 1981.

251. *Al-Da'wa,* no. 60, April 1981, 58–59. For example, the first "Friday Schools" conference was held in Alexandria, attended by approximately 450 people.

252. *Al-Da'wa,* no. 52, September 1980.

253. *Al-Da'wa,* no. 54, November 1980.

254. See Rutherford, 326.

255. Dekmejian, 97. Dekmejian presents a good look at Jihad's organizational structure, ideology, and recruitment techniques. See Dekmejian, 97–101.

256. Musa Sabri, 95–96.

257. Hala Mustafa, 151.

258. Ibid., 160.

259. Musa Sabri, 87.

260. Dekmejian, 99.

261. Musa Sabri, 94–98.

262. Ibid., 93–94.

263. Interview with Kemal Ibrashi.

264. Interview with Muhammad Fahim Amin.

265. Read *al-Guhmurriyya,* June 27, 1981 or *al-Ahram,* June 27, 1981.

266. Bianchi, 104; interviews with lawyers.

267. Interviews with numerous opposition lawyers, including Muhammad Fahim Amin.

268. Interview with Ashraf Ghorbal.

269. Interview with Noha Sadat.

270. Interview with Jehan Sadat.

271. Interview with Mustafa Khalil.

272. Interview with Anis Mansur. Mansur says Sadat told him that the shah had issued Sadat this word of warning.

273. Interviews with numerous secular opposition figures.
274. See the issues of *al-Sha'b* and *al-Ahali* throughout the summer of 1981.
275. Musa Sabri, 130, 136-138.
276. Interview with Mansur Hassan.
277. Farah, 3.
278. Ibid.
279. Thomas Philipp, "Copts and Other Minorities in the Development of the Egyptian Nation-State," in Shamir, ed., 130-150.
280. Mahmud Fawzi, 175. Interview with Pope Shenouda.
281. Interview with Sufi Abu Talib.
282. Ibid.
283. Musa Sabri, 118.
284. Ibid., 104; Sufi Abu Talib told me the same story during an interview with him.
285. Interview with Sufi Abu Talib.
286. In January, 1980, bombs exploded in several churches in Alexandria. See Farah, 3.
287. Ibid., 3.
288. Interviews with Pope Shenouda III and Milad Hanna.
289. Interview with Pope Shenouda III; see also Musa Sabri, 115.
290. Musa Sabri, 18-121.
291. *Al-Da'wa,* no. 49, June 1980, 60.
292. Interview with Milad Hanna.
293. Hamied Ansari, "Sectarian Conflict in Egypt and the Political Expediency of Religion," *The Middle East Journal,* vol. 38, no. 3, 1984, 397-418; *al-Ahram,* June 21, 1981 put the figures at 10 dead, 54 wounded, and 113 arrested; according to Heikal, *Autumn of Fury,* there were 17 dead, 54 wounded, and 113 arrested.
294. Interview with Daniel Petit.
295. Such stories were spread by word of mouth all over Cairo.
296. See *al-Da'wa,* July and August issues, 1981; also see Ansari, op. cit.
297. The author thanks Sa'd al-Din Ibrahim for this information.
298. Interview with al-Nabawi Isma'il. He intimated that this had indeed been the case.
299. Musa Sabri, 116-117.
300. Ibid.
301. Interview with Ashraf Ghorbal. The Americans had done much more to the shah. When push came to revolutionary shove in Iran, the Americans told the shah not to use military force to defend his regime. From the shah and his defender's perspective, they pulled the carpet out from under him.
302. Interview with Ahmed Beha al-Din.
303. Interview with Ambassador al-Reidi.
304. Interview with Ahmed Beha al-Din.
305. Interview with Ashraf Ghorbal.
306. Letter from Eilts to the author.
307. *Al-Sha'b,* no. 113, 8-9, published pictures of the SLP's national opposition conference to denounce the Israeli raid on the Iraqi nuclear reactor construction project. This form of intra-opposition assistance was very visible in the opposition press beginning in 1980.
308. Interview with Fuad Sirag al-Din.
309. Interview with Khalid Muhi al-Din.
310. Interview with Milad Hanna. See the issues of *al-Sha'b* during this period.
311. Interview with Anis Mansur.

312. Interview with Noha Sadat.
313. Interview with Pope Shenouda III.
314. Interview with Hamdi Fuad.
315. Interview with Ambassador al-Reidi.
316. Interview with Mustafa Kamel Murad.
317. Interviews with Jehan Sadat, Noha Sadat, Hassan Mar'ei, al-Nabawi Isma'il, among others.
318. Interview with 'Abd al-Razzaq 'Abd al-Magid.
319. Ibid.
320. Interview with Sufi Abu Talib.
321. Interview with Noha Sadat.
322. Interview with al-Nabawi Isma'il.
323. Musa Sabri, 80.
324. Ibid., 82.
325. Ibid., 78.
326. Ibid., 92.
327. Ibid., 90.
328. Ibid., 95-96; Kepel, 208-209.
329. Kepel, 211.
330. Ibid., 211-214.
331. Mahmud Fawzi, 184-187. Fawzi interviewed al-Nabawi Isma'il.
332. I wish to thank Ricky Romano for bringing this to my attention.
333. Interview with al-Nabawi Isma'il.
334. Interview with Kemal Hassan 'Ali; also with Ricky Romano. Romano was the CBS assistant bureau chief. He received the call from the CBS film crew that they had recorded Sadat's assassination. He astutely advised them to head immediately to the Cairo International Airport with the tape and catch the first available flight to any West European city, which they did. In this manner, CBS scooped the other networks. After carefully reviewing the tape, Romano and his colleagues believe that when Abu Ghazala tried to cover Sadat, al-Islambouli yelled, "I don't want you, I want that traitor, that dog." I failed to obtain verification from Abu Ghazala.
335. Interview with 'Abd al-Razzaq 'Abd al-Magid.
336. Interview with Hamdi Fuad.
337. Discussion with Robert LaTowsky.
338. Interview with Ibrahim Shukri.
339. Sa'd al-Din Ibrahim, *I'adat al-I'tibar li-l-Ra'is al-Sadat* (Cairo: Dar al-Shuruq, 1992).

Appendix A

Interviewees: name-date, position/title. (All interviews conducted in Cairo unless otherwise indicated.)

Wagih Abaza—6/15/91; Free Officer (FO), governor.
Berlinti 'Abd al-Hamid—12/14/90, 5/27/91; actress, 'Amer's wife.
Farid 'Abd al-Karim—3/31/83, 7/7/86; lawyer, Cairo ASU leader.
Muhsin 'Abd al-Khaliq—7/14/90, 7/16/90, 9/3/90, 9/5/90, 6/12/90, 6/17/90; FO, ambassador to Japan.
'Abd al-Razzaq 'Abd al-Magid—6/27/90; Sadat's economy czar.
Hoda 'Abd al-Nasser—12/4/90; Nasser's daughter; professor of political science at Cairo University.
Hussein 'Abd al-Razzeq—1/10/83; Marxist journalist, editor.
Tewfiq 'Abdu Isma'il—10/6/90; FO, minister under Sadat.
'Abd al-'Aziz 'Abdullah—2/5/83; Journalists' Syndicate elite.
Hassan Abu Basha—6/9/91; minister of interior under Mubarak.
Kemal Abu al-Magd—5/29/94; lawyer, minister under Sadat.
'Abd al-Muhsin Abu al-Nur—11/14/90; FO, general secretary ASU.
Sufi Abu Talib—6/28/94, 7/2/94; university president, speaker of People's Assembly under Sadat.
Kemal Hassan 'Ali—12/14/90; general, Sadat's director of GIA and minister of foreign affairs.
Mustafa Amin—3/14/83; journalist, editor of *al-Akhbar*.
Muhammad Fahim Amin—4/10/83, and other occasions; lawyer, Wafd Vanguard.
Gehad 'Auda—summer 1986; political scientist.
Galal Bashandi—numerous occasions in 1980-1982, 1985, 1987, 1990, 1994; businessman.
Ahmed Beha al-Din—1/24/82, 8/4/86; journalist, Sadat's speech-writer.
Hussein Kamel Beha al-Din—4/9/83; YO director.
Tahsin Beshir—6/14/93; minister under Sadat, ambassador to Canada.
'Abd al-Latif al-Boghdadi—11/5/90, 12/20,92, 5/8/93; FO, vice president.
Ahmed al-Bulkani—numerous occasions, 1990; Wafdist elite.
Ahmed Sayyid al-Darwish—6/19/86; minister under Sadat.
Dia al-Din Dawud—3/28/83; lawyer, ASU SEC member.

'Ali al-Din Hilal Dessouki—numerous occasions in 1980s, 1990s; political scientists, minister under Mubarak.

Salah Dessouki, numerous occasions in 1981-1983, 1990, 1992-1993, 5/30/94; police officer, governor of Cairo, ambassador to Finland.

Hermann Eilts—1985, 1991, 2000 in Boston; U.S. ambassador to Egypt.

Muhammad Fa'iq—3/19/83; minister of information under Nasser and Sadat.

Mahmud Fawzi—numerous occasions in 1990; journalist, autor.

Muhammad Fawzi—11/12/91; FO, general, minister of war under Nasser, Sadat.

Hamdi Fuad—5/31/86 and numerous occasions 1980-1982; journalist.

Yehiya al-Gamal—4/4/86, 5/23/94; lawyer, Arab nationalist leader.

'Adel Gazarin—5/26/94; president of Nasr automotive.

'Abd al-Ghani al-Gamassi—12/2/90; general, minister of war under Sadat.

Murad Ghalib—5/18/93; ambassador to Soviet Union.

Ashraf Ghorbal—summer 1994; foreign affairs ministry.

Nu'man Gum'a—6/22/86; lawyer, New Wafdist leader.

Salwa Gum'a—numerous occasions in 1990; political scientist at American University in Cairo, daughter of Sha'rawi Gum'a.

Sha'rawi Gum'a—4/10/83; minister of interior under Nasser, Sadat.

Naldo Haddad—numerous occasions in 1980-1982, 1985, 1987, 1990, 1994; businessman.

Galal al-Din al-Hamamsi—8/4/86; journalist.

Gamal Hammad—12/5/90; FO, author.

Ahmed Hamrush—7/17/86; officer, author, journalist.

Hassan Hanafi—1983; political philosopher and activist.

Milad Hanna—1982, 1990, 6/4/94; architect, political scientist.

Mansur Hassan—12/6/90; minister of information under Sadat.

Barbara Hatour—1981-1983, 1990, 1992, 1993; GTZ, German aid program.

Magdi Hatour—numerous occasions 1981-1983, 1990, 1992-1993; businessman.

'Abd al-'Aziz Higazi—7/8/86; prime minister under Sadat.

Samir Hilmi—7/12/86, 11/22/90; military general.

Kemal al-Din Hussein—4/5/83, 2/4/84; FO, minister of education, member of People's Assembly.

Amin Huweidi—11/10/90, 5/25/91; minister of war, intelligence.

Kemal Ibrashi—11/17/82; dentist, political cognoscente.

'Abdullah Imam—3/30/83; journalist, author.

Muhammad Mahmud al-Imam—5/28/93; minister of planning under Sadat.

Hafez Isma'il—5/11/93, 5/18/93; Sadat's foreign policy adviser.

Al-Nabawi Isma'il—6/8/94; minister of interior under Sadat.

'Aouni 'Izz al-Din—12/2/90, 6/9/94; journalist.

Erik Jensen—numerous occasions, 1999-2000; assistant secretary general of the United Nations.

Yehiya Kabil—6/94; dean of Cairo University Faculty of Engineering.

Mustafa Khalil—7/13/86, 6/15/93; prime minister under Sadat.

Ahmed al-Khawaga—3/12/83; lawyer, Bar Syndicate *naqib.*

Lutfi al-Kholi—3/26/83, 4/2,9/83; journalist, editor, Press Syndicate *naqib.*

Gamil Khouzzam—6/10/94; businessman.

Nadia al-Kilani—numerous occasions in 1992-1993; U.S. embassy.

Ahmed Lamlum—11/15,90, and other occasions; businessman.

Robert LaTowsky—numerous occasions; information guru.

Anis Mansur—6/94; journalist, Sadat speechwriter and confidant.

Yusuf Mansur—6/14/94; businessman.

Hassan Mar'ei—6/94; son of Sayyid Mar'ei, husband of Noha Sadat.

Sayyid Mar'ei—4/11/83; speaker of assembly under Sadat.

Samir Mas'ud—12/2/90; journalist.

John McDougal—1/18,19/77; witnessed the rioting.

Muhammad al-Mismari—3/17/83, 3/21/83; lawyer, MB elite.

Ahmed al-Misri—6/24/90, 6/11/91; FO, businessman.

Muhsin Muhammad—1982; editor.

Ibrahim Muhi al-Din—6/8/93; ministry of foreign affairs, son of Fuad Muhi al-Din.

Khalid Muhi al-Din—7/3/86, 1990; FO, editor, president of NPUG.

Zakariyya Muhi al-Din—4/7/93, 5/20/93; FO, vice president.

Muhammad Hilmi Murad—11/27/90; minister of education.

Mustafa Kamel Muard—6/30/86, 6/16/87, 1/30/90; FO, president of Liberal Party.

Ahmed Nasir—1990; New Wafd elite.

'Abd al-Hadi Nassef—2/25/83; journalist, SEC elite.

Richard Parker—telephone conversation, spring 2000.

Daniel Petit—numerous occasions; weapons salesman.

Henry Precht—conversations in Boston; U.S. State Department.

Leila Qassem—1983, 1985, 1991; psychologist.

'Abbas Radwan—6/4/91; FO, minister of interior under Nasser.

Wahid Ra'fat—6/28/86; lawyer, Wafdist leader.

'Umar Ragheb—1981-1983; businessman.

'Aisha Ratib—5/94; lawyer, cabinet minister under Sadat.

'Abd al-'Azim Ramadan—12/4/90; historian, author.

'Abd al-Ra'uf al-Reidi—5/31/94; Egyptian ambassador to the U.S. under Sadat.

Fa'iqa al-Rifa'i-5/24/93; economist, vice governor of Central Bank of Egypt.

Nadia Rizq—1981-1983; U.S. embassy, librarian.

Ricardo Romano—numerous occasions 1980-1983, 1990, 1999-2000; CBS News, Cairo.

Sa'id Roston—7/12/86; SLP elite.

'Ali Sabri—8/2/86; prime minister, ASU general secretary, vice president under Sadat.

Isma'il Sabri 'Abdullah—5/23/93 and 1983; author, minister of planning under Sadat.

Ibrahim Sa'd al-Din—1/31/83; economist.

Camelia Sadat—9/9/2000; Sadat's daughter by first wife Eqbal 'Afifi.

Jehan Sadat—phone interview March 3, 1999, July 1999; wife of Sadat.

Noha Sadat—6/94; Sadat's daughter.

Rif'at al-Sa'id—1983, 1985, 1987, 1990, 1992-1993, 6/16/94; author, secretary general of NPUG.

Jeswald Salacuse—spring 2000 phone conversation in Boston; former staff member at Ford Foundation in Cairo.

'Ali Ibrahim Salama—6/3/91; journalist.

Ibrahim Salih—12/2/90, 6/13/94; journalist.

Hussein al-Shaf'ei—4/13/83, 6/16/91; FO, vice president under Sadat.

Ahmed Sharaf—10/ 15,29/90; YO student leader.

Sami Sharaf—6/19/94, summer 1994; FO, director of Nasser and Sadat's Office of the President for Information.

'Abd al-Magid Shater—10/19/82; Liberal Party elite.

Pope Shenouda III—6/6/94; Pope of the Coptic Church.

'Adil Shuhdi—6/10k/93; officer in the Rangers.

'Abd al-Ghaffar Shukr—11/11/90; Higher Institute for Socialist Studies instructor.

Ibrahim Shukri—7/12/86 and 1982; president of SLP.

Mahmud al-Shurbagi—1983, 1992-1993; lawyer, son of Ahmed al-Shurbagi.

Mamduh al-Shurbagi—1983, 1992-1993; lawyer, son of Ahmed al-Shurbagi.

Muhammad Sid Ahmed—3/17/82, 6/13/91; journalist.

'Aziz Sidqi—9/12,26/1990; prime minister under Sadat.

Fuad Sirag al-Din—5/26/91, 6/3/91; prime minister, president of New Wafd.

Yassin Sirag al-Din—5/23/91, 5/18/94; businessman, New Wafd elite.

Bernd Siegfried—numerous occasions in 1990; economist.

Michael Sterner—telephone interview, spring 2000.

Ahmed al-Subtacy—6/16/87; secretary general of Liberal Party.

Fuad Sultan—6/6/94; minister under Sadat.

'Abbas al-Tunisi—numerous occasions in 1980-1982, erstwhile student activist.

Isma'il 'Uthman—5/28/91; businessman, Arab Contractors.

Yusuf Wali—8/5/84; minister of agriculture under Mubarak.

Al-Sayyid Yassin—numerous occasions in 1980-1982; director of al-Ahram's Center for Strategic Studies.

Hassan 'Abbas Zaki—5/29/93, 6/8/93; minister of finance under Nasser.

Muhammad 'Abd al-Salam al-Zayyat—7/15/86; minister of stte for National Assembly Affairs under Sadat.

Appendix B

Year	Popul.	GNP/cap	LE Gross Dom.I	$FDI	$Remitts	LE For. Debt
1973	37.4	280	2,381	—	116	2,563
1974	38.1	290	3,506	87	189	2,815
1975	38.8	320	5,484	225	366	5,477
1976	39.8	350	5,468	444	755	7,094
1977	40.7	380	6,166	477	897	12,760
1978	41.7	390	6,864	387	1,761	14,155
1979	42.7	420	7,671	1,375	2,445	16,637
1980	43.7	500	7,562	541	2,696	20,915
1981	44.6	530	8,181	747	2,180	23,947

N.B. Year, Population, per capita GNP, Gross Domestic Investment in L.E. 1987; Foreign Direct Investment; Workers' Remittances; Total Foreign Debt. All in millions except GNP/cap. Miscellaneous sources: CAPMAS Statistical Yearbooks, World Bank Reports.

Bibliography

'Abd al-Fattah, Fathi. *Shuyu'iyyun wa-l-Nasiriyyun.* Cairo: Rose al-Yusuf, 1975.

Abdalla, Ahmed. *The Student Movement and National Politics in Egypt.* London: Al Saqi Books, 1985.

'Abdel-Malek, Anouar. *Egypt: Military Society.* New York: Random House, 1968.

'Abd al-Razzaq, Hussein. *Misr fi 18 wa 19 Yanayir.* Cairo: Matba'at Ikhwan Muraftili, 1985.

'Abduh, Ibrahim. *Tatawwur al-Sahafa al-Misriyya, 1798-1981.* Cairo: Matabi'a Sagl al-'Arab, 1982.

Abu Basha, Hassan. *Muthakkirat Hassan Abu Basha.* Cairo: Dar al-Hilal, 1990.

Abu Fadl, 'Abd al-Fattah. *Kuntu Na'iban li-Ra'is al-Mukhabarat.* Cairo: Dar al-Hurriyya, 1979.

Abu-Settit, Muhammed Fouad. "Foreign Capital and Economic Performance: The Case of Egypt." Ph.D. thesis, University of Texas, Dallas, 1986.

Abu Taleb, Sufi Hassan. *Our Democratic Socialism: The Ideology of May Revolution 1971.* Cairo: Government Printing Offices, 1978.

Adams, Richard H., Jr. *Development and Social Change in Rural Egypt.* Syracuse, NY: Syracuse University Press, 1986.

Adamson, Walter L. *Hegemony and Revolution.* Berkeley: University of California Press, 1980.

Akhavi, Shahrough. "Egypt: Neo-Patrimonial Elite," in Frank Tachau, ed. *Political Elites and Political Development in the Middle East.* New York: John Wiley, 1975, pp. 69-113.

———. "Egypt: Diffused Elite in a Bureaucratic Society," in I. William Zartman, ed. *Political Elites in Arab North Africa.* New York: Longman, 1982, pp. 223-265.

'Ali, Kemal Hassan. *Mishawir al-'Umr.* Cairo: Dar al-Shuruq, 1994.

Alterman, Jon B., ed. *Sadat and His Legacy.* Washington, D.C.: Washington Institute for Near East Policy, 1998.

Althusser, Louis. *Positions.* Paris: Editions Sociales, 1976.

Amin, Mustafa. *Sanna Ula al-Sign.* Cairo: al-Maktab al-Misri al-Hadith, 1974.

———. *Sanna Thania al-Sign.* Cairo: al-Maktab al-Misri al-Hadith, 1975.

Amin, Samir. *Accumulation on a World Scale.* New York: Monthly Review Press, 1974.

———. *Unequal Development.* New York: Monthly Review Press, 1976.

Ansari, Hamied. "Sectarian Conflict in Egypt and the Political Expediency of Religion." *The Middle East Journal,* vol. 38, no. 3:397-418, 1984.

———. *Egypt: The Stalled Society.* Albany, NY: State University of New York Press, 1986.

Ayubi, Nazih N. M. *Bureaucracy and Politics in Contemporary Egypt.* London: Ithaca Press, 1980.

Ayubi, Shaheen. *Nasser and Sadat.* New York: University Press of America, 1994.

————. *Hawamish 'ala Qissat Muhammed Hassanein Heikal.* Beirut: Manshurat al-Maktaba al-'Asriyya, n.d.

Baker, Raymond. *Egypt's Uncertain Revolution Under Nasser and Sadat.* Cambridge, MA: Harvard University Press, 1978.

————. *Sadat And After.* Cambridge, MA: Harvard University Press, 1990.

Baran, Paul. *The Political Economy of Growth.* New York: Monthly Review Press, 1957.

Barron, John. *KGB.* New York: Reader's Digest Press, 1974.

Bayan 30 Maris, al-Lathi Ilqahu al-Ra'is Gamal 'Abd al-Nasser fi 30 Maris. Cairo: al-Hai'a al-'Amma li'l-Ist'alamat, n.d.

Beattie, Kirk J. *Egypt During the Nasser Years.* Boulder, CO.: Westview Press, 1994.

Beinin, Joel and Lockman, *Workers on the Nile.* Princeton: Princeton University Press, 1987.

Berger, Suzanne. "Problems and Prospects of Egyptian Small-Scale Industry." Unpublished paper. Massachusetts Institute of Technology, August 1978.

Berque, Jacques. *Egypt: Imperialism and Revolution.* London: Faber & Faber, 1972.

Betz, Hans-Georg. *Radical Right-Wing Populism in Western Europe.* New York: St. Martin Press, 1994.

Bianchi, Robert. *Unruly Corporatism.* New York: Oxford University Press, 1989.

Bill, James A. "Class Analysis and the Dialectics of Modernization in the Middle East." *International Journal of Middle East Studies,* 3:417-34, 1972.

Binder, Leonard. *In a Moment of Enthusiasm: Political Power and the Second Stratum in Egypt.* Chicago: University of Chicago Press, 1978.

————. *Islamic Liberalism.* Chicago: The University of Chicago Press, 1988.

Bishri, Tariq al-. *al-Dimuqratiyya wa-l-Nasiriyya.* Cairo: Dar al-Thaqafa al-Jadida, 1975.

Boghdadi, 'Abd al-Latif al-. *Muthakkirat, Volumes I and II.* Cairo: al-Maktab al-Misri al-Hadith, 1977.

Botman, Selma. *The Rise of Egyptian Communism, 1939-1970.* Syracuse: Syracuse University Press, 1988.

Boutros-Ghali, Boutros. *Egypt's Road to Jerusalem.* New York: Random House, 1997.

Brown, Donald S. "Egypt and the United States: Collaborators in Economic Development." *The Middle East Journal,* vol. 35, no. 1, pp. 3-14.

Bruton, Henry J. "Egypt's Development in the Seventies." *Economic Development and Cultural Change,* vol. 31, no. 4, pp. 679-7O4, July, 1983.

Buci-Glucksmann, Christine. *Gramsci and the State.* London: Lawrence and Wishart, 198O.

Burns, William J. *Economic Aid and American Policy Toward Egypt, 1955-1981.* Albany: State University of New York Press, 1985.

Cardoso, F.H. "On the Characterization of Authoritarian Regimes in Latin America," in David Collier, ed. *The New Authoritarianism in Latin America.* Princeton: Princeton University Press, 1979, pp. 33-60.

Carr, David William. *Foreign Investment and Development in Egypt.* New York: Praeger Publishers, 1979.

Carter, Jimmy. *Keeping Faith.* New York: Bantam Books, 1982.

Cohen, Youssef. *The Manipulation of Consent.* Pittsburgh, PA: University of Pittsburgh Press, 1989.

Cooper, Mark. *The Transformation of Egypt.* Baltimore, MD: Johns Hopkins University Press, 1982.

Cooper, Robert K., and Sawaf, Ayman. *Executive EQ: Emotional Intelligence in Leadership and Organizations.* New York: The Berkley Publishing Group, 1996.

Copeland, Miles. *The Game of Nations: The Amorality of Power Politics.* New York: Simon and Schuster, 1969.

Davis, Eric. "Islam and Politics in Modern Egypt," in S. Arjomand, ed. *Contemporary Social Movements in the Near and Middle East*. Albany: SUNY Press, 1982.

Dawud, Dia al-Din. *Sanawat 'Abd al-Nasser, Ayyam al-Sadat*. Cairo: Dar al-Khiyyal, 1998.

Dekmejian, Hrair. *Egypt under Nasir: A Study in Political Dynamics*. Albany, NY: SUNY Press, 1971.

———. *Islam in Revolution*. Syracuse, NY: Syracuse University Press, 1985.

Derrick, Michael. *The Portugal of Salazar*. New York: Campion Books, Ltd., 1939.

Dessouki, Ali E. Hillal, ed. *Democracy in Egypt: Problems and Prospects*. Cairo Papers in Social Science, vol. 1, Monograph 2. Cairo: American University in Cairo Press, January 1978.

Dessouki, Assem. "Land Tenure Policy in Egypt, 1952—1969, and its Effects on the Re-formation of the Peasantry," in Tarif Khalidi, ed. *Land Tenure and Social Transformation in the Middle East*. Beirut: American University in Beirut Press, 1984.

Domes, Jurgen. *The Government and Politics of the PRC: A Time of Transition*. Boulder: Westview Press, 1985.

Draz, 'Essam. *Dhubat Yuliu Yatakallimun*. Cairo: al-Minar al-Gadid li-l-Sahafa wa-l-Nashr, 1989.

Dunn, Michael Collins. "Fundamentalism in Egypt," *Middle East Policy*, vol. II, no. 3, 1993,

Dupuy, T.N. *The Almanac of World Military Power*. Harrisburg, PA: T.N. Dupuy Associates with Stockpile Books, 1970.

'Emari, 'Abd al-Galil al-. *Thikriyyat Iqtisadiyya...wa Islah al-Masar al-Iqtisadi*. Cairo: Dar al-Shuruq, 1986.

Enayat, Hamid. *Modern Islamic Political Thought*. Austin, TX: University of Texas Press, 1982.

Evans, Peter. *Dependent Development: The Alliance of Multinational State and Local Capital in Brazil*. Princeton, NJ: Princeton University Press, 1979.

Fahmi, Faruq. *Ightiyal 'Abd al-Hakim 'Amer*. Cairo: Dar Gharib li-l-Taba'a, 1988.

———. *I'tirafat Shams Badran wa Mu'amarat '67*. Cairo: Mu'ass'assit Amun al-Haditha, 1989.

Fahmy, Ismail. *Negotiating for Peace in the Middle East*. London: Croom Helm, 1983.

Faksh, Mahmud A. *The Future of Islam in the Middle East*. Westport, CT: Praeger, 1997.

Farah, Nadia Ramsis. *Religious Strife in Egypt*. New York: Gordon and Breach Science Publishers, 1986.

Farid, Abdel Magid. *Nasser: The Final Years*. Reading, MA: Ithaca Press, 1994.

Fawzi, Mahmud. *Al-Baba Shenouda wa-l-Mu'arida fi-l-Kanisa*. Cairo: Dar al-Nashr Hattiyyat, 1992.

———. *Hukkam Misr: al-Sadat*. Cairo: Markiz al-Raya li-l-Nashr wa-l-I'lam Ahmad Fawzi, 1997.

Fawzi, Muhammad. *Harb al-Thalath Sannawat, 1967-1970*. Cairo: Dar al-Mustaqbil al-'Arabi, 1984.

———. *Istratijiyyat al-Musaliha*. Cairo: Dar al-Mustaqbil al-'Arabi, 1986.

Fawzi, Su'ad, ed. *Dr. Mahmud al-Qadi: Rihlat al-Kifah*. Cairo: Dar al-Mawqif al-'Arabi, 1983.

Finklestone, Joseph. *Anwar Sadat: Visionary Who Dared*. London: Frank Cass, 1996.

Gaffney, Patrick Daniel. *Shaykh, Khutba and Masjid: The Role of the Local Islamic Preacher in Upper Egypt*. Ph.D. thesis, University of Chicago, 1982.

Gamassi, Muhammad 'Abd al-Ghani al-. *Muthakkirat al-Gamassi: Harb Uktubur 1973*. Cairo: al-Hai'at al-'Ammat l-il-Kuttab, 1998.

Gami'a, Mahmud. *'Araftu al-Sadat*. Cairo: al-Maktab al-Misri al-Hadith, 1998.

Gerschenkron, Alexander. *Economic Backwardness in Historical Perspective*. Cambridge, MA: Harvard University Press, 1962. Ghitani, Gamal al-, ed. *Mustapha Amin Yatathakkur*. Cairo: Maktabat Madbouli, 1983.

Goldschmidt, Jr., Arthur. *Modern Egypt*. Boulder, CO: Westview Press, 1988.

Gordon, Joel. *Nasser's Blessed Movement: Egypt's Free Officers and the July Revolution*. New York: Oxford University Press, 1992.

Hakim, Tewfiq al-. *'Awdat al-Wa'i.* second ed. Beirut: Dar al-Shuruq, 1975.

Hamamsi, Galal al-Din al-. *Hiwar Wara al-Aswar.* Cairo: al-Maktab al-Misri al-Hadith, 1975.

Hamrush, Ahmed. *Qissat Thawrat 23 Yuliu.* vol. 1: *Misr wa-l-Gaish* (1975); vol. 2: *Mugtam'a 'Abd al-Nasir* (1976); vol. 3: *'Abd al-Nasser wa-l-'Arab* (1977); vol. 4: *Shuhud Thawrat Yuliu* (1978); vol. 5: *Kharif 'Abd al-Nasser* (1979). Beirut: Arab Organization for Studies and Publishing.

———. *Qissat Thawrat 23 Yuliu.* Vol. 1: *Misr wa-l-'Askariyyun;* Vol.2: *Al-Gaish fi-l-Sulta.* Cairo: Dar al-Mawqif al-'Arabi, n.d.

Hamuda, 'Adil. *Nihayit Thawrat Yuliu.* Cairo: Maktabat Madbuli, 1983.

Hamuda, Hussein Muhammad Ahmed. *Asrar Harakat al-Dhubat al-Ahrar wa-l-Ikhwan al-Muslimin.* Cairo: al-Zahra li-l-'Ilam al-'Arabi, 1985.

Heba Handoussa, "The Impact of Foreign Aid on Economic Development: 1952-1986," Conference on AID Capital Flows and Dev't, Talloires, France, September 13-17, 1987: 10-14, unpublished.

Harik, Ilya, and Sullivan, Denis. *Privatization and Liberalization in the Middle East.* Bloomington: Indiana University Press, 1992.

Hassan, 'Abd al-Fattah. *Thikriyyat Siyasiyya.* Cairo: Dar al-Sha'b, 1974.

Heikal, Muhammed Hassanein. *Autumn of Fury.* New York: Random House, 1983.

———. *Li Misr....la li 'Abd al-Nasser.* second ed. Beirut: Skirikat al-Matbu'at li-l-Tawzi'a wa-l-Nashr, 1982.

———. *The Road to Ramadan.* New York: Ballantine Books, 1975.

———. *The Sphinx and the Commisar.* London: Collins, 1978.

———. *1967: al-Infigar.* Cairo: Markiz al-Ahram li-l-Targama wa-l-Nashr, 1990.

Hilal, 'Ali al-Din, al-Sayyid, Mustafa Kamel, and Badr al-Din, Ikram. *Tagrubat al-Dimuqratiyya fi Misr, 1970-1981.* Cairo: al-Markiz al-'Arabi li-l-Ba'th wa-l-Nashr, 1982.

Hinnebusch, Raymond A. "From Nasir to Sadat: Elite Transformation in Egypt," *Journal of South Asian and Middle Eastern Studies,* vol. VIII, no. 1, pp. 24-49, Fall, 1983.

Hirst, David and Beeson, Irene. *Sadat.* London: Faber and Faber, 1981.

Hopwood, Derek. *Egypt: Politics and Society, 1945-1981.* London: George Allen & Unwin, 1982.

Hudson, Michael. *Arab Politics: The Search for Legitimacy.* New Haven: Yale University Press, 1977.

Ibrahim, Saad Eddin. "Anatomy of Egypt's Militant Islamic Groups: Methodological Note and Preliminary Findings," *International Journal of Middle East Studies,* 12:423-453, 1980.

———. *Egypt, Islam, and Democracy.* Cairo: The American University in Cairo Press, 1996.

———. *I'adat al-I'tibar li-l-Ra'is Sadat.* Cairo: Dar al-Shuruq, 1992.

Imam, 'Abdullah. *'Abd al-Nasser wa-l-Ikhwan al-Muslimin.* Cairo: Dar al-Mawqif al-'Arabi, 1981.

———. *'Ali Sabri Yatathakkir.* Cairo: Dar al-Wihda, 1988.

———. *Inqilab 15 Mayo.* Cairo: Dar al-Mawqif al-'Arabi, 1983.

———. *Jehan, Sayyiddat Misr al-Ula wa-l-Akhira.* Cairo: Mu'ass'assat Rose al-Yusuf, 1985.

———. *Madhbahat al-Quda.* Cairo: Makatabat Madbuli, 1976.

———. *Salah Nasr Yatathakkur: al-Mukhabarat wa-l-Thawra.* Cairo: Mu'assassat Rose al-Yusuf, 1984.

———. *'Amer wa Berlinti.* Cairo: Sina li-l-Nashr, 1988.

'Ishmawi, Hassan al-. *al-Ikhwan wa-l-Thawra.* Vol. 1. Cairo: al-Maktab al-Hadith li-l-Taba'a wa-l-Nashr, 1977.

Ismael, Tareq Y. and El-Sa'id, Rifa'at. *The Communist Movement in Egypt, 1920-1988.* Syracuse, NY: Syracuse University Press, 1988.

Israeli, Raphael. *Man of Defiance: A Personal Biography of Anwar Sadat.* Totowa, NJ: Barnes & Noble Books, 1985.

Issawi, Charles. *Egypt in Revolution: An Economic Analysis.* London: Oxford University Press, 1963.

Ittihad al-Ishtiraki al-'Arabi al-. *al-Kitab al-Sannawi.* Dar wa-l-Matabi'a al-Sha'b, 1964.

'Izz al-Din, Ahmed. *Ahmed Kamel Yatathakkur.* Cairo: Dar al-Hilal, 1990.

Joll, James. *Antonio Gramsci.* New York: Penguin Books, 1977.

Kamel, Mohamed Ibrahim. *The Camp David Accords.* London: Routledge & Kegan Paul, 1986.

Kamel, Rashad. *Al-Mar'at al-Latti Hazzat 'Arsh Misr!* Cairo: Markiz al-Raya l-il-Nashr wa-l-I'lam, 1994.

———. *Thawrat Yuliu wa-l-Sahafa.* Cairo: Mu'assassat Rose al-Yusuf, 1989.

Kaplan, Robert D. *The Arabists.* New York: The Free Press, 1995.

Kassem, Laila Ahmed. "The Opposition in Egypt: A Case Study of the Socialist Labor Party." M.A. thesis, American University in Cairo, 1983.

Kepel, Gilles. *Muslim Extremism in Egypt: The Prophet and the Pharaoh,* translated by Jon Rothschild. Berkeley, CA: University of California Press, 1985.

Khurshid, I'timad. *Inhirafat Salah Nasr.* Cairo: Dar Gharif li-l-Taba'a, 1988.

———. *Hakayati ma'a 'Abd al-Nasser.* Cairo: Dar Gharib li-l-Taba'a, 1990.

Kissinger, Henry. *White House Years.* Boston, MA: Little, Brown and Co., 1979.

———. *Years of Upheaval.* Boston, MA: Little, Brown and Co., 1982.

Klaibur, S.J., Jeffrey, *The Church, Dictatorships, and Democracy in Latin America.* Maryknoll, NY: Orbis Books, 1998.

Korany, Bahgat, Brynen, Rex and Noble, Paul, eds. *Political Liberalization & Democratization in the Arab World,* vol. 2. Boulder, CO: Lynne Rienner, 1998.

———, and Dessouki, Ali E. Hillal. *The Foreign Policies of Arab States.* Boulder, CO: Westview Press, 1984.

Laclau, Ernesto. *Politics and Ideology in Marxist Theory.* London: NLB, 1977.

Lacouture, Jean. *Nasser.* Paris: Le Seuil, 1971.

———, Jean and Simonne. *Egypt in Transition.* New York: Criterion Books, 1958.

Lesch, Ann M. "The Muslim Brotherhood in Egypt: Reform or Revolution?" in Matthew C. Moen and Lowell S. Gustafson, eds. *The Religious Challenge to the State.* Philadelphia, PA: Temple University Press, 1992.

Levine, Daniel H. *Religion and Political Conflict in Latin America.* Chapel Hill, NC: University of North Carolina Press, 1986.

Linz, Juan J. "Totalitarianism and Authoritarian Regimes," in Fred I. Greenstein and Nelson W. Polsby, eds. *Macropolitical Theory.* Reading, MA: Addison-Wesley Publishing Co., 1975, 174-411.

Lipset, Seymour Martin and Rokkan, Stein. "Cleavage Structures, Party Systems, and Voter Alignments: An Introduction," in Lipset and Rokkan, eds. *Party Systems and Voter Alignments: Cross-National Perspectives.* New York: The Free Press, 1967, 1-64.

Mabro, Robert. *The Egyptian Economy: 1952-1972.* Oxford: Clarendon Press, 1974.

———, and Radwan, Samir. *The Industrialization of Egypt, 1939-1973: Policy and Performance.* Oxford: Clarendon Press, 1976.

Mahfouz, Afaf al-Kosheri. *Socialisme et Pouvoir en Egypte.* Paris: Librairie Generale de Droit et de Jurisprudence, 1972.

Malaff 'Abd al-Nasser. Cairo: Matabi'a al-Ahram al-Tugariyya, 1975.

Mar'ei, Sayyid. *Awraq Siyasiyya,* vol's. 1-3. Cairo: Matabi'a al-Ahram al-Tugariyya, 1978.

Mathhar, Sul'iman. *I'tirafat Qadat Harb Yuniu.* Cairo: Dar al-Hurriyya, 1990.

Mattar, Fuad. *Aina Asbaha 'Abd al-Nasser fi Gumhurriyyat al-Sadat?* Beirut: Dar al-Nahar li-l-Nashr, 1972.

Meyer, Gail E. *Egypt and the United States: The Formative Years.* Rutherford, NJ: Fairleigh Dickinson University Press, 1980.

Migdal, Joel S. *Strong Societies and Weak States.* Princeton, NJ: Princeton University Press, 1988.

Mitchell, Richard P. *The Society of Muslim Brothers.* London: Oxford University Press, 1969.

Mirel, Pierre. *L'Egypte des ruptures.* Paris: Editions Sindbad, 1982.

Moore, Clement H. "Authoritarian Politics in Unincorporated Society: The Case of Nasser's Egypt," *Comparative Politics,* 6:193-218, 1974.

————. *Images of Development: Egyptian Engineers in Search of Industry.* Cambridge, MA: MIT Press, 1980.

Mouffe, Chantal. "Hegemony and Ideology in Gramsci," in Chantal Mouffe, ed. *Gramsci and Marxist Theory.* Boston: Routledge & Kegan Paul, 1979, pp. 168-204.

Mullaney, Francis Cabrini. "The Role of Islam in the Hegemonic Strategy of Egypt's Military Rulers (1952-1990)." Ph.D. thesis, Harvard University, 1992.

Mursi, Fuad. *Hatha al-Infitah al-Iqtisadi.* Second Printing. Beirut: Dar al-Wahda li-l-Taba'a wa-l-Nashr, 1980.

Murad, Mahmoud. *Man al-Lathina Kanu Yahkimuna Misr?* Cairo: al-Ahram Press, 1975.

Mustafa, Hala. *Al-Islam al-Siyasi fi Misr: Min Harakat al-Islah illa Gama'at al-'Unf.* Cairo: Center for Political and Strategic Studies, 1992.

Nagib, Muhammad. *Kilmati li-l-Tarikh.* Cairo: Dar al-Kitab al-Gam'i, 1981.

Nasser, Gamal Abdel. *The Philosophy of the Revolution.* Buffalo, NY: Smith, Keynes & Marshall, 1959.

Nasser, Munir K. *Press, Politics, and Power: Egypt's Heikal and Al-Ahram.* Ames: Iowa State University Press, 1979.

Nathan, Andrew J. "A Factionalism Model for CCP Politics." *The China Quarterly,* no. 53. January/March 1973.

Nathan Associates, Robert R. "A Study of the Feasibility of a Private Investment Encouragement Fund for the Egyptian Private Sector." Submitted to U.S. Agency for International Development. September 1979.

Nixon, Richard M. *RN: The Memoirs of Richard Nixon.* New York: Grosset and Dunlap, 1978.

Nutting, Anthony. *No End of a Lesson: The Story of Suez.* London: Constable, 1967.

————. *Nasser.* London: Constable, 1972.

O'Brien, Patrick. *The Revolution in Egypt's Economic System: From Private Enterprise to Socialism, 1952-1966.* London: Oxford University Press, 1966.

O'Donnell, Guillermo A. *Modernization and Bureaucratic Authoritarianism.* Berkeley: Institute of International Studies, 1973.

————. "Tensions in the Bureaucratic-Authoritarian State and the Question of Democracy," in David Collier, ed. *The New Authoritarianism in Latin America.* Princeton: Princeton University Press, 1979, pp. 285-318.

Oweiss, Ibrahim M. *The Political Economy of Contemporary Egypt.* Washington, D.C.: Center for Contemporary Arab Studies, Georgetown University, 1990.

Palmer, Monte; Ali, Leila; and Yassin, El Sayyid. *The Egyptian Bureaucracy.* Syracuse, NY: Syracuse University Press, 1988.

Parkin, Frank. *Marxism and Class Theory: A Bourgeois Critique.* New York: Columbia University Press, 1979.

Perlmutter, Amos. *Egypt: The Praetorian State.* New Brunswick, NJ: Transaction Books, 1974.

Peters, Rudolph. *Jihad in Classical and Modern Islam.* Princeton, NJ: Markus Wiener Publishers, 1996.

Portelli, Hugues. *Gramsci et le bloc historique.* Paris: Presses Universitaires de France, 1972.

Posusney, Marsha Pripstein. *Labor and the State in Egypt.* New York: Columbia University Press, 1997.

Poulantzas, Nicos. *Political Power and Social Class.* London: NLB and Sheel & Ward, 1975.

Przeworski, Adam. "Material Bases of Consent: Economics and Politics in a Hegemonic System," in M. Zeitlin, ed. *Political Power and Social Theory*, vol. 1. Stamford, CT: JAI Press, 1980, 21-66.

Putnam, Robert D. *The Comparative Study of Political Elites*. Englewood Cliffs, NJ: Prentice-Hall, 1976.

Pye, Lucian W. "Identity and the Political Culture," in Lucien Pye and Sidney Verba, eds. *Political Culture and Political Development*. Princeton, NJ: Princeton University Press, 1965, 101-134.

———. "The Legitimacy Crisis," in Leonard Binder et al. *Crises and Sequences in Political Development*. Princeton, NJ: Princeton University Press, 1971, 135—158.

Quandt, William B. *Peace Process*. Washington, D.C.: The Brookings Institution, 1993.

Qutb, Sayyid. *Milestones*. Salimiah, Kuwait: International Islamic Federation of Student Organizations, 1978.

Rabin, Yitzhak. *The Rabin Memoirs*. Berkeley, CA: University of California Press, 1979.

Ramadan, 'Abd al-'Azim. *al-Fikr al-Thawri fi Misr Qabla Thawrat 23 Yuliu*. Cairo: Maktabat Madbuli, 1981.

———. *al-Ikhwan al-Muslimun wa-l-Tanthim al-Sirri*. Cairo: Matabi'a Rose al-Yusuf, 1982.

Ramazani, R.K. *Revolutionary Iran: Challenge and Response in the Middle East*. Baltimore, MD: Johns Hopkins University Press, 1988.

Reynolds, Nancy J. "Discourses of Social Change: An Analysis of the 1985 Personal Status Law Debate in Egypt." B.A. thesis, Harvard University, 1989.

Richards, Alan and Waterbury, John. *A Political Economy of the Middle East*. Boulder, CO: Westview Press, 1990.

Rizq, Gabr. *Madhabih al-Ikhwan fi Sugun Nasser*. Cairo: Dar al-I'tisam, 1977.

———. *Madhbahat al-Ikhwan fi Liman Tura*. Vol. 1. Cairo: Dar al-I'tisam, 1979.

Roosevelt, Kermit. *Arabs, Oil and History*. New York: Harper and Brothers, 1949.

Rubenstein, Alvin. *Red Star on the Nile*. Princeton, NJ: Princeton University Press, 1977.

Rutherford, Bruce K. *The Struggle for Constitutionalism in Egypt: Understanding the Obstacles to Democratic Transition in the Arab World*. Ph.D. thesis, Yale University, 1999.

Saaty, Hassan al-. "The New Aristocracized and Bourgeoisized Classes in the Egyptian Application of Socialism," in C.A.O. Van Nieuwenhuijze, ed. *Commoners, Climbers, and Notables*. Leiden: Brill, 1977, pp. 196-204.

Sabri, Musa. *Watha'iq 15 Mayo*. Cairo. n.d.

———. *Al-Sadat: al-Haqiqa wa-l-Astura*. Cairo: al-Maktab al-Misri al-Hadith, 1985.

Sadat, Anwar al-. *Revolt on the Nile*. New York: John Day, 1957.

———. *In Search of Identity*. Glasgow: Fontana/Collins, 1977.

———. *Those I Have Known*. New York: Continuum, 1984.

Sadat, Jehan. *A Woman of Egypt*. New York: Simon and Schuster, 1986.

Sadowski, Yahya M. *Political Vegetables?* Washington, D.C.: The Brookings Institution, 1991.

Safran, Nadav. *Egypt in Search of Political Community*. Cambridge, MA: Harvard University Press, 1961.

———. *Israel: The Embattled Ally*. Cambridge, MA: The Belknap Press of Harvard University Press, 1978.

Sa'id, Rif'at al-. *al-Hassan al-Banna: Mata..Kaif..wa Limatha?*. Cairo: Maktabat Madbuli, 1977.

Sayyid-Marsot, Afaf Lutfi al-. *Egypt's Liberal Experiment: 1922-1936*. Berkeley, CA: University of California Press, 1977.

Shamir, Shimon, ed. *Egypt: From Monarchy to Republic*. Boulder, CO: Westview Press, 1995.

Shoukri, Ghali, et al. *Misr Min al-Thawra...illa al-Ridda*. Beirut: Dar at-Tali'a lit-Taba'a wa-l-Nashr, 1981.

————. *Egypte: la contre-revolution.* Paris: Editions le Sycamore, 1979.

Sivan, Emmanuel. *Radical Islam: Medieval Theology and Modern Politics.* New Haven, CT: Yale University Press, 1985.

Skinner, Quentin and Price, Russell. *Machiavelli: The Prince.* New York: Cambridge University Press, 1988.

Skocpol, Theda. *States and Social Revolutions.* New York: Cambridge University Press, 1979.

Springborg, Robert. *Family, Power, and Politics in Egypt.* Philadelphia: University of Pennsylvania Press, 1982.

Stephens, Robert. *Nasser: A Political Biography.* London: Allen Lane, 1971.

Sul'iman, 'Abd al-'Aziz. *Mihnati.* Cairo: al-Maktab al-Masri li-l-Nashr, 1982.

Tilly, Charles. *The Formation of National States in Western Europe.* Princeton, NJ: Princeton University Press, 1975.

Truell, Peter, and Gurwin, Larry. *False Profits: The Inside Story of BCCI, the World's Most Corrupt Financial Empire.* Boston, MA: Houghton Mifflin, 1992.

'Uthman, 'Uthman Ahmed. *Safahat min Tagrubati.* Cairo: al-Sharika al-Misriyya li-l-Taba'a, 1976.

'Uthman, Wa'il. *Asrar al-Harakat al-Tulabiyya.* Cairo: al-Sharika al-Misriyya li-l-Taba'a, 1976.

Vatikiotis, P.J., ed. *Egypt Since the Revolution.* New York: Frederick A. Praeger, 1968.

————. *The Egyptian Army in Politics.* Bloomington: Indiana University Press, 1961.

————. *Nasser and His Generation.* London: Croom Helm, 1978.

Vogel, Ezra. *The Four Little Dragons.* Cambridge, MA: Harvard University Press, 1991.

Wahba, Mourad M. *The Role of the State in the Egyptian Economy, 1945-1981.* Reading, MA: Ithaca Press, 1994.

Waterbury, John. "Egypt: the Wages of Dependency," in A.L. Udovitch, ed. *The Middle East: Oil, Conflict and Hope.* Lexington, MA: Lexington Books, 1976, 291-351.

————. *The Egypt of Nasser and Sadat: The Political Economy of Two Regimes.* Princeton, NJ: Princeton University Press, 1983.

————. *Egypt: Burdens of the Past, Options for the Future.* Bloomington: Indiana University Press, 1978.

Woodward, Bob. *Shadow.* New York: Simon & Schuster, 1999.

World Bank. *The East Asian Miracle.* New York: Oxford University Press, 1993.

Youssef, Samir. *System of Management of Public Sector Enterprises.* Cairo: Center for Middle East Management Studies, American University in Cairo, 1983.

Zayyat, Muhammad 'Abd al-Salam al-. *Al-Qina'a wa-l-Haqiqa.* Cairo: Sharikat al-Amal li-l-Taba'a wa-l-Nashr, 1989.

Index